Susan B. Anthony

Susan B. Anthony
A Biographical Companion

Photograph of Susan B. Anthony taken around 1904.

Susan B. Anthony
A Biographical Companion

Judith E. Harper

ABC-CLIO
BIOGRAPHICAL
COMPANION

Library of Congress Cataloging-in-Publication Data

Harper, Judith E., 1953–
    Susan B. Anthony: a biographical companion / Judith E. Harper.
       p. cm. — (ABC-CLIO Biographical Companion)
    Includes bibliographical references and index.
    1. Anthony, Susan B. (Susan Brownell) 1820–1908—Encyclopedias.
2. Feminists—United States—Biography—Encyclopedias.
3. Suffragists—United States—Biography—Encyclopedias. I. Title. II. Series.
HQ1413.A55H37   1998   305.42'092—dc21   98-43287

ISBN 0-87436-948-7

04 03 02 01 00 99 98   10 9 8 7 6 5 4 3 2 1 (cloth)

ABC-CLIO, Inc.
130 Cremona Drive, P.O. Box 1911
Santa Barbara, California 93116-1911

This book is printed on acid-free paper ⊗.
Manufactured in the United States of America

For Ken

ABC-CLIO BIOGRAPHICAL COMPANIONS

Benjamin Franklin, by Jennifer L. Durham
Susan B. Anthony, by Judith E. Harper
Thomas Jefferson, by David S. Brown

ABC-CLIO Biographical Companions are encyclopedic guides to the lives of men and women who have had a significant impact on the social, political, and cultural development of the Western world. Each volume presents complete biographical information in an easily accessible format. An introduction and a chronology provide an overview, while the A to Z entries amplify a myriad of topics related to the person. A collection of documents and extensive illustrations give the reader an acute sense of the individual's life and times.

CONTENTS

PREFACE

*O*f all nineteenth-century social reformers, very few rivaled the prodi-
gious intensity and magnitude of Susan B.
Anthony's activism. For nearly 60 years, day
in and day out, she dedicated nearly every
waking moment to perfecting society. Although women's struggle for the ballot was
the central focus of her life after the early
1870s, she was not only a suffragist. During
her young adulthood, she was zealously immersed in an array of social and moral reform movements. As a result, navigating her
world can be an overwhelming and even
daunting task for those trying to familiarize
themselves with her life. This volume, arranged in an A to Z encyclopedic format, is
designed to assist those who wish both to
understand and to unravel her activism; to
learn more not only about her involvement
in the abolitionist, temperance, women's
rights, and woman suffrage movements but
also about these reforms as a whole and the
significance of her contributions to them.

The 123 entries in this volume present
the people, events, organizations, and important publications in Anthony's life and furnish more in-depth information about them
than a standard biography can provide. At
the end of each entry is a list of related entries and suggestions for further reading to
guide the reader to a deeper exploration of
each topic. For those wishing a more extensive scrutiny of a subject, the in-text cita-

tions and comprehensive bibliography are
guides to resources. Citations identifying the
sources of excerpted letters and other documents, to be used in conjunction with the
Abbreviations for Manuscript Collections
and Repositories, will help readers to locate
specific unpublished documents.

This volume also examines Anthony's personal life, especially as it influenced her activism. Although her story unfolds on every
page of this volume, her biographical entry
"Anthony, Susan B." discusses her childhood;
young adulthood; family relationships; and
most problematic conflicts, defeats, and tri-
umphs. Readers will discover that Elizabeth
Cady Stanton is as integral a part of this volume as she was in Anthony's life and work.
In addition to the biographical entry
"Stanton, Elizabeth Cady," the two women's
unique partnership and friendship receive
special attention in the entry "Anthony/Cady
Stanton Partnership." Similarly, the biographical entries on Anthony's male and female
colleagues, friends, and family illustrate her
many rich, multifaceted relationships and
create a fascinatingly complex portrayal of
Anthony the woman, the suffragist, the politician, the friend, the sister, and the daughter.
This volume also includes entries dedicated
to a number of reformers who played a vital
role in Anthony's life and who have never
been included or examined closely in previous biographies. Among this group are Parker

Pillsbury, her closest and most devoted male friend and fellow reformer, Clara Bewick Colby, Olympia Brown, Samuel Joseph May, Clara Barton, Charles Lenox Remond, Robert Purvis, Matilda Joslyn Gage, Lillie Devereux Blake, and Frances Willard.

ACKNOWLEDGMENTS

A writer of history cannot progress on any project without being made aware of the crucial importance of libraries. My most profound gratitude is reserved for the directors and staff of the Margaret Clapp Library at Wellesley College. A scholar of American women's history could not find a more comprehensive collection from which to launch explorations, nor a more congenial, helpful, nurturing atmosphere in which to conduct research. My thanks go also to the dedicated specialists of the Boston Athenaeum for obtaining the books and dissertations on interlibrary loan that I needed to make this volume as complete and as up-to-date as possible.

Perhaps the most astounding discovery I made in the course of researching and writing this book was the 45-reel microfilm collection *The Papers of Elizabeth Cady Stanton and Susan B. Anthony*. Compiled by the historians and archivists Patricia G. Holland and Ann D. Gordon and their assistant editors Gail K. Malmgreen and Kathleen A. McDonough, this microfilm series, published in 1991, represents well over a decade of work involving archivists of manuscript collections all over the country. Now available in a number of university and public library collections around the country, it is as comprehensive a collection of both Anthony's and Cady Stanton's speeches, writings, letters, and other documents as has ever been gathered. Scholars, students, and those intrigued by these two compelling American women can now uncover the most intricate details of their legacy. For a writer without the funds or the time to travel to distant libraries, the *Papers* were a dream come true. I would like to thank Northeastern University for purchasing this collection and making it accessible to an unaffiliated scholar.

Special thanks also go to Stacey Marie Robertson of Bradley University in Peoria, Illinois, for her generosity in sharing her work, expertise, and enthusiasm for the abolitionist movement and Parker Pillsbury. The following people also generously assisted me in the research for this volume: Mary M. Huth of the Department of Rare Books and Special Collections at the University of Rochester Library; Colleen Hurst of the Susan B. Anthony House Museum and National Historic Landmark in Rochester, New York; Meghan Lodge at the Rochester Historical Society; Ruth Rosenberg-Naparsteck, City Historian of the Rochester Public Library and editor of the journal *Rochester History;* Robert A. Holt of the Leavenworth Historical Society in Leavenworth, Kansas; Keith Jones at the Mabel Smith Douglass Library at Rutgers University; and Robert Cooney, curator of the Woman Suffrage Media Collection in Point Reyes, California. I would also like to express my gratitude to Mary Anthony Coughlin for permission to quote extensively from Anthony's unpublished speeches, letters, and other documents.

Finally, for their nurturance, editorial assistance, and good fellowship, I heartily thank my fellow writers Jan Gardner, Stephen Fox, Elizabeth Hinchliffe, Steven Marks, Christine Ammer, and Richard Jacobs as well as the National Writers Union, the National Council of Independent Scholars, and the incomparable H-Net network of historians. An abundantly exuberant thank-you goes to Ken Whitney for his indefatigable computer assistance, irrepressible good humor, and, most of all, for his belief in me.

ABBREVIATIONS FOR MANUSCRIPT COLLECTIONS AND REPOSITORIES

ARCHIVES AND REPOSITORIES

BPL Department of Rare Books and Manuscripts, Boston Public Library, Boston, Mass.

CHS Colorado Historical Society, Denver, Colo.

HL Huntington Library, San Marino, Calif.

LCMD Library of Congress, Manuscript Division, Washington, D.C.

LCRBD Library of Congress, Rare Books Division, Washington, D.C.

MSDL Mabel Smith Douglass Library, Rutgers, The State University of New Jersey, New Brunswick, N.J.

SL Arthur and Elizabeth Schlesinger Library on the History of Women in America, Radcliffe College, Cambridge, Mass.

SSC Sophia Smith Collection, Smith College, Northampton, Mass.

SUL Department of Special Collections, Syracuse University Library, Syracuse, N.Y.

URL Department of Rare Books and Special Collections, University of Rochester Library, Rochester, N.Y.

ABBREVIATIONS FOR INDIVIDUAL MANUSCRIPT COLLECTIONS

A-A Anthony-Avery
BF Blackwell Family
CB Clara Barton
CBC Clara Bewick Colby
DC Dillon Collection
EM Ellis Meredith
GC Galatea Collection
GF Garrison Family
GS Gerrit Smith
IH Ida Harper
LS Lucy Stone
OB Olympia Brown
SBA Susan B. Anthony
TS Theodore Stanton
WLG William Lloyd Garrison
WP Wendell Phillips

BOOKS

DAB Johnson, Allen, and Dumas Malone, eds. *Dictionary of American Biography.* New York: Scribner's, 1964.

HWS History of Woman Suffrage, vol. 1, 1881, ed. Elizabeth Cady Stanton, Susan B. Anthony, and Matilda Joslyn Gage; vol. 2, 1882, ed. Stanton, Anthony, and Gage; vol. 3, 1886, ed.

Stanton, Anthony, and Gage; vol. 4, 1902, ed. Anthony and Ida Husted Harper; vols. 5 and 6, 1922, ed. Husted Harper. Reprint edition: New York: Arno Press, 1969. (Vol. 3 of *HWS* contains an index to vols. 1–3.)

NAW James, Edward T., Janet Wilson James, and Paul S. Boyer, eds. *Notable American Women 1607–1950: A Biographical Dictionary*. Cam-bridge, Mass.: Belknap Press of Harvard University Press, 1971.

Papers The Papers of Elizabeth Cady Stanton and Susan B. Anthony, ed. Patricia Holland and Ann D. Gordon. Wilmington, Del.: Scholarly Resources, 1991. (All *"Papers"* citations refer to series 3 of this 45-reel microfilm series unless otherwise noted.)

INTRODUCTION

One hundred and fifty years ago, in the tiny village of Seneca Falls, New York, five women organized the first convention that advocated equality and justice for women in all areas of society. It was at this 1848 gathering that Elizabeth Cady Stanton first publicly demanded that women be given the right to vote. Suffragists, including Susan B. Anthony, traced the history of the woman suffrage movement back to this groundbreaking meeting of 300 white and African-American women and men. Anthony, a respected schoolteacher in Canajoharie, New York, never attended the Seneca Falls Convention. In fact, at that time she was not even interested in women's rights issues. Yet the year 1848 marked a profound turning point in her life, one that ultimately inspired her to transform U.S. democracy and revolutionize the status of women in society.

By the fall of 1848, Anthony was dissatisfied with the limitations of teaching. In a letter to her mother, she articulated the intensity of her desire to dedicate herself to the work of reform. She set her sights on improving the world through temperance activism and embarked on a 58-year career during which she would help women achieve the political power that would ensure their personal safety, financial security, and equality in the workplace and the home.

To become immersed in the day-to-day life of Susan B. Anthony during those 58 years is to realize with a startling clarity that the woman suffrage movement was a momentously important reform at the heart of U.S. history. But despite the excellent histories focusing on the woman suffrage movement, the majority of traditional historians regard women's struggle to gain the most fundamental right of a democracy as completely detached from the American story. As the noted suffrage historian Ellen Carol DuBois explains, unlike most political and social reform movements of the nineteenth and twentieth centuries, the woman suffrage movement "has not been accorded the historic recognition it deserves, largely because woman suffrage has too frequently been viewed as an isolated institutional reform" (DuBois 1978, 17). As a result, its vital connections to other reform movements, historical events, political issues, and cultural trends have been ignored, as if they had no impact on the evolution of U.S. government, society, and culture. Most U.S. history textbooks, encyclopedias, traditional histories, and film and television documentaries promote the view that the most extensive democratic reform in U.S. history—a mass political movement that in its final decade involved more than a million women—mysteriously appeared, occupied a remote corner of the American scene for 72 years, and vanished after the Nineteenth Amendment was adopted.

How does it happen that a reform as pervasive and as integrally connected to all aspects of nineteenth- and twentieth-century culture is dismissed so easily? It has long been observed that historians have persisted in devaluing and ignoring women's contributions. Yet popular culture has also been instrumental in neglecting women's role in history. Although Anthony is often remembered as the tough suffrage leader she was, the media frequently misrepresents the woman suffrage movement as a frivolous reform. Popular images create a composite picture of suffragists as a curiously impassioned group of genteel ladies who filled the void of their leisure time by dabbling with suffrage parades and protest teas.

To examine Anthony's life and the activism of her fellow suffragists is to witness the shattering of these confabulated images. Women became involved in the woman suffrage movement because they desperately sought relief from the effects of their powerless position in society. They were not merely seeking a privilege that men jealously guarded; they demanded a right that the Constitution guaranteed them because they were citizens of the United States. Suffragism offered the possibility of a better world than the one they inhabited—in which women were uniformly denied economic equality and a living wage, rights to their children and their own property, and the right to a trial by a jury of their peers. Hundreds of thousands of women fought for the ballot so that they could vote for prohibition and thereby eliminate the alcohol abuse and domestic violence threatening their families and communities. Mothers joined the ranks of suffragists so that they could have a voice in the education of their children. Still others desired the vote as a means to end war and brutality, child labor, and inhumane treatment in prisons and asylums.

Anthony's real life (as this volume, her many biographies, and the massive collection of her papers illustrate) is proof that she was not the leader of a trivial, isolated reform but the commander of a dynamic political and social movement. To examine her life closely

Engraving of Susan B. Anthony by G. E. Perins.

is to discover that she was not only a suffragist. As a Garrisonian abolitionist, she risked her life to emancipate the slaves and to convince Northerners to abolish racial prejudice. During the Civil War, she and Cady Stanton organized thousands of women in the largest petition drive that had ever been presented to Congress to achieve passage of a Thirteenth Amendment ensuring the slaves' freedom. After the war, Anthony organized relief for the emancipated slaves in Kansas and helped them establish new lives and assert their civil and political rights. As a women's rights reformer in the 1850s, she led an exhaustive, statewide, six-year campaign that gave New York women more legal rights over their children, their property, and their employment than ever before. She was a dedicated scholar of constitutional law and American legal history. It was a well-known fact in Washington that her command of constitutional law far exceeded the knowledge of the congressmen and presidents she lobbied year in and year out. Although the press ridiculed and harassed her, she was highly respected by government officials. By the late nineteenth century, her opinions on all matters of national and international affairs were sought after and published.

Although she is often remembered as the embodiment of the sour-faced, dour visage imprinted on the Susan B. Anthony dollar, she defied this stereotype. She was as much the witty, funny, warmhearted, generous, vulnerable, and lovable woman as she was the determined, domineering activist, shrewd political strategist, and manipulative propagandist. People who met her often expected the worst, fearing that they would confront the severe, man-hating horror the newspapers told them they would find. Instead they were shocked and delighted to meet a down-to-earth, gracious woman deeply interested in their problems and just as thoroughly committed to persuading them that woman suffrage was the best way to remedy them.

Whatever the origins of modern misperceptions about the woman suffrage movement and Susan B. Anthony, might not twentieth-century Americans' pessimistic and apathetic attitudes toward the vote also have an impact? Even Americans who consider themselves civic-minded report that they find it too difficult to get to the polls for every election. According to Congressional Quarterly's 1996 edition of *America Votes*, only 49 percent of Americans of voting age cast ballots in the 1996 national election. Many voters state that they become discouraged when they elect candidates who do not or cannot institute the changes they promised. Low voter turnout, voting statistics, and analyses of voter behavior suggest that whether late-twentieth-century Americans vote or not, most believe that their ballots have very little influence on the course of government.

Nineteenth-century Americans, especially educated, middle-class men and women like Anthony, lived in a completely different world. For the most part they were convinced that voters commanded a superior power and that the ballot was the crux of government. They believed that government hinged on the consent of the governed, as embodied in

Susan B. Anthony's study in the south wing of the second floor of the Madison Street house in Rochester, New York. On the wall are images of William Lloyd Garrison, Wendell Phillips, Gerrit Smith, Ernestine Potowski Rose, Abby Kelley Foster, Harriet Beecher Stowe, Lucy Stone, and others. The family record, sampler, and quilt shown in the picture were made by Susan Anthony when she was a young girl.

the will of the voter. Anthony's supreme confidence in the power of the ballot to revolutionize society was so extreme by today's standards as to make her and the cause of woman suffrage almost impossible for modernists to comprehend. What is often forgotten is that Anthony was not seeking the vote for women as much as she was pursuing the perfection of society. She was convinced that once women achieved the suffrage, they would use their ballots to participate in government and institute universal justice and economic equality, abolish racism and prejudice, remove corruption from government, and cure the ills caused by industrialization.

The woman suffrage movement was only one facet of the grand world of nineteenth-century reform. Reformers of all persuasions were dazzled by the conviction that they could create and shape an ideal world. Since their deaths, most activists have become associated with only one of their many reform interests. Yet Anthony, Cady Stanton, William Lloyd Garrison, Clara Barton, Wendell Phillips, and others like them focused on improving not just one corner of society but all of it. They passionately contributed their money, time, and energies to multiple movements: among them, political, constitutional, religious, and educational reforms; prison and asylum reform; temperance; and pacifism. They also possessed an astounding longevity. In an era when the average life expectancy was less than 50 years, Anthony and the vast majority of her colleagues endured well into their eighth, ninth, and tenth decades. What accounts for such uniform hardiness? To be sure, anyone seriously pursuing the life of a reformer needed a sturdy constitution. Traveling incessantly, being exposed to extremes of weather, regularly consuming insufficient and improperly cooked food, working night and day for long periods—all exacted their toll. Reformers became ill, yes; but what

emerges from a study of their lives is the evidence of a galvanizing force that they all shared—an impetus that pushed them from their sickbeds and kept them vital and committed to social change well into their seventies. Like Anthony, nineteenth-century reform women and men were an impassioned group. The strength of their commitment to others, their inexhaustible belief in themselves and their individual crusades, their refusal to perceive failures as overwhelming, and the confidence in their power to change society are rejuvenating antidotes to twentieth-century feelings of powerlessness.

Finally, what is most enduring about Anthony's legacy is the rock-solid power of her unshakable certitude that national woman suffrage would usher in a new enlightenment. The Nineteenth Amendment and the votes of millions of women have not fulfilled her expectations; nor have they paved the way to universal justice, economic equality, or racial harmony. Yet this fact is the least relevant aspect of her legacy because it is the nobility of her dedication to the cause, on which she lavished her every thought, dream, and action, that is most significant about her life. The quest filled her with a light so brilliant and a fire so unquenchable that no obstacle could compete with her near-fanatical determination to blast open the doors of democracy. And in her vision of this new, true republic, the full participation of all the nation's citizens could not fail to institute a perfect society. That women and men have not yet chosen to walk through the doors she opened is an enigma that she would have found unfathomable. Yet were she alive today, she would have refused to accept this outcome as a failure. Perhaps the most heartening part of her legacy is her conviction that all one needs to overcome an obstacle is boundless determination and more hard work.

Susan B. Anthony

Susan B. Anthony
A Biographical Companion

Abolitionist Movement

A bolitionism, a dominant political and social reform movement of the mid-nineteenth century, was dedicated to the eradication of slavery. Although Susan B. Anthony is primarily remembered for her work in the women's rights and woman suffrage movements, she was a zealous abolitionist, well known for her years of uncompromising, passionate work to gain the slaves' freedom.

In the United States, antislavery sentiment became organized as early as the eighteenth century, especially among Quakers. In fact, the first document to protest slavery in the United States was written by the Germantown Friends in 1688 (Lutz 1968, 4). Abolitionist activity became more widespread in the early nineteenth century, and in 1833, the formation of the American Anti-Slavery Society (AASS) signaled the inception of abolitionism as an established reform movement. In 1839, the more radical of the AASS's two factions, led by William Lloyd Garrison, took control of the AASS, forcing some of its more conservative members to form a separate organization, the American and Foreign Anti-Slavery Society. In 1840, those committed to pursuing political solutions to slavery organized the Liberty Party. Despite the firestorm of national debate that the abolitionists created, only a small minority of Americans were ever actively involved in the movement. Although most were white

middle-class northerners, a majority of free African Americans were also integral to abolitionism.

In addition to demanding the immediate emancipation of the slaves, Garrison's followers, who became known as Garrisonian abolitionists, were convinced that women should take a more active role in the abolitionist movement. They also fervently believed that "moral suasion"—persuading, cajoling, and whipping the public into a frenzy with the moral righteousness of their cause—was the one true means of convincing northerners to demand the abolition of slavery, not political activity or compromise, as the majority of abolitionists thought.

THE ROLE OF WOMEN IN THE ABOLITIONIST MOVEMENT

In the 1830s both white and free African-American women became increasingly involved in antislavery reform. Throughout New England and the Northeast, the Middle Atlantic seaboard and the Midwest, women formed female antislavery societies, raising consciousness about the evils of slavery among themselves and throughout their communities. Antislavery women played a vital role in the abolitionist movement—raising funds to support abolitionist lecturers in the field, writing and disseminating abolitionist literature and propaganda, combating the effects of racial discrimination, and drafting and circulating petitions to pressure state legislatures and Congress to enact antislavery laws. A number of women, most of them Garrisonians, gave lectures. Sarah and Angelina Grimké, Lucretia Coffin Mott, Abby Kelley Foster, Lucy Stone, Susan B. Anthony, and the African-American activists Sarah Parker Remond, Sojourner Truth, and Frances Ellen Watkins Harper traveled widely and consistently attracted large audiences. They proved to be a powerful draw, at least partly because people were curious to see them brave the cultural prohibition against women speaking in public. Coffin Mott, Kelley Foster, and Maria Weston Chapman (secretary of the AASS and a founder of the Boston Female Anti-Slavery Society) performed key decisionmaking roles in the central executive committees of the predominantly male antislavery societies.

SUSAN B. ANTHONY AND ABOLITIONISM

As the daughter of Daniel Anthony, a liberal Hicksite Quaker noted for his antislavery views, Susan B. Anthony grew up discussing slavery and abolitionism. She occasionally spent her vacations from teaching at the Albany home of her Quaker friend Lydia Mott (a cousin of Coffin Mott's husband), who was deeply involved in abolitionism. Their discussions about antislavery issues and Mott's abolitionist work influenced the young Anthony. As a young woman in her twenties, Anthony was an avid reader of Garrison's newspaper the *Liberator* and was well aware of the work and struggles of women abolitionists.

Unlike many of the female abolitionists whom she admired, Anthony had the devoted support of her parents and siblings throughout her career in reform. And as a Quaker, she was accustomed to being free to speak publicly, whether at Quaker meetings or at school. Although Anthony began her reform work in the temperance movement, she maintained a keen interest in the abolitionist movement and, through the Rochester community of Hicksite Quakers, was well

acquainted with many leading abolitionists. She regularly attended antislavery meetings and conventions and longed to one day become an abolitionist herself, though she doubted her ability to do so.

In the spring of 1854, after more than five years as a temperance reformer and two as a women's rights activist, Anthony traveled south with abolitionist and women's rights activist Ernestine Potowski Rose, who was conducting a women's rights lecture tour. Because the Kansas-Nebraska Act was being debated in Congress throughout their trip, proslavery sentiment was rampant in Washington, D.C., and in the other border and southern cities they visited. In Washington, Anthony attended the debates, but her first face-to-face encounter with slavery made the deepest impression on her. Surrounded by slaves in her hotel, in restaurants, and in transit from city to city, she became extremely concerned about how her contact with slavery affected her sensibility. In her diary entry for March 20, 1854, she wrote:

> This noon I ate my dinner without once asking myself, are these human beings, who minister to my wants, slaves to be bought & sold & tired out at the will of a master? And when the thought first entered my mind, I said, even I am getting accustomed to slavery, so much so that I have ceased continually to be made to feel its blighting, cursing influence, so much so that I can sit down & eat from the hands of the bondman, without being once mindful of the fact. . . . Oh slavery hateful thing that thou art, thus to blunt the keen edge of men's conscience, even while they strive to shun thy poisonous touch.

By halfway through the tour, she had concluded:

> I have had ProSlavery People tell me just go South once, & see Slavery as it

is, & then you will talk very differently. I can assure all such, that contact with Slavery has not a tendency to make one hate it less, no, no, the ominous effect of the institution, upon the white man alone, causes me to hate it. (SBA Diary, March 1854, SBA-SL, in *Papers*)

Anthony's experience as a general agent for the AASS in the state of New York from 1856 to 1861 broadened and focused the direction of her abolitionist rhetoric and ideology. She quickly adopted the fiery, confrontational style of her fellow Garrisonians.

What is American Slavery? It is the Legalized Systematized robbery of the bodies and souls of nearly four millions of men, women and children. . . . It is theft, robbery, piracy, murder, it is avarice, covetousness, lust, licentiousness, concubinage, polygamy; it is atheism, blasphemy, and sin against the Holy Ghost. ("What is American Slavery?" Speech, 1857, SBA-LCMD, in *Papers*)

In her speeches she continually sought to convey the humanity and personhood of the slave to northerners, most of whom had never seen a slave and could only perceive of slavery in the abstract.

Let us, my friends, for the passing hour, make the slaves' case our own . . . let us feel . . . that it is our own backs that are bared to the slavedriver's lash, that it is our own flesh that is lacerated & torn, that it is our own life-blood that is poured out. ("Make the Slaves Case Our Own," Speech, 1857, SBA-LCMD, in *Papers*)

Anthony and a number of her fellow Garrisonians were not only concerned with the abolition of slavery; they were equally disturbed by the severity of racial prejudice in the North, a condition Anthony believed to be as pernicious and intractable as slavery in the South. In 1858, Anthony delivered a stinging attack on northerners, pointing a critical finger at their holier-than-thou attitude and the questionable superiority of their treatment of African Americans. Anthony believed that the "help" northerners gave to African Americans not only failed to camouflage their blatant racial discrimination but crippled free northern blacks as much as slavery ensnared African Americans in the South.

As the nation endured one crisis after another—the Kansas-Nebraska Act of 1854, the Border War in Kansas, the *Dred Scott* decision of 1857, the raid on Harpers Ferry, and the execution of abolitionist John Brown in 1859—each sledgehammer of an event heightened tensions between North and South, and between proslavery and antislavery factions in the North. Although northern mob violence had plagued abolitionists from the beginning of the movement, as more and more northerners blamed the impending national crisis on the abolitionists, their confrontations with enraged mobs increased in frequency and severity.

During the late 1850s, while Anthony was consumed by her role as a lecturer and general agent for the AASS, the extreme hardships that male and female Garrisonians endured in the face of violent mobs caused them to depend on each other to a degree not before experienced. A convivial spirit of camaraderie and trust developed that rarely flagged even in the midst of their usual squabbles and misunderstandings. Their letters to each other reveal relationships based on mutual respect for each reformer's strengths and talents. This level of gender cooperation, extremely rare in the nineteenth century, reached its height among Garrisonians in the years immediately preceding the Civil War.

The letters the Garrisonians sent to each other also portray the harrowing daily life of the abolitionist agent. In addition to their focus on the content of their speeches and their reception from audiences, their letters

Heralds of Freedom, *published by C. H. Brainard in Boston, 1857, pictures prominent male abolitionist leaders and colleagues of Susan B. Anthony. Clockwise from top: Ralph Waldo Emerson, Wendell Phillips, J. R. Gibbings, Theodore Parker, Gerrit Smith, Samuel Joseph May, and, at center, William Lloyd Garrison.*

are filled with descriptions of their struggles with transportation, foul weather, pest-ridden lodging, and inedible food. The primary topics, however, were detailed reports of their own health mixed with news and concern for the health problems of fellow abolitionists, a testament to the fact that a strong con-

stitution was a prerequisite for success as a Garrisonian agent.

Once the Civil War had commenced, Garrison and his followers deliberately stopped their agitation and maintained a low profile, corresponding with one another about the progress of the war and how it might influence the future of the slaves and of slavery. They also pressed President Abraham Lincoln to abolish slavery. After the Emancipation Proclamation of 1863, Susan B. Anthony's and many other feminist abolitionists' work for the Woman's National Loyal League (WNLL) led to the ratification of the Thirteenth Amendment in 1865, which formally eradicated slavery and protected the freedom of African Americans. After the Civil War, Anthony and the majority of Garrisonian reformers continued the struggle to obtain and protect the civil and political rights of African Americans and to eliminate or alter institutions, laws, and policies that perpetuated racial barriers and prejudice.

Related entries:

Suggestions for further reading:
Aptheker, Herbert. 1989. *Abolitionism: A Revolutionary Movement*. Boston: Twayne Publishers.
Hersh, Blanche Glassman. 1978. *The Slavery of Sex: Feminist-Abolitionists in America*. Urbana: University of Illinois Press.
Quarles, Benjamin. 1969. *Black Abolitionists*. New York: Oxford University Press.

American Anti-Slavery Society

The American Anti-Slavery Society (AASS), formed by William Lloyd Garrison and Arthur and Lewis Tappan at a Philadelphia antislavery convention in 1833, was one of the primary national abolitionist organizations in the United States. Much of the work and activity of the AASS was achieved through its auxiliary societies. These regional, state, and local organizations sponsored lectures and conventions to rally support for abolitionism; published antislavery newspapers; disseminated antislavery literature; organized fund-raising events; gathered petitions on abolitionist issues; combated racial prejudice; and, in many areas, assisted local African Americans with education and housing. AASS members believed that if they bombarded the public with enough information about the evils of slavery, northerners would realize that it must be abolished and demand that the government prohibit it.

Susan B. Anthony's involvement in the AASS, particularly her years as an antislavery agent (1856–1861) and her close working relationships with other AASS activists, was crucial to her development as an abolitionist and as a women's rights and suffrage reformer. Her association with the AASS and its members swept her into the vanguard of Garrisonian abolitionism and promoted the development and expression of her radical egalitarianism, which formed the basis of her emerging political ideology. The alliances and important friendships that emerged from her AASS experience included those with William Lloyd Garrison, Wendell Phillips, Parker Pillsbury, Samuel May, Jr., and Charles Remond. Her AASS activism also strengthened previously formed bonds with Abby Kelley Foster, Stephen Symonds Foster, Lucy Stone, and Samuel Joseph May.

From the founding of the AASS, Garrison was unique among male abolitionists for his recognition of the value of having women actively involved in the antislavery movement. At the formative meeting of the AASS in 1833, he urged the proliferation and expansion of female antislavery societies. By the late 1830s, he promoted women's rights and advocated a policy of women activists having an equal voice in AASS government, to the consternation of the society's conservative members who, because of this and other issues, separated to form their own society.

In her young adulthood, Susan B. Anthony was well aware of the activities of the AASS and its industrious auxiliary societies through her reading of Garrison's newspaper, *The Liberator,* and other antislavery journals. She had long admired women involved in the AASS, particularly Kelley Foster, Lucretia Coffin Mott, and Stone. For Anthony, a long-cherished dream of a career in abolitionism was realized in 1856 when Samuel May, Jr. (a cousin of Samuel Joseph May), general agent of the Massachusetts Anti-Slavery Society, wrote to her, stating that the society's executive committee wished to employ her as an agent for the state of New York.

I really think the efficiency and success of our operations in New York this winter will depend more on your personal attendance and direction than upon that of any other of our workers. We need your earnestness, your practical talent, your energy and perseverance to make these conventions successful. (Harper 1899, 1:148)

Anthony eagerly accepted, and for $10 a week, from 1856 through the winter of 1861, under the most arduous conditions, she organized antislavery lectures and meetings from Albany to Buffalo.

Like the majority of AASS activists, Anthony reacted with alarm when Garrison proposed disbanding the AASS in 1865. Garrison reasoned that since the proposed Thirteenth Amendment would ensure the freedom of all African Americans, the work of the society was finished. Despite the urging of his male and female colleagues, Garrison could not be persuaded to reconsider. In May 1865, Garrison stepped down and Wendell Phillips assumed leadership until the AASS disbanded in 1870. From 1865 to 1870, during the early years of the Reconstruction era, AASS members continued the struggle to secure the civil and political rights of African Americans.

Related entries:
Abolitionist Movement
American Equal Rights Association
Civil War
Garrison, William Lloyd
The Liberator
Mott, Lucretia Coffin
Phillips, Wendell
Pillsbury, Parker
Stone, Lucy
Thirteenth Amendment

Suggestions for further reading:
Friedman, Lawrence J. 1982. *Gregarious Saints: Self and Community in American Abolitionism, 1830–1870.* New York: Cambridge University Press.
Mabee, Carleton. 1970. *Black Freedom: The Nonviolent Abolitionists from 1830 through the Civil War.* Toronto: Macmillan.

American Equal Rights Association

The American Equal Rights Association (AERA) was organized at the Eleventh National Woman's Rights Convention in New York City in May 1866, and was pledged to agitate for universal suffrage, that is, securing the ballot for African-American males and all women. A few months previously, Theodore Tilton, the Republican abolitionist editor of the *Independent* and a women's rights advocate, first suggested the idea of merging the American Anti-Slavery Society (AASS) and the women's rights movement into one organization. Although Susan B. Anthony was filled with optimism at the prospect, Wendell Phillips, the new leader of the AASS, balked at the idea and pointed out that no merger could occur without a change in the constitution of the AASS. Phillips, because of his fervent commitment to securing citizenship and suffrage for African-American males, became a leading opponent of Anthony and Elizabeth Cady Stanton's efforts to campaign for woman suffrage during the late 1860s.

At the 1866 AASS annual convention held in New York just prior to the Eleventh National Woman's Rights Convention, Anthony and Cady Stanton discovered that the merger proposal had not been included on the AASS convention agenda as they had been led to believe, and therefore no action could be taken. Anthony was determined not to be thwarted by this mishap. Days later at the woman's rights convention, she proposed the formation of the American Equal Rights Association (AERA), which would campaign for the enactment of universal suffrage. On May 10, 1866, this convention adopted the AERA constitution.

Most of the original members of the AERA were feminist abolitionists who had been prominent in the antebellum women's rights movement. Besides organizers Anthony, Lucy Stone, and Cady Stanton, there were Lucretia Coffin Mott, Martha Coffin Wright, Paulina Wright Davis, Ernestine Potowski Rose, Antoinette Brown Blackwell, and Lydia Mott as well as African-American activists Frances Watkins Harper, Sojourner Truth, and Sarah Parker Remond, to name a few. Several white and African-American male abolitionist leaders were also members, including Frederick Douglass, Parker Pillsbury, Samuel Joseph May, Theodore Tilton, Stephen Symonds Foster, Robert Purvis, and Henry Blackwell. There was also a significant group of women who had not been active in either the antebellum women's rights movement or in abolitionism.

The press censured and ridiculed the AERA just as it had harassed the AASS and the women's rights movement. One newspaper described the AERA membership as a "caravan" of "mummified and fossilated females"; "crack-brained, rheumatic, dyspeptic, henpecked men"; and "self-educated, oily-faced, insolent, gabbling negroes" (Harper 1899, 1:264).

The AERA initially aimed to change state constitutions, specifically, to erase constitutional race and gender restrictions on the franchise. AERA members labored to remove restrictive language from state constitutions in New York, Kansas, Maine, Massachusetts, Ohio, Missouri, and the District of Columbia (DuBois 1978, 65–66). Anthony and Cady Stanton played a pivotal role in the two biggest constitutional campaigns related to woman suffrage, in New York and in Kansas.

Although Wendell Phillips was not an active AERA member, he participated in discussions concerning the campaign to amend the New York state constitution. Completely absorbed by his quest to attain rights for African-American males, he was blind to Anthony and Cady Stanton's woman suffrage efforts, including their expressed plan to have the word *male* deleted from the state constitution. When he suggested that the two women commence a statewide campaign to have the word *white* removed from the constitution, Anthony became enraged and retorted that she would "sooner cut off her right hand than ask the ballot for the black man and not for the woman" (Harper 1899, 1:261). She could not comprehend how Phillips, a man she respected and whom she believed respected her, could expect her and Cady Stanton to trek all over New York state demanding the ballot for African-American men without claiming it for women.

Despite Anthony's, Cady Stanton's, and other AERA activists' well-organized New York campaign, the report of Horace Greeley's suffrage committee (which stated its opposition to woman suffrage) caused the New York Constitutional Convention to reject the measure by a vote of 125 to 19 (DuBois 1978, 88). In Kansas, the AERA campaign for the woman suffrage referendum failed as well, but not before chalking up an encouraging total of 9,000 votes in favor of the measure.

After the Kansas campaign, Republican AERA members were distressed by Anthony and Cady Stanton's alliance with the racist Democrat George Francis Train and by their ardent anti-Republicanism during the mission. This conflict dominated the AERA for the remaining two years of its existence and prevented the organization from effectively mounting any additional campaigns.

In 1868, Republican AERA members Lucy Stone, Henry Blackwell, and Stephen Foster accused Anthony of misusing AERA funds. They objected to her having used the AERA office for arrangements connected with Train's lecture tour and for the establishment of her and Cady Stanton's newspaper, *The Revolution*, activities that were judged to be counter to the mission of the AERA. Anthony responded by submitting her financial accounts to her accusers' scrutiny. Although no problems were found and she was cleared of the allegation, Republican AERA members resurrected the complaint again and again at meetings.

By this time, Anthony and Cady Stanton were completely estranged from most AERA members, and they ceased to use this organization as the basis for their woman suffrage activities. Yet they continued to attend annual meetings and remained outspoken, constantly reminding the AERA membership that it had been organized to fight for women's political rights as well as African Americans'.

In the weeks prior to the May 1869 AERA annual convention, Anthony and Cady Stanton became optimistic that they could convince AERA members to support a Sixteenth Amendment guaranteeing woman suffrage in addition to AERA's already announced endorsement of the Fifteenth Amendment, which ensured the ballot for African-American males. When Anthony proposed the idea at the beginning of the May meeting, it was immediately rejected as members insisted on the precedence of the Fifteenth Amendment. This final meeting of the AERA made it clear to Anthony, Cady Stanton, and their supporters that if they planned to pursue woman suffrage, they would have to do it in an independent organization that would be solely devoted to the cause. Two days later, Anthony, Cady Stanton, and a group of women activists from 19 states formed the National Woman Suffrage Association.

Related entries:
Abolitionist Movement
American Anti-Slavery Society
Blackwell, Henry Browne
Douglass, Frederick
Fifteenth Amendment
Foster, Stephen Symonds
Fourteenth Amendment
Greeley, Horace
Harper, Frances Ellen Watkins
Kansas Campaign of 1867
National Woman Suffrage Association
Phillips, Wendell
Purvis, Robert
Reconstruction
Stone, Lucy
Tilton, Theodore
Truth, Sojourner

Suggestions for further reading:
Kugler, Israel. 1987. *From Ladies to Women: The Organized Struggle for Woman's Rights in the Reconstruction Era*. Westport, Conn.: Greenwood Press.
DuBois, Ellen Carol. 1978. *Feminism and Suffrage: The Emergence of an Independent Women's Movement in America 1848–1869*. Ithaca, N.Y.: Cornell University Press.

American Woman Suffrage Association

The American Woman Suffrage Association (AWSA), led principally by Lucy Stone, Henry Blackwell, and Julia Ward Howe, was formed in November 1869, in reaction to Susan B. Anthony and Elizabeth Cady Stanton's establishment of the National Woman Suffrage Association (NWSA) in May 1869. AWSA organizers and original members, primarily from New England, were disturbed by the NWSA's rejection of the Fifteenth Amendment, Anthony and Cady Stanton's radicalism as expressed in their newspaper *The Revolution*, and the unorthodox political alliances Anthony and Cady Stanton had formed. Personal disagreements and animosity between Anthony and Cady Stanton on the one hand and Stone, Henry Blackwell, and other New England Republicans on the other intensified the rift and made mediation impossible. In particular, the hostility between Stone and Anthony, forged in the furor over Anthony and Cady Stanton's alliance with the racist George Francis Train during the AERA Kansas campaign of 1867 and over Anthony's use of AERA funds for this mission, compounded preexisting misunderstandings and negatively influenced all attempts at reconciliation.

Despite the bitterness between the two factions, Anthony attended the founding convention of the AWSA in Cleveland, Ohio, in late November 1869. After suffering through speeches denouncing the NWSA and *The Revolution*, Anthony boldly asked to speak. Holding firmly to her purpose to do whatever she believed necessary to achieve woman suffrage, she attempted to convince the convention that she knew the best method of achieving the franchise. She exhorted AWSA members to go with her to Washington to demand that Congress enact a Sixteenth Amendment ensuring woman suffrage. Although the membership responded enthusiastically to her speech, the AWSA remained steadfast to its primary strategy—pursuing woman suffrage on a state-by-state basis (Lutz 1959, 172–173). Even so, the AWSA did not completely abandon work for a federal suffrage amendment. It organized members all over the country to circulate petitions in favor of a Sixteenth Amendment, which were then regularly submitted to Congress.

From the start, the AWSA was more conservative than the NWSA, avoiding issues that might distract from the principal objective of woman suffrage or that might alienate its majority of white middle-class male and female members. The AWSA also had stronger financial support than the NWSA. Unlike the NWSA's paper *The Revolution*, the AWSA's *Woman's Journal*, established by Stone and Blackwell in 1870, was launched with sound financial backing and soon attained status as the foremost women's rights newspaper in the nation. Stone, Blackwell, and other AWSA leaders were adamant about maintaining membership on a delegate basis. They urged state and local suffrage associations to become auxiliaries of the AWSA and each to send delegates to AWSA conventions. The AWSA not only permitted men to be members but also allowed them to hold leadership positions. Influential Congregational minister Henry Ward Beecher served as the AWSA's first president, followed by Massachusetts reformer Thomas Wentworth Higginson. Of all the men involved in the AWSA, however, Blackwell consistently held the most power and influence.

The AWSA always had more African-American members than the NWSA. Frances Ellen Watkins Harper, Sojourner Truth, Caroline Remond Putnam (sister of Sarah Parker Remond), Josephine St. Pierre Ruffin, and a number of New England African-American activists attended AWSA conventions and meetings, but like their fellow African Americans in the NWSA, AWSA African-American suffragists believed that white feminists deliberately ignored the special needs and problems of African-American women. By the late 1880s, they became increasingly disgruntled as white suffrage leaders found it politically expedient to reject the political needs of all African Americans in their single-minded pursuit of national woman suffrage.

Although the AWSA and the NWSA shared the same goals—to achieve woman suffrage and women's political and social equality—their political agendas and strategies differed. The AWSA believed that waging one state campaign at a time was the most efficacious method of achieving national woman suffrage and a federal suffrage amendment. AWSA leaders were convinced that they could prove to the nation the benefits of woman suffrage by first obtaining it in individual states and then publicizing its successful operation. In addition to supporting state suffrage associations in their own statewide campaigns, the AWSA disseminated massive amounts of suffrage literature wherever it was campaigning. The AWSA was also unique in its use of paid lecture agents to canvass campaign areas (*HWS*, 2:763–764).

From the time the AWSA was organized, a number of male and female suffragists attempted to reunite the two factions of the woman suffrage movement. Lucretia Coffin Mott, Theodore Tilton, Isabella Beecher Hooker, Anthony, and others made repeated attempts at reconciliation during the first few years after the 1869 split. None succeeded, however, because neither organization was willing to compromise or to relinquish its most highly valued characteristics and priorities. Stone, Blackwell, and other AWSA leaders were adamant about retaining their delegate organization and maintaining the state-by-state strategy as their principal tactic. Anthony and NWSA leaders were equally firm in their insistence on the priority of a federal suffrage amendment and their rejection of a delegate system. It was not until 1887 that NWSA and AWSA leaders, egged on by a younger, rising generation of suffragists, consented to reconciliation meetings. In 1890, the NWSA and the AWSA merged to form the National American Woman Suffrage Association (NAWSA).

Related entries:
American Equal Rights Association
Beecher, Henry Ward
Blackwell, Henry Browne
Fifteenth Amendment
Harper, Frances Ellen Watkins
Mott, Lucretia Coffin
National American Woman Suffrage Association
National Woman Suffrage Association
The Revolution
Stone, Lucy
Tilton, Theodore
Truth, Sojourner
Woman Suffrage Movement
The *Woman's Journal*

Suggestions for further reading:
Flexner, Eleanor. 1975. *Century of Struggle: The Woman's Rights Movement in the United States.* Cambridge, Mass.: Belknap Press of Harvard University Press.
Kerr, Andrea Moore. 1992. *Lucy Stone: Speaking Out for Equality.* New Brunswick, N.J.: Rutgers University Press.
————. 1995. "White Women's Rights, Black Men's Wrongs: Free Love, Blackmail, and the Formation of the American Woman Suffrage Association." In *One Woman, One Vote: Rediscovering the Woman Suffrage Movement,* ed. Marjorie Spruill Wheeler. Troutdale, Oreg.: New Sage Press.

Anthony, Daniel (1794–1862)

Susan B. Anthony's father, Daniel Anthony, was the oldest of the nine children of the Quakers Humphrey and Hannah Lapham Anthony of Adams, Massachusetts, a farming village in the northwest corner of the state. Humphrey Anthony was a wealthy farmer whose family had settled in the Hoosac River valley on the slopes of Mount Greylock in the late eighteenth century. Lapham Anthony, a high-ranking Quaker from a prominent family, arranged for Daniel to attend the renowned Nine Partners, a Quaker boarding school in Dutchess County in eastern New York. Daniel, who knew his father expected him to become a farmer, was exhilarated by his education and soon became a teacher at Nine Partners. When he returned to Adams in 1814, he reluctantly joined his father in working on the family farm but also became schoolmaster of his own school on the Anthony homestead.

In 1817, he married one of his students, Lucy Read, a non-Quaker he had known all his life. During their engagement, he built a new home from lumber his father had given him on a parcel of land that was a gift from Lucy's father. Daniel established a small general store in the front corner room of the house, where he sold the usual dry goods and liquor.

"Marrying out of meeting" was not only frowned upon but forbidden. When the adventurous couple embarked on their honeymoon trip across the wilderness frontier of western New York state, Daniel undoubtedly knew that when he returned he would have to face the Quaker elders. Not long after they arrived home, the elders censured Daniel for selling alcohol in his store and for his marriage to a non-Quaker. Daniel's response to the ruling may have mollified the Quaker establishment because, in the end, they elected not to disown him. As he later told his wife and family, in addition to agreeing never to sell hard liquor, he told the elders, "I was sorry that in order to marry the woman I loved best, I had to violate a rule of the religious society I revered most" (Harper 1899, 1:10). Susan always believed that Daniel's family's high standing in the Quaker community and its respect for Daniel's integrity and education influenced them to retain him as a member.

In the early years of his marriage, Daniel farmed his land and operated the store. In 1822, he put into action a dream that had long intrigued him—building and operating his own cotton textile mill. He harnessed the water power in Tophet Brook, which traversed his father-in-law's property, and constructed a three-and-one-half-story mill powered by the stream. He also supervised the building of more than 20 cotton looms. His textile mill was very successful and was soon weaving the profitable cotton cloth. The success imbued him with confidence and increased his desire to expand his operation, but because he lacked capital, he was not able to relocate to a site that would support a larger mill.

John McLean, a businessman and judge from Battenville, New York, visited Daniel's mill and offered him the opportunity he had been hoping for. McLean owned an old mill in Battenville on the Battenkill River. He had been searching for a man to reconstruct and re-outfit it for cotton production. McLean had plenty of capital, and Daniel enthusiastically accepted the offer to manage his mill. His wife and both sets of parents were devastated at the prospect of Daniel moving his family out of the area, but he was determined to seize this opportunity. In 1826, Lucy, Daniel, and their young children Guelma, Susan, Hannah, and Daniel Read Anthony moved to Battenville and lived for a time with John McLean in his grand home until they found a home of their own.

The Battenville mill was exceptionally prosperous through the mid-1830s, and

Daniel Anthony, father of Susan B. Anthony.

Daniel attained status as one of the area's most esteemed citizens. But by 1836 a national economic disaster was looming. Vast economic changes, exacerbated by factors in the cotton industry, caused the Panic of 1837 and the resulting economic depression of 1838–1843 (*see* Panic of 1837). By 1838, Daniel was in deep financial trouble and knew that bankruptcy was imminent. He lost the mill and many of his business concerns. The Anthony family had to move to the less auspicious village of Hardscrabble, 2 miles down the Battenkill River. The business reversal was a devastating loss for Daniel, as national economic forces beyond his control eliminated the enterprises he had so carefully constructed. Despite repeated attempts to launch new businesses and investments, he never again achieved the prosperity he and his family had enjoyed when they had lived in Battenville. In 1845, he gave up the quest for an economic comeback and, with the money Lucy Read Anthony had inherited from her family, arranged their purchase of a farm in Rochester, New York. Daniel farmed for a time, but, as in years past, his heart was not invested in an agricultural lifestyle. He soon became a salesman for the New York Life Insurance Company. He made a success of this business and pursued it for the rest of his life.

Daniel's interests were not confined to business and industry. Upon moving to Battenville in 1826, he became interested in the temperance movement and organized temperance meetings for his employees. As he had promised the Quaker elders when he lived in Adams, he never again sold hard liquor. According to Susan, another incident in Adams had also influenced his decision to refrain from selling liquor. In this story, Daniel was horror-struck when a man was discovered frozen to death in the Adams area next to an empty jug of whisky. Although Daniel had not sold him the liquor, from that time on, he felt a moral responsibility to cease all his sales of hard liquor (Harper 1899, 1:17–18).

After the move to Hardscrabble, Daniel's temperance convictions took precedence over his adherence to Quaker law. The young people of the community asked him if they could hold their dancing classes in the old tavern ballroom, a large room on the top floor of the Anthony home. At first Daniel rejected their request. As a Quaker, he could not condone dancing by allowing it in his own house. But, as Susan recalled, the teenagers pointed out that the only other place available was a tavern where alcohol was sold. When they insisted that they did not want to be subjected to the temptations of that environment, Daniel relented, and the dancing school was established at the Anthonys' home. The Quaker elders soon terminated his membership. He was aggrieved to be disowned but believed that he had done the only thing that was morally right. Though rejected from membership, he continued to attend Quaker meetings but became increasingly secure in following the dictates of his own conscience and morality.

For Daniel, the most exciting part of the move to Rochester was his new Hicksite

Quaker neighbors. Rochester was home to a radical group of freethinking, reform-oriented Quakers, and Daniel, with his fervent temperance views and antislavery sentiments, was immediately at home among them. Isaac and Amy Kirby Post, Elias and Rhoda De Garmo, and a new Rochester resident, the African-American abolitionist Frederick Douglass, were among his close friends. By the time Susan was teaching in the distant community of Canajoharie, New York, in the late 1840s, Daniel was growing ever more zealous in his abolitionist activism.

With the most radical members of this community, Daniel withdrew from the Rochester Friends Meeting because the elders discouraged and tried to restrain their activism. The Rochester abolitionists attended Sunday afternoon gatherings, often at the Anthony farm, where touring abolitionist agents and lecturers were frequent guests.

Historians and scholars have questioned the impact of Daniel Anthony's activism on his daughter Susan's life as a reformer. Despite all the debate on this issue, Susan never doubted the crucial importance of his influence. In letters to family and friends and in the authorized biography written by Ida Husted Harper, Susan repeatedly acknowledged the pivotal significance of her father's interest, encouragement, and financial support of her activism.

Related entries:
Abolitionist Movement
Anthony, Lucy Read
Anthony, Susan B.
Civil War
Douglass, Frederick
Kansas-Nebraska Act
Panic of 1837
Quakerism (Society of Friends)

Suggestions for further reading:
Anthony, Katharine. 1954. *Susan B. Anthony: Her Personal History and Her Era.* Garden City, N.Y.: Doubleday.
Harper, Ida Husted. 1899, 1908. *The Life and Work of Susan B. Anthony.* 3 vols. Indianapolis: Bowen-Merrill (vols. 1 and 2) and Hollenbeck Press (vol. 3).

Anthony, Daniel Read
(1824–1904)

*D*aniel Read Anthony, the older of Susan B. Anthony's two younger brothers, was a newspaper publisher and journalist, a respected Kansas Republican Party leader, and a successful businessman in the Kansas frontier town of Leavenworth. An important historical figure in his own right, he was a vibrant personality, known for his fervent antislavery and Radical Republican convictions. He became a legend in local Kansas history, which abounds with tales of his exploits during the settlement of the towns of Lawrence and Leavenworth, the Border War, the abolitionist era, and the Civil War and throughout his career as a journalist and politician.

D. R. Anthony, as he was known to his friends and family, was four and a half years younger than his famous sister. He was the youngest of the Anthony children who were born in Adams, Massachusetts, in the years before the family moved to Battenville, New York. Anthony was always close to D. R., as she was to each of her siblings, and D. R. never stopped showing his affection for her. Despite the nearly 1,000 miles between them, they corresponded regularly throughout their lives. Anthony visited him and his family whenever she was in the West, and she highly valued his opinions and advice, even though she frequently disagreed with them.

Following his high school education, D. R. worked as a clerk in Lenox, Massachusetts. He also was a teacher in the Battenville, New York, area and in western Massachusetts. In 1854 he traveled to Kansas with the New England Emigrant Aid Company, an experience that changed his life. D. R. loved the freshness and drama of Kansas Territory, where free-soil settlers, many from the Northeast, were determined to stake out new lives and communities against tremendous obstacles. When he returned home later that year to Rochester, New York, he reported on Kansas's bitter struggle for freedom and

delivered his first political speech protesting the Kansas-Nebraska Act in Saratoga Springs, New York. Like his younger brother, Jacob Merritt Anthony, D. R. was a follower of John Brown, the militant abolitionist who was a defender of the Kansas free-soilers.

In 1857, D. R. Anthony returned to Kansas to make the town of Leavenworth his permanent home. In 1861, he purchased his first newspaper, the *Leavenworth Conservative*. It was an odd choice for a man who, by his own admission, had already gained renown for being "one of the most radical men in Kansas." He served briefly during the Civil War as a lieutenant colonel in the First Kansas Cavalry (later renamed the Seventh Kansas Cavalry). D. R. created an enormous controversy when he ordered his troops to prevent southern men from reclaiming fugitive slaves who had passed through Union lines, a directive that was in opposition to federal law. He was arrested and imprisoned when he refused to countermand the order. Following an investigation by the U.S. Senate, he was permitted to return to active duty, but in September 1862 he resigned from the army and returned home to receive accolades from Leavenworth's antislavery advocates.

He became mayor of Leavenworth for the first time in 1863 and remained active in city politics throughout his life. In 1864, he bought the *Leavenworth Evening Bulletin* and, in 1871, the *Leavenworth Times*. In addition to his career as publisher and editor of the *Leavenworth Times*, he was a leader in Kansas Republican Party politics and served in the Kansas state legislature. An astute businessman, he invested in real estate and was director and trustee of several railroad corporations.

Life in a frontier boomtown was nothing like the staid Quaker world in which D. R. had been raised. Particularly in Leavenworth, forged in the bloodshed of the Border War, living in the midst of violence was an accepted fact of life. His Quaker upbringing abandoned, D. R. always carried a gun, as was the norm for men in Leavenworth. His rabidly outspoken editorial opinions frequently made him a target of violence. In 1865, while Susan B. Anthony was visiting, D. R. criticized a Leavenworth citizen in the *Evening Bulletin,* who then assaulted him with an umbrella. Not satisfied by this attack, the outraged man gathered all his friends to stake out D. R., who likewise had collected all his comrades. A feud ensued, putting D. R.'s life in jeopardy for more than two weeks. In 1868, he was implicated in a fatal shooting incident, and in 1875, he was nearly killed by a rival Leavenworth newspaper owner during a performance at the Leavenworth Opera House. When Susan received the news of her brother's injury, she rushed to Leavenworth, and with her brother Merritt and her sister-in-law, helped to save his life. Leavenworth's reputation for lawlessness was legendary among easterners. Anna Dickinson, the abolitionist orator and friend of Susan B. Anthony, remarked after lecturing in Leavenworth, "It will take one generation here to forget the lessons of barbarism and another to learn those of civilization" (Anthony 1954, 232).

D. R. traveled east to marry Anna E. Osborne of Martha's Vineyard, Massachusetts, in January 1864. They had five children, only two of whom lived to adulthood, Maude Anthony Koehler and Daniel Read Anthony, Jr., who later became a U.S. congressman from Kansas. D. R.'s daughter and her aunt's cherished namesake, Susan "Susie" B. Anthony, was tragically killed in a skating accident in 1889 while still a teenager.

In 1904, when Susan was 84 years old, she and her sister Mary Stafford Anthony traveled to Leavenworth to visit D. R., whose health was rapidly deteriorating. They remained two weeks, knowing all the while that it was probably for the last time. Weeks after the sisters returned to Rochester, the telegram announcing his death arrived, and Susan and Mary once again boarded a train for Leavenworth to attend his funeral. It was a painful passing for them both and very difficult for them to comprehend that of their large and loving family, they now had only each other.

Related entries:
Anthony, Jacob Merritt
Anthony, Susan B.
Brown, John
Civil War
Kansas-Nebraska Act

Suggestions for further reading:
Anthony, Katharine. 1954. *Susan B. Anthony: Her Personal History and Her Era.* Garden City, N.Y.: Doubleday.
Gordon, Ann D., and Tamara Gaskell Miller, eds. 1997. *The Selected Papers of Elizabeth Cady Stanton and Susan B. Anthony.* Vol. 1. New Brunswick, N.J.: Rutgers University Press.
Harper, Ida Husted. 1899, 1908. *The Life and Work of Susan B. Anthony.* 3 vols. Indianapolis: Bowen-Merrill (vols. 1 and 2) and Hollenbeck Press (vol. 3).

Anthony, Guelma Penn

See **McLean, Guelma Penn Anthony**

Anthony, Hannah Lapham

See **Mosher, Hannah Lapham Anthony**

Anthony, Jacob Merritt (1834–1900)

Jacob Merritt Anthony, Susan B. Anthony's youngest sibling, was born in Battenville, New York, when she was 14 years old. As a young man in the mid–1850s, Merritt was strongly influenced by the militant abolitionist John Brown, who frequently visited Frederick Douglass and the rest of the abolitionist community in Rochester, New York. In 1856, Merritt followed John Brown to Osawatomie, Kansas Territory, to defend its settlers in maintaining Kansas's status as a free territory against marauding proslavery Missouri "border ruffians." Though extremely ill, Merritt helped to repel the Missouri forces when they raided Osawatomie that same year. Following the battle, Merritt struggled back to his cabin, where for weeks he lay incapacitated and alone while recovering, his family not knowing if he had survived the raid (*see* Kansas–Nebraska Act).

Merritt settled permanently in Kansas, at first living in Osawatomie. He married a cousin, Mary Almina Luther, in 1858. Prior to the Civil War, he farmed for a brief time in Pikes Peak, Colorado, but soon returned to Kansas. A little more than two months after Kansas entered the Union as a free state on January 29, 1861, the Civil War erupted. Merritt served as a captain in the Union army for the entire duration of the war. At war's end, he resumed his family life in Leavenworth, Kansas, living near his brother Daniel Read Anthony. In 1869, Merritt and his family settled permanently in Fort Scott, another large town in Kansas Territory.

Susan often visited Merritt, Mary, and their four children (all of whom lived to adulthood) when she was traveling in the Midwest. She maintained close relationships with Merritt's children all of her life, but of them all, she was closest to the oldest, Lucy Elmina Anthony, who became a suffragist.

Like all of Anthony's siblings, Merritt cared deeply about his brothers and sisters. In 1875, when Daniel Read Anthony was in critical condition following a near-fatal shooting in Leavenworth, Merritt rushed to his brother's home and kept a vigil by his bedside until Daniel emerged from the crisis.

In June 1900, Susan was shocked to receive a telegram informing her of Merritt's sudden, unexpected death. At 80 years of age, she found it hard to accept that Merritt, who had been in excellent health and was only 66 years old, should die before her. Although her brother D. R. and sister Mary shared her grief, Anthony found it extremely difficult to carry on. She cried day after day. In her diary she wrote, "I have shed more tears than in years and years before" (Harper 1908, 3:1217–1218).

Related entries:
Anthony, Susan B.
Brown, John
Kansas–Nebraska Act

Suggestions for further reading:
Anthony, Katharine. 1954. *Susan B. Anthony: Her Personal History and Her Era.* Garden City, N.Y.: Doubleday.
Lutz, Alma. 1959. *Susan B. Anthony: Rebel, Crusader, Humanitarian.* Boston: Beacon Press.

Anthony, Lucy Read (1793–1880)

*T*he mother of Susan B. Anthony, Lucy Read was born in Adams, Massachusetts, the second child and daughter of Daniel and Susannah Richardson Read's seven children. Like Daniel Anthony and his family, the Reads were farmers, living 1 mile outside of the village of Adams. Richardson Read raised her children as Baptists. Her husband Daniel Read, though also reared as a Baptist, adamantly adhered to the Universalist faith, another Protestant denomination.

Lucy Read and the Quaker Daniel Anthony fell in love during the years when she was a student in his school. Although Lucy readily agreed to marry Daniel in 1817, she was less sure about marrying into the Society of Friends. She could have converted to Quakerism but chose not to and even claimed that she was "not good enough" to be a Quaker. Although it is not clear exactly what she meant, she adored singing and dancing, two pastimes forbidden to Quakers. She knew that marrying Daniel meant that she would have to give up both activities, whether she decided to become a Quaker or not. During their engagement, she insisted that she attend one final dancing party before their wedding. Daniel agreed, and on a July evening, Lucy danced until four in the morning with one young man after another as Daniel watched from the sidelines.

All descriptions of Read Anthony agree that she was a shy, reserved woman who kept

Lucy Read Anthony, mother of Susan B. Anthony.

ter woman's rights convention in August 1848, two weeks after the historic Seneca Falls Convention. She also signed the Rochester convention's *Declaration of Sentiments*. She always supported her husband's temperance and abolitionist activism as well as Susan's reform work, even though it was extremely unusual for a mother in the nineteenth century to approve a daughter's life choice that did not include marriage.

More than a year after Daniel Anthony's death, Read Anthony sold the Rochester farm that she had bought with Daniel in 1845. As much as it pained her to abandon a home so full of the memory of Daniel, she realized that she and Mary could not manage the farm on their own. During this time, Susan wrote a letter to Mary in which she expressed some of her deepest feelings about their mother and her role in their lives.

her feelings to herself. Susan B. Anthony described her as a loving, caring mother but also one who communicated little. Read Anthony was said to have been extremely embarrassed by each of her pregnancies. Even as she approached the time of birth, she refused to acknowledge or discuss her condition except with her mother. She gave birth to eight children, six of whom lived to lead productive, healthy adult lives. One child was stillborn and another, Eliza Tefft Anthony, died of scarlet fever at age two. Susan and her sisters Guelma, Hannah, and Mary all worried about Read Anthony's overwhelming workload—managing the household for their own large family and for the many boarders who worked in Daniel Anthony's mill. Her daughters eagerly assisted her with the endless cooking, cleaning, baking, sewing, and laundry. Despite her never-ending household duties, Read Anthony always made the time to care for sick neighbors and the poverty-stricken in their community.

With Daniel and her youngest daughter Mary, Read Anthony attended the Roches-

The rest of us have our work to engross us . . . , but mother now lives in her children, and I often feel as if we did too little to lighten her heart and cheer her path. Never was there a mother who came nearer to knowing nothing save her own household, her husband and children. . . . If we sometimes give her occasion to feel that we prized father more than her, it was she who taught us ever to hold him thus above all others. Our high respect and deep love for him, our perfect trust in him, we owe to mother's precepts and vastly more to her example. . . . we shall live in remembrance of her wise counsel, tender watching, self-sacrifice and devotion not second to that we now cherish for the memory of our father—nay, it will even transcend that in measure, as a mother's constant and ever-present love and care for her children are beyond those of a father. (Harper 1899, 1:232)

Read Anthony wanted to move closer to the center of Rochester but did not purchase a home immediately, choosing to stay awhile with her oldest daughter Guelma and her son-in-law Aaron McLean in Rochester. In 1866 she bought a large brick house on Madison Street in Rochester, large enough for the entire McLean family and her daughter Mary Anthony to live with her.

In the months after Guelma's death in 1873 and as Hannah's tuberculosis progressed, Read Anthony, now 80 years of age, withdrew from reality and was no longer aware of the losses occurring within her family (Anthony 1954, 325). Mary and Susan remained as devoted to her as ever. During the final months of her mother's life, Susan did not undertake any extensive travel but remained close at hand to help nurse her mother. Read Anthony died in 1880 at the age of 86.

Related entries:
Anthony, Daniel
Anthony, Susan B.
New York Married Women's Property Law of 1860
Read, Joshua

Suggestions for further reading:
Anthony, Katharine. 1954. *Susan B. Anthony: Her Personal History and Her Era.* Garden City, N.Y.: Doubleday.
Harper, Ida Husted. 1899, 1908. *The Life and Work of Susan B. Anthony.* 3 vols. Indianapolis: Bowen-Merrill (vols. 1 and 2) and Hollenbeck Press (vol. 3).

Anthony, Mary Stafford (1827–1907)

*M*ary Stafford Anthony, Susan B. Anthony's youngest sister, was an educator, women's rights advocate, and suffragist. The youngest daughter of Daniel and Lucy Read Anthony, she was born in Battenville, New York, six months after Daniel Anthony settled his family there. Mary be-

gan her teaching career at age 17 when she accepted a job in the town of Fort Edward, New York, for $1.50 per week. In 1856, she returned home to Rochester, New York, to begin teaching in the city's public schools. Like Susan, she supported equal employment opportunities for women in education. In 1860, when she was asked to temporarily replace a school principal, she refused to accept the job if it meant that she would receive a fraction of his salary. The school board agreed to pay her the full salary.

In 1848, when she was 21 years old, she attended the second woman's rights convention, held in Rochester, just two weeks after the first woman's rights convention in Seneca Falls, New York. Mary and both her parents signed the convention's *Declaration of Sentiments.* When Susan arrived home for her summer vacation from teaching in Canajoharie, New York, Mary piqued her sister's curiosity about the new women's rights movement with her enthusiastic report of the convention and its feminist activists.

Mary was a self-sacrificing, dutiful daughter who devoted her life to the service of others, particularly those in her own family. During the years that she was a teacher and principal in the Rochester schools, she cared for her mother and managed the Anthony household. During her sisters Guelma's and Hannah's illnesses, she also supervised the Mosher household next door, nursed her sick sisters, and cared for her brothers-in-law Aaron M. McLean and Eugene Mosher and an extended tribe of nieces and nephews. She managed all this uncomplainingly and seems never to have considered her own needs or wishes as being separate from her family's.

Although too busy to be deeply involved in the woman suffrage movement for most of her life, Mary strongly supported Susan's suffrage work. Mary sacrificed one entire summer vacation to work in the office of *The Revolution,* Anthony and Elizabeth Cady Stanton's women's rights newspaper, and she donated $500 to keep the newspaper afloat.

After her retirement from education in 1883 at the age of 56, she had more time to devote to social reform. She was a member of the Woman's Christian Temperance Union (WCTU); volunteered for the Red Cross; assisted Clara Barton after a devastating flood destroyed Johnstown, Pennsylvania; and was an officer of the Committee of Charities in Rochester. In 1892, she became president of the Political Equality Club in Rochester, a post she held for 11 years. She was also an active suffragist in the New York State Woman Suffrage Association. In 1893, she was elected to serve as its corresponding secretary, just as the society inaugurated a campaign to persuade state legislators to adopt a woman suffrage amendment in the new state constitution. Mary spared no effort in her management of the central campaign office established at the Anthony homestead in Rochester. She worked unceasingly from December 1893 through July 1894 preparing thousands of letters, pamphlets, and suffrage tracts for mailing, while Susan crisscrossed the state on a massive lecture tour.

In 1904, Mary accompanied Susan, who was becoming too feeble to travel alone, on a trip to Europe to the International Council of Women and the International Woman Suffrage Alliance in Berlin. During Susan's last few years, as her strength diminished, Mary assisted her so that she could carry on her work for woman suffrage. In 1905, during the year that she and Anthony traveled to Oregon, Mary began to suffer the dizziness and fainting spells that were the warning signs of her final illness. Nevertheless, she remained hearty enough to care for Susan through her final illness in the early months of 1906. After Susan's death, while Mary's health continued to fail, she pushed herself to return to Oregon, as she had promised Susan, to assist in the 1906 Oregon suffrage campaign. By the time she arrived back in Rochester that summer, she was truly ill, and her health declined steadily until her death in early February 1907. She left almost all of her estate to the woman suffrage and women's

rights causes, but the house and $5,000 went to her niece Lucy Elmina Anthony, the daughter of her brother Jacob Merritt Anthony and Anna Howard Shaw. As Mary's will stated, Lucy was "the only niece who has given her time and labor for the Suffrage Cause."

Related entries:
Anthony, Susan B.
State Suffrage Campaigns—New York, Oregon
University of Rochester

Suggestions for further reading:
Anthony, Katharine. 1954. *Susan B. Anthony: Her Personal History and Her Era.* Garden City, N.Y.: Doubleday.
Harper, Ida Husted. 1899, 1908. *The Life and Work of Susan B. Anthony.* 3 vols. Indianapolis: Bowen-Merrill (vols. 1 and 2) and Hollenbeck Press (vol. 3).

Anthony, Susan B. (1820–1906)*

CHILDHOOD

Susan Brownell Anthony was born in Adams, Massachusetts, on February 15, 1820. The second child and second daughter of Daniel and Lucy Read Anthony, she was named for Daniel's sister Susannah Anthony Brownell, who died when Susan was about a year old. In the early nineteenth century, Adams was a quiet farming village in the northwestern part of the state, in the shadow of its largest mountain, Mount Greylock. Both the Anthony and the Read families had lived in the region since the late eighteenth century.

Lucy Read Anthony gave birth to eight children, six of whom lived to adulthood.

---

*Since this entire volume encompasses Susan B. Anthony's life and work, this entry is not a comprehensive biography but a discussion of aspects of Anthony's life that have not been fully treated in other entries—her childhood and young adulthood, the impact of her family relationships upon her life, her personality, her relationships with other reformers, her leadership style, and her final years and death.

Almost all of Susan's early childhood memories include the two sisters closest to her in age. Her sister Guelma was 20 months older and her sister Hannah was 19 months younger than she. The only other sibling born while the family lived in Adams was Daniel Read Anthony, born in 1824. Besides her parents, the other people most important to Susan were her grandparents, all of whom lived nearby. The Anthony girls frequently visited their maternal grandparents, Daniel and Susannah Richardson Read, who indulged and doted on their beloved grandchildren. Susan's earliest recollections are filled with the details of the delicious foods her grandmother Read served whenever they stopped by. Her grandfather Read entertained them with stories of his days as a soldier in the Revolutionary War when he had fought under Benedict Arnold in Quebec and Ethan Allen at Fort Ticonderoga. Her Quaker grandparents, Humphrey and Hannah Lapham Anthony, also lived in Adams. Her grandmother Anthony was a strong, highly respected, top-ranking Quaker, an elder in the Quaker Meeting and a member of the High Seat, as was her mother before her.

Susan recalled that she learned to read when she was about three or four years old while staying at her grandmother Anthony's house. When she was six years old, Daniel Anthony uprooted his family and moved them to Battenville, New York, a village 35 miles north of Albany, where he managed and modernized a mill on the Battenkill River. In 1833, the Anthony family moved into their new, beautiful brick home, a symbol of Daniel Anthony's business success and prosperity. Susan's three youngest siblings—Mary, Eliza, and Jacob Merritt, were all born in Battenville.

At first Susan and her sisters attended the local district school in Battenville, but the education there proved to be of the most rudimentary variety. When Susan longed to learn long division, her male teacher told her she could not learn it. In fact, he did not have sufficient mathematical knowledge to teach her. Susan persisted in her determination to learn the skill and persuaded a local farm boy to teach her.

Whether impelled by the long-division fiasco or not, Susan's father resolved that he must provide an exemplary education for all his children regardless of gender, a very unusual decision for a middle-class parent in the 1830s. In general, girls of the early nineteenth century attended school for only a few years and were instructed in only the most basic skills—reading, writing, and simple arithmetic. They were deprived of the opportunity to study mathematics, the sciences, Latin, and Greek—all considered essential to a boy's education. But Daniel Anthony wanted much more for his daughters. He established a school for his children and for the children of his neighbors who were willing to contribute to the teacher's salary. The school was first housed in Daniel Anthony's store. When the Anthonys' new home was completed, a special schoolroom was set aside for the "home-school." Daniel Anthony employed only the most highly educated women teachers for his school. Almost all were graduates of the most respected female seminaries, including a young woman who had studied with Mary Lyon, the renowned educator who would soon found her own female seminary at Mount Holyoke, Massachusetts.

During her girlhood years, Susan's days were filled with school, her chores, and her needlework. Her mother, besides having to cook, clean, and do laundry for her own large family, also had to board the schoolteacher and the Vermont "Green Mountain" girls employed in her husband's mill and factory. Even before the Anthony girls were old enough to attend school, they were helping their mother with the cooking and cleaning. As Susan later recalled, she and her sisters were eager to help. Susan always worried about how hard her mother had to work and was eager to lighten her load. No matter how busy Read Anthony was, she made sure that her daughters' sewing and needlework skills were top-notch. Susan loved sewing and was extraordinarily skilled. She created a beautiful sampler at age 11 and eventually completed a quilt.

As part of his children's Quaker upbringing, Daniel Anthony wanted them to attend Quaker meetings. A year after he became a member of the meeting in Easton, New York, he applied for all his children to become members. Since Susan's mother was a Baptist and never became a Quaker, this formal application was necessary. In January 1833, the Anthony children were all accepted as members. Not long afterward, Daniel Anthony asked permission to hold Quaker meetings in his home. Since Battenville was 10 miles from Easton, his request was approved. As Quakers, the Anthony children were not allowed to sing or to dance, which was a hardship since many of their friends and neighbors were not Quakers. Even though Read Anthony supported her husband's decision to raise their children as Quakers, she did occasionally permit Susan and her siblings to attend children's parties.

In 1834, when Susan was 14 years old, her youngest sister Eliza, born in 1832, died as a result of scarlet fever, a common cause of death among babies and young children in the days before antibiotics. (Read Anthony also gave birth to a child that was stillborn when Susan was very young.) In her elder years, Susan was fond of recalling the antics of little Eliza. She declared that she was the "cunningest" child she had ever known (Anthony 1954, 19).

At her father's direction, Susan began her career as a teacher during the summer that she was 15 years old. She taught the summer session in her father's home school, which, because the busiest agricultural season was under way, was composed of very young children only. During the winter of 1837, she boarded briefly with a Quaker family in Easton and taught their children at a salary of $1.00 per week. She then taught in the local district school for $1.50 per week. Guelma and Hannah each took teaching jobs as well, which was all part of Daniel Anthony's

master plan for his daughters. Although criticized by the other middle-class adults of their community, who believed that it was improper for a man of his social standing to allow his daughters to work, Daniel Anthony was wholeheartedly committed to ensuring that all his children possessed the skills to be self-sufficient, independent adults.

Susan had not been teaching long when she discovered that women teachers received a fraction of a male teacher's salary, even though women taught just as many students and worked as hard and as many hours as men. Throughout her career as a teacher, it frustrated her beyond measure whenever she replaced an inadequate male teacher and only received a quarter of his salary. Achieving equality in teacher salaries as well as equality for women in education were causes that she pursued all her life, especially while she was a young reformer in the 1850s at state teachers' conventions.

Daniel Anthony also wanted his daughters to attend one of the excellent female seminaries that were rising in prominence during the 1830s. In 1836, Guelma began attending Quaker Deborah Moulson's boarding school outside Philadelphia. In the fall of 1837, Susan also enrolled as a student there. For a girl who had never been far from home, the trip to Deborah Moulson's school was an eye-opening, thrilling adventure and one that used nearly every mode of transportation available at that time. She and her father traveled by wagon to Albany, by steamboat down the Hudson River to New York City, and by boat to board a train bound for Bordentown, New Jersey. Then they traveled on another boat down the Delaware River to Philadelphia, at which point they boarded a horse-drawn omnibus. They completed their journey to Deborah Moulson's seminary in the village of Hamilton, Pennsylvania, on foot. Separating from her father was a wrenching experience for Susan. In fact, the months away from her entire family were extremely painful for her. She coped by writing frequent, long letters to her parents.

Deborah Moulson's style of teaching, though in keeping with the age, did not make Susan's adjustment to boarding school life any easier. The brochure advertising Moulson's school stated that "the inculcation of the principles of Humility, Morality and a love of Virtue will receive particular attention," an indication that Moulson took her responsibility as moral mentor seriously. She was extremely strict and insisted that her students constantly strive to perfect their moral natures. Under her tutelage, Susan became obsessed with her imperfections and her inability to meet Moulson's and her own expectations. Her diary provides a clear insight into these preoccupations. "I have been guilty of much levity and nonsensical conversation and have also permitted thoughts to occupy my mind which should have been far distant," Susan wrote. "Perhaps the reason I can not see my own defects is because my heart is hardened. O, May it become more and more refined until nothing shall remain but perfect purity" (Harper 1899, 1:29).

Moulson instructed her students to keep diaries, but they were intended to be records of a student's struggle to achieve self-perfection rather than a personal refuge. She also carefully monitored students' letters to their families and friends. The girls first wrote their letters on slates. As soon as Moulson had edited them, they wrote their final drafts on paper. After receiving Moulson's approval, they were mailed.

No matter how hard Susan tried, she could not please Moulson. According to Susan's recollections, Moulson approved of everything Guelma did. When Susan confronted Moulson about this discrepancy, the teacher explained that Guelma was doing her best, but Susan, who was much more capable, was not. On one occasion, when Moulson was examining the girls' writing, Susan asked her to read her work. Confident that her work was sound, she was overwhelmed when Moulson criticized precisely what Susan believed was best about her writing. Moulson then pointed to the dot of an *i* and asked

Susan to repeat the rule for the dotting of *i*'s. When Susan admitted she was ignorant of it, Moulson said that "it was no wonder she [Moulson] had undergone so much distress in mind and body, and that her time had been devoted to us in vain." In her diary, Susan wrote, "This was like an Electrical shock to me. I rushed upstairs to my room where, without restraint, I could give vent to my tears. . . . If I am such a vile sinner, I would that I might feel it myself" (Harper 1899, 1:29).

No explanation makes sense of Moulson's repeatedly harsh treatment of Susan. By the time Susan entered the seminary, Moulson knew that her tuberculosis was progressing rapidly. As Moulson's health swiftly deteriorated during the winter of 1837–1838, she probably knew that she was dying, a reality made all the more painful because, after decades of teaching, she had only recently realized her dream of establishing her own school. Yet even this personal tragedy does not explain why she singled out Susan for such severity.

Despite the anguish of her months at Moulson's seminary, Susan managed to enjoy all she was learning. She loved the sciences and mathematics, especially algebra. She also relished the camaraderie and the light-hearted moments she shared with the other girls. But in the end, Moulson's severe moral training left Susan emotionally crippled for many years. Susan wrote, "We were cautioned by our dear Teacher to-day to beware of self-esteem," an instruction that sums up the legacy of Moulson's teaching for Susan. For many years, Susan would not only doubt her goodness but would continue to be obsessed with her imperfections. Instead of feeling confident about her many strengths—her intelligence, her compassion for others, her refusal to give up, her many outstanding skills—she felt beleaguered by her imagined moral failures, her selfishness, and her lack of humility and piety and by what she had been led to believe were her poor communication skills. A profound sense of inferiority plagued her for many years after leaving

Moulson's school and would hinder her early years as a reformer.

YOUNG ADULTHOOD

Susan's departure from Moulson's seminary in May 1838 signaled the abrupt end of her childhood. When she and Guelma returned home, they discovered with full force what their father had been preparing them for all spring—Daniel Anthony faced bankruptcy. The Panic of 1837 had become the economic depression of 1838, affecting manufacturers and businesspeople throughout the country. Daniel Anthony lost his factory, his store, their handsome home, and most of their furniture and other belongings. Thanks to Susan's uncle, Joshua Read, they were able to salvage their most treasured possessions. Ever sensitive to the feelings of others, Susan was keenly aware of her father's agony over his business losses and longed to help.

In March 1839, the Anthony family moved to a house that had once been a hotel in Hardscrabble, a village 2 miles down the Battenkill River. Unlike Battenville, Hardscrabble was a poor, somewhat dilapidated little hamlet. The Anthonys particularly detested the name of the village, which no doubt symbolized for them the way its poorer inhabitants were forced to eke out a living. When Daniel Anthony later became postmaster of Hardscrabble, he used his authority to change its name to Center Falls.

In May 1839, Susan accepted a position as teacher at Quaker Eunice Kenyon's boarding school in New Rochelle, New York. Over the next five years, she would contribute all her earnings from her teaching toward the support of her family. Although she was lonely being away from home, the situation was a pleasant one, and Kenyon's manner was not at all reminiscent of Deborah Moulson's overbearing ways. She remained only a few months, however, returning home in the late summer of 1839.

During her months away from home, she corresponded avidly with her family and with Aaron McLean, Guelma's fiancé and grandson of Judge John McLean, Daniel's business partner. From the Anthonys' first days in Battenville, both Susan and Guelma had admired Aaron and enjoyed his company. He was a caring, intelligent, fun-loving older brother to them. In 1838, when Aaron and Guelma suddenly became a twosome, Susan was stunned to discover that they now considered her company superfluous. She did not record her feelings about Aaron and Guelma's budding relationship but appeared outwardly to accept it. She continued to be friendly with Aaron and to correspond with him when she was away from home. Yet considering how fond Susan was of Aaron and how much she enjoyed debating social and political issues with him, it is likely that Guelma and Aaron's attachment was a great loss for Susan. In September 1839, after Susan arrived home from New Rochelle, Aaron and Guelma were married. What Susan thought about the possibility of her own marriage is not clear. She did thoroughly enjoy male company, however, and had plenty of admirers, though she did not become close to any one young man.

When Daniel Anthony decided to move to a farm in Rochester, New York, in 1845, purchased with money Read Anthony had inherited from her family, Susan helped with the move, an exhausting but fascinating journey westward by barge from Albany to Rochester via the Erie Canal. With help from her uncle Joshua Read, in 1846 she was offered a position as the headmistress of female students at Canajoharie Academy, a well-known boarding school in Canajoharie, New York. Susan's three years there marked a turning point in her life. Now 26 years old, she was a mature young woman and an experienced, successful teacher, which boosted her self-confidence. She enjoyed spending time with her Read family cousins in the Canajoharie area. And for the first time, her wages were her own to spend. She reveled in the opportunity. She became fascinated by fashion and was able to allocate much of her earnings toward the purchase of new dresses, capes,

Susan B. Anthony at age 28, when she was a Canajoharie Academy teacher.

and hats. Without the presence or the influence of a Quaker community, Susan freely explored a different way of life. She attended parties and dances and dressed colorfully and stylishly.

But her life was not all pleasure and frivolity. She pursued her active interest in the temperance movement, which dated back to the days of her father's temperance involvement in Battenville when she was a girl. While Susan was becoming invested in the Daughters of Temperance organization in Canajoharie, her father's letters were filled with his vehement protests against slavery and news of the activities of his fellow Rochester Hicksite Quaker abolitionists. Daniel's antislavery fervor activated Susan's own abolitionist sentiment, but since Canajoharie residents were dead-set against abolitionism, she did not have an opportunity to become involved in the movement while living there. As a result, she focused her desire to perfect society toward the temperance movement and the abolition of alcohol consumption.

Both her father and her mother encouraged Susan's participation in the Daughters of Temperance and, in the early 1850s, her founding of the Woman's State Temperance Society. In fact, as long as Daniel and Lucy Read Anthony were alive, they fully approved of all of Susan's reform work. Daniel occasionally contributed money to her temperance, abolitionist, and women's rights projects and campaigns. Susan was unusual among women reformers in this regard. Her parents also allowed her the freedom to follow her own path without making demands that she marry, visit them frequently, or help with their household affairs, which was unusual for parents of daughters during the nineteenth century.

THE BEGINNINGS OF A REFORM CAREER

The 1850s were years of incessant activism for Anthony. The temperance movement, abolitionism, the women's rights movement, and women's labor issues attracted her attention and consumed all of her time. Throughout this decade she was rarely at home in Rochester and kept in touch with her family by mail. Women reformers became her closest friends and companions and formed another nurturing family for her. In the early 1850s, her friendships with Elizabeth Cady Stanton, Lucy Stone, and Antoinette Brown (Blackwell) were extremely important. Her associations with these women taught her about the world of reform, feminism, and the art of oratory. Most of all, the four women loved and respected each other, and because of that approval and regard, Anthony's self-confidence soared. However, the marriages of Stone in 1855 and Brown in 1856 severely altered her relationships with them. And once again, as was the case with her sisters Guelma and Hannah (who married in the spring of 1845), Stone's and Brown's nuptials forced Anthony to confront her own ambivalent feelings about marriage and her single status.

By the time of Stone's marriage, Anthony was 35 years old, and although Stone was three years older, Anthony must have realized that her own chances of finding a man who would respect and uphold her reform career were negligible. By this time, Anthony was solidly wedded to her women's rights work, and it appears that she had accepted this career path for herself. But it is essential to point out that she never swore off marriage, as Stone had prior to her relationship with Henry Blackwell. Judging from Anthony's letters and diaries, it seems most likely that she remained open to the possibility of marriage for many years. Although she is known to have refused several marriage proposals, she later emphasized that she did not marry because she never became romantically involved with a man she could respect morally and intellectually.

Yet despite her growing resolution to have an independent life, she was enraged when she discovered that Stone planned to marry. She found it extremely difficult to part with her dream of a united, tightly knit sisterhood of single women reformers who would devote all their energies to their cause. Anthony also realized that Stone's and Brown Blackwell's marriages and Cady Stanton's child-rearing and domestic responsibilities left her alone in the world of women's rights reform. To compensate, she deepened her connection with another close single woman friend and reformer, Lydia Mott. In 1859, after struggling to keep the women's rights movement afloat on her own, Anthony complained to Mott, "There is not one woman left who may be relied on, all have 'first to please their husband,' after which there is but little time or energy left to spend in any other direction." Then she explained her personal rejection of the institution of marriage: "In the depths of my soul there is a continual denial of the self-annihilating spiritual or legal union of two human beings. Such union, in the very nature of things, must bring an end to the free action of one or the other" (Harper 1899, 1:171).

For the rest of her life, Anthony maintained her conviction that for women, marriage and a leadership role in reform were not compatible. When Anthony was in her seventies, her friend and fellow African-American suffragist Ida Wells-Barnett reported that she confronted Anthony about her feelings about women reformers and marriage. Wells-Barnett observed:

> I had been with her several days before I noticed the way she would bite out my married name in addressing me. Finally I said to her, "Miss Anthony, don't you believe in women getting married?" She said, "Oh, yes, but not women like you who had a special call for special work. I too might have married but it would have meant dropping the work to which I had set my hand." (Wells-Barnett 1970, 255)

When Anthony became an abolitionist agent for the American Anti-Slavery Society (AASS) in 1856, she had the opportunity to work side by side with many male abolitionists whom she had previously admired, respected, and viewed only from a distance. She luxuriated in her warm friendships with William Lloyd Garrison, Wendell Phillips, Parker Pillsbury, Charles Lenox Remond, Samuel Joseph May, and other abolitionists (most of whom were married) whom she shepherded on lecture tours throughout New York state. They stimulated her passion, ignited her oratory, and by their example molded her into a lecturer of consequence. The camaraderie they developed during the late 1850s and during the infamous 1861 "winter of mobs" lecture tour forged powerfully strong personal relationships that lasted the rest of their lives. Her male friends admired her toughness and her refusal to give up despite the harshest weather and most violent mobs.

During the Civil War, the enormous success of Anthony and Cady Stanton's Woman's National Loyal League (WNLL), the first national political organization of women, heartened and emboldened them both. The strong support of male Republican leaders and their fellow abolitionists convinced them that achieving women's political equality was not only attainable but could be realized in the very near future.

YEARS OF STRUGGLE

During the early years of Reconstruction immediately after the Civil War, the Radical Republican drive to amend the Constitution to protect the rights and freedom of African-American males made Anthony and Cady Stanton optimistic about the future of woman suffrage. In 1865–1866, Anthony did not perceive any significant obstacle to achieving national woman suffrage. Since plans were already under way to revise the Constitution, she reasoned that adding a clause enabling women to vote would not be difficult. Then, in 1867–1868, when the obstacles to woman suffrage became overwhelming, the shock waves were enormous.

For Anthony, the most staggering blow was her discovery that most of her trusted male abolitionist comrades would not lift a finger to help women get the vote—to help *her* get the vote. Their total rejection of women's claim to the ballot, a cause they had championed all through the women's rights movement of the 1850s, hit Anthony right between the eyes, and she, like Cady Stanton, experienced it as a personal injury. The hurt stung them deeply while powerfully influencing their decisions and reactions during the late 1860s.

One of the most perplexing episodes in Anthony's life occurred at this time, when she canvassed Kansas with the infamous racist Democrat George Francis Train on behalf of the American Equal Rights Association's (AERA's) mission to have a Kansas woman suffrage referendum enacted. She did not seek out Train's help; he was sent to her by Kansas Republicans who believed that he would help capture the votes of the state's Democrats (Barry 1988, 178). But why, when she first witnessed his anti–African-American invective at rallies, did she continue to campaign with him? Although it is true that no man in Kansas was more pro–woman suffrage than he, this fact does not explain how Anthony, after her years combating slavery and northern racial prejudice, tolerated his speeches designed to stimulate racial hatred in their audiences (*see* Kansas Campaign of 1867).

As she and Cady Stanton later explained, they accepted Train's help because there was no one else. They had been brushed aside by Kansas Republicans, northern Republicans, and most of their abolitionist colleagues. Their pleas for assistance and press publicity were consistently ignored, even though the majority of Kansas voters were amenable to woman suffrage until late in the campaign. But regardless of their need, their mission in Kansas fell under the auspices of the AERA, an organization dedicated to obtaining suffrage for African-American men as well as all women. Even though Anthony supported African-American rights in her speeches,

how did she, as an AERA member on an AERA campaign, justify stumping with a professed racist? Anthony and Cady Stanton's actions reveal the fierce intensity of their desperation, as well as their anger at the Radical Republicans and their abolitionist friends who had washed their hands of woman suffrage to devote all their energy to securing the rights of African-American men.

The consequences of Anthony and Cady Stanton's partnership with Train dominated their lives for decades and contributed greatly to the split in the women's rights movement. Neither woman ever admitted that the alliance with Train had been a mistake, but Anthony could not have escaped the realization of how ill-conceived a decision she had made or avoided the pain of knowing that she had compromised her principles. The experience and its consequences would haunt her for the rest of her life. No wonder that she was plunged into depression when she and Cady Stanton were writing about the events of the late 1860s for the *History of Woman Suffrage* and later, when she and Ida Husted Harper were reconstructing this period for her biography. While her biography was being written in the 1890s, Anthony decided that she must report her side of the Train fiasco and the massive betrayal of her former friends, something she had never done publicly.

Whatever her own responsibility in the Train affair, Anthony never forgot the scourging she received for it from her old friends. What she found most unjust about their attacks was the way that they allowed this one event—her alliance with Train—to erase all the good she had done in the past. In a letter to Massachusetts abolitionist, women's rights reformer, and Stone and Henry Blackwell's ally Thomas Wentworth Higginson, Anthony made an appeal to reason and fairness while firmly asserting her righteousness and her belief in herself and her work.

But even if not one old friend had seemed to have remembered the past—and all been swallowed up, overshadowed by the Train cloud, I should still have rejoiced that I had done the work—for no *human* prejudice or power can rob me of the joy, the compensation I have stored up therefrom—That it is wholly spiritual—I need but tell you that this day, I have not *two hundred dollars more* than I had the day I entered upon the public work of woman's rights and AntiSlavery.

I don't know why I trouble you with this scribble—but that I want you to *know* that it is *impossible* for me to lay a straw in the way of any one who *personally wrongs me*—if only that one will work nobly for the cause in their own way & time—They may try to hinder my success, but *I never* theirs. (SBA to TWH, May 20, 1868, GC-BPL, in *Papers*)

After the chaos, misery, and floundering of the years 1865–1870 and the failure of her and Cady Stanton's newspaper, *The Revolution*, Anthony looked hopefully to the future and the fledgling National Woman Suffrage Association (NWSA) as she resolved to invest her entire being in the work of woman suffrage. As the 1870s progressed, she deepened and strengthened her commitment to securing the ballot for all women.

The cause was Anthony's life. As precious as her family and friends were to her, the struggle for woman suffrage was her central focus. Because she fervently believed that women would never achieve equality or a decent standard of living until they attained the ballot, she devoted every fiber of her being toward advancing the cause. She also developed a unique style of leadership that was consistent with that dedication.

Anthony was a powerful leader. She was accustomed to taking charge of a goal, mustering the resources to attain it, and then plowing through all obstacles until she achieved it. The intensity of her single-minded focus and her incomparable drive made her extraordinary among reformers. These qualities led her to adopt a leadership style that enabled her to accomplish more than most people, although it also alienated some reformers. Her critics within the suffrage movement reproached her for her dictatorial style. The criticisms were not entirely without justification; she was not known as the "General" of the suffrage movement for nothing. But unlike many true dictators, Anthony was not interested in power for its own sake or for self-aggrandizement. She possessed a glorious vision of a future society in which women would be the equals of men, and she believed that she must harness every available resource toward that goal. Those reformers who did not care to be directed by her strong, firm hand or who preferred to be their own bosses did not thrive under Anthony's direction. Yet she had excellent working relationships with many suffragists. As long as her followers understood that they must work hard, cooperate with the entire suffrage team, and use their individual talents to the utmost for the sake of the cause, relations were harmonious.

Unlike many dictatorial leaders, Anthony had a high tolerance for dissent. She listened carefully to the ideas and criticisms of her fellow suffragists and acted on many of them. Carrie Chapman Catt, whom Anthony regarded with the highest esteem, frequently disagreed with her strategies. But as was typical among Anthony's strong working relationships, she and Chapman Catt strove to work through their differences. The African-American suffragist and civil rights reformer Ida Wells-Barnett reflected on this aspect of Anthony's liberal broad-mindedness. She and Anthony disagreed on many subjects, particularly Anthony's handling of racial issues. Wells-Barnett observed that Anthony "never in any way showed resentment of my attitude. She gave me rather the impression of a woman who was eager to hear all sides of any question, and that I am sure is one of the reasons for her splendid success. . . ." (Wells-Barnett 1970, 230).

As Anthony aged, her search for exceptional young women to form the next generation of suffrage leaders became a major preoccupation. Always on the lookout for impassioned women orators and indefatigable reformers, she cultivated relationships with a number of capable young activists, the most promising of whom she affectionately called her "nieces." Many of Anthony's hopefuls did not sustain their interest or their stamina, made other life choices, or could not meet her exceedingly demanding standards. But the most treasured inner circle of her elite corps of young lieutenants—Rachel Foster Avery, Anna Howard Shaw, and Carrie Chapman Catt—surpassed her expectations.

Anthony could be very controlling in her relationships with her young lieutenants. The bulk of her correspondence with Clara Bewick Colby clearly displays forceful efforts to mold the young activist into a future suffrage leader. To Anthony's frustration, Bewick Colby was a competent, hardworking, cooperative worker who stubbornly refused to be shaped into an obedient future Susan B. Anthony. The way that Anthony pushed Bewick Colby and her other hopefuls demonstrates how fiercely and desperately Anthony pursued the goal of selecting a first-rate successor.

In the late 1880s, Rachel Foster's marriage crushed Anthony's dream that Foster would succeed her. She had groomed the young woman so painstakingly, nurtured her development so closely, that Foster's decision to marry came as a staggering blow. What becomes clear is that as much as Anthony hoped Foster would lead the NWSA and the later National American Woman Suffrage Association (NAWSA), Foster harbored doubts. Although Foster (Avery) devoted her entire life to a leadership role in the suffrage movement, she did not want to be the supreme leader, though she found it impossible to disappoint Anthony by telling her directly. Anthony's overbearing behavior toward her potential successors was the direct result of her realization that she was aging. She knew that she would not be able to direct the suffrage movement forever, and she realized that without an outstanding leader, the cause was lost.

Anthony's frustration in preparing a future suffrage leader stemmed from the fact that she tried to find an activist exactly like herself. She searched for a young woman who would sacrifice everything to the cause as she had—money, a home, marriage, personal time, food, sleep, and, if need be, health. By 1900, when she retired as president of NAWSA, she had accepted that she would never find a reformer who matched her skills, talents, knowledge, passion, and stamina and who also possessed the skills she lacked—in oratory and writing. Nevertheless, she realized that Carrie Chapman Catt and, to a somewhat lesser degree, Anna Howard Shaw possessed the strength and skills necessary to carry NAWSA into the twentieth century and to a woman suffrage victory.

FAMILY AND FRIENDS

Throughout her career, Anthony's demanding work and travel schedule did not permit much leisure. Yet she made the time to visit friends and family whenever possible. Her frequent travel fostered this habit. While on the way to Washington, D.C., on suffrage business, she sometimes stopped in Philadelphia to visit her friends Lucretia Coffin Mott and Anna Dickinson. And while lecturing in the Midwest, she often made a detour to Kansas, spending time with her brothers Daniel Read Anthony in Leavenworth and Jacob Merritt Anthony in Fort Scott. No matter how busy she was, she kept in touch with her entire family by mail. A determined, prolific letter writer, Susan and her parents and siblings shared their lives and concerns for each other in their correspondence.

Anthony was always very close to her parents, her siblings, and their families. She fretted over each family illness and grieved deeply at each loss. She also suffered painful anniversary reactions for years following the deaths of loved ones. In November 1862, her father died after a severe two-week illness.

Anthony's suffering was acute and lasted for months. Many years later, in a letter of condolence to Ellen Wright Garrison, the daughter of her recently deceased friend Martha Coffin Wright, Anthony expressed how her father's death had affected her and how his life and influence continued to be a source of inspiration.

> Twelve years ago when my dear Father died—aged 69—in the full strength & vigor of body & mind . . . it seemed to me the world and everybody in it must stop—It was months before I could recover myself—and at last it came to me; that the best way I could prove my love & respect for his memory, was to try to do more & better work for humanity than ever before—and from that day to this the feeling, in my triumphs and defeats, that my Father rejoiced and sorrowed with me—has been a constant stimulus to urge me ever to rally to new effort. (SBA to EWG, January 22, 1875, GF-SSC, in *Papers*)

As the years passed, the death of each family member and friend affected her profoundly. After her sister Guelma's death from tuberculosis in 1873, Anthony revealed the depth of her grief in a letter to her mother.

> How continually . . . is the thought of you and your loss and my own with me! How little we realize the constant presence in our minds of our loved and loving ones until they are forever gone . . . Our Guelma, does she look down upon us, does she still live, and shall we all live again and know each other, and work together and love and enjoy one another? (Harper 1899, 1:447)

Despite her extensive work commitments, she nursed Guelma, Hannah, and her mother through the final weeks of their fatal illnesses.

Few who knew her understood how she suffered over the loss of each person who had been close to her. As she herself once explained, "I doubt if there be any mortal who clings to loved ones with greater tenacity than do I" (quoted in Barry 1988, 157).

To cope with loss, Anthony did not rely on religion to support her as did most nineteenth-century men and women, nor did she believe in spiritualism, as was the rage among many of her fellow reformers. Despite an intellectual interest in the spiritualistic idea that the dead communicated with the living, she did not find the possibility a consolation. In her grief, she consistently turned to the work of improving society. In 1889, she explained why religious musings were not an important part of her life in a letter to her dear friend and colleague, Universalist minister Olympia Brown. "I am content to do all I can to make the conditions of this life better for the next generation to live in—assured that right living here is not only the best thing for me and the world here—but for the best possible fitting for whatever is to come in the hereafter" (SBA to OB, March 11, 1889, OB-SL, in *Papers*).

Whenever Anthony took time off from her hectic schedule, she enjoyed literature. Her most beloved literary work was Elizabeth Barrett Browning's narrative poem *Aurora Leigh*. She treasured this volume of poetry more than any other book in her possession, often traveled with it, and identified strongly with its main character. Barrett Browning's female character Aurora Leigh was the literary embodiment of Anthony's conception of a "true woman," an ideal that she articulated in her "True Woman" speech of the late 1850s (*see* Women's Rights Movement). Like Anthony, Aurora Leigh chose independence and self-fulfillment in her work over marriage.

HOW OTHERS VIEWED HER

From the late 1860s through the 1880s, the press presented such a distorted picture of Anthony that when people met and talked with her, they were stunned to discover that she was not the shriveled-up, sour, man-hating old crone that the newspapers portrayed. An article in an Adrian, Michigan, newspaper declared that "Miss Anthony typifies the typical old maid, tall, angular and inclined to be vinegar visaged" (April 9, 1870, *Times and Expositor*, SBA Scrapbooks, LCRBD, in *Papers*). Having read similar testimonials, people all over the country were surprised when they came face-to-face with the genuine article.

In 1867, a Kansas suffragist who had been expecting to shelter Cady Stanton was furious when told that she would house Anthony instead. Vowing not to accept her, the woman was not prepared when she met "a dignified Quaker-looking lady with a small satchel and a black and white shawl on her arm." She went on to explain:

Half disarmed by her genial manner and frank, kindly face, I led the way into the house and said I would have her stay to tea and then we would see. . . . While I was looking after things she gained the affections of the babies; and seeing the door of my sister's sick-room open, she went in and in a short time had so won the heart and soothed . . . the nervous sufferer . . . that by the time tea was over I was ready to do anything if Miss Anthony would only stay with us. And stay she did for over six weeks, and we parted from her as from a beloved and helpful friend. (Harper 1899, 1:286)

In 1877, another reporter observed:

I was entirely won by her genial manners, and sunny spirit. Miss Anthony is certainly a noble and elegant appearing woman. Arrayed in a rich black silk[,] her large fine figure presents on the lecture platform quite a stylish appearance while her voice and manner betray so much culture and refinement, one's prejudice is melted away almost unconsciously, and there is a wonderful magnetism about the woman that draws and attracts irresistibly. I felt as sorry to part with her as from an old and dear friend. (*Ballot Box*, November 25, 1877, SBA Scrapbooks, LCRBD, in *Papers*)

Without doubt, at least part of the misconception about Anthony's nature was derived from her physical appearance. Photographs reveal the same stern countenance her audience viewed, the result of the natural, downward curve of her mouth. She lamented this facial feature, which was in stark contrast to her pleasant, genial personality. Her eyes also distressed her. Although it was not apparent in photographs, Anthony had a strabismus defect, which made her eyes appear to cross. As a young woman she endured an operation to correct the problem, but when the procedure failed, it worsened the condition. She was extremely self-conscious about her eyes' appearance and wore eyeglasses in an attempt to conceal the flaw.

In 1869, a male editor from the *Hartford Post* commented:

Miss Anthony is a resolute, substantial woman of forty or fifty [she was nearly fifty], exhibiting no signs of age or weariness. Her hair is dark, her head well formed, her face has an expression of masculine strength. If she were a man you would guess that she was a schoolmaster, or a quiet clergyman, or perhaps a business man and deacon. She pays no special attention to feminine graces, but is not ungraceful or unwomanly. In speaking her manner is self-possessed without ranting or unpleasant demonstrations, her tones slightly monotonous. Long experience has taught her a candid, kindly, sensible way of presenting her views, which wins the good will of her hearers whether they accept them or not. (Harper 1899, 1:333)

Of course, her fellow reformers' descriptions of Anthony emphasize her inner qualities rather than her physical appearance. Mary Ashton Livermore, who assisted in the formation of the NWSA, observed that Anthony

> is a woman whom no one can know thoroughly without respect. Entirely honest, fearfully in earnest, energetic, self-sacrificing, kind-hearted, scorning difficulties of whatever magnitude and rigidly sensible, she is the warm friend of the poor, oppressed, homeless and friendless of her own sex. . . . Let the press laugh at her as it may, she is a mighty power among both men and women. (Harper 1899, 1:316)

HER FINAL YEARS

Anthony remained physically and mentally active as she aged, working hard into her eighties. Even though she occasionally slackened her customarily frenetic pace after 1891, she was still much more active than most adults half her age. In her seventies and eighties, she continued to travel from coast to coast, lecturing and attending suffrage conventions and campaigning in state suffrage campaigns. But a collapse on the lecture platform in July 1895, when Anthony was seventy-five, let her know for the first time in her life that her body was not indestructible. The "fainting spell" was most likely a mild stroke, the first she was to suffer. After a month in bed, she made a complete recovery. Gradually her stamina returned, and by 1896 she was engrossed in the California suffrage campaign, taxing her energies to the full. But despite a return to health, her body had made its point—she would not live forever. Shortly after the California campaign, she and Ida Husted Harper began work on her biography.

In 1900, Anthony experienced another stroke. Again she spent weeks regaining her strength, and this time she did not make a full recovery. Her legendary inexhaustible energy did not return. Her doctor informed her that another, more severe stroke could strike at any time. He urged her to take better care of herself and warned her to avoid excessive cold and crowds of people. Although Anthony seriously considered his advice, she soon decided that it would be better to "die in the harness" than to abandon everything that made her life worth living—her work for the cause (Harper 1908, 3:1228). No longer the president of NAWSA, Anthony was still deeply involved in its work, as she continued to be for the next four years.

During the early weeks of 1906, Anthony knew that her health was failing rapidly. She desperately wanted to attend the NAWSA convention in Washington, D.C., in February and focused her will on gathering the strength to make the trip. When a howling blizzard descended on Rochester as she and Mary prepared to embark on their journey, Anthony refused to consider remaining at home. Mary swaddled her sister in blankets, and they set off to meet their train. Before they reached Baltimore, Anthony had succumbed to a severe cold that soon became a life-threatening illness. Although she had to miss almost all of the convention, she managed to rally enough to attend one session. She was also able to be present at her eighty-sixth birthday celebration, held at the conclusion of the convention. She listened stoically as messages from well-wishers were read aloud to those assembled, including one from President Theodore Roosevelt. Anthony, despite her feebleness, rose from her chair and walked to the front of the platform to address the gathering. "When will the men do something besides extend congratulations?" she demanded. "I would rather have President Roosevelt say one word to Congress in favor of amending the Constitution to give women the suffrage than to praise me endlessly!" (Harper 1908, 3:1408). Her audience roared with laughter and applause, no doubt joyous to see Anthony strong enough to display her usual feistiness. At the end of the festivities, Anthony rose to speak once more, supported by her closest living friend, NAWSA president Anna Howard Shaw. After praising the work of NAWSA leaders and suffragists, she concluded, "There have been others also just as true and devoted to the cause—I wish I could name every one—but with such women consecrating their lives . . . failure is impossible!" (Harper 1908, 3:1409).

Shortly after arriving home, Anthony developed double pneumonia, and her weak heart began to fail. As the days passed, she showed no sign of improvement. On March 7, 1906, Shaw arrived to stay with her dear friend through her final illness. They passed the hours reminiscing together, and Anthony regaled Shaw with stories from her abolitionist days. At one point, she remarked, "Just think of it, Anna, I have been striving for over sixty years for a little bit of justice no bigger than that, and yet I must die without obtaining it! Oh, it seems so cruel!" As painful as this realization was, Anthony was reassured that Shaw was at the helm of NAWSA. But she knew that Shaw would have to be very strong to continue surviving the criticism and the struggles among NAWSA's battling factions. To this end, Anthony imparted to Shaw the essence of the course she had tried to take throughout her life.

No matter what is done or is not done, how you are criticized or misunderstood, or what efforts are made to block your path, remember that the only fear you need have is the fear of not standing by the thing you believe to be right. Take your stand and hold it: then let come what will, and receive the blows like a good soldier. (Shaw 1915, 209–210)

On March 11, Anthony lost consciousness, with her sister Mary and Shaw by her side. Less than an hour after midnight, on March 13, Anthony died.

Although the Anthony family wished to have her funeral service at the Unitarian Church in Rochester, which Anthony had attended for so many years, it was not large enough for all who hoped to attend. The Central Presbyterian Church was chosen instead. In the hours before the funeral, Anthony lay in state. An estimated 10,000 people filed past her casket, and another 2,500 attended her funeral.

Of the hundreds of laudatory editorials published immediately after Anthony's death, the testimonial of her oldest foe and rival, Henry Blackwell, in the *Woman's Journal* deserves special mention, not only because it is the expression of a suffragist who feuded most acrimoniously with her over a period of decades, but because it so eloquently and accurately captures the essence of her as a reformer.

For many years, both in early and later times, I saw much of Miss Anthony. I have been impressed not only by her absolute devotion to the suffrage cause, but also by a certain magnanimity and large-heartedness. While she had her strong preferences and predilections, she held them secondary to her main object, and was willing to accept suggestions from any quarter. . . . Whether in the palace of the rich or the tenement of the poor, in the society of Queen or seamstress, of the luxurious millionaire or the hardy frontiersman, she, like Benjamin Franklin, remained simple, unembarrassed and sincere. It is said that most men and women cease to grow after they reach maturity, but Miss Anthony grew steadily in quality of mind and heart with advancing age, mellowing but not weakening as the years went by.

Miss Anthony had qualities of leadership such as are possessed by few women or men. With rare devotion and unflinching tenacity of purpose, she has identified herself for years with the suffrage movement, growing steadily in public esteem. Her name will always be identified with this greatest of all political reforms. (Harper 1908, 3:1547–1548)

Suggestions for further reading:
Anthony, Katharine. 1954. *Susan B. Anthony: Her Personal History and Her Era.* Garden City, N.Y.: Doubleday.
Barry, Kathleen. 1988. *Susan B. Anthony: Biography of a Singular Feminist.* New York: New York University Press.
Sherr, Lynn. 1995. *Failure Is Impossible: Susan B. Anthony in Her Own Words.* New York: Times Books.

Anthony/Cady Stanton Partnership

The relationship of Susan B. Anthony and Elizabeth Cady Stanton was one of the most productive and fascinatingly complex working partnerships in U.S. history. From their first meeting in Seneca Falls, New York, in 1851 until the death of Cady Stanton in 1902, their half-century of friendship and collaboration inspired and galvanized each woman to achieve her most pressing goals. Through the years, their relationship was never static—it ebbed and flowed, characterized by periods of intimacy and close collaboration followed by years of distance and independent, solitary striving. Yet even when

they were apart or were most at odds with each other, both women acknowledged the enduring strength of their rock-solid, unbreakable connection. Following the failure of their newspaper *The Revolution* in 1870, Cady Stanton informed Anthony that since she believed their partnership was for life, they had better "make the best of it."

When Anthony and Cady Stanton first met in Seneca Falls, each woman had already embarked on her career in reform. Anthony was a temperance activist, and Cady Stanton was a leader in the emerging women's rights movement. Through her abolitionist husband, Henry Brewster Stanton, she also had a detailed knowledge of the abolitionist movement. Because Cady Stanton was five years older and was more experienced politically than Anthony, she was an inspiration to the young Rochester activist, who craved information on how to become a dynamic reformer. In the early years of their friendship, Cady Stanton acted as Anthony's adviser, giving her valuable tips and information on the art of public speaking, reform strategies, politics, the law, and the legislative process.

Anthony reveled in her new relationship with Cady Stanton. Finally she had met someone with whom she could talk at length about reform and who was full of knowledge about women's rights, philosophy, religion, spirituality, and politics. But as much as Anthony gained from the friendship, Cady Stanton was equally nourished by Anthony. The young Quaker woman was the best sounding board for her ideas that Cady Stanton had ever encountered. Anthony listened to her thoughts and opinions, read her writings, and asked questions that stimulated Cady Stanton to clarify her thinking. When Anthony critiqued her writing, she never failed to point out where her friend was being unclear or unfair. And, unlike almost all of Cady Stanton's other friends, Anthony's time was her own. As a single woman without a husband, children, or a home that she was expected to maintain, Anthony was able to spend days and sometimes weeks at a time as a guest at the Stantons' house. When Cady Stanton had an important speech or article to write, Anthony cared for the Stanton children and took charge of the cooking. Then, as soon as the children were abed, they had the long evenings to themselves, to talk and strategize by the fireplace. Throughout the 1850s, they worked closely together, collaborating to form and lead the Woman's State Temperance Society (WSTS); planning national, state, and regional woman's rights conventions; and campaigning for an expanded New York Married Women's Property Law.

Despite their closeness, their relationship was not always harmonious. Anthony was disgruntled whenever Cady Stanton failed to appear at conventions or to deliver an important speech, and she despaired whenever Cady Stanton reported that she was pregnant again. Anthony longed for her colleague to be free to become as active a reformer as she was. But all through the 1850s, Cady Stanton was tied to her home, raising her seven children. As a result, Anthony had to be the activist for the two of them—she delivered the speeches that her colleague wrote, read the letters that her friend addressed to the conventions she could not attend, and carried out the strategies that they devised by the Stanton fireplace.

Anthony's and Cady Stanton's biographers as well as scholars of U.S. women's history have long pondered the nature of their partnership. All have emphasized the fact that each woman's talents and skills complemented the other's. Anthony was the incomparable administrator, the doer, the propulsive force pushing them both toward greater achievement. Cady Stanton was the thinker, the writer, and the rhetorician. There is no question that throughout Anthony's career, she relied on Cady Stanton's outstanding writing talent. Anthony never overcame her painfully acute sense of her own inadequacy as a writer. Once she started collaborating with Cady Stanton, Anthony put less pressure on herself to perfect her own writing skills. She continued to write her own speeches and articles, but whenever possible asked for Cady Stanton's editorial assistance. In many cases, she asked Cady Stanton to write the speeches for her, all under Anthony's critical eye, of course. Later, as the years passed and especially after 1870, as they each pursued their separate agendas—Cady Stanton as lecturer on the lyceum circuit and Anthony as suffrage leader—Cady Stanton was not available to supervise Anthony's writings. Then Anthony, although never able to match her friend's brilliance with the pen, had to write her own speeches and documents. Despite her growing self-reliance, however, she never missed an opportunity to coax Cady Stanton to draft documents for the National Woman Suffrage Association (NWSA) and the National American Woman Suffrage Association (NAWSA), to pen addresses to Congress and to state legislatures, and to help her edit her speeches. To Anthony's mind and to many of their generation, Cady Stanton had an exceptional talent, and Anthony believed that it was her duty to expose the world to her brilliance, her philosophy, and her convictions about the status of women in society.

In her *Reminiscences*, Cady Stanton emphasized the collaborative nature of their written work.

> In writing we did better work than either could alone. While she [Anthony] is slow and analytical in composition, I am rapid and synthetic. I am the better writer, she the better critic. She supplied the facts and statistics, I the philosophy and rhetoric, and, together, we have made arguments that have stood unshaken through the storms of long years. . . . Our speeches may be considered the united product of our two brains. (E. Stanton 1973, 166)

If Anthony benefited from Cady Stanton's reform experience and writing abilities, what did Cady Stanton gain from her friendship with Anthony? During the 1850s, Cady

Stanton's self-esteem was at a low point. Her father, her husband, and her friends harshly criticized her work and her devotion to the women's rights movement. Before she met Anthony, Lucretia Coffin Mott was one of very few people supporting her efforts, but theirs was by necessity a long-distance relationship. From the first, Anthony believed in Cady Stanton's abilities and her enormous potential. Anthony regarded her friend's work seriously, critiqued it shrewdly and honestly, and thereby bolstered Cady Stanton's image of herself as an intellectual and leader of consequence. Equally important, Anthony was on fire with her purpose to improve women's condition in society, just as Cady Stanton was.

In addition to her commitment to temperance, women's rights, and abolitionist reform, Anthony relentlessly pursued Cady Stanton's greatness. Anthony refused to allow her partner to be idle. She pushed and prodded her to produce speeches, letters, and articles and shoved her into the limelight of the women's rights and woman suffrage movements, insisting that Cady Stanton serve as president of the NWSA and NAWSA and that she chair NWSA delegations to Congress. As much as Cady Stanton complained about Anthony's slave-driving tactics, she realized from the beginning of their relationship that without Anthony to push her, she achieved much less. Unlike Anthony, who drove herself mercilessly and to exhaustion, Cady Stanton enjoyed relaxation, and as she herself often admitted, luxuriated in being "lazy." She did not feel ashamed or burdened by this character trait, but nevertheless was thankful for Anthony's constant reminders about the pressing nature of her goals. At Anthony's seventieth birthday celebration, Cady Stanton announced:

Sub rosa, dear friends, I have had no peace for forty years, since the day we [Anthony and Cady Stanton] started together on the suffrage expedition in search of woman's place in the National Constitution. She has kept me on the war-path at the point of the bayonet so long . . . that I have often wished . . . that I might spend the sunset of my life in some quiet chimney-corner.

Then, on a more serious note, Cady Stanton concluded her remarks, saying, "I do believe that I have developed into much more of a woman under her jurisdiction than if left to myself reading novels in an easy chair" (Harper 1899, 2:667).

After their women's rights lecture tour of California in 1871, they parted company. Cady Stanton returned home, and Anthony joined Abigail Scott Duniway on a lecture tour of Oregon and Washington Territory. After being in Cady Stanton's company every day for months, Anthony enjoyed her independence and her freedom from the continual reminder of her friend's greatness. In a letter to her family in Rochester, Anthony acknowledged the huge price she paid for promoting Cady Stanton. If she suffered, however, it was a prison she had created herself. This letter also revealed that, in at least one sense, Anthony perceived her relationship with Cady Stanton as her duty.

I miss Mrs. Stanton, still I can not but enjoy the feeling that the people call on *me*. . . . I have an opportunity to sharpen my wits a little by answering questions and doing the chatting, instead of merely . . . listening to the brilliant scintillations as they emanate from her never-exhausted magazine. There is no alternative—whoever goes into a parlor or before an audience with that woman does it at the cost of a fearful overshadowing, a price which I have paid for the last ten years, . . . because I felt that our cause was most profited by her being seen and heard, and my best work was making the way clear for her. (Harper 1899, 1:396)

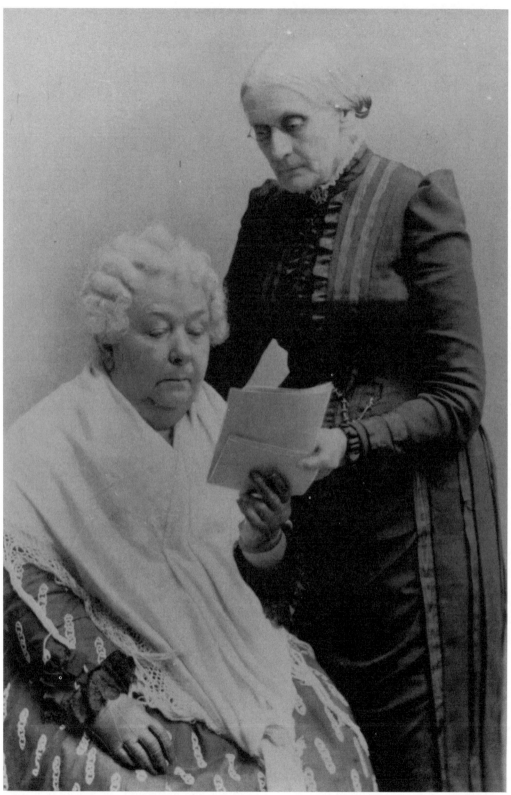

Elizabeth Cady Stanton, seated, with Susan B. Anthony.

Although Anthony and Cady Stanton worked together closely, cared deeply for each other, and thoroughly knew each other's personalities, strengths, and weaknesses, neither woman was the true intimate of the other. They each had friends who were their confidantes, to whom they unburdened their most troublesome personal problems and their deepest insecurities, secrets, and resentments. Cady Stanton's closest personal friend was her cousin Elizabeth Smith Miller, with whom she had been friends since girlhood. In the first few decades of Anthony's friendship with Cady Stanton, Anthony's confidante was the Quaker reformer Lydia Mott, whom Anthony had first met at Deborah Moulson's Quaker seminary. Both Mott and Smith Miller were very warm, nurturing women who provided the uncritical, unconditional love that Anthony and Cady Stanton both craved. Much later in life, Anthony formed deep, emotional bonds with younger women—her relationships with Rachel Foster (Avery) and Anna Howard Shaw being the most intimate.

Anthony experienced occasional bouts of depression that Cady Stanton could not fathom. Anthony took to heart each failure and defeat and fretted over each one. Following their withdrawal from the Woman's State Temperance Society (WSTS) in 1853, the feud with Lucy Stone and Henry Blackwell in the late 1860s, and Anthony's decision to terminate publication of *The Revolution* in 1870, Anthony was devastated for months. Cady Stanton suffered no such pangs and had no patience for what she perceived as Anthony's wallowing in defeatism. Her method for dealing with her own moods reveals why she may not have been able to empathize with Anthony's depressions. In a letter to her daughter Harriot Stanton, she explained, "I never encourage these moods [sadness], but by some active work and practical thinking try to cheat myself into the thought that all is well, grand, glorious, triumphant" (ECS to HS, August 20, 1880, TS Papers, MSDL, in *Papers*).

Despite the fact that Anthony and Cady Stanton had other close friends, they loved each other deeply and enjoyed expressing their love with frequent hugs and long embraces, a common practice among middle-class female friends of the nineteenth century. In 1865, when Anthony spent more than six months in Kansas working for the relief of the freed slaves, Cady Stanton wrote her, "I long to put my arms around you once more and hear you scold me for my sins and shortcomings. . . . Oh, Susan, you are very dear to me. I should miss you more than any other living being on this earth." Anthony fully requited Cady Stanton's affection. During their travel by train to the Far West in 1871, Anthony recorded in her diary, "We have a drawing-room all to ourselves, and here we are just as cozy and happy as lovers." But the rest of Anthony's diary entry makes clear that she is describing a spiritual love, not a union based on physical attraction. "It is not the outside things which make life, but the inner, the spirit of love which casteth out all devils and bringeth in all angels" (Harper 1899, 1:388).

After the crushing defeats of the late 1860s, their formation of the NWSA in 1869, and the failure of *The Revolution* in 1870, Anthony's and Cady Stanton's paths truly diverged. Anthony was faced with repaying a mountain of debt from *The Revolution*, a responsibility that Cady Stanton stubbornly refused to share with her, and with the necessity of building and guiding the NWSA. From this point on, the sole focus of Anthony's life was the pursuit of national woman suffrage. Although Cady Stanton had pioneered the suffrage struggle, she had no intention of making it the center of her life. Her feminist interests were much more eclectic than Anthony's. They included marriage and divorce reform, the education of girls and young women, and the oppression of women by organized religion and other institutions, to name only a few. As Cady Stanton explained in a letter to their mutual friend Olympia Brown, "I am a leader of thought rather than numbers. . . . Lucy [Stone] and Susan [Anthony] alike see suffrage only. They do not see woman's religious and social bondage"(ECS to OB, May 8, 1888, OB Papers, SL, in *Papers*). From the 1870s on, their independent interests and travel drew them apart for months at a time.

The early 1870s were a particularly rocky period in Anthony and Cady Stanton's relationship. They disagreed about Cady Stanton's lack of attendance at conventions, her refusal to help with the day-to-day work of NWSA, the role of Victoria Claflin Woodhull in NWSA (a feud that led to Cady Stanton's resignation as president), and Cady Stanton's outspokenness on the Beecher-Tilton Scandal. Her tendency to say to the press whatever was on her mind without thinking through the potential consequences for Anthony or for the NWSA was a serious problem, considering that both were struggling to overcome negative public images. Despite the anger they unleashed on each other, their connection was never severed. In the worst of times, they avoided each other, waiting months and sometimes years for the crisis to pass. When the storm eventually lifted, they found themselves corresponding more, visiting, and reconnecting. In 1876, Cady Stanton observed, "Our friendship is of too long standing and has too deep roots to be easily shattered. I think we have said worse things to each other, face to face, than we have ever said about each other. Nothing that Susan could say or do could break my friendship with her; and I know nothing could uproot her affection for me" (Harper 1899, 1:488–489).

During the late 1870s and early 1880s, they enjoyed a period of harmony and closeness once more as they cooperated on the compiling and writing of the first three volumes of the *History of Woman Suffrage*. Although they squabbled and debated contentiously about issues and dates, they were of one mind and purpose as to what they hoped to accomplish by recording the history of the women's rights and woman suffrage movements. Cady Stanton's daughter, Margaret Stanton

Lawrence, observed the two suffragists at work and provided the clearest portrayal of their collaboration.

> It is as good as a comedy to watch these souls from day to day. They start off pretty well in the morning, fresh and amiable. They write page after page with alacrity, they laugh and talk, poke the fire by turn, and admire the flowers on their desk. . . . Everything is harmonious for a season, but after straining their eyes over the most illegible, disorderly manuscripts . . . suddenly the whole sky is overspread with dark and threatening clouds, and from the adjoining room I hear a hot dispute about something. . . . Susan is punctilious on dates, mother on philosophy, but each contends as stoutly in the other's domain as if equally strong on all points. Sometimes these disputes run so high that down go the pens, one sails out of one door and one out the other, walking in opposite directions around the estate, and just as I have made up my mind that this beautiful friendship of forty years has at last terminated, I see them walking down the hill, arm in arm. . . . When they return they go straight to work where they left off, as if nothing had ever happened. . . . The one that was unquestionably right assumes it, and the other silently concedes the fact. They never explain, nor apologize, nor shed tears, nor make up, as other people do. (Margaret Stanton Lawrence, "As a Mother," in *The New Era*, November 1885, as quoted in Griffith 1984, 178)

In the late 1880s and 1890s, as Anthony and NWSA leaders welcomed temperance and religious conservative women into the woman suffrage movement, Cady Stanton increasingly criticized Anthony's tactics and her growing conservatism. In contrast, Cady

Stanton's increasing attacks on the clergy and her refutations of Christian theology made her appear to grow more radical. Although she did nothing to interfere with the merger of the NWSA and its former rival, the American Woman Suffrage Association (AWSA), in 1890, she and Anthony disagreed over the movement's increasing conservatism and its overall direction. Cady Stanton disapproved of Anthony's highly prized young lieutenants Carrie Chapman Catt and Rachel Foster Avery, much preferring the freethinking liberalism of Lillie Devereux Blake and Clara Bewick Colby. But since Cady Stanton was not at all involved in the work of the NWSA or NAWSA, Anthony did little more than listen to her old friend's complaints. After 30 years of being immersed in the day-to-day operation of the movement, Anthony understood that her colleague simply could not comprehend all that the leadership or the administration of the NAWSA entailed.

In 1891, Anthony finally realized her dream of settling in her own home, when she and her sister Mary Anthony set up housekeeping together in the Anthony home in Rochester, New York. But to Anthony's mind, the place where she planned to spend her final days would never be complete without Cady Stanton's presence. Anthony knew that her friend was footloose, visiting among her children rather than maintaining a home for herself. Anthony wrote to Cady Stanton, asking her to consider making a home with her and Mary. To Anthony's deep disappointment, Cady Stanton decided to establish a permanent home with her widowed daughter, Margaret Stanton Lawrence, and her unmarried son, Robert Stanton, in an apartment in New York City. When she heard this news, Anthony wrote her old friend that she experienced an "inner wail in my soul." She then revealed what she had been hoping would come from their living together.

[M]y constant thought was that you would come here, where are the documents necessary to our work, and stay for as long . . . as we must be together to put your writings into systematic shape to go down to posterity. I have no writings to go down, so my ambition is not for myself, but it is for one by the side of whom I have wrought these forty years. (Harper 1899, 2:712)

Interestingly enough, Anthony had not stopped to consider the kind of life that Cady Stanton might have wanted. From Cady Stanton's letters and her diary, it is evident that she was anticipating a more leisurely lifestyle and an opportunity to read, explore, and write on the topics of interest to her in the present, not to rehash or refurbish her old work. Cady Stanton knew Anthony well enough to realize that she would drive her in their old age as she had pushed her all through their youth and middle age. Cady Stanton agreed to visit, but for the rest of the time, Anthony would be on her own. Anthony was not at loose ends for long, however. In 1891, she still had nearly a decade of all-out suffrage activism ahead of her and some of the most grueling state suffrage battles. Later, when "relaxing" at home in Rochester, she would assist Ida Husted Harper in the writing of the first two volumes of her biography, *The Life and Work of Susan B. Anthony,* and volume 4 of the *History of Woman Suffrage.*

Anthony visited Cady Stanton on two occasions during the first half of 1902 and promised that she would return in November to celebrate her friend's eighty-seventh birthday. Two weeks prior to that event, Anthony received a telegram informing her that her cherished comrade was dead. She was inconsolable. When newspaper reporters hounded her for comments on Cady Stanton's death, the grief-stricken Anthony replied, "I cannot express myself at all as I feel. I am too crushed to speak. If I had died first, she would have found beautiful phrases to describe our friendship, but I cannot put it into words." The next day, after she arrived in New York City to await the funeral, she described her profound sense of isolation and loss to Husted Harper.

> Oh, this awful hush! It seems impossible that voice is stilled which I have loved to hear for fifty years. Always I have felt that I must have Mrs. Stanton's opinion of things before I knew where I stood myself. I am all at sea. . . . What a world it is, it goes on and on just the same no matter who lives or who dies! (Harper 1908, 3:1263–1264)

Yet even as Anthony mourned her personal loss, thoughts of her and Cady Stanton's work for woman suffrage were not far from her mind. Along with Anthony's memories of their decades of struggle to obtain political and social equality for women came the realization that she must not delay continuing her suffrage activism or her efforts to make the world understand their legacy through the written record of the history of the movement. In the final weeks of 1902 and in 1903, as she completed and then awaited the publication of the fourth volume of the *History of Woman Suffrage,* she attacked the gargantuan task of distributing the *History*—which she believed was the culmination of her and Cady Stanton's life work—to libraries, newspapers, magazines, schools, and organizations.

Related entries:
Anthony, Susan B.
The History of Woman Suffrage
National American Woman Suffrage Association
National Woman Suffrage Association
New York Married Women's Property Law of 1860
The Revolution
Stanton, Elizabeth Cady
Woman Suffrage Movement
Woman's National Loyal League
Woman's State Temperance Society
Women's Rights Movement

Suggestions for further reading:
Barry, Kathleen. 1988. *Susan B. Anthony: Biography of a Singular Feminist.* New York: New York University Press.

DuBois, Ellen Carol, ed. 1992. *The Elizabeth Cady Stanton–Susan B. Anthony Reader: Correspondence, Writings, Speeches.* Boston: Northeastern University Press.
Griffith, Elisabeth. 1984. *In Her Own Right: The Life of Elizabeth Cady Stanton.* New York: Oxford University Press.

Avery, Rachel G. Foster (1858–1919)

Throughout the 1880s, Rachel Foster Avery was Susan B. Anthony's most cherished young lieutenant in the National Woman Suffrage Association (NWSA). The two suffragists were close colleagues but also shared a deep emotional bond. Anthony, in particular, had a strong maternal connection with Foster Avery, who was nearly 39 years her junior. Yet despite the age difference, Anthony had the highest respect for Foster Avery's abilities, opinions, insights, and decisions in the administration of NWSA affairs.

Rachel Foster was born a Quaker in Pittsburgh, Pennsylvania, the daughter of Julia Manuel Foster, a devout women's rights activist who had been ushered into the movement by Elizabeth Cady Stanton. Her father J. Heron Foster, a former abolitionist, was the prominent editor of the *Pittsburgh Dispatch,* the newspaper he founded.

Foster first met Anthony when she was 20 years old at the 1879 NWSA convention. She had just completed her education, which had included study in political economy at the University of Zurich. She was instantly captivated by Anthony and became immediately engrossed in the drive for woman suffrage. In 1880 she was elected corresponding secretary of NWSA, a post she occupied until 1901. She first demonstrated her considerable executive potential and her reformer's zeal when she organized a number of woman suffrage conventions in the Midwest, also in 1880. In 1882, she led the NWSA Nebraska suffrage campaign, where she and Anthony confronted intense antisuffrage and antifeminist hostility. Anthony was extremely concerned about how Foster would cope with the pressures of campaigning. She wanted to nurture and cultivate Foster into an ideal suffrage leader, not overwhelm her into a state of nervous collapse. "How I wish you were made of *iron*—so you couldn't tire out," Anthony wrote her. "I fear all the time you will put on that *added ounce* that breaks even the camel's back—You understand just how to make agitation & that's the secret of successful work" (SBA to RF, April 5, 1882, A-A Papers, URL, in *Papers*). But Anthony needn't have worried because Foster proved she could manage all the rigors of the campaign trail.

In 1883, Foster was eager to resume her European travels. In need of a chaperone, she invited Anthony to accompany her as her guest. Foster suggested that they visit Elizabeth Cady Stanton in England as well as other noted feminists in Europe. Anthony gladly accepted, and the two women toured England, France, Germany, and Italy, the multilingual Foster acting as Anthony's translator. It was on this trip that Foster and Anthony developed their close personal relationship.

Throughout the mid-1880s, as Anthony gave Foster more and more responsibility in the management of the NWSA, it became apparent that Anthony was grooming her for future leadership. But in 1887, Foster stunned Anthony when she adopted a baby girl. Anthony was not shocked that the unmarried Foster adopted a daughter. Instead, she was mortified that her young associate had deceived her by keeping the impending adoption a secret from her but not from other NWSA suffragists, and she was distressed beyond measure because she had been hoping that Foster eventually might succeed her. Anthony knew from her vast experience as a reformer that the demands of motherhood precluded a woman's single-minded, 24-hour-a-day devotion to work. She responded to the news by writing a letter to the baby, followed by a letter to Foster two days later. The letter to little Miriam Alice Foster clearly

Rachel Foster at age 21.

conveys Anthony's primary concern about Foster's decision.

It is doubtful whether Aunt Susan welcomes your little ladyship to the home of 748 N. St. . . . ! She is thinking whether you will not divert all the love of the Foster Mamas [Foster's sister Julia was also a suffragist] from the great work for the emancipation of *woman*—to the little business of caring for the . . . wants of the one wee one—your little self. So my dear . . . do deport yourself as to help the junior Aunties to be more— to do more—for the *woman general* than ever before you came to them. (SBA to MAF, June 22, 1887, A-A Papers, URL, in *Papers*)

Foster reassured Anthony over and over that motherhood would not interfere with her activism, and she lived up to that promise. But, in Foster's mind, pledging continued devotion to woman suffrage did not mean that she shared Anthony's ambitions for her. On the contrary, the adoption and Foster's subsequent marriage in 1888 signified that she wanted both a family life and suffrage activism, which, from Anthony's and Foster's point of view, meant that a top leadership position was out of the question.

In March 1888, Foster and May Wright Sewall executed the groundbreaking International Council of Women (ICW), an event for which she and Sewall had spent years in preparation. At this event, Foster met Cyrus Miller Avery, the son of Rosa Miller Avery, a well-known Chicago suffragist and NWSA member. The young couple soon became romantically involved. In November 1888, Foster married Avery, to Anthony's consternation. She had managed to adjust to Foster's motherhood, and since she seemed as devoted to woman suffrage as ever, Anthony had clung to the hope that Foster might succeed her, providing she adopted no more children. But to Anthony, Foster Avery's marriage was the death knell of her future leadership, and Anthony immediately went into mourning. Once again, Foster Avery tried to console Anthony by pointing out that she intended to continue her role as corresponding secretary of NWSA and that her husband wholly supported her work. Indeed, she fulfilled this plan, despite the births of two more daughters. During the intense merger negotiations between the NWSA and the American Woman Suffrage Association (AWSA), Foster Avery played a primary leadership role. She and Anthony also maintained their mutually nourishing friendship. By this time, following the deaths of Foster Avery's mother and sister, she regarded Anthony as her closest family member. Nevertheless, Anthony had already begun searching for another young woman to lead the NWSA. She cultivated a close working and personal relationship with the famed orator Anna Howard Shaw and kept her ever-watchful eyes on the ablest of her young lieutenants.

Foster Avery, a wealthy woman and philanthropist, was also generous toward her friends. At Anthony's seventy-fifth birthday celebration, Foster Avery presented her mentor with an $800 annuity, which ensured that Anthony would receive $200 every three months for the rest of her life. Foster Avery organized the annuity by collecting $5,000 from 200 contributors toward the establishment of a trust fund. Anthony was surprised and thrilled by the unusual gift and by Foster Avery's extraordinary thoughtfulness and understanding of her needs.

Anthony and Foster Avery's relationship weathered a crucial crisis in December 1895 and January 1896, shortly after the publication of Elizabeth Cady Stanton's *The Woman's Bible*. Foster Avery was prominent among National American Woman Suffrage Association (NAWSA) members who voted to censure *The Woman's Bible* at the 1896 NAWSA convention in late January. Foster Avery, like many of the younger NAWSA suffragists, was extremely concerned that Cady Stanton's radical religious views would harm NAWSA's already deteriorating public image and further deplete its dwindling membership. Because of NAWSA's religious conservative majority, Foster Avery, Carrie Chapman Catt, and others believed that the organization could not withstand the fallout from another controversy that would certainly alienate conservative supporters and financial contributors.

Anthony was furious with Foster Avery, as she was with the other ringleaders of the controversial and unprecedented action, Chapman Catt, Shaw, Henry Blackwell, and Alice Stone Blackwell among them. But of all who participated, Anthony had been the closest to Foster Avery, and her dear friend's attack on Cady Stanton wounded her deeply. Although Foster Avery later apologized to Anthony, she appears not to have realized that by castigating Cady Stanton, she was, in effect, personally attacking Anthony. A passage from Anthony's diary reveals how thoroughly she lost all objectivity on this issue. "Rachel is a wonderfully strong woman in many directions," Anthony wrote. "If only she hadn't put that censure of Mrs. Stanton's *Bible* in her last year's report as corresponding secretary!—I should say in all directions. But that was caused by a weak or wicked spirit, I can not divine which, even at this distance" (Anthony 1954, 439–440). Anthony's diary entry clearly indicates that she found it impossible to understand the purpose of those who agreed to the censure resolution. That Anthony could only imagine her friend's actions as the result of weakness or wickedness of character rather than the expedient political maneuver it was emphasizes the depth of her personal anguish over Cady Stanton's rejection.

In 1901, a year after Anthony's retirement as president of NAWSA, Foster Avery resigned her position as corresponding secretary but maintained her active role in NAWSA. From 1904 to 1909, she was corresponding secretary of the International Woman Suffrage Alliance, and from 1907 to 1910, she served as vice president of NAWSA. Foster Avery's disagreements with NAWSA president Shaw and her frustration over her inept leadership led to Foster Avery's resignation from NAWSA in 1910. In the last decade of her life, she became more deeply involved in the Pennsylvania state suffrage struggle. She died of pneumonia in 1919 when she was 60 years old, less than a year away from the ratification of the Nineteenth Amendment.

Related entries:
American Woman Suffrage Association
Anthony, Susan B.
International Council of Women
National American Woman Suffrage Association
National Woman Suffrage Association
Woman Suffrage Movement
The Woman's Bible

Suggestions for further reading:
Barry, Kathleen. 1988. *Susan B. Anthony: Biography of a Singular Feminist.* New York: New York University Press.
Lasch, Christopher. 1971. "Rachel Foster Avery." In *NAW,* 1:71–72.
"Mrs. Rachel Foster Avery." 1893. In *A Woman of the Century*, edited by Frances E. Willard and Mary A. Livermore. Buffalo, New York: Charles Wells Moulton, pp. 37–38.

B

Barton, Clara (1821–1912)

Clara Barton, founder and high-powered leader of the American Red Cross, was a devout supporter of women's rights and the woman suffrage movement as well as a good friend of Susan B. Anthony. Although Barton never became closely associated with any one suffrage organization, her advocacy of women's rights through her lectures and her decades of commitment to social reform inspired many generations of U.S. women to assume vital, humanitarian roles in the public sphere.

Clarissa Harlowe Barton was born and raised in central Massachusetts. Like many young middle-class women of her generation, she became a teacher at age 18. In 1852, after teaching in Bordentown, New Jersey, she convinced the town's school committee to allow her to create one of New Jersey's first "free," or public, schools. The school soon thrived and quickly attained an enrollment of more than 600 pupils. When the school committee decided to hire a principal, they denied her the opportunity to fill the high-paying position and engaged a man instead. She resigned and immediately relocated to Washington, D.C., where she became the first female clerk in the U.S. Patent Office and one of the first women civil servants in the United States.

At the beginning of the Civil War, she discovered that soldiers on the front lines had no medical supplies and insufficient food. She immediately began gathering and distributing these supplies to the makeshift hospitals on the battlefields outside of Washington. Soon she was also nursing wounded soldiers on the front lines. Working entirely as a volunteer, she kept her work separate from the United States Sanitary Commission and the Union army's organization of nurses.

In 1867, Barton met Anthony and Elizabeth Cady Stanton at a train station in Cleveland, Ohio, at a time when all three women were engaged in lecture tours. Anthony greatly admired Barton, who had struggled against great odds to forge a unique role for herself in public life. Anthony publicized her new friend's lectures in *The Revolution*, frequently asked her to speak at woman suffrage conventions, and kept trying to enlist her to active duty in the woman suffrage movement. Despite Barton's unequivocal commitment to women's rights and her vocal support of woman suffrage, she resisted all of Anthony's and other suffragists' entreaties. As much as Barton believed in women's need for the ballot, she was even more convinced that women needed to thrust themselves into public life, in whatever capacity they chose, and move onward. Barton saw no point in waiting for the vote to give women permission to take their places in the public sphere.

When Anthony witnessed Barton's successful five-year campaign to convince the

U.S. government to sign the Geneva Treaty (an international agreement dictating the humanitarian treatment of the wounded in wartime) and her organization of the American Red Cross in 1881, she could not help but bemoan the loss of Barton's talents and ferocious energy to the woman suffrage movement. "How gloriously our movement would go on," she wrote Barton, "if it had the like of your hand, brain & heart to organize, systematize, vitalize & marshall its forces" (SBA to CB, September 19, 1876, CB-LCMD, in *Papers*).

Throughout the 1880s and 1890s, Barton continued to lecture at national woman suffrage conventions but remained ever cautious to keep the American Red Cross completely separate from the woman suffrage movement. Barton remained president of the Red Cross until 1904, when internal dissatisfaction with her leadership caused her to resign at the age of 83. In her last years, she involved herself in the Christian Science religion and in spiritualism while maintaining an active interest in the woman suffrage movement.

Suggestions for further reading:

Burton, David Henry. 1995. *Clara Barton: In the Service of Humanity*. Westport, Conn.: Greenwood Press.
Oates, Stephen B. 1994. *A Woman of Valor: Clara Barton and the Civil War*. New York: Free Press.
Pryor, Elizabeth Brown. 1987. *Clara Barton: Professional Angel*. Philadelphia: University of Pennsylvania Press.

Beecher, Henry Ward (1813–1887)

*L*iberal Congregational minister Henry Ward Beecher was the most influential clergyman of the mid–nineteenth century. A member of the prominent Beecher family, he was the son of the renowned evangelical Presbyterian minister Lyman Beecher, the brother of Harriet Beecher Stowe and Catharine Beecher, and the half-brother of NWSA suffragist Isabella Beecher Hooker. Beecher rose to national fame through the popularization of his "Gospel of Love," a doctrine he developed while minister at Plymouth Church in Brooklyn, New York. Like many of the clergy of his day, Beecher rejected the harsh, punitive Calvinist theology of his father's generation. Beecher's Gospel of Love stressed personal freedom, love, and salvation instead of damnation for one's sins (Waller 1982, 24).

Unlike the fiery lectures of the social reformers of his era, Beecher was dynamic without being dogmatic. His sermons were replete with wit and humor and were characterized by his casual, direct manner of personally connecting with his audiences. Beecher's charisma and hopeful message attracted 2,500 worshippers to Plymouth Church each week. His sermons were printed and distributed nationally.

Beecher resisted becoming involved in social reform movements in the 1850s, but in 1860 he became firmly associated with the women's rights movement when he delivered a critically acclaimed speech on women's rights in New York City. During the Civil War, in 1863 and 1864, he supported Susan B. Anthony and Elizabeth Cady Stanton in the work of their Woman's National Loyal League (WNLL). After the Civil War, he maintained his pro–women's rights position and was a member of the American Equal Rights Association (AERA).

In 1866, at the Eleventh National Woman's Rights Convention, Beecher declared, "It is more important that woman should vote than that the black man should vote," claiming that although African-American men needed the vote, "it is God's . . . idea of a true human society that man and woman should not be divorced in political affairs" (*HWS,* 2:159). And at the AERA convention in May 1867, Beecher perfectly expressed the views of Anthony, Cady Stanton, Parker Pillsbury, and other women's rights activists who were pushing for national recognition and adoption of universal suffrage.

Henry Ward Beecher pictured with his father, Lyman Beecher, and sister, Harriet Beecher Stowe.

If any say to me, "Why will you agitate the woman question when it is the hour for the black man?" I answer, it is the hour for every man and every woman, black or white. . . . The truth that I have to urge is not that women have the right of suffrage . . . but that suffrage is the inherent right of mankind. (Harper 1899, 1:276)

But by 1869, Anthony and Cady Stanton's high hopes for Beecher's continued support collapsed. In a complete about-face, Beecher withdrew his advocacy of universal suffrage to adopt the position of the majority of New England Republican AERA members who supported the ballot for African-American men through the Fifteenth Amendment. In 1869, he was chosen president of Lucy Stone and Henry Blackwell's American Woman Suffrage Association (AWSA), rival to Anthony and Cady Stanton's National Woman Suffrage Association (NWSA).

As the Beecher-Tilton Scandal raged through the early to mid-1870s, Anthony hoped that she, Cady Stanton, and the NWSA would remain uninvolved. They were too closely connected with all the parties involved to escape unscathed, however. Amazingly enough, Beecher, although he was accused of committing adultery with Elizabeth Richards Tilton, emerged from the turmoil with his reputation and power only slightly tarnished, a testament to his dominant political and social position.

Related entries:

Suggestions for further reading:
Clark, Clifford E., Jr. 1978. *Henry Ward Beecher: Spokesman for a Middle-Class America.* Urbana: University of Illinois Press.
Waller, Altina L. 1982. *Reverend Beecher and Mrs. Tilton: Sex and Class in Victorian America.* Amherst: University of Massachusetts Press.

Beecher-Tilton Scandal

*T*he Beecher-Tilton Scandal was one of the most infamous U.S. scandals of the nineteenth century. Its intricate, convoluted history, from the first exposé to the conclusion of the nearly seven-month-long trial, dominated the press for several years from November 1872 until 1875. The heart of the scandal involved the alleged extramarital relationship between the nationally renowned liberal Congregational minister Henry Ward Beecher and Elizabeth Richards Tilton, the wife of Theodore Tilton, an influential writer and editor and Beecher's closest friend. Because Beecher was president of the American Woman Suffrage Association (AWSA) and Theodore Tilton had served as president of the National Woman Suffrage Association (NWSA), both factions of the woman suffrage movement were severely affected by the furor even though neither organization was directly involved. Susan B. Anthony was a close friend and colleague of both the Tiltons, visiting them frequently at their home throughout the late 1860s and early 1870s. She was also a longtime friend and admirer

of Henry Ward Beecher. Her close associations with all the individuals involved ensured that the scandal would affect her deeply.

The public had an insatiable appetite for news about the scandal. Americans were both captivated and horrified by the tales of betrayal, subterfuge, blackmail, free-love philosophies, and unbridled sexuality. Although the affair became public in early November 1872, when Victoria Claflin Woodhull published a complete exposé in her journal *Woodhull and Claflin's Weekly,* rumors of Beecher and Richards Tilton's liaison had been circulating in the social reform community for several years. In fact, Richards Tilton confided her involvement with Beecher to several friends, including Anthony and Elizabeth Cady Stanton. (Richards Tilton was poetry editor of *The Revolution,* Anthony and Cady Stanton's newspaper). Anthony kept the confession to herself, believing that a friend's extramarital affair was an intensely private issue. Cady Stanton felt no such compunction and passed the confidence along to Claflin Woodhull in 1871. At this time Claflin Woodhull was highly respected by Cady Stanton, Anthony, and NWSA suffragists. Cady Stanton's indiscretion may have stemmed from her dislike of Beecher and her loathing of his conservative sisters Harriet Beecher Stowe and Catharine Beecher for voicing their public disapproval of Cady Stanton's radical views on women's rights, woman suffrage, and marriage and divorce reform (Griffith 1984, 157).

Claflin Woodhull did not reveal what she knew about Beecher and Richards Tilton until her sudden rise to fame reversed itself. Her fledgling Equal Rights Party (ERP) crumbled after she was selected its presidential candidate. This failure combined with an unrelentingly hostile press and concomitant financial reversals made Claflin Woodhull a desperate woman by June 1872. Her plan to expose Beecher and her scheme to extort money from members of the NWSA and the AWSA sealed her ruin, but not before she had set in motion the volatile events that destroyed the reputations and fortunes of nearly everyone involved and that reduced the membership and impeded the functioning of both the NWSA and the AWSA.

By 1874, just as Anthony was beginning to believe that the Beecher-Tilton news was quieting down and the public once again might renew their interest in woman suffrage, Theodore Tilton stirred the media cauldron. He condemned Beecher in several New York newspapers in June 1874 and in August initiated legal proceedings to sue Beecher. The adultery trial, which ran for 112 days in 1875, mesmerized Americans and turned them even more solidly against women's rights and woman suffrage. Just as the press had linked the much-hated free-love movement with woman suffrage in the public's mind in 1872, the newspapers continued to profess Beecher's innocence and claimed that Claflin Woodhull and Tilton's evil, free-love variety of women's rights and woman suffrage activism was at the root of the entire scandal. By repeatedly connecting Claflin Woodhull and Theodore Tilton's free-love theories with NWSA and AWSA suffragists, the press invented a popular image of a tainted, immoral, untouchable woman suffrage movement (Kerr 1992, 164–165, 176). This fabrication decimated the membership of both organizations during the mid-1870s, crippling woman suffrage agitation.

The Beecher-Tilton trial was agonizing for Anthony. Wherever she went throughout the country on lecture engagements or in her own hometown, the press mercilessly harassed her, pressuring her to tell what she knew about the affair. Even her friends pestered her for answers. She refused to budge, but as the weeks wore on, she became increasingly distressed about what the affair was costing the cause. As long as the public was wrapped up in the scandal, no one would consider the woman suffrage movement's plans, agenda, or successes.

Before the trial, Beecher's self-appointed church investigation committee cleared him of Tilton's charge of adultery. The trial itself resulted in a hung jury, nine in favor of Beecher and three against. Although Beecher emerged with his reputation only slightly marred by the scandal, those of both the Tiltons and Claflin Woodhull were destroyed.

Related entries:
American Woman Suffrage Association
Beecher, Henry Ward
Equal Rights Party
Free-Love Controversy
Hooker, Isabella Beecher
National Woman Suffrage Association
Tilton, Theodore
Woodhull, Victoria Claflin

Suggestions for further reading:
Arling, Emanie Sachs. 1928. *"The Terrible Siren": Victoria Woodhull (1838–1927)*. New York: Harper and Bros.
Clark, Clifford E., Jr. 1978. *Henry Ward Beecher: Spokesman for a Middle-Class America*. Urbana: University of Illinois Press.
Waller, Altina L. 1982. *Reverend Beecher and Mrs. Tilton: Sex and Class in Victorian America*. Amherst: University of Massachusetts Press.

Blackwell, Alice Stone (1857–1950)

*R*adical political reformer and suffragist, the only child of woman suffrage leaders Lucy Stone and Henry Blackwell, Alice Stone Blackwell wholly invested her talents in the woman suffrage movement and in an array of humanitarian causes. She is frequently credited as the suffragist most responsible for driving the 1890 merger of the suffrage organization her parents founded, the American Woman Suffrage Association (AWSA), and Susan B. Anthony and Elizabeth Cady Stanton's National Woman Suffrage Association (NWSA) into the National American Woman Suffrage Association (NAWSA). Although Blackwell was never close to Anthony personally, perhaps the result of her parents' long-standing feud with the suffrage leader, she was a determined, hardworking NAWSA suffragist who served as its recording secretary from 1890 to 1908.

Alice Stone Blackwell, who is credited with being the driving force behind the formation of the National American Woman Suffrage Association (NAWSA).

Blackwell grew up in an extraordinary family, surrounded by a circle of strong, publicly achieving female relatives. In addition to the vigorous women's rights and woman suffrage activism of her parents, her aunt Elizabeth Blackwell (Henry Blackwell's sister) was the first woman to receive a medical degree and the first person to found a school of nursing in the United States. Her aunt Emily Blackwell (Henry's sister) also became a medical doctor, and her aunt Antoinette Brown Blackwell (wife of Henry's brother Samuel Blackwell) was the first woman to be ordained as a minister in the United States as well as being a published scholar and suffragist.

Alice Blackwell had an outstanding education, primarily in coeducational institutions. She attended a renowned college preparatory school in Boston, the Chauncy Hall School, and was admitted to Boston University in 1877, one of only two women in her class. Although she was painfully shy as a child, she had overcome this trait by the time she attended college. A scholar and intellectual, she was popular among her classmates and was elected president of her class. Following graduation, she entered the family

business of suffrage activism by becoming an editor of her parents' acclaimed women's rights and suffrage newspaper, the *Woman's Journal*. Until 1917, editing and publishing the *Woman's Journal* was her chief preoccupation. In 1887, she became the editor and publisher of a new publication, the *Woman's Column*, which consisted of prosuffrage articles and editorials. Blackwell distributed the journal to newspaper editors throughout the country for republication in the nation's leading newspapers. Blackwell's writings about the suffrage movement received accolades, even from antisuffragists.

After her mother's death in 1893, Blackwell truly came into her own. Although her mother's final words to her were "Make the world better," Stone did not specify how or in what capacity her daughter should improve society, thereby freeing Blackwell from a full-time commitment to suffrage activism. Consequently, Blackwell became immersed in the struggle to free people from political oppression, both in the United States and around the world. She involved herself in numerous liberal and radical social and political reform organizations. The Friends of Russian Freedom (a prosocialist organization), the American Peace Society, the Women's Trade Union League, the National Association for the Advancement of Colored People (NAACP), the New England Anti-Vivisection Society, and the Woman's Christian Temperance Union (WCTU) were among her most esteemed causes. She also was instrumental in the development of the League of Women Voters. As a result of an important relationship with an Armenian theological student in the early 1890s, she also dedicated herself to assisting Armenian refugees who had escaped the Turkish genocide, a cause she pursued for the rest of her life.

Following World War I, Blackwell became increasingly concerned about rampant nativist and antisocialist sentiment in American society, which deprived the foreign-born of their civil liberties and their political freedom. She strenuously protested the deportation of socialist immigrants and the incarceration and eventual executions of Italian immigrant anarchists Nicola Sacco and Bartolomeo Vanzetti. She supported the two men throughout their trial and imprisonment and maintained a lengthy correspondence with Vanzetti, forever believing in the two men's innocence.

After 40 years of effort, Blackwell finally published the long-awaited biography of her mother, *Lucy Stone: Pioneer of Women's Rights,* in 1930. Then in 1935, an unscrupulous business manager lost most of Blackwell's savings. Thousands of her friends, colleagues, and supporters established an annuity for her, which helped her sustain a modest lifestyle. In 1945, Boston University granted her an honorary Doctor of Humanities degree, an acknowledgment of her lifelong contributions to the women's rights and woman suffrage movements and to her international humanitarian social reform.

Related entries:
American Woman Suffrage Association
Blackwell, Henry Browne
National American Woman Suffrage Association
Stone, Lucy
The *Woman's Journal*

Suggestions for further reading:
Blackwell, Alice Stone. 1930. *Lucy Stone: Pioneer of Women's Rights.* Boston: Little Brown.
Blodgett, Geoffrey. 1971. "Alice Stone Blackwell." In *NAW,* 1:156–158.
Merrill, Marlene Deahl, ed. 1990. *Growing Up in Boston's Gilded Age: The Journal of Alice Stone Blackwell, 1872–1874.* New Haven, Conn.: Yale University Press.

Blackwell, Antoinette Louisa Brown (1825–1921)

The first woman to be ordained a minister in the United States, Antoinette Brown Blackwell was also a religious scholar, philosopher, social reformer, popular lecturer, and activist in the temperance, antislavery, women's rights, and woman suffrage movements. While a student at Oberlin College, Brown decided to prepare to enter the ministry. Although dissuaded by her family and Oberlin administration and faculty, Brown persisted until the college allowed her to enroll in its theological program. She successfully completed the course of study in 1850, but the college refused to grant its theological degree to a woman. After leaving Oberlin, she became a regular on the reform lecture circuit, speaking on temperance, antislavery, and women's rights issues. She soon gained renown for refuting the orthodox clergy's use of biblical scriptures to instruct women to confine their activities to their homes and families. In September 1853, she was ordained as a Congregational minister in Wayne County, New York.

Anthony and Brown first met and became friends at the Third National Woman's Rights Convention in Syracuse, New York, in 1852. For the next four years Anthony and Brown enjoyed a close, personal correspondence and friendship—advising, encouraging, and challenging each other to overcome the internal and external impediments that blocked them from achieving their goals as women's rights activists. Brown, Anthony, and Amelia Jenks Bloomer conducted a brilliantly successful temperance lecture tour in 1853, and Brown lectured on behalf of Anthony and Elizabeth Cady Stanton's crusade for married women's property rights in 1854.

Brown's marriage in 1856 to Samuel Blackwell (the brother of Henry Blackwell, fellow Oberlin College alumna Lucy Stone's husband-to-be) forever altered her relationship with Anthony. Anthony was extremely disappointed by Brown's and Stone's decisions to marry, in part because both women had determined never to marry and also because Anthony had gloried in the vision of a sisterhood wholly devoted to advancing women's rights. Despite Brown Blackwell's and Stone's protests to the contrary, Anthony knew that marriage and family responsibilities would necessitate their absence from the vanguard of women's rights activism. Brown Blackwell returned to the lecture circuit for a brief time after the birth of her first child, but the task of juggling her family life with financial concerns, travel difficulties, and the stresses of regular speaking engagements forced her to retreat from public life. She then devoted herself to her scholarly interests while also continuing to support the women's rights and suffrage movements.

During the post–Civil War years of confusion and conflict in the women's rights movement, Brown Blackwell struggled to remain impartial in the dispute between her brother- and sister-in-law Henry Blackwell and Lucy Stone, and her old friends Anthony and Cady Stanton. She accomplished this by completely distancing herself from the political issues driving the split in the women's rights movement and by steering clear of any intensive involvement in either Anthony and Cady Stanton's National Woman Suffrage Association (NWSA) or Stone and Blackwell's American Woman Suffrage Association (AWSA).

Brown Blackwell's distaste for political wrangling reflected her personal conviction that the battles that erupted over the Fourteenth and Fifteenth Amendments were trivial distractions from the real work of achieving women's equality in society. Although Brown Blackwell supported the woman suffrage movement throughout her entire life (voting for the first time in 1920 at the age of 95), she believed that promoting women's education and expanding women's role outside the home were more crucial to achieving equality than the ballot (Cazden 1983, 139–140).

Related entries:
Anthony, Susan B.
Blackwell, Henry Browne
Bloomer, Amelia Jenks
Stone, Lucy
Syracuse Woman's Rights Convention of 1852
Temperance
Woman's Rights Conventions
Women's Rights Movement

Suggestions for further reading:
Cazden, Elizabeth. 1983. *Antoinette Brown Blackwell: A Biography.* Old Westbury, N.Y.: Feminist Press.
Lasser, Carol, and Marlene Deahl Merrill, eds. 1987. *Friends and Sisters: Letters between Lucy Stone and Antoinette Brown Blackwell, 1846–1893.* Urbana: University of Illinois Press.

Blackwell, Henry Browne (1825–1909)

Henry Browne Blackwell's career in social reform primarily revolved around his dedication to women's rights and the woman suffrage movement. Despite his considerable acumen as an activist in his own right, Blackwell continues to be most often remembered as the husband and closest colleague of Lucy Stone, a principal leader of the women's rights and woman suffrage movements, and as the brother of Elizabeth Blackwell, the first woman doctor in the United States.

When he was seven years old, Blackwell and his family emigrated from England to the United States, settling eventually in Cincinnati, Ohio. From the family's early days in the United States, Blackwell's father, Samuel, was immersed in the antislavery movement. As a young man, Blackwell, too, became an active abolitionist while also pursuing a career in the hardware trade. Although he made frequent attempts throughout his life to launch businesses and to invest in real estate and other inventive moneymaking schemes, these ventures were rarely profitable. He experienced his greatest success as a leader of the American Woman Suffrage Association (AWSA) and as an adept, courageous manager and executor of woman suffrage projects and campaigns.

Blackwell first met Lucy Stone in 1850 when she stopped in Cincinnati to receive funds from the Ohio Anti-Slavery Society, but it was not until 1853, when he became reacquainted with her on a trip to Boston, that he decided to offer her friendship and the possibility of marriage. He spent most of the next two years relentlessly pursuing her and coaxing her to marry him. Stone, fervently committed to remaining single, discouraged him while sustaining a voluminous written correspondence with him. Blackwell eventually extracted her agreement to marry by promising to support all her women's rights work, to give her freedom to manage her own career, and to allow her to retain total control over her own body (Kerr 1992, 81). When they married in 1855, their marriage ceremony included, at his suggestion, a jointly authored "Marriage Protest" of the body of laws that endowed husbands with complete legal power in the marital relationship and that deprived women of the property and other legal rights they enjoyed prior to marriage (Kerr 1992, 82).

Although Blackwell attended and addressed woman's rights conventions of the 1850s, he first became prominent in the women's rights movement through his involvement in the American Equal Rights Association (AERA). Stone and Blackwell canvassed Kansas during the AERA woman suffrage campaign in 1867. Like Stone, Blackwell was indignant about Anthony and Elizabeth Cady Stanton's partnership with the racist Democrat George Francis Train during the final months of the Kansas campaign. Blackwell and Stone castigated Anthony for associating the AERA with Train and for using AERA funds to pay for a campaign that was, at least in Train's execution of it, anti–African-American. After all, they reasoned, the AERA was dedicated to obtaining suffrage not only for women but for African-American males. Most New England Republican reformers agreed with Stone and Blackwell and went so far as to blame Anthony for the failure of the entire campaign.

In *Susan B. Anthony: A Biography of a Singular Feminist*, historian Kathleen Barry states that her scrutiny of some recently discovered correspondence of suffragist Isabella Beecher Hooker uncovered a letter in which Beecher Hooker describes a conversation she had with Blackwell in December 1869. According to Beecher Hooker, Blackwell confided to her that he and Kansas Republican leaders had cooperated to arrange Anthony's campaign with Train in 1867. According to Blackwell, they created this odd couple so that Train's appeal among Kansas Democrats would earn more votes for the woman suffrage referendum. They also hoped that Anthony would temper Train's undesirable anti–African-American diatribes (Barry 1988, 178, 181–182). Beecher Hooker's report of Blackwell's conversation with her is significant because it directly contradicts Blackwell's repeated public accusations, throughout the late 1860s and again in 1899, that Anthony was wholly responsible for Train's involvement in the Kansas campaign. These charges alienated Anthony and Cady Stanton from their close friends Stone, Wendell Phillips, William Lloyd Garrison, Stephen Symonds Foster, Abby Kelley Foster, and the majority of AERA members and their former Garrisonian abolitionist colleagues, and were a major factor contributing to the split in the women's rights movement.

When Blackwell acknowledged to Beecher Hooker that his Train scheme had been a grievous error, he swore her to silence, a vow she appears to have broken only when she communicated the details in this letter. Public knowledge of Blackwell's involvement in the Train affair would have marred the reputation of a Republican reformer as politically ambitious as Blackwell.

Anthony, however, seems to have been oblivious of the source of the plan to have Train accompany her during the Kansas campaign. She always maintained that she had never known, nor had she thought to question, who had originated the idea to send Train to her, but in her desperation for able-bodied assistance she had wholeheartedly welcomed his arrival.

Blackwell continued to create unique political strategies that contributed to his growing reputation as a politically savvy reformer. In 1867, hoping to advance both African-

American and woman suffrage, he wrote and distributed *What the South Can Do: How the Southern States Can Make Themselves Masters of the Situation*, a pamphlet printed from a letter he sent to southern state legislatures. This document reassured southern legislators that if they extended the suffrage to southern white women, they need not fear enfranchising African-American males. He argued that the resultant increase in white voters would prevent the black vote from overwhelming the white vote (Walker 1983, 24). In 1890, Blackwell again used this strategy of appealing to the racial fears and prejudices of white southerners to manipulate support for woman suffrage, this time with greater success. He bombarded southern legislators with pamphlets advocating the enfranchisement of literate southern women to decrease what he described as the political "power of semi-barbarous illiteracy" that the African-American vote had created (quoted in Kerr 1992, 230). Although his racist and nativist strategies were not unusual among white turn-of-the-century suffragists, they were a radical departure for a former abolitionist and champion of African-American rights.

In the late 1860s, Blackwell came to agree with Wendell Phillips, Frederick Douglass, and former New England Republican abolitionists that securing the Fourteenth and Fifteenth Amendments must take precedence over attempts to achieve woman suffrage. In this struggle, he was bitterly opposed to Anthony and Cady Stanton's rejection of the Fifteenth Amendment, and he frequently denounced them at AERA meetings.

Blackwell ably assisted Stone in the formation of the New England Woman Suffrage Association (NEWSA) in 1868, the AWSA in 1869, and the Massachusetts Woman Suffrage Association (MWSA) in 1870, assuming and fulfilling a leadership position in each organization. He helped Stone launch the *Woman's Journal,* assisted her in the management of its business affairs, and acted as editor after Mary Livermore resigned

in 1872, although Stone and eventually their daughter Alice Stone Blackwell took over in his frequent, lengthy absences for business trips and suffrage campaigns. Blackwell's love of adventure and his irrepressible enjoyment of overcoming the hardships and obstacles of frontier travel made him an ideal campaigner. When Stone (seven years his senior) became too feeble for cross-country campaigns, he engineered the trips alone—making valuable contributions to the suffrage campaigns in Vermont, Nebraska, South Dakota, Montana, Rhode Island, Colorado, and Washington state.

As exemplary a reformer as Blackwell was, he is reported to have suffered from being in Stone's shadow. Despite his political astuteness, he could never compete with Stone, whose name was a household word by the time they married, nor could his skills or reputation match or exceed her oratorical brilliance, her incomparable stature in the suffrage movement, or her sound, balanced executive management and leadership of AWSA affairs. After Stone's death in 1893, Blackwell remained committed to his woman suffrage activism while also continuing on as editor of the *Woman's Journal* until his death in 1909.

Related entries:
Abolitionist Movement
American Equal Rights Association
American Woman Suffrage Association
Blackwell, Alice Stone
Fifteenth Amendment
Hooker, Isabella Beecher
Kansas Campaign of 1867
National American Woman Suffrage Association
National Woman Suffrage Association
Reconstruction
Stone, Lucy
Train, George Francis
Woman Suffrage Movement
The *Woman's Journal*

Suggestions for further reading:
Hays, Elinor Rice. 1967. *Those Extraordinary Blackwells: The Story of a Journey to a Better World.* New York: Harcourt Brace.
Kerr, Andrea Moore. 1992. *Lucy Stone: Speaking Out for Equality.* New Brunswick, N.J.: Rutgers University Press.

Wheeler, Leslie, ed. 1981. *Loving Warriors: Selected Letters of Lucy Stone and Henry B. Blackwell, 1853–1893*. New York: Dial Press.

Blake, Lillie Devereux (1833–1913)

National Woman Suffrage Association (NWSA), National American Woman Suffrage Association (NAWSA), and New York state suffrage leader Lillie Devereux Blake was a vibrant, tireless worker for woman suffrage and was integrally involved in nearly every major project of the NWSA and NAWSA from 1869 until 1900.

Born in North Carolina, Elizabeth Johnson Devereux was raised in Connecticut and resided in New York City for most of her adult life. Following the death of her first husband, she supported herself and her two daughters with the income from her writing. A popular author of novels, stories, and nonfiction articles, Devereux Blake was drawn to the woman suffrage movement in 1869 several years after her marriage to her second husband, Grinfill Blake. From her first exposure to the movement, she was eager for intense involvement. By the mid-1870s, Devereux Blake was active in nearly every phase of NWSA efforts—assisting Susan B. Anthony in the planning and execution of NWSA conventions, working on the NWSA finance committee, acting as recording secretary at meetings, addressing conventions, lobbying members of Congress, testifying at congressional hearings, and participating in state suffrage campaigns. Although Devereux Blake luxuriated in the time she spent in the limelight and had an intense ambition to lead the movement, she did not shirk the tedious, menial drudgery of suffrage activism.

Devereux Blake was equally dedicated to the woman suffrage movement in New York state. President of the New York State Woman Suffrage Association from 1879 until 1890 and the New York City Woman Suffrage League from 1886 until 1900, she was the successful commander of state suffrage campaigns and efforts to persuade legislators to enact women's rights legislation.

Devereux Blake emphatically pressed her views on NWSA and NAWSA leaders and members when her ideas conflicted with the majority. She was consistently in favor of aggressive suffrage agitation and often grew impatient with Anthony and other suffrage leaders when they counseled prudence and patience. In 1880 she persisted in her campaign to persuade leaders of the NWSA to steer away from further petition campaigns until the majority finally agreed to abstain from them. In the 1880s and 1890s, just as Devereux Blake was becoming increasingly convinced that the ballot should not be the sole object of their efforts, Anthony was growing more and more certain that the ballot must be the supreme and only focus of NWSA and NAWSA activism, a dynamic that may have set the two women on a collision course.

Anthony's numerous letters to Devereux Blake reveal the two suffrage leaders' shared devotion to executing the minutiae of NWSA business matters as well as Anthony's confidence that her colleague would faithfully execute Anthony's directions. Conspicuously absent from this correspondence, however, are Anthony's customary expressions of warmth, concern, and goodwill. Nor do Anthony's letters contain her usual offerings of personal information, which characterize her letters to most of her fellow reformers and young lieutenants. Many have speculated on the reasons for Anthony's cool treatment of Devereux Blake, though none are based on any clear evidence. Whatever Anthony's reasons for her opinion and feelings toward Devereux Blake, it is clear that she did not regard the younger woman as the ideal future leader of NAWSA, as many other suffragists did.

When Anthony began planning to retire from the presidency of NAWSA, she wished Carrie Chapman Catt to succeed her, though

Elizabeth Cady Stanton and many other NAWSA leaders expected that Devereux Blake should fill the position because of her three decades of flawless, uninterrupted activism. Deeply hurt by Anthony's lack of confidence and support, Devereux Blake managed to campaign for the presidency for a brief time, but before the vote was taken, she withdrew her candidacy. She remained exceedingly bitter toward Anthony for the rest of her life.

Following this crisis, Devereux Blake established the National Legislative League in 1900 to continue the agitation for women's rights legislation that she had undertaken through the New York suffrage associations and NAWSA. Her declining health, however, prevented her from fulfilling her legislative goals, and beginning in 1906, she was forced to retire from her career as an activist.

Related entries:
Anthony, Susan B.
Centennial Exposition
National American Woman Suffrage Association
National Woman Suffrage Association
Woman Suffrage Movement

Suggestions for further reading:
Blake, Katherine Devereux, and Margaret Louise Wallace. 1943. *Champion of Women: The Life of Lillie Devereux Blake.* New York: Fleming H. Revell.
HWS, Vols. 2–3, 3:408.
Taylor, William R. 1971. "Lillie Devereux Blake." In *NAW,* 1:167–169.

Bloomer, Amelia Jenks (1818–1894)

Although Amelia Jenks Bloomer is best known for her role in publicizing the Bloomer costume, she was an active contributor to the temperance, women's rights, and woman suffrage movements. In the 1840s and early 1850s, Jenks Bloomer was a resident and deputy postmaster of Seneca Falls, New York (her husband, Dexter Bloomer, was

postmaster). In 1848 she attended the Seneca Falls Convention. Jenks Bloomer's most significant contribution to the women's rights movement was the publication of her newspaper the *Lily*, which was launched in 1849 and soon became the leading women's temperance newspaper in the Northeast. The *Lily* eventually embraced a broad range of women's rights issues.

Susan B. Anthony became friends with Jenks Bloomer through their temperance work, and it was during a visit to her in 1851 that Anthony first met Elizabeth Cady Stanton. Although Cady Stanton warned Anthony to steer clear of Jenks Bloomer's conservative views, Anthony maintained a friendship with her and never missed a chance to praise the *Lily* highly, promoting it wherever she traveled on temperance business.

Bloomer and Anthony were named secretaries of the Woman's State Temperance Society (WSTS) at its first convention in 1852. In 1853, they embarked on a successful temperance lecture tour of New York state with *New York Tribune* editor Horace Greeley and temperance activist Antoinette Brown, speaking to packed houses wherever they traveled.

Jenks Bloomer did not cease publication of the *Lily* when she moved to Mount Vernon, Ohio, in 1854 but was forced to sell it when she and her husband settled in Council Bluffs, Iowa, in 1855. In Iowa, Bloomer continued to work on behalf of women's rights and woman suffrage until her death in 1894, although not on a national level. In 1856, she endorsed a woman suffrage measure in a speech to the Nebraska Territory's state legislature. She fought for married women's property rights in Iowa, and in 1871 became president of the Iowa Woman Suffrage Society.

Related entries:
Blackwell, Antoinette Louisa Brown
Bloomer Costume
The *Lily*
Temperance
Woman's State Temperance Society

Suggestions for further reading:
Lewis, W. Davis. 1971. "Bloomer, Amelia Jenks." In *NAW,* 1:179–181.
Solomon, Martha M., ed. 1991. *A Voice of Their Own: The Woman Suffrage Press, 1840–1910.* Tuscaloosa: University of Alabama Press.

Bloomer Costume

The Bloomer costume, modeled on the loose-fitting pantaloons and short dress common at water-cure spas in the mid-nineteenth century, became the predominant style of dress for the most radical of women's rights activists in the early 1850s. Although the Bloomer costume became a popular symbol of the women's rights movement in the early 1850s, its wearers never intended it to be. They donned the "short dress," as they called it, because it freed them from whalebone corsets and the cumbersome, crippling layers of long petticoats and skirts that trailed to the ground, accumulating dirt and mud, and that made stairs, manure-laden streets, and outhouses difficult to negotiate.

Elizabeth Smith Miller, the first feminist to design and wear the short dress, and her cousin Elizabeth Cady Stanton were both enthusiastic supporters of the new style. One after the other, women's rights reformers adopted the costume. In her newspaper the *Lily,* Amelia Jenks Bloomer described Cady Stanton's attire at the Woman's State Temperance Society (WSTS) Convention in Rochester in 1852. She proceeded to publicize the new dress in the *Lily,* including dress patterns so that readers could make their own. Soon the short dress became popularly known as "the Bloomer," the "Bloomer Dress," and the "Bloomer Costume," to Jenks Bloomer's dismay.

When Susan B. Anthony first met Cady Stanton in March 1851 in Seneca Falls, New York, Cady Stanton was attired in the short dress (Griffith 1984, 72). By 1852, as the two women became friends, Cady Stanton wasted no time in persuading her new friend to join her, but Anthony was not easily converted.

She remarked in a letter to fellow feminist Lucy Stone in May 1852 that although the dress had its merits, she didn't think it was a change she needed. Cady Stanton did not give up. Throughout 1852, as she began wearing the short dress to public meetings and conventions, she kept the pressure on Anthony. After anguished soul-searching, Anthony decided to wear the Bloomer costume by the end of that year.

Yet the Bloomer costume never caught on as Anthony and her fellow women's rights activists hoped. The public's reaction to the costume was overwhelmingly negative. Women who wore the Bloomer dress in public were subjected to ridicule, harassment, and the wrath of angry mobs, comprising mostly boys and men. Anthony, Stone, and other women reformers who traveled frequently suffered the most, yet their letters reveal that although they found the public's reaction bothersome, they tried to take the harassment in stride. Oddly enough, they did not seem to perceive the potential danger in their confrontations with the public. In New York City, as Anthony and Stone were on their way to the post office, they were surrounded by a horde of boys and men who, though described by Stone as "good-natured," taunted and jostled them. When someone hailed the police and a carriage for them, they escaped "with only a little rough treatment at the last" (Blackwell 1930, 105).

Time and persistence did not alter the public's reception of the costume. Cady Stanton was the first to abandon wearing the Bloomer dress in public, and once she had made the decision that the dress was not worth the trouble, she immediately began urging her fellow feminists to do the same. She summed up her position in a postscript she added to a letter Anthony sent to Stone: "for your own sake lay aside the short dress. We put it on for greater freedom; but what is physical freedom compared with mental bondage? By all means, have the new dress made long" (ECS to LS, February 23, 1854, ECS Papers, LCMD, in *Papers*).

As was characteristic of Anthony, once she had made the commitment to wear the Bloomer costume, she could not easily reverse the decision in good conscience. Although she later acknowledged that she "found it a physical comfort but a mental crucifixion," she believed that determinedly wearing the Bloomer dress had a value that extended far beyond the decision to wear simpler attire (Harper 1899, 1:117). In a letter to Stone, Anthony sympathized with Cady Stanton's wish to avoid persecution, yet observed:

> Everyone who drops the dress, makes the task a harder one for the few left. . . . I have been so pressed by those who are perhaps better and wiser than myself, to lay aside the short dress, so implored for the sake of the Cause, etc. etc., that for the last ten days my heart has almost failed me, and but for my reliance on my own convictions of right and duty, must have sat down disheartened and discouraged. It is hard to stand alone,

but no doubt good discipline for us. (SBA to LS, February 9, 1854, BF-LCMD, in *Papers*)

For the feminists in Anthony's circle, wearing the Bloomer costume had come to signify something about their status, position, and role as women, and for each woman the meaning was slightly different. For Anthony, the freedom to choose and wear attire that made her all-important reform work physically easier to perform was a direct expression of one of her most fundamental beliefs—the right of women to ordain their own lives. Even so, Cady Stanton's pressure coupled with Anthony's realization that the Bloomer dress had become "an intellectual slavery" convinced her to reassume a conventional form of dress by mid-1854 (Harper 1899, 1:117).

Related entries:
Bloomer, Amelia Jenks
The *Lily*
Stone, Lucy
Woman's State Temperance Society
Women's Rights Movement

Suggestions for further reading:
Barry, Kathleen. 1988. *Susan B. Anthony: Biography of a Singular Feminist.* New York: New York University Press.
HWS, 1:469–471.

Engraving of a classic Bloomer costume, composed by William Dessier. Published by Wm. Hall & Son, circa 1851.

Brown, John (1800–1859)

On October 16, 1859, militant abolitionist John Brown led a raid on the U.S. Arsenal at Harpers Ferry, Virginia, in an unsuccessful attempt to obtain firearms with which to ignite a sweeping slave insurrection. Unlike the Garrisonian abolitionists, who rejected violent solutions to slavery, Brown was an extremist among the many abolitionists who were convinced that only armed force could destroy slavery. As a loyal Garrisonian and as a Quaker, Susan B. Anthony did not condone the use of violence to achieve abolitionist ends, yet she possessed

Militant abolitionist John Brown, leader of the October 1859 raid on the federal arsenal at Harpers Ferry, Virginia.

for the memorial and bravely sold tickets door-to-door. When no one responded to her request to preside or to lecture at the meeting, she prevailed on her loyal friend and fearless fellow Garrisonian, Parker Pillsbury, who eagerly accepted and who, according to Anthony, delivered "the speech of his life." The meeting passed smoothly, with approximately 300 people in attendance. Once the hall was paid for, Anthony sent the remaining proceeds to Brown's widow and his children.

Related entries:
Abolitionist Movement
Anthony, Jacob Merritt
Douglass, Frederick
Kansas-Nebraska Act
Pillsbury, Parker

Suggestions for further reading:
Oates, Stephen B. 1984. *To Purge This Land with Blood: A Biography of John Brown.* Amherst: University of Massachusetts Press.
Rossbach, Jeffrey. 1982. *Ambivalent Conspirators: John Brown, the Secret Six, and a Theory of Slave Violence.* Philadelphia: University of Pennsylvania Press.

enormous sympathy for Brown's ideals and respect for his uncompromising pursuit of his goals. Anthony experienced the raid and its aftermath keenly because John Brown was no stranger to the Anthony family. From the mid-1850s on, he had been a regular visitor to Rochester, to the home of the Anthonys' friend Frederick Douglass. It was at his home that Anthony's youngest brother, Jacob Merritt Anthony, first met and became deeply influenced by Brown, following him to Kansas in 1856 to defend free-state settlers in the battle against Missouri proslavery forces at Osawatomie.

Antiabolitionist feeling exploded after the Harpers Ferry raid as northern proslavery sympathizers, Democrats, and conservatives blamed the raid on abolitionists. When John Brown was executed on December 2, 1859, Anthony felt compelled, as did a number of abolitionists throughout the North, to organize a public meeting to mourn him despite the volatile antiabolitionist mood of the public. She rented Corinthian Hall in Rochester

Brown, Olympia (1835–1926)

Radical suffrage pioneer and Universalist minister Olympia Brown first entered the woman suffrage movement during the chaotic Reconstruction era, when her intense devotion to woman suffrage and her extraordinary stamina and vitality earned her the lifelong admiration, respect, and close friendship of Susan B. Anthony.

Brown's parents ensured that their daughter, born in Michigan and raised in the Universalist faith, obtained an outstanding education. She graduated from Antioch College in Ohio in 1860 and from St. Lawrence University's school of theology in 1863. Less than a month after graduation, Brown became the first woman in the United States to be ordained by the leadership of a recognized denomination (Universalist). During the 1860s and much of the 1870s, she served as minister in several New England Universalist congregations.

Brown first met Anthony, Elizabeth Cady Stanton, and other women's rights reformers in 1866 at the Eleventh National Woman's Rights Convention in New York City, which established the American Equal Rights Association (AERA). Brown became instantly attached to the AERA's cause of universal suffrage and by 1867 was canvassing New York and Kansas on behalf of woman suffrage. A passionate, sought-after speaker, Brown's relentless campaign on the Kansas frontier in the summer and fall of 1867 won her the accolades of Anthony and Henry Blackwell and ensured her a place in the leadership of the woman suffrage movement.

Brown attempted to remain independent of any factionalism that occurred during the schism in the women's rights movement. She helped organize Lucy Stone and Blackwell's New England Woman Suffrage Association in 1868 and became a charter member of Anthony and Cady Stanton's National Woman Suffrage Association (NWSA) and Stone and Blackwell's American Woman Suffrage Association (AWSA) in 1869. She adhered most closely, however, to the NWSA.

Brown, her husband, and their young family moved to Racine, Wisconsin, in 1878 so that Brown could assume the pastorship of a congregation in that city. (Like Lucy Stone, Brown retained her birth name after marriage.) Although Brown remained active in the NWSA and participated regularly in national conventions, she also became deeply entrenched in Wisconsin's state suffrage movement. Over the years she was an active member, vice president, and president of the Wisconsin Woman Suffrage Association (WWSA).

Her most ambitious suffrage project was her test of a Wisconsin suffrage law. Because the law's most notable characteristics were its baffling lack of clarity and definition, Wisconsin suffragists and male liberal legislators and reformers decided to interpret it broadly—as fully enfranchising women, enabling them to vote in all elections. Brown and the WWSA urged Wisconsin women to test the law by voting not only in school elections as the law specified but also in local, municipal, state, and national elections. Anthony, based on her own and Virginia Minor's clash with the judicial system over their voting, warned Brown against this action and cautioned her to proceed slowly (Harper 1899, 2:624), but she ignored the warnings and forged ahead. When voting officials prevented her from casting a ballot in a Racine municipal election in 1887, she sued the city in what she hoped would be a successful test case of the suffrage law. Although the lower court judge ruled in her favor, the Wisconsin Supreme Court overturned the original decision on appeal. This outcome not only eliminated Wisconsin women from gaining access to full suffrage but also severely limited their ability to vote in school and municipal elections statewide and froze Wisconsin's suffrage movement for many years (McBride 1993, 131). As a result of the Wisconsin suffrage law disaster, Brown grew increasingly disenchanted with state suffrage work but continued to engage in state suffrage campaigns in South Dakota, Iowa, Kansas, and Maryland.

Anthony, unlike many of her freethinking and headstrong colleagues, tolerated and accepted Brown's idiosyncrasies, her stubborn independence, and her adamant insistence that she go her own way. Even when Brown led a vocal protest in 1889 against the NWSA-AWSA merger, which flaunted her opposition to Anthony's authority, the two women managed to maintain friendly relations. Anthony was well accustomed to Brown's singularities from her early days in the movement and appears to have resisted taking Brown's actions personally, in complete contrast to the manner in which she responded to Lucy Stone's behavior. Anthony also knew that Brown posed no threat to her leadership. In 1890, mere months after Brown's divisive merger protest, Anthony wrote her, "Come what may my dear—I shall always believe in Olympia Brown—and I trust come what may she will always believe in her special friend Susan B. Anthony" (SBA to OB, September 3, 1890, OB-SL, in *Papers*). Both Brown and Anthony were inspired by the other's admiration. For Anthony's seventieth birthday celebration in February 1890, Brown wrote:

> I think I express the feeling of most if not all the workers in our cause when I say that the women of America owe more to Susan B. Anthony than to any other woman living. While Mrs. Stanton has been the standard bearer of liberty, announcing great principles, Miss Anthony has been the power which has carried those principles on toward victory and impressed them upon the hearts of the people. (Harper 1899, 2:670)

In 1892, Brown formed the Federal Suffrage Association (FSA) at a time when Anthony and National American Woman Suffrage Association leaders had abandoned the Sixteenth Amendment campaign to concentrate on state suffrage battles. Among the FSA's more prominent proposals was its quest to persuade Congress to enfranchise women to vote in congressional elections. Brown remained committed to obtaining federal suffrage through the FSA (as did her friend and colleague Clara Bewick Colby), and later became a militant advocate of Alice Paul and Lucy Burns's Congressional Union and National Woman's Party.

In 1920, Brown was one of the very few survivors of the first generation of suffragists to vote in the first national election following ratification of the Nineteenth Amendment. In her final years, Brown continued her career as a radical reformer through the American Civil Liberties Union and the Women's International League for Peace and Freedom.

Related entries:
American Equal Rights Association
Anthony, Susan B.
Colby, Clara Dorothy Bewick
Kansas Campaign of 1867
National Woman Suffrage Association
Sixteenth Amendment Campaign
State Suffrage Campaigns
Woman Suffrage Movement

Suggestions for further reading:

Brown, Olympia. 1917. *Democratic Ideals: A Memorial Sketch of Clara B. Colby.* n.p. A Federal Suffrage Association Publication.
DuBois, Ellen Carol. 1978. *Feminism and Suffrage: The Emergence of an Independent Women's Movement in America 1848–1869.* Ithaca: Cornell University Press.
Graves, Lawrence L. 1971. "Olympia Brown." In *NAW,* 1:256–258.
McBride, Genevieve G. 1993. *On Wisconsin Women: Working for Their Rights from Settlement to Suffrage.* Madison: University of Wisconsin Press.

C

Catt, Carrie Lane Chapman (1859–1947)

Carrie Chapman Catt was a leading suffragist and president of the National American Woman Suffrage Association (NAWSA) from 1900 to 1904 and from 1916 to 1920. From her entrance into the woman suffrage movement in the late 1880s until the final passage of the Nineteenth Amendment in 1920, Chapman Catt committed herself to woman suffrage activism in the United States and abroad. Early in the 1890s, following Chapman Catt's exemplary leadership in state suffrage campaigns, Susan B. Anthony came to admire her no-nonsense, businesslike approach to suffrage work, her extraordinary administrative skills, and her ability to rally thousands of women to agitate for suffrage. Her shrewd understanding of the male political and business worlds was a boon to the suffrage cause. Her charismatic oratory inspired people to contribute funds to NAWSA and women to initiate local suffrage societies. For all of these reasons, Chapman Catt was Anthony's chosen successor as president of NAWSA in 1900.

Carrie Clinton Lane was born on a farm in Ripon, Wisconsin. In 1866, when she was seven years old, her family moved westward to a farm on the northern Iowa prairie. Following her graduation from high school, her father refused to help her finance a college education. Not to be dissuaded, she taught school for a year and earned enough to matriculate at Iowa State Agricultural College at Ames, Iowa, in 1877. She worked her way through college and graduated with a science degree in 1880. For the next two years she was a high school principal in Mason City, Iowa, and in 1883 became its superintendent of schools, one of the first women to do so in the United States.

When Lane married Leo Chapman in 1885, she became assistant editor of his newspaper, the *Mason City Republican*. After he died of typhoid fever the following year in San Francisco, she spent a year as a newspaper reporter in that city. In 1887, she returned home to Iowa to make her living as a lecturer. She joined the Iowa Woman Suffrage Association in that year, becoming its recording secretary and director of field activities in 1889. She attended the 1890 NAWSA convention and soon rose to prominence as one of its most zealous western suffragists. Also in 1890, she married her second husband, George Catt, who strongly supported her career as an activist. Most sources reveal that prior to marriage, the couple drew up an agreement that stipulated that Chapman Catt would devote four months of each year to her suffrage work. But in a speech delivered in 1936, she recalled that because of her husband's devout advocacy of her involvement, no restrictions were ever placed on the time she allotted to it, since her husband agreed that she was to do "reform work enough for both" (Fowler 1986, 16).

Throughout the 1890s, Chapman Catt channeled her writing and oratorical talents as well as her incomparable organizational skills toward winning state suffrage campaigns. Her leadership of the successful Colorado suffrage campaign of 1893 cemented her position as a principal NAWSA suffragist. When she became chair of NAWSA's National Organization Committee, a position she held from 1895 to 1900, she wielded considerable power as the chief director of state suffrage battles.

Through working closely with Chapman Catt on state campaigns, Anthony discovered her protégé's multifaceted talents. But unlike other NAWSA leading suffragists Lillie Devereux Blake, Abigail Scott Duniway, and Clara Bewick Colby, Anthony observed that Chapman Catt possessed the all-important ability to listen and to respond to the concerns of the NAWSA leadership. When her opinions differed from others', she worked at negotiating an agreement. Anthony soon learned that she could trust Chapman Catt's judgment completely, but paradoxically, they never formed the close, personal friendship that developed between Anthony and many of her most favored young lieutenants. Many suffragists admitted that Chapman Catt's aloof manner made it difficult to know her. As far as her relationship with Anthony was concerned, the fact that Chapman Catt was highly critical of NAWSA's disorganization, lack of momentum, and sparse membership also may have been a barrier to their intimacy (Fowler 1986, 20).

In the late 1890s, Anthony worried endlessly about who would succeed her when she retired from the NAWSA presidency in 1900. As much as she admired and loved Anna Howard Shaw, Anthony realized that she was not the strongest possible candidate. Shaw was a brilliant speaker, but there was no denying that she lacked the organizational abilities of Chapman Catt. Anthony tormented herself with the decision process. But given the huge

Carrie Chapman Catt in 1905.

amount of coordination necessary to wage the increasingly competitive state suffrage campaigns and the intricate strategizing needed to win congressional support, Anthony knew that Chapman Catt was the best choice.

At the NAWSA convention in 1900, Chapman Catt received Anthony's blessing and was elected president by an overwhelming majority. Although Anthony was no longer president, she continued to exert control on NAWSA and on Chapman Catt, who spent her time boosting NAWSA's membership, fund-raising, and traveling from state to state to urge legislators and the public to adopt woman suffrage. In addition to directing NAWSA, Chapman Catt pursued her dream of establishing an international woman suffrage association. In 1902, she was a leading founder of the International Woman Suffrage Alliance and became its first president in 1904.

All of this activity took its toll on Chapman Catt's health. When she decided to step down as NAWSA's president in 1904, she was literally worn out. She was also worried about her husband's increasing ill health. Without the weight of NAWSA matters pressing upon her, she had the time to immerse herself in her international woman suffrage efforts. Her husband's unexpected death in 1905 plunged her into a deep depression. When she recovered, she turned again to her passion for international suffrage work. Because her husband had left her financially well off, she was freed from having to earn a living and was able to dedicate the next ten years to international woman suffrage.

When Anna Howard Shaw resigned from the presidency of NAWSA in 1915, the membership demanded that Chapman Catt take her place. The only problem was that she did not want the job. Exhausted from her work on the unsuccessful 1915 New York state suffrage campaign, she knew she had taxed herself beyond her endurance. But when at least 100 NAWSA members cornered her at a December 1915 NAWSA convention and insisted that she assume the presidency, she caved in to the pressure and accepted. According to her close friend and biographer Mary Gray Peck, when Catt entered her hotel room after leaving the convention hall, she sobbed on her bed for hours. The next day, however, she threw herself into the task at hand—to be president of NAWSA and to push on to a final suffrage victory (Van Voris 1987, 130).

During the next year (1916) Chapman Catt toured the country, talking with as many state suffragists as possible. At the 1916 NAWSA convention, she presented to NAWSA leaders her carefully orchestrated, secret proposal for achieving national woman suffrage. It became known as the "Winning Plan." Under this strategy, through a combined all-out effort at both the state and federal levels, the woman suffrage amendment would be achieved. The plan necessitated a winning campaign in at least one southern state to destroy the southern states' unified antisuffrage bloc. It also called for victories in several midwestern states and in New York and Maine. She reasoned that the momentum of these state victories, strategically located around the nation, would propel the House and Senate to pass the amendment and put pressure on state legislatures to ratify it. Chapman Catt's Winning Plan was just that. The soundness of her strategies, her pragmatic leadership, and her astute political maneuvering were instrumental to the enactment of the Nineteenth Amendment.

Beginning in 1919, the year prior to the ratification of the Nineteenth Amendment, Chapman Catt began publicizing her conception of a national, nonpartisan League of Women Voters that would educate and organize women to be independent, politically informed citizens. She founded the league in 1920 and served as its honorary chair until her death in 1947. But working toward world peace proved to be her primary postsuffrage passion. Concerns about international peace dominated her reform activities for the rest of her life as she campaigned arduously for the League of Nations and for the Kellogg-Briand Pact in 1928.

Related entries:
Anthony, Susan B.
National American Woman Suffrage Association
Shaw, Anna Howard
State Suffrage Campaigns—Colorado, South Dakota
Woman Suffrage Movement
The Woman's Bible

Suggestions for further reading:
Catt, Carrie Chapman, and Nettie Rogers Shuler. 1926. *Woman Suffrage and Politics: The Inner Story of the Suffrage Movement.* New York: Charles Scribner's Sons.
Flexner, Eleanor. 1971b. "Carrie Clinton Lane Chapman Catt." In *NAW,* 1:309–313.
Fowler, Robert Booth. 1986. *Carrie Catt: Feminist Politician.* Boston: Northeastern University Press.
Van Voris, Jacqueline. 1987. *Carrie Chapman Catt: A Public Life.* New York: Feminist Press at the City University of New York.

Centennial Exposition (1876)

In the mid-1870s the nation eagerly awaited the 1876 celebration of the first 100 years of the United States. The Centennial Commission, appointed by President

Ulysses S. Grant, began preparations for the nationwide celebration more than three years prior to the event. As the commission's plans unfolded before the public, Susan B. Anthony, Matilda Joslyn Gage, Elizabeth Cady Stanton, and other National Woman Suffrage Association (NWSA) leaders recognized the irony and the injustice of a democratic republic commemorating the rights and privileges it determinedly denied to one-half of its citizens. In the aftermath of the failure of the NWSA's "New Departure" strategy to achieve national woman suffrage, Anthony, Joslyn Gage, and Cady Stanton realized the crucial importance of asserting the inalienable rights of women as citizens on this historic occasion.

In January 1876, NWSA president Joslyn Gage penned the NWSA's militant protest against the Centennial, which was published and broadly circulated: "We protest against this government of the United States as an oligarchy of sex, and not a true republic; and we protest against calling this a centennial celebration of the independence of the people of the United States" (*HWS,* 3:4).

During the spring of 1876, Anthony prepared for the Centennial Exposition, which was to be held in Philadelphia beginning in May. In June, Anthony, Cady Stanton, and Joslyn Gage labored together, often up to 16 hours a day, to draft the *Declaration of the Rights of Woman.* They hoped to present this proclamation at the Independence Day celebration to be held in Independence Hall. When the commission refused to grant the NWSA leaders admission to the program, Anthony secured a press pass from her brother Daniel Read Anthony's newspaper, the *Leavenworth Times.* Then, when the commission finally decided to issue the women four seats on the platform in Independence Hall, the women repeatedly requested permission to read the *Declaration* during the proceedings. They were refused each time. In frustration and disgust, Lucretia Coffin Mott and Cady Stanton decided to boycott the program, opting to hold a women's rights meeting si-

multaneously in a nearby Unitarian church. Anthony and her equally militant NWSA cohorts Joslyn Gage, Sara Andrews Spencer, Lillie Devereux Blake, and Phoebe Couzins refused to retreat. They vowed to attend, to be seen, and not to be silent at Independence Hall.

In the blistering, sweltering heat of that July Fourth, Anthony and her comrades patiently waited on the platform in Independence Hall for the right moment to deliver their declaration to the podium. As soon as the reader of the *Declaration of Independence* was finished, Anthony and her fellow suffragists rose from their seats and proceeded to the podium to hand their declaration to Thomas W. Ferry, acting vice president of the United States, a known supporter of women's rights. Anthony hoped Ferry might read the document aloud, but when he did not, the women strode out of the hall to reconvene on a musicians' platform a short distance away. There Anthony read the *Declaration of the Rights of Woman* to the crowd that assembled.

In the declaration, Cady Stanton, Anthony, and Joslyn Gage emphasized women's integral involvement in the creation of the republic and listed the gross injustices to which women citizens were still subjected 100 years later. The declaration asserted that even though women have "shown equal devotion with man to the building and the defense of the nation's freedom," they are continually denied the rights that male citizens value most highly—the right of a trial by a jury of one's peers, freedom from discriminatory legal codes, taxation only with representation, and the right to suffrage. Anthony then emphasized that the refusal to grant women their rights as citizens only served to weaken the nation and its institutions (*HWS,* 3:34).

Although a number of eastern newspapers reported on the militancy of the NWSA activities at the Centennial, Anthony was well aware that the declaration would not ring in any significant change. That, she knew, would only come about through concerted, relentless political agitation among the nation's lawmakers and citizens. Following the Centennial events in Philadelphia, Anthony immediately immersed herself in laying the groundwork so that she, Cady Stanton, and Joslyn Gage could begin writing a history of the women's rights movement. While thus engaged in the latter half of 1876, the women also devised a huge shift in NWSA suffrage strategy—away from the "New Departure" activism of the early to mid-1870s toward a full-fledged commitment to securing a Sixteenth Amendment guaranteeing national woman suffrage.

Related entries:
Gage, Matilda Joslyn
National Woman Suffrage Association
Sixteenth Amendment Campaign
Woman Suffrage Movement

Suggestions for further reading:
Barry, Kathleen. 1988. *Susan B. Anthony: Biography of a Singular Feminist.* New York: New York University Press.
Blake, Katherine Devereux, and Margaret Louise Wallace. 1943. *Champion of Women: The Life of Lillie Devereux Blake.* New York: Fleming H. Revell.
HWS, 3:1–56.

Civil War (1861–1865)

THE OUTBREAK OF WAR HALTS ALL REFORM WORK

*I*n the spring of 1861, Susan B. Anthony was deeply involved in preparations for the upcoming Eleventh National Woman's Rights Convention, when one by one, a succession of southern states began to secede from the Union. Despite the national political chaos and uncertainty, she persevered with her plans because she believed that no matter what the state of the nation, women must continue the struggle to achieve equality with men, just as abolitionists must keep the pressure on Congress and the president to free the slaves. She was stunned when she learned that the American Anti-Slavery Society

(AASS) had canceled its May 1861 convention (which was to be held the same week as the woman's rights convention). William Lloyd Garrison, Wendell Phillips, and most Garrisonians had decided to halt all abolitionist activity because they believed that creating further divisiveness in the North would be harmful to the Union. As a group, almost all women's rights activists and abolitionists believed that nothing should distract from the nation's rallying together in this crisis. Anthony disagreed and protested but eventually was persuaded to cancel the woman's rights convention.

Throughout the early months of the war, Anthony was annoyed, confused, and disappointed by this decision and by the new stance of her abolitionist and women's rights colleagues. She could not fathom how her fellow Garrisonians could suddenly support the federal government when for decades they had castigated it and vowed to dissolve it. Nor could she comprehend how the peace-loving Garrison, renowned for his allegiance to the philosophy of nonresistance, could endorse the government's war, which he described as a "grand uprising of the manhood of the North" (Lutz 1959, 92). To Anthony, the outbreak of war between North and South meant that the emancipation of the slaves was within reach, but only if abolitionists continued to fight for it.

Pressured by her peers to desist from all abolitionist and women's rights work, Anthony returned home to the family farm in Rochester, New York. She was immediately disturbed by the enforced idleness and responded by filling her hours with incessant labor—plowing the fields, planting the crops, and cleaning the house. She also used the time to read extensively, studying the political news and enjoying literature (Harper 1899, 1:215). But no matter how busy she kept herself, the isolation and the lack of reform work whittled away at her self-confidence and her sense of mission. She soon found herself doubting her ability as a reformer.

ANTHONY SPEAKS OUT FOR EMANCIPATION

Undoubtedly inspired by the brilliant oratory of the young Quaker Anna Dickinson, whom she heard lecture in New York City, Anthony was itching to be agitating again by the spring of 1862. She alone embarked on a lecture tour of western New York, boldly speaking out for the immediate emancipation of all African Americans. She also broached the emancipation issue most disturbing to northerners—the northern migration of freed slaves—which many northerners believed would displace white workers and disturb the precarious social order.

> "What will you do with the Negroes?" Do with them precisely what you do with the Irish, the Scotch, and the Germans. Educate them. Welcome them to all the blessings of our free institutions—to our schools and churches, to every department of industry, trade and art. "Do with the Negroes?" What arrogance in *us* to put the question, what shall *we* do with a race of men and women who have fed, clothed and supported both themselves and their oppressors for centuries. (SBA Lecture, October 1862, SBA-SL, in *Papers*)

She also criticized President Abraham Lincoln's policies, especially his failure to come out strongly against slavery. To Anthony, the national conflict was a war for freedom, and she resented politicians who tried to avoid the issue of the slaves' future.

A NEW, PATRIOTIC MISSION FOR WOMEN

On a visit with Elizabeth Cady Stanton at her new home in Brooklyn, New York, both women expressed their need to push beyond their inactivity and feelings of uselessness to contribute to this war for freedom. Anthony and Cady Stanton were especially concerned

by the attitudes of women devoting themselves to war-related work. Women were nursing the wounded, serving on sanitary commissions (sending clothing, food, and supplies to Union regiments), assisting the freedmen, and replacing men in business and in farming occupations. Yet most devalued their labor and their sacrifices. Anthony cringed whenever she heard women say that they were "just helping out" or "just giving the brave soldiers some comfort." She wished that women would realize that their war labor was just as valuable to the Union cause as the enlisted men's contributions (Lutz 1959, 100). What use was all the effort that women expended in this war, Anthony wondered, if women refused to recognize the value of their own contribution to freedom, to the Union, to democracy?

Anthony and Cady Stanton agreed—in addition to attaining immediate emancipation for African Americans, there was much work to be done to awaken the hearts and minds of the nation's women. Could they conceive of a mission that would further both goals? Out of these discussions emerged Anthony and Cady Stanton's plan to create a national, political organization—the Woman's National Loyal League (WNLL)—which would unite thousands of women into a vital, political mission to guarantee the freedom of all African Americans.

THE 1864 PRESIDENTIAL ELECTION— ANTHONY BACKS FRÉMONT

Consumed by work for the WNLL in 1863 and 1864, Anthony and Cady Stanton had time for little else. Early in 1864, however, they were increasingly dissatisfied with Lincoln's proposals for the reconstruction of the South after the war. Anthony and Cady Stanton were concerned about the impact that Lincoln's weak, unstructured, and excessively lenient treatment of the Confederate leadership would have on the masses of politically powerless African Americans. For these reasons, both women supported the candidacy of John C. Frémont, the Missouri general whom they admired for his efforts to free the slaves in his state. This presidential election also marked the first in which Anthony actively backed a candidate, an action that reflected her developing politicization. Frémont, chosen the candidate of the Radical Democratic Party in May 1864, championed causes that Anthony and Cady Stanton could wholeheartedly accept. He called for a constitutional amendment that would liberate all enslaved African Americans and a policy of reconstruction that would redistribute Confederate-owned land while guarding the new civil and political rights of freed African Americans (Venet 1991, 137). But once again, as Frémont supporters, Anthony, Cady Stanton, and Wendell Phillips were in the minority among their abolitionist and women's rights friends.

As critical of Lincoln as the abolitionist majority was, it was even more wary of Frémont, whom it considered an unknown and potentially dangerous political entity. When Lincoln's 1864 Republican Party platform also endorsed a constitutional amendment to end slavery, most abolitionists saw no compelling reason to abandon Lincoln. In the fall of 1864, with the Democratic Party's nomination of General George McClellan and the Union army's recent successes on southern battlefields, Frémont's candidacy lost strength, and he pulled out of the race. Anthony, Cady Stanton, and Phillips, however, continued to criticize Lincoln publicly and demanded legal protection for emancipated slaves, though they officially supported no candidate.

ANTHONY WORKS TOWARD A NEW BEGINNING FOR AFRICAN AMERICANS IN KANSAS

With the success of the WNLL's mission late in 1864 and final congressional approval of the Thirteenth Amendment in January 1865, Anthony was once again at loose ends. She traveled west to visit her brother Daniel Read Anthony, the mayor of Leavenworth, Kansas. It was a harrowing journey through the chaos and devastation that the war left behind in Missouri. Despite her discomfort at being confined in a railroad car crammed with families of white northerners emigrating to Kansas and Nebraska (which she described as being as clean as "any decent farmer's pigpen"), she was fascinated by the drama unfolding in the war's final months. The spectacle of huge Union army supply trains, Union troops marching in the streets, and large bands of freed African Americans pouring into Leavenworth—all spoke to the possibility of a glorious new beginning for the nation (Harper 1899, 1:242–243). She had not been in Kansas long before she found reform work urgently needing her attention. As thousands of freed slaves settled in Kansas, she was soon assisting in the effort to organize relief as well as employment and educational opportunities for them. Because Kansas was rife with racial prejudice, she also helped a group of African Americans establish an equal rights league.

In April, the surrender of the Confederates was followed a week later by the assassination of Lincoln. At a memorial gathering of Leavenworth citizens, Anthony spoke in words that must have shocked the grieving assemblage. Following a series of laudatory speeches and eulogies for Lincoln, she told the crowd that just prior to receiving the telegram announcing Lincoln's death, she had been reading his latest speech. "My soul was sad and sick," she said, "at what seemed his [Lincoln's] settled purpose—to consign the ex-slaves back to the tender mercies of the disappointed, desperate, sullen revengeful ex-lords of the lash [the Confederates]." This most recent of Lincoln's "crime of crimes" appalled her. His decision "to disarm and send home [to the South] the 200,000 brave, black Union soldiers" without the protection of civil or political rights while simultaneously "re-arming the former, our enemies with the ballot," was unforgivable.

She then explained that upon reading of Lincoln's death, "my first thought was that God had spoken to the nation in His thunder tone to 'Stand Still And Know That I Am God' " (*Evening Bulletin* [Leavenworth, KS], April 24, 1865, SBA Scrapbooks, LCRBD, in *Papers*). To loyal, mourning Lincoln supporters, Anthony's conjured image of God striking down Lincoln because he proposed abandoning African Americans must have landed like a thunderbolt. Her speech revealed the depth of her horror at both Lincoln's and the newly sworn-in president Andrew Johnson's lack of concern about the fate of millions of freed slaves. True to her abolitionist identity, she felt she must shock her listeners to awaken them to this new evil.

All during the spring of 1865, Anthony received a flurry of correspondence from her abolitionist colleagues, all alarmed at Garrison's declaration that he would dissolve the AASS as soon as the Thirteenth Amendment was ratified. Anthony responded by communicating her overwhelming support for a continuation of the work of the AASS. Even though Cady Stanton, Parker Pillsbury, and others urged her to return home, she lingered in Kansas through the summer, finding enormous satisfaction in meeting the needs of the emancipated. It was not until August 1865, when she read in the newspaper that the House of Representatives had heard resolutions proposing that gender determine a citizen's right to the franchise, that she suddenly headed north. Soon she would be embroiled in the struggle to attain universal suffrage, a battle that she would later acknowledge was the most difficult and painful of her life.

Related entries:
Abolitionist Movement
American Anti-Slavery Society
Dickinson, Anna Elizabeth
Emancipation Proclamation of 1863
Garrison, William Lloyd
Phillips, Wendell
Pillsbury, Parker
Reconstruction
Stanton, Elizabeth Cady
Thirteenth Amendment
Woman's National Loyal League
Women's Rights Movement

Suggestions for further reading:
Lutz, Alma. 1968. *Crusade for Freedom: Women in the Antislavery Movement.* Boston: Beacon Press.
Massey, Mary Elizabeth. 1966, 1994. *Women in the Civil War.* Lincoln: University of Nebraska Press.
Venet, Wendy Hamand. 1991. *Neither Ballots nor Bullets: Women Abolitionists and the Civil War.* Charlottesville: University Press of Virginia.

Colby, Clara Dorothy Bewick (1846–1916)

*P*rominent national suffragist, chief Nebraska suffrage leader, and publisher and editor of the *Woman's Tribune,* Clara Dorothy Bewick was born in England and emigrated to the United States with her family in 1849. Raised in Wisconsin, she was the first woman to study at the University of Wisconsin and graduated as her class valedictorian. After her marriage, she and her husband Leonard Wright Colby made their home in Beatrice, Nebraska. She first met Susan B. Anthony and Elizabeth Cady Stanton in 1877 when both suffrage leaders delivered speeches as part of a lecture series Bewick Colby had arranged. In 1881, she helped institute the Nebraska Woman Suffrage Association and was chosen its president in 1885, a post she filled through 1898.

In addition to publishing the *Woman's Tribune,* a highly acclaimed woman suffrage newspaper, from 1883 until 1909, Bewick Colby was active in the National Woman Suffrage Association (NWSA) and the National American Woman Suffrage Association (NAWSA). She served on the NWSA merger negotiation committee that cooperated with the American Woman Suffrage Association (AWSA) to form NAWSA in 1890. She was actively involved in the planning and execution of NWSA and NAWSA conventions and also managed to engage in a number of state suffrage campaigns, including those in Kansas, Wisconsin, Nebraska, South Dakota, and Oregon.

Although Anthony fully acknowledged Bewick Colby as one of the select group known as her "lieutenants" or "best girls," the two women's relationship was not trouble-free. Bewick Colby never managed to penetrate Anthony's inner circle, reserved for her special "nieces" Rachel Foster Avery, Carrie Chapman Catt, and Anna Howard Shaw, at least partly because the Nebraska suffragist persisted in pursuing her own independent suffrage projects. She also had a habit of publicizing her personal views on suffrage issues when they conflicted with those of Anthony and other suffrage leaders.

Anthony, who corresponded extensively with Bewick Colby, attempted from time to time to rein in the younger woman and groom her for higher office in the NWSA and the NAWSA, but Bewick Colby proved unsuitable in this regard, being loyal first and foremost to the advancement of her own ideas and convictions. Anthony especially wished she could harness Bewick Colby's writing skill on national suffrage projects because the NAWSA lacked writing talent. As Anthony told her, not one of her three top lieutenants (Foster Avery, Chapman Catt, and Shaw), for all their sterling qualities, was a "pen boomer" like Bewick Colby.

To Anthony's consternation, Bewick Colby became involved in advancing a controversial federal suffrage plan. Its adherents argued that the Constitution endows Congress with the power to determine the election of its members. They asserted that Congress, by a simple majority vote, may enfranchise women to cast ballots for its members. Francis Minor (whose legal arguments formed the basis of the NWSA's "New Departure" strategy in the early 1870s) and suffragists Olympia Brown, Bewick Colby, and others pursued this program through the Federal Suffrage Association, first organized by Brown in 1892.

Anthony and the NAWSA leadership chose not to become involved in endorsing the federal suffrage plan because they believed that Congress would never approve it and the Supreme Court would never uphold it. They also rejected pursuing a plan that would consume valuable resources that could be spent more effectively on state suffrage battles. On a more personal level, Anthony resented the loss of Bewick Colby's talents whenever she squandered her energies on what Anthony believed were fruitless missions: "There is not any one of our girls who seems to me so 'wasting her powers upon the desert air' as do you," Anthony wrote her, "and it is simply because you are perpetually trying to do half a dozen things at the same time, when the only way to do any one of them well, would be to drop the other five!" (SBA to CBC, November 20, 1899, CBC-HL, in *Papers*).

Bewick Colby habitually voiced realities that Anthony and other leading suffragists brushed aside in their hell-bent pursuit of the ballot. At the 1886 NWSA convention, Bewick Colby tried to alert members to "The Relation of the Woman Suffrage Movement to the Labor Question" and in so doing struck at the heart of a major dilemma facing the late-nineteenth-century woman suffrage movement. She expressed concern that the movement had come to define its women's rights focus so narrowly that it was ignoring the pressing economic needs of a majority of the nation's women. By abandoning the needs of the NWSA's constituency, she argued, the movement was in danger of losing the support of most American women (*HWS*, 4:70–71).

In 1904, Bewick Colby settled in Portland, Oregon, where she continued to publish the *Woman's Tribune* while immersing herself in the Oregon woman suffrage campaigns. After the 1906 Oregon suffrage defeat and Anthony's death, Bewick Colby distanced herself from NAWSA, traveled in Europe, and participated in several international conventions. She served as a delegate to the International Woman Suffrage Alliance convention in 1913. She also maintained an active interest in the peace movement.

Suggestions for further reading:
Brown, Olympia. 1917. *Democratic Ideals: A Memorial Sketch of Clara B. Colby*. n.p. A Federal Suffrage Association Publication.
HWS, 3:670–695.
Jerry, E. Claire. "Clara Bewick Colby and the *Woman's Tribune*, 1883–1909." In *A Voice of Their Own: The Woman Suffrage Press, 1840–1910*, ed. Martha M. Solomon. Tuscaloosa: University of Alabama Press.

Couzins, Phoebe Wilson (1839?–1913)

*L*oyal suffragist, lawyer, and friend of Susan B. Anthony, Phoebe Wilson Couzins was primary among National Woman Suffrage Association (NWSA) leaders from the organization's inception in May 1869 until it merged with the American Woman Suffrage Association (AWSA) in 1890. Couzins was born in St. Louis, Missouri, and graduated from a St. Louis public high school when she was only 15 years old. Her English-born mother, Adaline Weston Couzins, was an impassioned Union supporter in proslavery Missouri. Both she and her daughter volunteered as nurses for the Western Sanitary Commission during the Civil War. As the young Couzins nursed the wounded in battle after battle, she soon became a pacifist. Stimulated by the example of the strong, active women in the Sanitary Commission, Couzins believed that if women were to acquire political power, they would prove a powerful force to end all war.

After the war, Couzins became interested in the woman suffrage question and by 1869 was a member of the Woman Suffrage Association of Missouri. She served as a delegate to the 1869 American Equal Rights Association (AERA) convention in New York City, and with Anthony and Elizabeth Cady Stanton helped found the NWSA. At the time of her entrance into the national woman suffrage movement, Couzins decided to study for a law degree. She was the first woman student and woman graduate of Washington University's Law School, receiving her degree in 1871. Although she enjoyed the study of law and was admitted to the bar in the states of Missouri, Arkansas, Utah, and Kansas and in Dakota Territory, Couzins never actually practiced. She devoted herself instead to her suffrage activism. From the late 1870s until the late 1880s, she frequently traveled and lectured with Anthony, who greatly admired Couzins's abilities. In 1887, Couzins succeeded her father as U.S. Marshal for the eastern district of Missouri, and though she kept the post only two months, she was the first woman to be a federal marshal.

During the late 1880s, Couzins developed a severe rheumatism that was almost totally disabling. Anthony's correspondence with other NWSA suffragists reveals that she sorely missed Couzins's presence and deeply regretted the tragedy of her ill health, in large part because she realized how difficult it was to find top-quality, amenable colleagues who were willing to sacrifice all their time and energy for woman suffrage.

Although Couzins's health rallied at times over the next ten years, she lost standing among national suffrage leaders following the NWSA's merger with AWSA in 1890, at least partly because she had alienated many AWSA suffragists in the past. Then in 1897, in an abrupt and baffling about-face, Couzins turned against woman suffrage and became a paid lobbyist for the United Brewers' Association, a powerful antisuffrage and antitemperance organization. She also publicly denounced Anthony and her three top lieutenants, Rachel Foster Avery, Anna Howard Shaw, and Carrie Chapman Catt, in the *New York Herald*.

When interviewed about Couzins's defection and the attack upon her, Anthony responded, "Miss Couzins is a sick, unhappy, disappointed woman in every respect. The disease that affects her body undoubtedly influences her mind, and because she is in that condition I do not care to answer her attacks upon me or to say anything against her." She then added, "It is simply the difference between Phoebe Couzins in her younger days, when she was recognized as one of the most prominent women of the country, and Phoebe Couzins of to-day, in ill-health, disappointed and, I think, irresponsible." In the interview, Anthony also pointed out that many suffragists, herself included, had personally contributed to Couzins's meager financial resources (April 7, 1897, Rochester *Democrat and Chronicle*, SBA Scrapbooks, LCRBD, in *Papers*). When the United Brewers' Association dismissed Couzins a year later, she attempted to revive her lecturing career, but due to her constant ill health and increasing physical disabilities, she found it difficult to make a living. In the last several years of her life, she was truly poverty-stricken. She died in 1913.

Related entries:
Centennial Exposition
National Woman Suffrage Association

Suggestions for further reading:
HWS, Vols. 2, 3.
"Miss Phoebe Couzins." 1893. In *A Woman of the Century*, eds. Frances E. Willard and Mary A. Livermore. Buffalo, N.Y.: Charles Wells Moulton, p. 211.
Thomas, Dorothy. 1971. "Phoebe Wilson Couzins." In *NAW*, 1:390–391.

𝒟

Daughters of Temperance

Susan B. Anthony's first involvement in a reform organization occurred when she joined the Daughters of Temperance in 1848 in Canajoharie, New York, where she was employed as a teacher. The Canajoharie Daughters of Temperance was an all-female society that was an auxiliary of the Sons of Temperance, a major national temperance organization. It is estimated that the Daughters of Temperance had 30,000 members in 1848 (Blocker 1989, 49). Anthony was immediately invigorated by her membership and soon displayed her aptitude as an organizer, becoming secretary, or "Presiding Sister," of the Canajoharie chapter.

On March 1, 1849, Anthony braved the taboo against women speaking in public by delivering her first public speech at a supper given by the Canajoharie Daughters of Temperance. In her speech, Anthony emphasized her core belief that because women suffered the most serious consequences of men's intemperance through unemployment, poverty, and domestic violence, women should take their place at the forefront of the temperance movement. (For the complete text of this speech, see the "Daughters of Temperance Speech" in the Documents section.)

When Anthony returned home to Rochester, New York, in the fall of 1849, she became involved in the Daughters of Temperance in that city. Because she recognized that successful fund-raising was essential to disseminating information about temperance issues, she organized suppers and festivals to raise the necessary money. Anthony's active involvement in the Daughters of Temperance came to a close in January 1852, when she tried to speak at a Sons of Temperance meeting in Albany. Even though delegates from the Daughters of Temperance had been especially invited to this gathering, the presiding officer rebuffed her attempt, saying, "the sisters were not invited . . . to speak but to listen and learn" (Harper 1899, 1:65). Anthony and several other women responded by walking out of the meeting. At that point, acting on the advice of her respected friend Lydia Mott, Anthony and the women who had walked out as well as several supportive, reform-minded men started their own organization, which came to be known as the Woman's State Temperance Society.

Related entries:
Anthony, Susan B.
Mott, Lydia
Temperance
Woman's State Temperance Society

Suggestions for further reading:
Barry, Kathleen. 1988. *Susan B. Anthony: Biography of a Singular Feminist.* New York: New York University Press.
Lutz, Alma. 1959. *Susan B. Anthony: Rebel, Crusader, Humanitarian.* Boston: Beacon Press.

Davis, Paulina Kellogg Wright (1813–1876)

Prominent women's rights activist, suffragist, and first historian of the women's rights movement, Paulina Wright Davis played an integral, executive role in the women's rights movement in the early 1850s, remaining active in this and in the woman suffrage movement until her final illness and death in 1876. She first became involved in social reform in the 1830s, working with her husband Francis Wright in temperance, abolitionism, and women's rights. Independently of her husband, she helped found the Female Anti-Slavery Society in Utica, New York. And as early as the late 1830s, Wright and the early women's rights reformer Ernestine Potowski Rose petitioned the New York state legislature for a married women's property law.

In 1850, Wright Davis (recently remarried to Thomas Davis) was the chief organizer of the First National Woman's Rights Convention held in Worcester, Massachusetts, in October 1850. She was a principal organizer of the Second National Convention in Worcester in 1851 and the third in Syracuse, New York, in 1852. Throughout the early 1850s she was instrumental in organizing, executing, addressing, and presiding over the national woman's rights conventions. From 1853 to 1855, in addition to her convention work, she was owner, publisher, and editor of the *Una*, a prominent women's rights journal.

Susan B. Anthony first met Wright Davis at the Third National Woman's Rights Convention. Early in the proceedings, Wright Davis selected Anthony to be a member of the nominating committee. Although she was well aware of Wright Davis's sterling reputation as a committed activist, Anthony was taken aback by her and her close friend Elizabeth Oakes Smith's glamorous, somewhat flashy attire—a style that Anthony considered frivolous. As a product of the austere social reform tradition of the Hicksite Quakers, Anthony could not imagine how common, working women would be able to relate to women's rights leaders dressed in such a fashion. When she broached this concern to the convention, however, she referred only to Oakes Smith's attire, suggesting that it disqualify her for nomination as president (Lutz 1959, 33). This experience could not have endeared Anthony to Wright Davis and may have been the root of the latter's remark decades later that she once held a prejudice against Anthony (Barry 1988, 196). Despite their completely different backgrounds, however, neither woman allowed her first impressions to prevent her from developing a close working relationship and friendship with the other.

Throughout the late 1860s, as the women's rights movement split apart over the Fifteenth Amendment, Wright Davis was one of the few New Englanders who never wavered in her support of Anthony and Elizabeth Cady Stanton (Barry 1988, 272). Wright Davis believed that Lucy Stone, Henry Blackwell, and other New Englanders who opposed Anthony and Cady Stanton had created an organization (the American Woman Suffrage Association [AWSA]) "whose purpose, aim, and object is to destroy Elizabeth C. Stanton and S. B. Anthony." Although Wright Davis was not as impartial an observer as she claimed to be, she was not alone in the belief that Cady Stanton and Anthony were ostracized and "sacrificed to envy and jealousy—to the pettiness of a clique" (PWD to Gerrit Smith, November 7, 1869, GS-SUL). Wright Davis was among those who helped Anthony and Cady Stanton establish the National Woman Suffrage Association (NWSA) in 1869. She also supported, financed, worked briefly as a contributing editor, and wrote articles for Anthony and Cady Stanton's newspaper, *The Revolution*.

When the feminist activist Isabella Beecher Hooker organized a woman's rights convention in Hartford, Connecticut, in October 1869, both factions in the women's rights struggle were invited. Wright Davis, never afraid to take an unpopular stance, decided to capitalize on her stature in the movement. She braved the tense, uneasy audience and praised Anthony and Cady Stanton's efforts on behalf of women's rights and woman suffrage. She then infuriated many of the New Englanders further, including William Lloyd Garrison, by strongly advocating the NWSA and *The Revolution* (Barry 1988, 197).

Anthony and Wright Davis did not always agree despite their strong association. As a devoted supporter of the feminist activist Victoria Claflin Woodhull, Wright Davis continued to promote her long after Anthony had concluded that Claflin Woodhull was using her and the NWSA for her own self-aggrandizement. Nevertheless, Wright Davis continued to back Woodhull and her presidential candidacy through the Equal Rights Party in 1872 while also maintaining her NWSA involvement.

Related entries:
Abolitionist Movement
American Equal Rights Association
American Woman Suffrage Association
Equal Rights Party
National Woman Suffrage Association
New York Married Women's Property Law of
    1860
The Revolution
Stone, Lucy
Syracuse Woman's Rights Convention of 1852
The *Una*
Woman Suffrage Movement
Woman's Rights Conventions
Women's Rights Movement
Woodhull, Victoria Claflin

Suggestions for further reading:
Derbyshire, Lynne. 1993. "Paulina Kellogg Wright Davis." In *Women Public Speakers in the United States, 1800–1925: A Bio-Critical Sourcebook,* ed. Karlyn Kohrs Campbell. Westport, Conn.: Greenwood Press.
Solomon, Martha M., ed. 1991. *A Voice of Their Own: The Woman Suffrage Press, 1840–1910.* Tuscaloosa: University of Alabama Press.
Tyler, Alice Felt. 1971a. "Davis, Paulina Kellogg Wright." In *NAW,* 1:444–445.

Declaration of the Rights of Woman

See **Centennial Exposition**

Dickinson, Anna Elizabeth (1842–1932)

Brilliantly successful abolitionist orator of the Civil War and immediate postwar era, Anna Elizabeth Dickinson was the first woman public speaker to achieve both critical and popular acclaim lecturing on the political issues of abolitionism. Unlike most of the women reformers who preceded her, Dickinson had enormous popular appeal among both women and men and also earned the respect of prominent male politicians outside the abolitionist movement.

Dickinson, from a Quaker abolitionist family in Philadelphia, began speaking publicly at the age of 17. Her early speeches were so well executed that they sparked the interest of two leading abolitionists who eventually mentored her—Lucretia Coffin Mott and later William Lloyd Garrison. Garrison was so impressed by Dickinson's extraordinary raw talent that he adopted her as his protégé. He then instructed her in abolition and the art of oratory and arranged lecturing engagements for her.

Dickinson's powerful extemporaneous speeches on abolition, the foibles of national political leaders, and the follies of the president's proposed postwar reconstruction policy led to her national recognition as the "Joan of Arc of the Union Cause" (Venet 1991, 53). By 1863, she was formally enlisted by the Republican Party to stump for some of their candidates. Dickinson electrified audiences with her rare ability to combine an acute understanding of political issues with a dramatic, deeply emotional presentation.

Susan B. Anthony first met Dickinson after hearing her lecture in New York City in the spring of 1862. Anthony was wildly enthusiastic about Dickinson's talent and abilities and, after meeting the young orator, immediately drew her into her inner circle of friends. Twenty-two years younger than Anthony, Dickinson became the focus of Anthony's emotional life, particularly during the late 1860s and early 1870s. Although it is true that Dickinson aroused Anthony's mothering instincts, their relationship was far too complex to be classified solely as a mother-daughter bond. Their frequent letters, filled with expressions of love and endearment, reveal their deep, mutual affection. Their relationship exemplified the warm, intimate, romantic friendships that were common among many nineteenth-century women.

Anthony was also in love with Dickinson's talent. Anthony had always had enormous respect and admiration for public speakers who were masters of the art of oratory—Garrison, Wendell Phillips, Lucy Stone, Coffin Mott, and Parker Pillsbury among them. Anthony valued eloquent oratory more than any other skill or art form. Not only that, she believed that Dickinson perfectly exemplified the "True Woman," Anthony's ideal modern woman, who she hoped would lead the battle "as an evangel" for universal suffrage and, later, for the woman suffrage movement.

Although Anthony had grand plans for her friend's future, Dickinson did not share them. From the surviving letters, it is clear that Dickinson was ambivalent about assuming any role in the woman suffrage movement. She regularly refused most of Anthony's proposed speaking engagements and avoided Anthony's pleas for involvement in the American Equal Rights Association (AERA) and, later, the National Woman Suffrage Association (NWSA). Although Dickinson explained that she did not feel called to the work of suffrage, Anthony persisted. As the years passed and as it became clearer that

Dickinson had no intention of offering her services to the cause of woman suffrage, Anthony slowly let go of the relationship. By the time Dickinson had embarked on a theatrical career in 1876, Anthony had moved on to close friendships with other women, including other potential young "evangels" who showed promise that they might one day propel the suffrage movement forward.

Related entries:
Abolitionist Movement
American Equal Rights Association
Anthony, Susan B.
Civil War
Garrison, William Lloyd
Mott, Lucretia Coffin
National Woman Suffrage Association
Reconstruction
Women's Rights Movement

Suggestions for further reading:
Campbell, Karlyn Kohrs. 1993. "Anna E. Dickinson." In *Women Public Speakers in the United States, 1800–1925: A Bio-Critical Sourcebook*, ed. Karlyn Kohrs Campbell. Westport, Conn.: Greenwood Press.
Massey, Mary Elizabeth. 1966, 1994. *Women in the Civil War*. Lincoln: University of Nebraska Press.
Venet, Wendy Hamand. 1991. *Neither Ballots nor Bullets: Women Abolitionists and the Civil War*. Charlottesville: University Press of Virginia.
Young, James Harvey. 1971. "Dickinson, Anna Elizabeth." In *NAW*, 1:475–476.

Douglass, Frederick (1817–1895)

*F*ormer slave, abolitionist, orator, publisher, author, women's rights activist, and key "conductor" on the Underground Railroad, Frederick Douglass was an important colleague and friend of Susan B. Anthony from the time of his arrival in Rochester, New York, in 1847 until his death in 1895. Following an illustrious oratorical career as an agent of the Massachusetts and the American Anti-Slavery Societies,

Douglass arrived in Rochester not long after the Anthony family settled there. He was befriended by Anthony's father, Daniel Anthony, as he was by the entire group of Rochester Hicksite Quakers.

Immediately upon arriving in Rochester, he established his own antislavery newspaper, the *North Star,* a rival to Garrison's *The Liberator.* In addition to publishing news and editorials on abolitionist activities and national events, the *North Star* (renamed *Frederick Douglass's Paper* in 1851) published articles relating to the women's rights movement. Anthony submitted notices of forthcoming temperance and women's rights meetings to Douglass's paper as well as letters, news items, and information about her temperance and women's rights activities. Douglass, a strong supporter of women's rights, participated in the Seneca Falls Convention of 1848 and signed the convention's *Declaration of Sentiments.* He was also the only man to support Elizabeth Cady Stanton's resolution demanding the franchise for women.

Douglass was also one of the very few men who fully appreciated and publicly acknowledged the pivotal role women played in the abolitionist movement. In his autobiography, *The Life and Times of Frederick Douglass,* he wrote: "When the true history of the antislavery cause shall be written, women will occupy a large space in its pages; for the cause of the slave has been peculiarly woman's cause" (Douglass 1994, 903). In the harsh winter of 1861, he responded to Anthony's call to join her and an elite corps of speakers who braved some of the fiercest antiabolitionist, proslavery mobs in the movement's history.

There is no question that Douglass and Anthony mutually admired each other's strengths, talents, and commitment to the cause of African-American freedom and women's rights. In spite of the controversies and scandals that caused Douglass to become alienated from William Lloyd Garrison's in-

Frederick Douglass, prominent abolitionist, civil rights leader, and women's rights activist.

ner circle of antislavery activists, Anthony did not spurn him as many did. When Daniel Anthony died in 1862, it was Frederick Douglass who delivered the eulogy, an act that reflected the enduring bond between the two families.

The political chaos that erupted immediately after the Civil War raised issues that all but annihilated Douglass and Anthony's friendship. Although Douglass had always supported woman suffrage, during the all-out campaign of 1865–1870 to secure civil and political rights for freed African Americans through the Fourteenth and Fifteenth Amendments, he found it necessary to withdraw temporarily from the woman suffrage struggle. He intensely resented Anthony's and Cady Stanton's refusal to endorse the amendments, and they were equally offended by his defection from their cause. The ultimate and final confrontation between Douglass and Anthony on the Fifteenth Amendment occurred at the final meeting of the American Equal Rights Association (AERA) in May

1869. The rift was very public and resulted in a painful rupture in their friendship.

Immediately following ratification of the Fifteenth Amendment in 1870, Douglass resumed his women's rights activism. He urged that a campaign for a Sixteenth Amendment to secure woman suffrage be initiated, and in his newspaper, *The New National Era*, he regularly advocated the franchise for women. In his editorial "Woman and the Ballot," which was published in October 1870, he stressed not only women's natural right to the ballot but the nation's urgent need for the participation of all its citizens. He especially emphasized that depriving women of the ballot weakened the nation and denied the government of the "intelligences" of one-half of its population (Douglass 1955, 235–239).

Although Anthony resumed a warm relationship with Douglass, she never fully recovered from the abandonment by the male colleague who had fully understood women's enslavement and degradation yet had turned his back on woman's cause at a critical moment. Their relationship never regained the closeness and sense of partnership that they had enjoyed prior to the events of 1865–1870, but they stayed in touch. Douglass continued his ardent support of woman suffrage throughout the remainder of his life and often lectured at woman suffrage conventions.

On February 20, 1895, the day of Douglass's death, he attended a meeting of the National Council of Women in Washington, D.C. Anthony and suffrage leader Anna Howard Shaw ushered him to the platform. Although he refused their invitation to speak, he gratefully received the standing ovation from several generations of suffragists who wished to acknowledge his commitment to woman suffrage and women's rights.

At Douglass's funeral, Anthony delivered a eulogy prepared by Cady Stanton. Near the closing of the address, Cady Stanton identified the basis of the bond that had cemented Douglass's and women's mutual struggles for political freedom, a commonality that also explains why the rupture of that bond in 1869 had caused so much pain: "He [Douglass] was the only man I ever knew," Cady Stanton had written, "who understood the degradation of disfranchisement of woman" (unidentified clipping, February 26, 1895, SBA Scrapbooks, LCRBD, in *Papers*).

Related entries:
Abolitionist Movement
American Anti-Slavery Society
American Equal Rights Association
Equal Rights Party
Fifteenth Amendment
Fourteenth Amendment
Garrison, William Lloyd
The *North Star*
Phillips, Wendell
Reconstruction
Remond, Charles Lenox
Seneca Falls Convention of 1848
Underground Railroad
Woman Suffrage Movement
Women's Rights Movement

Suggestions for further reading:
Kimmel, Michael S., and Thomas E. Mosmiller, eds. 1992. *Against the Tide: Pro-Feminist Men in the United States, 1776–1990: A Documentary History.* Boston: Beacon Press.
McFeely, William S. 1991. *Frederick Douglass.* New York: W. W. Norton.
Walker, S. Jay. 1983. "Frederick Douglass and Woman Suffrage." *The Black Scholar* 14 (September–October): 18–25.

Dred Scott Decision (1857)

Susan B. Anthony was more infuriated by the *Dred Scott* decision than by almost any other single event in the years preceding the Civil War. If the Fugitive Slave Act of 1850 and the Kansas-Nebraska Act of 1854 aroused northern abolitionists to concerted action against slavery, then the Supreme Court's delivery of the *Dred Scott* decision in March 1857 inflamed them to new heights of fiery protest against the federal government and a Constitution that blatantly supported southern slaveowners. The *Dred Scott* decision delivered the ultimatum that African Americans did not have the protection of the provisions set forth in the Constitution because they were not citizens at the time the Constitution became law. Consequently, they were not citizens of any state, nor could they sue in the courts. The decision also held that Congress did not have the jurisdiction to outlaw slaveholding in the territories.

The *Dred Scott* decision prompted Anthony to deepen her commitment to the principles of disunionism, the conviction that the Union must be dissolved as long as federal institutions and laws supported slavery. For the first time in her speaking career, she was so inspired by her indignation that she felt able to lecture extemporaneously, referring only occasionally to a few notes (Lutz 1959, 60). Her tone turned harsh and militant, and in her newfound confidence, she demanded that her audiences abandon their passivity and withdraw their support from a proslavery government.

> Again, it is argued, that we of the North, are not responsible for the crime of slave holding—that the guilty ones dwell in the South, . . . Thus, do we put the slaves case far away from us;—forgetting that he is a human being like ourselves,—forgetting that we, ourselves are bound up with the slave-holder, in his guilt, forgetting that we of the North stand pledged to the support of the Federal Government, the tenure of whose existence is vested in the one idea of protection to the slave-holder, in his slave property. ("Make the Slaves Case Our Own" speech, 1857, SBA-LCMD, in *Papers*).

It is questionable whether such rhetoric actually changed many people's opinions. Yet this kind of abolitionist agitation was enormously successful in heightening tensions between both proslavery and antislavery factions, and pro-union and disunion supporters in the North.

Related entries:
Abolitionist Movement
Kansas-Nebraska Act

Suggestions for further reading:
Aptheker, Herbert. 1989. *Abolitionism: A Revolutionary Movement*. Boston: Twayne Publishers.
Sewall, Richard H. 1976. *Ballots for Freedom: Antislavery Politics in the United States, 1837–1860*. New York: Oxford University Press.

Duniway, Abigail Jane Scott (1834–1915)

*P*rincipal suffragist of the Pacific Northwest and publisher of *The New Northwest*, a women's rights newspaper, Abigail Scott Duniway spent more than 40 years promoting woman suffrage throughout Oregon, Washington, and Idaho. A protégé and longtime friend of Susan B. Anthony, Scott Duniway's rigid independence and determination to steer her own suffrage campaigns prevented her from rising to the leadership of the National Woman Suffrage Association (NWSA) and later, the National American Woman Suffrage Association (NAWSA).

Abigail Jane Scott was born into an Illinois farm family in 1834. She attended school irregularly, as was the norm for children in farming communities during the antebellum era. In March 1852, when she was 17 years old, her father resolved to move his family to Oregon Territory. They traveled as part of an ox-driven wagon train that her father organized. Her mother, who protested that her health was not equal to the arduous journey, died of cholera en route. Upon settling in Lafayette, Oregon, in the Willamette Valley, Scott (Duniway) worked as a teacher until she married fellow Illinois farmer Benjamin Charles Duniway in 1853.

She bore and raised two of their six children while she and her husband endured the backbreaking labor of trying to create a farm from virgin forest. In 1862, they lost the farm they had purchased in Lafayette in 1857 because her husband, against Scott Duniway's wishes, signed several promissory notes to cover a neighbor's debts. When the man defaulted, the Duniways had to sell their property. She bemoaned her existence as a "legal nonentity" because she completely lacked the power to control her family's finances. When her husband was disabled permanently in an accident, she squarely faced the challenge of supporting her family. After running a boarding school and teaching for a time, she discovered that a career in education would not sustain them. She then established a successful millinery shop, which she owned and operated for five years.

Scott Duniway's experiences, her mother's, and those of the Oregon frontier women she knew sparked her decision to remedy society's oppression of women. With the full support of her husband, she moved to Portland, Oregon, to start her own women's rights newspaper in 1871, *The New Northwest*. In that same year, she persuaded Susan B. Anthony to lecture throughout Oregon and Washington Territory. In the process of introducing Anthony to each of her audiences on this tour, Scott Duniway developed her oratorical skills and, after Anthony's departure, continued to lecture on women's rights and woman suffrage throughout the Pacific Northwest. In 1873, she organized the Oregon Equal Suffrage Association and soon became its president. Throughout the 1870s and 1880s, she struggled to persuade state and territorial legislators to enact women's rights legislation and woman suffrage.

Anthony and Scott Duniway regularly exchanged letters after their 1871 tour. Anthony believed that Scott Duniway, with some guidance, could develop into a forceful leader for the woman suffrage cause. The Oregon suffragist's indomitable energy, courage, and lecturing ability demonstrated that she possessed all the earmarks of a successful suffragist. Anthony mentored Scott Duniway through her letters, offering friendly advice on her suffrage activism. As the decades passed, however, Anthony grew increasingly disturbed as she observed Scott Duniway's caustic demeanor toward other NWSA suffragists at conventions. As a result, Anthony eventually dismissed Scott Duniway's potential as an NWSA leader. Her tendency to shirk criticism, her refusal to consider other points of view, and her conviction that her suffrage strategies were the only methods with any merit made her cooperation with NWSA suffragists almost impossible. Although revered by suffragists in the Northwest, her resistance to working with temperance women and her tendency to blame them for suffrage failures made her unpopular with many women in her home state.

Furthermore, Scott Duniway's "still hunt" strategy, in which she secretly cajoled legislators and prominent business leaders into accepting state woman suffrage measures, aroused the ire of many Oregonians as well as national suffrage leaders. Despite the criticism, Scott Duniway stood by her still hunt method, declaring that the elimination of the highly visible "hurrah" campaigns ensured that the powerful antisuffrage groups did not mobilize, thereby giving woman suffrage amendments a fighting chance.

Although Scott Duniway was mortified when the NAWSA took control of the 1906 Oregon suffrage campaign, she did not let it defeat her. She continued to lecture and work for suffrage regardless. In 1912, when Oregon finally won woman suffrage after six referenda, Scott Duniway at last received recognition for her 41 years of suffrage activism. At age 77, confined to a wheelchair, she wrote and signed Oregon's woman suffrage proclamation and was honored by becoming the state's first registered woman voter.

Related entries:
Anthony, Susan B.
Colby, Clara Dorothy Bewick
State Suffrage Campaigns—Idaho, Oregon, Washington
Woman Suffrage Movement

Suggestions for further reading:

Beeton, Beverly. 1986. *Women Vote in the West: The Woman Suffrage Movement 1869–1896.* New York: Garland Publishing.

Duniway, Abigail Scott. 1971. *Path Breaking: An Autobiographical History of the Equal Suffrage Movement in the Pacific Coast States.* New York: Schocken Books.

Edwards, G. Thomas. 1990. *Sowing Good Seeds: The Northwest Suffrage Campaigns of Susan B. Anthony.* Portland: Oregon Historical Society Press.

Johnson, L. C. 1971. "Abigail Scott Duniway." In *NAW,* 1:531–533.

Emancipation Proclamation of 1863

I n September 1862, President Abraham Lincoln announced that as of January 1, 1863, all slaves in states or regions still under the control of the Confederates "shall be then, thenceforward, and forever free." The majority of abolitionists rejoiced, believing that Lincoln had taken an irreversible step toward total emancipation. Abolitionist Theodore Tilton expressed the predominant Garrisonian viewpoint in a letter to his friend and colleague Susan B. Anthony: "Well, what have you to say to the proclamation? Even if not all one could wish, it is too much not to be thankful for. It makes the remainder of slavery too valueless and precarious to be worth keeping. . . . Three cheers for God!" (Harper 1899, 1:225–226).

But Anthony, Elizabeth Cady Stanton, Wendell Phillips, and a few other more radical abolitionists found the proclamation to be no cause for jubilation. From Lincoln's perspective, the Civil War was waged to preserve the Union. But to Anthony and Cady Stanton, the conflict was unquestionably a war to eradicate slavery, and they would offer no prayer of thanksgiving until immediate, total emancipation was achieved. Anthony was dismayed at how easily her colleagues were placated. Although it was true that Lincoln had freed the slaves in Washington, D.C.,

in June 1862 and in the nation's territories in July, the proclamation did not liberate the African Americans still enslaved in the border states and in areas of the South occupied by Union forces. And what about the slaves the proclamation did free? They resided in Confederate-controlled areas where the federal government had no power to enforce their freedom. In Anthony's opinion, Lincoln issued the Emancipation Proclamation for political purposes, not for moral ones, and she resented the way each announcement of freedom was timed for maximum political benefit. As a Quaker and a Garrisonian, she loathed the actions of politicians who manipulated human lives to advance their own political agenda.

In early January 1863, while Anthony was still immobilized by grief following the death of her father, Daniel Anthony, the previous November, she was stirred to action by an urgent letter from Henry Stanton, Cady Stanton's husband. Stanton, a loyal Republican who had campaigned hard for Lincoln and was a member of his administration, wrote her: "The country is rapidly going to destruction. The army is almost in a state of mutiny for want of its pay and for lack of a leader. . . . You have no idea how dark the cloud is which hangs over us." He then added what he knew would goad Anthony into concerted activism. He explained that if the Union lost the war, what little good the Emancipation Proclamation had achieved would vanish. He added: "Here then is work for you. Susan, put on your armor and go forth!" (Harper 1899, 1:226).

Although it is unclear from Henry Stanton's letter what he thought Anthony might do to help this situation, within a month she was at Cady Stanton's side. Both were soon involved in the discussions that led to the birth of the Woman's National Loyal League (WNLL), an organization that would engage hundreds of thousands of citizens in the battle to constitutionally guarantee the freedom of all African Americans.

Related entries:
Abolitionist Movement
Civil War
Phillips, Wendell
Thirteenth Amendment
Tilton, Theodore
Woman's National Loyal League

Suggestions for further reading:
Foner, Eric. 1988. *Reconstruction: America's Unfinished Revolution, 1863–1877.* New York: Harper and Row.
Venet, Wendy Hamand. 1991. *Neither Ballots nor Bullets: Women Abolitionists and the Civil War.* Charlottesville: University Press of Virginia.

Equal Rights Party

The Equal Rights Party (ERP), established by Victoria Claflin Woodhull in 1872, consisted of a diverse group of social reformers, including former abolitionists, women's rights reformers and suffragists, temperance activists, anarchists, communists, proponents of greenbackism (those who endorsed an increase in the circulation of paper currency), and advocates of Native American rights. At the People's Convention held May 9–11, 1872, in New York City, approximately 500 members convened to approve its platform and nominate its candidate

for president. The platform was decidedly socialistic, with assorted demands for government protection "from the cradle to the grave." The one commonality bonding all members was the conviction that the present U.S. political system was incapable of solving the nation's social problems (Kugler 1987, 113).

Although Susan B. Anthony wholeheartedly agreed with the ERP's organizing premise, she would have nothing to do with any organization founded by Claflin Woodhull. Elizabeth Cady Stanton, Isabella Beecher Hooker, Paulina Wright Davis, and Belva Lockwood—Claflin Woodhull's devout National Woman Suffrage Association (NWSA) advocates—attended and supported the convention and her presidential candidacy. Frederick Douglass was nominated for vice president without his knowledge or consent, a distinction he later declined.

The party was not able to sustain itself in the weeks and months following the convention. Distress over her lagging campaign and various legal and financial disasters spurred Claflin Woodhull to publish the exposé that instigated the notorious Beecher-Tilton Scandal, an act that only served to cripple her presidential campaign. Nor did Claflin Woodhull's name ever appear on a ballot—she was a year shy of the age of 35 required for a presidential candidate.

Related entries:
Beecher-Tilton Scandal
Davis, Paulina Kellogg Wright
Free-Love Controversy
Hooker, Isabella Beecher
National Woman Suffrage Association
Woodhull, Victoria Claflin

Suggestions for further reading:
Arling, Emanie Sachs. 1928. *"The Terrible Siren": Victoria Woodhull (1838–1927).* New York: Harper and Bros.
Underhill, Lois Beachy. 1995. *The Woman Who Ran for President: The Many Lives of Victoria Woodhull.* Bridgehampton, N.Y.: Bridge Works Publishing.

Fifteenth Amendment

*T*he Fifteenth Amendment was the final element in the Radical Republicans' program of Reconstruction following the Civil War. Passed by Congress in February 1869 and ratified in 1870, the Fifteenth Amendment prevented states from prohibiting the right to vote on the basis of "race, color, or previous condition of servitude." Although the Fifteenth Amendment ensured the suffrage for African-American males, it was written so as to give the states the opportunity to restrict the extension of suffrage to other groups of citizens, among them women, illiterate men, or men who didn't pay taxes.

In 1869, the Fifteenth Amendment proved to be the divisive issue that finally split the women's rights movement into two separate factions, the National Woman Suffrage Association (NWSA) organized by Susan B. Anthony and Elizabeth Cady Stanton, and the American Woman Suffrage Association (AWSA), formed principally by New England activists Lucy Stone and Henry Blackwell.

In 1866, several years before the Fifteenth Amendment was created, women's rights activists had organized the American Equal Rights Association (AERA) to uphold universal suffrage. By 1868, the AERA had become controlled by both male and female Republican members who insisted that agitating for the ballot for African-American males must take precedence over woman suffrage. They made it impossible for Anthony, Cady Stanton, and other women's rights activists to advocate for woman suffrage within the AERA. Frederick Douglass, Wendell Phillips, and a large contingent of New England Republican members stressed the African Americans' urgent need of the franchise and the Fifteenth Amendment to protect them from grave dangers in the newly reconstructed, war-ravaged South.

Anthony and Cady Stanton refused to support the Fifteenth Amendment because it denied women the vote, not because they did not support African-American suffrage. Indeed, they continued to support universal suffrage until the disintegration of the AERA in 1869. But they could not condone an amendment that, as Cady Stanton described it, created an "aristocracy of sex," in which the Constitution upheld the right of all men to vote while denying the vote to all women (DuBois 1978, 175).

The divisive issues concerning the Fifteenth Amendment came to a head at the final, explosive convention of the AERA in May 1869 in New York City. At this meeting, debate over the amendment ripped the membership apart. Most of Anthony's and Cady Stanton's former abolitionist coworkers stood firmly in favor of the amendment, whereas Anthony, Cady Stanton, and a number of loyal women's rights supporters were just as fervently opposed. Frederick Douglass started the fireworks by declaring:

> I must say that I do not see how any one can pretend that there is the same urgency in giving the ballot to woman as to the negro. With us, the matter is a question of life and death, at least, in fifteen States of the Union. When women, because they are women, are hunted down through the cities of New York and New Orleans; when they are dragged from their houses and hung upon lamp-posts . . . when they are in danger of having their homes burnt down over their heads . . . then they will have an urgency to obtain the ballot equal to our own. (*HWS,* 2:382)

Lucy Stone then attempted to find a middle ground between the extremes of Douglass and Anthony, but loyal New England Republican that she was, she backed Douglass. "Woman has an ocean of wrongs too deep for any plummet, and the negro, too," she said. "But I thank God for that XV. Amendment, and hope that it will be adopted in every State" (*HWS,* 2:384).

Anthony clarified her and Cady Stanton's position. She stressed that the Fifteenth Amendment was flawed because it was not "Equal Rights," and she boldly confronted her opponents for destroying the basic principle of the AERA's universal suffrage platform.

> The question of precedence has no place on an equal rights platform. The only reason it ever forced itself here was because certain persons insisted that woman must stand back and wait until another class should be enfranchised. In answer we say: "If you will not give the whole loaf of justice to the entire people, if you are determined to extend the suffrage piece by piece, then give it first to women, to

the most intelligent and capable of them at least." (Harper 1899, 1:323)

Yet it took Phoebe Couzins, a young female law student from Missouri, to distill what Anthony, Cady Stanton, and other woman suffrage advocates found most repugnant about the amendment, namely, "that every intelligent, virtuous woman is the inferior of every ignorant man" (*HWS,* 2:388).

When AERA members voted to endorse the Fifteenth Amendment, Anthony and Cady Stanton withdrew with their supporters. They immediately called a meeting at the Women's Bureau, and with women representing 19 states, organized the National Woman Suffrage Association.

Related entries:
American Equal Rights Association
American Woman Suffrage Association
Blackwell, Henry Browne
Couzins, Phoebe Wilson
Douglass, Frederick
Fourteenth Amendment
National Woman Suffrage Association
Phillips, Wendell
Reconstruction
Stone, Lucy

Suggestions for further reading:
DuBois, Ellen Carol. 1978. *Feminism and Suffrage: The Emergence of an Independent Women's Movement in America 1848–1869.* Ithaca, N.Y.: Cornell University Press.
Foner, Eric. 1988. *Reconstruction: America's Unfinished Revolution, 1863–1877.* New York: Harper and Row.

Foster, Abby Kelley (1811–1887)

One of the early Quaker feminist abolitionists, Abigail (Abby) Kelley Foster had an enormous influence on Susan B. Anthony and many other young women of the rising generation of women activists who emerged in the 1840s and 1850s. She is best known for her pioneering work as one of the first women public speakers, succeeding Quakers Sarah and Angelina Grimké in their brief struggle to assert women's right to publicly address the evils of slavery.

From her first speech in 1838 through the early 1840s, Abby Kelley endured ridicule, harassment, and physical danger as she tenaciously maintained her right to speak out about slavery. In addition to her constant lecturing and traveling for the American Anti-Slavery Society (AASS), she was among those women's rights reformers who planned the First National Woman's Rights Convention held in Worcester, Massachusetts, in 1850. Although abolitionism was always her predominant interest, she strongly supported and actively participated in women's rights activities.

In 1851, Anthony first met Kelley Foster and her fellow Garrisonian abolitionist husband, Stephen Symonds Foster (whom she married in 1845), when they were delivering antislavery lectures in Rochester, New York. Anthony admired Kelley Foster's eloquent and assured command of her audience and identified closely with her Quaker ways. Upon meeting and talking with Anthony, the Fosters recognized Anthony's intense interest in abolitionist issues. They invited her to accompany them on a week of lectures through northern New York. Anthony gladly accepted, but when the week had passed she was convinced that she lacked the skills and knowledge necessary to be a Garrisonian abolitionist. Kelley Foster urged Anthony to join them on a more permanent basis, but Anthony declined, believing that she was not a sufficiently skilled speaker to do so.

In 1855, while Anthony was recuperating from severe back strain at a water-cure spa in Worcester, she visited the Fosters several times at their farm on the outskirts of Worcester, Massachusetts. Kelley Foster observed that she was pleasantly surprised by the woman Anthony had become: "She has grown, intellectually, more than any other person of my acquaintance within the last four years" (Sterling 1991, 299).

Following the Civil War in 1866, when male abolitionists insisted that priority be given to African-American rights over women's rights, Kelley Foster sided with Wendell Phillips and the male majority. She believed that the immediate needs of the freed slaves must take priority over women's claim to suffrage. She opposed Anthony and Elizabeth Cady Stanton and even her husband Stephen, who supported universal suffrage at that time.

Kelley Foster, in poor health throughout the late 1860s, was not present when her husband denounced Anthony and Cady Stanton at meetings of the American Equal Rights Association (AERA). When the final schism in the women's rights movement occurred in 1869, Kelley Foster joined Stephen in supporting Lucy Stone, Henry Blackwell, and other New England abolitionists in the formation of the American Woman Suffrage Association (AWSA) instead of Anthony and Cady Stanton's more radical National Woman Suffrage Association (NWSA). With her husband, Kelley Foster was active in the AWSA throughout the 1870s.

Related entries:
Abolitionist Movement
American Anti-Slavery Society
American Equal Rights Association
American Woman Suffrage Association
Foster, Stephen Symonds
Phillips, Wendell
Quakerism (Society of Friends)
Stanton, Elizabeth Cady
Woman's Rights Conventions
Women's Rights Movement

Suggestions for further reading:
Hersh, Blanche Glassman. 1978. *The Slavery of Sex: Feminist-Abolitionists in America.* Urbana: University of Illinois Press.
Sterling, Dorothy. 1991. *Ahead of Her Time: Abby Kelley and the Politics of Antislavery.* New York: W. W. Norton.

Foster, Stephen Symonds (1809–1881)

*G*arrisonian abolitionist and social reformer Stephen Symonds Foster was renowned for his volcanic antislavery oratory.

Susan B. Anthony's decades-long relationship with Foster was representative of her associations with many male abolitionists, in which the antebellum years of cooperation and fellowship were followed by the post–Civil War period of misunderstandings, alienation, and shattered relationships.

A native of New Hampshire, Foster attached himself to abolitionism while a student at Dartmouth College. In 1839, he was hired as a lecturing agent of the New Hampshire Anti-Slavery Society and soon thereafter became involved with William Lloyd Garrison and the American Anti-Slavery Society (AASS). He married fellow abolitionist and women's rights reformer Abby Kelley in 1845.

Foster's aggressive, no-holds-barred oratorical style impressed audiences, but when carried into antislavery meetings, his flamboyance tended to alienate both male and female abolitionists. Though AASS leaders Wendell Phillips and William Lloyd Garrison publicly acknowledged how difficult Foster was to deal with, he was admired by them and the rest of his peers for his extraordinary talent, his relentless abolitionist fervor, and his never-say-die approach to the podium.

Anthony first met Foster when he and Kelley Foster traveled to Rochester on an antislavery lecture tour in 1851. In the winter of 1861, during the months preceding the Civil War, Anthony organized a series of lectures given by the strongest, most fearless abolitionist orators she could muster, in a gutsy, risky venture to keep abolitionism before the public as proslavery sentiment strengthened. Stephen Foster eagerly accepted the challenge and faced one virulent mob after another as they crossed New York state.

As a member of the newly formed American Equal Rights Association (AERA) in 1866, Stephen Foster upheld universal suffrage even when Kelley Foster did not. She aligned with the majority of male abolitionists in proclaiming the precedence of the claim of African-American men to the suffrage. His support of Anthony and Elizabeth Cady Stanton did not survive the events of 1867, however. Foster was outraged when they accepted the support and financial aid of George Francis Train while promoting woman suffrage in Kansas. Like most Garrisonians, he considered Train a racist demagogue. Foster could not accept their alliance with Train because he believed it betrayed abolitionist principles, African Americans, and universal suffrage. In retaliation, Foster and fellow AERA reformer Henry Blackwell accused Anthony of misusing AERA funds. Even when Anthony completely cleared herself of this charge, Foster's antipathy toward Anthony and Cady Stanton continued unabated. At the AERA's climactic final meeting in May 1869, Foster accused them of racism and attacked both women so unfairly that Lucy Stone and Blackwell, who were no longer their allies, defended the two women's long record of efforts on behalf of African-American rights. Although Foster refused to back down and demanded that Anthony and Cady Stanton step down as officers of the AERA, the rest of the membership did not act upon his recommendation.

Although Stephen and Kelley Foster did not collaborate with Anthony and Cady Stanton from this time on, throughout the 1870s the Fosters continued their involvement with woman suffrage as active members of the American Woman Suffrage Association (AWSA), the New England–based rival to Anthony and Cady Stanton's National Woman Suffrage Association (NWSA).

Related entries:
Abolitionist Movement
American Anti-Slavery Society
American Equal Rights Association
American Woman Suffrage Association
Blackwell, Henry Browne
Fifteenth Amendment
Foster, Abby Kelley
Reconstruction
Train, George Francis

Suggestions for further reading:
Pease, Jane H., and William H. Pease, eds. 1972.
*Bound with Them in Chains: A Biographical
History of the Antislavery Movement.* Westport,
Conn.: Greenwood Press.
Sterling, Dorothy. 1991. *Ahead of Her Time: Abby
Kelley and the Politics of Antislavery.* New York:
W. W. Norton.

Fourteenth Amendment

Although the Fourteenth Amendment ensures the civil rights of all citizens of the United States, it was passed by Congress in 1866 and ratified by the states in 1868 to secure the freedoms of African Americans. Because the Radical Republicans of the Reconstruction era realized that a constitutional amendment provided the most powerful legal protection available to guarantee the liberties of African Americans, they initiated the drive for the Fourteenth and, later, the Fifteenth Amendments.

Susan B. Anthony favored protecting citizens' rights by constitutional amendment. Yet when she read about the proposed Fourteenth Amendment in August 1865, while she was still in Kansas, she was horrified to discover that members of Congress had included the word *male* in the second section of the amendment, to specify the gender of voters. She was extremely alarmed because the gender of citizens had never been established in the Constitution before. In the 1850s, women's rights advocates had predicated women's claims to civil, legal, and political rights on their conviction that the Constitution recognized women as citizens of the United States. Anthony was well aware that inserting the qualifier *male* into the Fourteenth Amendment would weaken women's claims to their rights as citizens.

Anthony immediately returned north and conferred with many of her women's rights colleagues, including her closest friend and ally, Elizabeth Cady Stanton, who was equally dismayed by the potential legal ramifications of the Fourteenth Amendment. The two women immediately began devising plans that would encourage legislators to make woman suffrage part of the Fourteenth Amendment. They urged Senator Charles Sumner to add woman suffrage to the amendment and pleaded with him to delete the word *male*. Both efforts were unsuccessful. They also drafted a petition for woman suffrage to be presented to Congress. In a few months, they managed to collect 10,000 signatures. Yet in so doing, they encountered extreme resistance among many of their abolitionist colleagues and Radical Republican leaders, who were adamant that this was "the negro's hour" and that woman suffrage would have to wait until after African-American males were enfranchised. In fact, some Radical Republican congressmen went so far as to refuse to present to Congress the petitions they received.

By the spring of 1866, Anthony, Cady Stanton, and Lucy Stone realized that their petitions and other strategies had not had any impact on the wording of the Fourteenth Amendment. They then shifted their focus toward constructing a political organization that would press for suffrage for both African-American males and all women. They were convinced that this new group, the American Equal Rights Association (AERA), would persuade their reluctant abolitionist colleagues to join them in the effort to obtain universal suffrage.

Related entries:
Abolitionist Movement
American Equal Rights Association
Fifteenth Amendment
"New Departure" Strategy
Reconstruction
Stone, Lucy
Women's Rights Movement

Suggestions for further reading:
Foner, Eric. 1988. *Reconstruction: America's
Unfinished Revolution, 1863–1877.* New York:
Harper and Row.
Kugler, Israel. 1987. *From Ladies to Women: The
Organized Struggle for Woman's Rights in the
Reconstruction Era.* Westport, Conn.:
Greenwood Press.

Free-Love Controversy

*I*n the mid-nineteenth century, as Americans sought to perfect many social and political institutions, a tiny percentage of radical social reformers became intrigued with the idea of transforming the conventional marriage relationship. These adherents of "free love," many of them abolitionists, proclaimed that expressions of love and sexuality in the marriage relationship should not be performed solely as a legal obligation but as an offering of the mutual love between husband and wife. Although there was enormous variation among free-love philosophies, most advocates protested the use of legal power and conjugal authority to coerce or subjugate a marital partner sexually, particularly a wife (Sears 1977, 3–4).

Prior to the Civil War, most Americans ignored the few reformers who promoted free-love theories. In the postwar era, however, as the nation's social climate became more conservative, Americans increasingly perceived free-love ideas as a threat to the stability of the social order (Waller 1982, 2). With the press propagating misconceptions of free love, falsely defining it as licentiousness and promiscuity, few Americans had any factual knowledge of what the free-love movement was about.

Susan B. Anthony and Elizabeth Cady Stanton long endured the onus of the free-love label. Because of Cady Stanton's advocacy of marriage and divorce reform, she was mistakenly associated with the free-love movement, although she was never involved and was in sympathy with only a few of their ideas. Anthony, too, was no free-love advocate. Both women revered the sanctity of the monogamous marriage bond, believing that it bound men and women equally. Anthony supported divorce reform as a means to free women from abusive husbands who jeopardized their wives' and their children's lives.

In any event, even though the woman suffrage movement never espoused free-love ideas, it became increasingly linked with the free-love movement, particularly after Victoria Claflin Woodhull became prominent in the National Woman Suffrage Association (NWSA) in 1871. Horace Greeley, an arch-opponent of Cady Stanton's marriage and divorce reform proposals, incontrovertibly meshed free love and women's rights in a *New York Tribune* headline and in his editorials, a marriage of his own invention.

Claflin Woodhull was not the only feminist activist who championed free love, but she was the most notorious. Anthony had no quarrel with fellow suffragists' involvement in radical reforms—she only wished that they would keep their free-love ideas separate from their work for woman suffrage. Claflin Woodhull did this until the press and vocal critics within and without the suffrage movement increased their harassment of her. She reacted to the attacks by openly professing the litany of her free-love beliefs, which were radical even by free-love advocates' standards. Claflin Woodhull's most controversial stand was her endorsement of an individual's freedom to engage in loving, extramarital sexual relationships, a view that scandalized and repelled both male and female nineteenth-century Americans.

The public's vehement rejection of Claflin Woodhull's free-love beliefs and lifestyle not only ruined her political aspirations but severely affected both the NWSA and the American Woman Suffrage Association (AWSA). The furor decimated membership and curtailed activism in both wings of the movement for several years. It also caused Lucy Stone to lead the AWSA into an extremely conservative position on marriage in an attempt to shun both the taint of free love and Cady Stanton's radical divorce reform proposals.

Related entries:
American Woman Suffrage Association
Beecher, Henry Ward
Beecher–Tilton Scandal
Greeley, Horace
National Woman Suffrage Association
Stone, Lucy
Woodhull, Victoria Claflin

Suggestions for further reading:
Sears, Hal D. 1977. *The Sex Radicals: Free Love in High Victorian America*. Lawrence: The Regents Press of Kansas.
Stoehr, Taylor. 1979. *Free Love in America: A Documentary History*. New York: AMS Press.
Waller, Altina L. 1982. *Reverend Beecher and Mrs. Tilton: Sex and Class in Victorian America*. Amherst: University of Massachusetts Press.

G

Gage, Matilda Joslyn
(1826–1898)

Women's rights activist, leading suffragist of the National Woman Suffrage Association (NWSA), and accomplished author Matilda Joslyn Gage was among the most competent and hardworking of all NWSA suffrage leaders and a close personal friend of Susan B. Anthony and Elizabeth Cady Stanton.

Matilda Joslyn's father, a prominent doctor in Cicero, New York, ensured that his daughter received a comprehensive education. In addition to her formal schooling, he tutored her in Greek, mathematics, and physiology. Her father was also an avid supporter of the temperance, abolitionist, and women's rights movements, which influenced her to engage in a reform career. After her marriage in 1845 to Henry Gage, a businessman, the couple made their permanent home in Fayetteville, New York. Like most married women reformers, Joslyn Gage's reform ambitions were limited by the responsibility of raising her four children. She was also burdened by chronic bouts of ill health. Her frequent illnesses and her overall lack of stamina were additional obstacles that she struggled to overcome.

Anthony first met Joslyn Gage at the Third National Woman's Rights Convention in Syracuse, New York, in September 1852. Several years later, Gage endeared herself to Anthony when she came to her rescue at a woman's rights convention that Anthony had organized in Saratoga Springs, New York. When all of Anthony's scheduled women speakers failed to arrive, she was desperate for a lecturer. Joslyn Gage agreed to fill in at the last minute and telegraphed home, asking a family member to wire one of her speeches. Anthony recalled many years later that thanks to Joslyn Gage, the meeting was a huge success (Rochester *Democrat and Chronicle*, March 20, 1898, SBA Scrapbooks, LCRBD, in *Papers*).

With Anthony and Cady Stanton, Joslyn Gage was a founding member of the NWSA in May 1869. She was also involved in the woman suffrage movement at the state level, serving as vice president and secretary of the New York State Woman Suffrage Association. Because Joslyn Gage's speaking voice was barely audible to an audience, she concentrated on her strongest assets—her clear, forceful writing ability and her administrative skills. In May 1875, she was elected president of NWSA, a post she held for only one year. Her tenure likely would have been longer, but the membership agreed that because of NWSA's high visibility during the nation's centennial year of 1876, the veteran women's rights leader Cady Stanton should hold the office.

Like many other women, Joslyn Gage attempted to cast a ballot in the 1872 presidential election but was obstructed from doing so. A few weeks later, when she learned that Anthony was arrested for having voted, she offered her friend her assistance. When Anthony lectured throughout Ontario County, New York, to garner popular support for her constitutional position, Joslyn Gage delivered her speech, "The United States on Trial, Not Susan B. Anthony," in those communities that Anthony did not have time to visit. Until the end of her life, Anthony was grateful that Joslyn Gage came to her rescue when so many of her friends were not able to do so.

Joslyn Gage regularly contributed articles to Anthony and Cady Stanton's newspaper *The Revolution* and, with them, was coauthor of the NWSA's *Declaration of the Rights of Woman,* which was presented at the 1876 Centennial Exposition in Philadelphia. She also contributed three lengthy essays to the *History of Woman Suffrage* and was listed as one of its coauthors. From 1878 to 1881, she published her own suffrage newspaper, the *National Citizen and Ballot Box.*

From the late 1870s on, Joslyn Gage grew increasingly frustrated at being unable to secure a top leadership position in the NWSA. She eventually discussed the issue with Anthony, who tried to reassure Joslyn Gage by reminding her that she (Anthony) had always tried to give her leadership roles. Yet Anthony appears to have misunderstood, perhaps deliberately, that what Joslyn Gage most wanted was the opportunity to share power with Anthony, an arrangement that the "General" may have found impossible to consider or even to discuss.

Like Cady Stanton, Joslyn Gage protested the growing conservatism of the woman suffrage movement and the NWSA during the 1880s. Ever a radical thinker, she was an ardent opponent of Anthony's plan to draw temperance women and religious conservatives into the suffrage movement. In the late 1880s, she urgently opposed the merger of the American Woman Suffrage Association (AWSA) and the NWSA. Joslyn Gage, Olym-

pia Brown, and a group of NWSA suffragists issued a formal protest of the merger and accused the leadership of undemocratic, dictatorial methods in imposing its decisions on the membership. Joslyn Gage also accused Anthony of deliberately thwarting the will of the majority. Anthony tolerated all her accusations until Joslyn Gage claimed that Anthony had arranged the merger in order to make herself president of the new National American Woman Suffrage Association (NAWSA). Anthony was so outraged by this attack that she openly protested its unfairness before the entire membership, without naming her accuser. Her relationship with Joslyn Gage, which had been eroding over the last 14 years, was officially over.

Shortly after the first NAWSA convention in 1890, Joslyn Gage resigned her membership and established her new suffrage organization, the Woman's National Liberal Union, which she promised would maintain the liberal principles on which the NWSA was founded. Ever a scholar, in 1893 her book *Woman, Church, and State* was published. In it she presented her opposition to all national efforts to merge church and state and also voiced her protest against organized religion's opposition to women's advancement. Despite the turmoil characterizing the final years of Anthony's relationship with Joslyn Gage, Anthony never criticized Joslyn Gage in either her authorized biography or when speaking in public, choosing only to recall Joslyn Gage's considerable contribution to the women's rights and woman suffrage movements.

Related entries:
Centennial Exposition
The *History of Woman Suffrage*
National Woman Suffrage Association
Syracuse Woman's Rights Convention of 1852
The *United States v. Susan B. Anthony*
Women's Rights Movement

Suggestions for further reading:
Barry, Kathleen. 1988. *Susan B. Anthony: Biography of a Singular Feminist.* New York: New York University Press.

Blake, Katherine Devereux, and Margaret Louise Wallace. 1943. *Champion of Women: The Life of Lillie Devereux Blake.* New York: Fleming H. Revell. (This book includes biographical data about Joslyn Gage.)

HWS, 1:465–466.

Warbasse, Elizabeth B. 1971. "Matilda Joslyn Gage." In *NAW,* 2:4–6.

Garrison, William Lloyd (1805–1879)

To the young Susan B. Anthony embarking on a career in social reform in the late 1840s and early 1850s, William Lloyd Garrison was the ideal embodiment of the fervent radical activism to which she aspired. He would become one of her most important role models. As one of the nation's foremost radical abolitionists, Garrison first became involved in antislavery activism in the 1820s. By 1830, his confrontational, inflammatory rhetoric, which exposed the evils of slavery and demanded immediate emancipation, had earned him a reputation as an extremist and a fanatic. Garrison's fire-breathing oratory soon became his trademark, a style that inspired and rallied antislavery sympathizers to the cause while alienating many others. When Samuel Joseph May criticized him for an overly acrimonious speech, Garrison explained, "Brother May, I have need to be *all on fire,* for I have mountains of ice about me to melt" (as quoted in Lutz 1968, 24). In January 1831, he founded and became publisher and editor of *The Liberator,* one of the most influential antislavery periodicals. A champion of many social reforms, Garrison was most active as leader and principal activist of the American Anti-Slavery Society (AASS), the New England Anti-Slavery Society (NEASS), and the Massachusetts Anti-Slavery Society (MASS).

Anthony first became aware of Garrison through the pages of *The Liberator,* as did the majority of those who became antislavery reformers. She strongly identified with Garrison's brand of radicalism, particularly his uncompromising stand on antislavery and women's rights issues. In 1851, Anthony first heard Garrison lecture in Syracuse, New York, where she shared the podium with the British abolitionist George Thompson. She was so deeply moved by Garrison's and Thompson's passionate elocution that she followed them to the next stop on their lecture tour. Although Anthony was not involved in the abolitionist movement at this time, she was in complete sympathy with the abolitionist agenda. Given that Anthony was sorely aware of her inadequacy as a public speaker in 1851, Garrison proved a powerful role model, and his white-hot, no-holds-barred verbosity was a style that she and many other abolitionist orators emulated.

Anthony's admiration of Garrison also stemmed from his support and promotion of women's rights. He had not only urged women to be actively involved in the abolitionist movement from its earliest days but had also demanded that female activists in the AASS, the NEASS, and the MASS be given the same rights, privileges, and authority as male members. He attended and supported woman's rights conventions throughout the 1850s and after the Civil War, and staunchly supported equal opportunities for women in all areas of political and social life.

By 1855, Anthony had established her reputation as a strong, capable activist through her work in the temperance and women's rights movements. When she was hired to be New York agent for the AASS in 1856, she joined the ranks of Garrisonian abolitionists as she had long dreamed. Like Garrison and his followers, she was soon expounding Garrison's credo of "Immediate Emancipation" and "No Union with Slaveholders." Although she never became as totally committed to nonresistance as Garrison was, she completely agreed with Garrison's rejection of the use of violence and armed force to achieve the abolition of slavery.

There is no question that throughout the 1850s, Anthony and many (though not all)

Wood engraving of William Lloyd Garrison in 1846, at age 30.

of her feminist-abolitionist colleagues idolized Garrison—frequently deferring to him and his opinions. Since he had been instrumental in engineering the path that enabled them to participate fully in abolitionist reform, many women Garrisonians were undoubtedly influenced by their awareness of the debt they owed him.

In 1860, however, Garrison and Wendell Phillips's strong, negative reaction to Anthony's efforts to help a woman escape the cruel, abusive tyranny of her husband and brothers proved the harbinger of an abrupt change in her relationships with her male mentors. When the woman's husband and her male relatives, all prominent politicians, threatened to sue Anthony and bring charges against her, both Garrison and Phillips immediately penned letters of reprimand, ordering Anthony to tell them the whereabouts of the woman and her child. Anthony refused. Although she understood that they were concerned about the effect the negative publicity about her would have on the abolitionist movement, she was appalled that Garrison and Phillips, who had devoted their lives to helping enslaved African Americans, refused to support her efforts to save an enslaved woman.

Garrison was affronted when Anthony declined to do as he indicated. He cornered her at a meeting and demanded, "Don't you know the law of Massachusetts gives the father the entire guardianship and control of the children?" Anthony grabbed the opportunity to make Garrison understand what he had been ignoring in his effort to protect the movement's reputation. "Yes, I know it," she replied, "and does not the law of the United States give the slaveholder the ownership of the slave? And don't you break it every time you help a slave to Canada?" Garrison admitted that he did. She then added, "You would die before you would deliver a slave to his master, and I will die before I will give up that child to its father" (Harper 1899, 1:203–204). Garrison, however, was not persuaded by the analogy.

The entire incident distressed Anthony because, as she wrote, "Only to think that in this great trial I should be hounded by the two men whom I adore and reverence above all others" (Harper 1899, 1:204). But beyond her shock at her beloved colleagues' treatment of her, the event, like Garrison and Phillips's unexpected rejection of Elizabeth Cady Stanton's resolution on divorce in 1860, highlighted the gaps in the two men's support for women's rights (*see* Phillips, Wendell). As much as she had come to rely on their undivided advocacy of all women's rights concerns, their lack of support in this instance gave her one of the first indications that their sympathy and understanding were not limitless and that their past wholehearted support in no way guaranteed approval of all her future activism.

Although Garrison was not directly involved in the calamitous events of 1865–1870, when Wendell Phillips and most male abolitionists abandoned the cause of woman suffrage to enhance the possibility of achieving political rights for African-American males, Garrison's support of Phillips's position angered and frustrated Anthony and Cady Stanton. Then, in a letter to Anthony in January 1868, Garrison castigated her and Cady

Stanton for their association with the Democrat George Francis Train, questioning their judgment in a manner that Anthony and Cady Stanton found insulting and condescending.

> In all friendliness, and with the highest regard for the Women's Rights movement, I cannot refrain from expressing my regret and astonishment that you and Mrs. Stanton should have taken such leave of good sense, as to be travelling companions and associate lecturers with that crack-brained harlequin and semi-lunatic George Francis Train! . . . He may be of use in drawing an audience; but so would a kangaroo, a gorilla or a hippopotamus. (WLG to SBA, *The Revolution*, January 29, 1868, in *Papers,* series 1)

The final blow occurred in October 1869, when Cady Stanton, determined to assert a woman's right to direct her own movement, lambasted Garrison for being "despotic in spirit and purpose" in an editorial in *The Revolution* (*The Revolution*, October 28, 1869, in *Papers*, series 1). A month later, it came as no surprise to Anthony or Cady Stanton when Garrison backed Lucy Stone and Henry Blackwell in the formation of the American Woman Suffrage Association (AWSA), an organization intended to rival Anthony and Cady Stanton's National Woman Suffrage Association (NWSA), established in May 1869.

By 1870, Anthony and Garrison occupied completely opposite camps, with much bitterness on both sides. Garrison's letter to abolitionist Theodore Tilton in April 1870 conveyed that he was still overwrought about the Anthony–Cady Stanton issue. He confided to Tilton that he could not work with the two suffragists who were so "untruthful, unscrupulous, and selfishly ambitious" (WLG to TT, April 5, 1870, WLG-BPL). Garrison never seemed to fathom how his attempts to strong-arm Anthony and Cady

Stanton cost him the fond devotion and fealty he had once valued. Long accustomed to his leadership position, Garrison became resentful and truculent when his attempts to shape, control, and execute veto power within the women's rights movement were rejected.

Although Cady Stanton and Garrison never resolved their estrangement, Anthony did not give up on her relationship with him. During the 1870s she corresponded with him on occasion. In 1878, when she asked him to write a letter in favor of the Sixteenth Amendment suffrage campaign, he refused, explaining her strategic errors and why the campaign would surely fail. Yet the relationship continued because Anthony was able to accept Garrison's limitations while continuing to value his past contributions to society, to abolitionism, and to her own development as a social activist and orator. On the occasion of Garrison's death in 1879, in a letter of condolence to the Garrison family, she wrote:

> It is impossible for me to express my feelings of love and respect, of honor and gratitude, for the life, the words, the works, of your father; but you all know, I trust, that few mortals had greater veneration for him than I. His approbation was my delight; his disapproval, my regret. . . . Blessed are you indeed, that you mourn so true, so noble, so grand a man as your loved and loving father. (Harper 1899, 1:508)

Related entries:
Abolitionist Movement
American Anti-Slavery Society
Civil War
The Liberator
Phillips, Wendell
Thirteenth Amendment
Train, George Francis
Women's Rights Movement

Suggestions for further reading:
Cain, William E., ed. 1995. *William Lloyd Garrison and the Fight against Slavery.* New York: Bedford Press.

Merrill, Walter M. 1963. *Against Wind and Tide: A Biography of William Lloyd Garrison.* Cambridge, Mass.: Harvard University Press.

Stewart, James Brewer. 1992. *William Lloyd Garrison and the Challenge of Emancipation.* Arlington Heights, Ill.: Harlan Davidson.

Greeley, Horace (1811–1872)

Editor of the liberal *New York Tribune* for 31 years, political leader, member of Congress, and presidential candidate, Horace Greeley is widely acknowledged as the most influential journalist of the mid-nineteenth century. Through the pages of the *New York Tribune*'s "penny daily" and weekly editions, he informed readers about the leading political and social questions of the day, including such social reform issues as antislavery, temperance, and women's rights issues.

Greeley, a temperance advocate, admired Susan B. Anthony's organizational skill in the temperance movement in New York state. He published her notices of upcoming women's rights meetings, conventions, and lectures free of charge from 1854 until 1856, at which time he became concerned that Anthony and Elizabeth Cady Stanton's increasing radicalism would taint his public image (Lutz 1959, 47, 57). Although Anthony appreciated Greeley's journalistic support in the mid-1850s and respected him for his liberal stands on social reform issues, by the late 1850s their positions increasingly conflicted. In 1860, Greeley vehemently protested the divorce bill Anthony and Cady Stanton were promoting before the New York state legislature. Although the bill asked only for divorce in "cases of desertion and cruel and inhuman treatment," Greeley was outraged. Just as Wendell Phillips and William Lloyd Garrison objected to divorce being a part of the women's rights platform, Greeley also insisted that it was not a women's rights issue but a matter that concerned women and men equally (Barry 1988, 145).

Greeley strongly supported Anthony and Cady Stanton's efforts to secure the Thirteenth Amendment through the Woman's National Loyal League (WNLL). After the Civil War, he briefly supported universal suffrage, but by 1867 he abruptly turned against the ballot for women, proclaiming his oft-repeated adage, "the best women I know do not want to vote." When Anthony and Cady Stanton discovered that Greeley would be present at the New York Constitutional Convention to be held in the summer of 1867, they were deeply concerned. They knew and had heard from others that the powerful Greeley would oppose their attempts to persuade the delegates to delete the word *male* from the state constitution, an essential preliminary step to obtaining woman suffrage in New York state. They then decided to take a risky course of action that might strengthen their shaky political position but would also earn them the enmity of Horace Greeley.

Unbeknownst to Greeley, Anthony visited his wife, Mary Cheney Greeley. Just as she asked dozens of other women to help her circulate petitions, Anthony asked Cheney Greeley to sign and gather signatures to be presented to the delegates at the constitutional convention. She agreed. On June 27, 1867, weeks before the convention and the execution of their plan, they presented their position on woman suffrage at the convention's preliminary hearing on the subject. The delegates confronted them with the argument that women should not have access to the ballot because they do not militarily defend the nation. Then Greeley (chair of the committee on woman suffrage) asked, "Miss Anthony, you know the ballot and the bullet go together. If you vote, are you ready to fight?" Instantly she retorted: "Yes, Mr. Greeley, just as you fought in the late war— at the point of a goose-quill!" (Harper 1899, 1:278).

In mid-July, just as Anthony and Cady Stanton had planned, their male representative announced to the crowded galleries of the New York Constitutional Convention that Mrs. Horace Greeley and 300 other women from Westchester had petitioned the delegates to have the word *male* removed from the constitution. The crowd burst into laughter, and Greeley, mortified by the public humiliation, became enraged at Anthony and Cady Stanton's subterfuge. He cornered them at a party two weeks later and said, "You two ladies are the most maneuvering politicians in the State of New York." To Cady Stanton, he added, "I have given positive instructions that no word of praise shall ever again be awarded you in the *Tribune*" (Harper 1899, 1:280).

Greeley remained to the last an ardent opponent of woman suffrage but, curiously enough, retained a stubborn, though distant, admiration of Anthony. He opposed all her political efforts, but words of praise for her did find their way into the *New York Tribune* in 1870: "through these years of disputation and struggling, Miss Anthony has thoroughly impressed friends and enemies alike with the sincerity and earnestness of her purpose" (quoted in Lutz 1959, 176–177).

Kind, personal words or not, in 1872, when Greeley, the leader of the Liberal Republican Party, became the Democratic Party candidate for president, Anthony opposed him. She made it clear that despite Greeley's support in the early years, the balance of their nearly 20-year relationship was overwhelmingly negative. In *An Appeal to the Women of America from the National Woman Suffrage Association,* Anthony urged women to vote for the Republican Ulysses S. Grant. She did not hesitate to point out that "Horace Greeley . . . has for years been our most bitter opponent. Both by tongue and pen he has heaped abuse, ridicule, and misrepresentation upon our leading women, while the whole power of the *Tribune* has been used to crush our great reform" (*HWS*, 2:519). Following Grant's victory, Greeley's health and spirit collapsed, and he became severely ill. He died a few weeks after the election.

Related entries:
American Equal Rights Association
Beecher-Tilton Scandal
Free-Love Controversy
National Woman Suffrage Association
The *New York Tribune*
Reconstruction
Temperance
Woman's National Loyal League
Woman's Rights Conventions
Women's Rights Movement

Suggestions for further reading:
Kimmel, Michael S., and Thomas E. Mosmiller, eds. 1992. *Against the Tide: Pro-Feminist Men in the United States, 1776–1990: A Documentary History.* Boston: Beacon Press.
Robbins, Peggy. 1990. "Where Do You Stand Horace Greeley?" *Civil War Times Illustrated* 29 (5):50–55.
Schulze, Suzanne. 1992. *Horace Greeley: A Bio-Bibliography.* New York: Greenwood Press.

H

Harper, Frances Ellen Watkins (1825–1911)

Foremost among African-American poets and novelists of the nineteenth century and one of the most productive of African-American reformers, Frances Ellen Watkins Harper was born free in the slave city of Baltimore, Maryland. Raised and educated by her uncle, a minister, Watkins embarked on a teaching career in Ohio in 1850. In 1853, after moving to Pennsylvania, she became engrossed in the abolitionist movement and, in 1854, began a career as an abolitionist lecturer, poet, and writer in the Northeast and Ohio, primarily through the Maine and Pennsylvania Anti-Slavery Societies.

A tireless advocate and a financial supporter of the Underground Railroad, Watkins was associated with abolitionists Frederick Douglass, Susan B. Anthony, Sojourner Truth, and Henry Highland Garnet. Married to Fenton Harper in 1860, she briefly retired from public life until her husband's death in 1864, when she resumed an active lecturing career. As ardent an abolitionist as she was, Watkins Harper also found time for women's rights activism, especially in the years following the Civil War. A loyal member of the American Equal Rights Association (AERA), Watkins Harper assumed a highly visible role in the decisive proceedings of the final meeting of the AERA in May 1869, when Anthony and Elizabeth Cady Stanton withdrew to form the National Woman Suffrage Association (NWSA).

In 1869, the proposed Fifteenth Amendment, which promised to bestow the franchise on African-American men only, polarized AERA members. Anthony, Cady Stanton, and a number of other women's rights activists rejected the amendment and maintained that women should be enfranchised first, whereas Frederick Douglass and most male and female New England members agreed that the African Americans' desperate need for the ballot's protection superseded women's claim to suffrage. As one of the very few AERA members who was both an African American and a woman, Watkins Harper's views were closely attended. She supported Douglass, stating that "she would not have the black women put a single straw in the way, if only the men of the race could obtain what they wanted." Anthony then challenged her position, pointing out that the Fifteenth Amendment would change relations between African-American men and women and "put two million more men in position of tyrants over two million women who had until now been the equals of the men at their side" (*HWS*, 2:391–392).

There is no record of Watkins Harper responding to Anthony's retort at the AERA meeting, but in her 1869 serialized novel *Minnie's Sacrifice*, she reframed her position on the issue of suffrage for African-American males. Minnie, the novel's main female character, states, "But I cannot recognize that the negro man is the only one who has pressing claims at this hour. . . . And while I would not throw a straw in the way of the colored man, even though I know that he would vote against me as soon as he gets his vote, yet I do think that woman should have some power to defend herself from oppression" (Boyd 1994, 127). Although Watkins Harper acknowledged women's right to vote and their need for the franchise, she could not forward women's claim if it meant disfranchising African-American men.

Also during the late 1860s, Watkins Harper courageously undertook a lecture tour of the war-ravaged South, speaking on the challenges of Reconstruction for African Americans and on women's rights. Watkins Harper became increasingly involved in women's rights and woman suffrage after 1870, particularly concerning herself with the role of African-American women in the movement. She was active in the American Woman Suffrage Association (AWSA), rival to Anthony and Cady Stanton's National Woman Suffrage Association (NWSA). She also served on the executive boards of the Woman's Christian Temperance Union (WCTU), the International Council of Women (ICW), the Woman's International Temperance Society (WITS), the Association for the Advancement of Women (AAW), and the Universal Peace Union (UPU). When attempts to gain recognition from white feminists of African-American women's special needs and issues proved fruitless, Watkins Harper became involved in efforts to organize African-American women. She helped form the National Association of Colored Women (NACW) and served for a time as its vice president.

Related entries:
Abolitionist Movement
American Equal Rights Association
American Woman Suffrage Association
Fifteenth Amendment

National Woman Suffrage Association
Underground Railroad
Woman Suffrage Movement
Woman's Christian Temperance Union
Women's Rights Movement

Suggestions for further reading:
Boyd, Melba Joyce. 1994. *Discarded Legacy: Politics and Poetics in the Life of Frances E. W. Harper, 1825–1911.* Detroit: Wayne State University Press.
Collier-Thomas, Bettye. 1997. "Frances Ellen Watkins Harper: Abolitionist and Feminist Reformer 1825–1911." In *African American Women and the Vote, 1837–1965,* ed. Ann D. Gordon. Amherst: University of Massachusetts Press.
Hine, Darlene Clark. 1993. "Harper, Frances Ellen Watkins." In *Black Women in America: An Historical Encyclopedia,* ed. Darlene Clark Hine, Elsa Barkley Brown, and Rosalyn Terborg-Penn. Brooklyn, N.Y.: Carlson Publishing, pp. 532–537.

Harper, Ida Husted (1851–1931)

Woman suffrage historian, journalist, suffrage activist, and the only authorized biographer of Susan B. Anthony, Ida Husted Harper was undoubtedly one of the National American Woman Suffrage Association's (NAWSA's) best and most accomplished writers. Her laudatory three-volume biography of Anthony, *The Life and Work of Susan B. Anthony,* is one of the most extensively detailed on any U.S. historical personage. As editor of volumes 5 and 6 of the *History of Woman Suffrage* and as coeditor with Anthony of volume 4, she is noted as one of the primary historians of the woman suffrage movement. Husted Harper was also an outstanding propagandist and an indispensable member of NAWSA president Carrie Chapman Catt's "Winning Plan," NAWSA's carefully orchestrated program to achieve national woman suffrage.

Ida Husted was born and raised in Indiana. After receiving her high school diploma, she attended Indiana University for one year before accepting a position as the high school principal in Peru, Indiana. Several decades later, she attended Stanford University, but she never completed a degree. In 1871, she married Thomas Harper, an attorney and labor reformer, with whom she settled in Terre Haute, Indiana. Husted Harper launched her lifelong career in journalism when she began submitting articles to a Terre Haute newspaper using a male pseudonym. She soon contributed articles under her own name and had her own column, entitled "A Woman's Opinions." After she and her husband divorced in 1890, she was hired as editor in chief of the *Terre Haute Daily News*. After moving to Indianapolis, she became an editor at the *Indianapolis News*.

Husted Harper first met Anthony when the suffrage leader was lecturing in Terre Haute. The Indiana journalist had long been a supporter of woman suffrage, a cause that increasingly absorbed her during the 1880s. By 1887, she was secretary of a leading Indiana woman suffrage society. But Husted Harper's most significant work for the woman suffrage movement did not begin until she met Anthony again, in San Francisco, during the California suffrage campaign of 1896. Anthony was immediately impressed by Husted Harper's intuitive grasp of the campaign's publicity needs, especially her ingenious schemes to use the press to publicize woman suffrage. Anthony also admired her in-depth understanding of newspaper editorial hierarchies. She asked Husted Harper to command the press publicity for the California campaign, a task she managed with Anthony's help. Even though the campaign failed to secure woman suffrage for California, the newspapers were almost totally prosuffrage, largely due to Husted Harper's efforts.

During the California campaign, Anthony persuaded Husted Harper to be her official biographer. Although the journalist was reluctant at first, she finally agreed as long as Anthony promised to work with her and to refrain from traveling during the compiling and writing of the book. In March 1897,

Husted Harper arrived at Anthony and her sister Mary Anthony's home in Rochester, New York, where she would live for much of the next two years. Although Anthony had explained that she stored all of her documents in her two-room attic, Husted Harper was flabbergasted when she entered the attic for the first time and confronted the staggering volume of amassed material—20,000 letters and box upon box of newspaper clippings, scrapbooks, pamphlets, and other records that Anthony had collected over a lifetime. Husted Harper detailed Anthony's attic treasures in her biography.

> Ranged around the walls were trunks, boxes and bags of letters and other documents. . . . There were piles of legal papers, accounts, receipts and memoranda . . . and the diaries and note-books of sixty years. The shelves were filled with congressional, convention and other reports; there were stacks of magazines and newspapers, large numbers of scrap-books and bushels of scraps waiting to be pasted. (Harper 1899, 2:909)

Anthony and Husted Harper worked together from early morning into the evening hours and found that they were very compatible. Anthony was enormously pleased with Husted Harper's work and meticulous methods, praising her in letters to her friends and colleagues. When the biography was completed, she prevailed upon Husted Harper to assist her in writing volume 4 of the *History of Woman Suffrage*, a work Anthony had been organizing for years. Husted Harper declined, but Anthony, true to her well-practiced arm-twisting methods, managed to persuade her to edit and write volume 4 by threatening to destroy all the data she had collected over the years.

After the biography and volume 4 of the *History of Woman Suffrage* was published, Anthony had to execute another promise she had made to Husted Harper—that she (Anthony) would destroy all her original manuscripts as soon as the book was published. Anthony had already sent her scrapbooks and many of her old books and journals to the Library of Congress to be archived there as the Susan B. Anthony Papers, but thousands of letters and other documents had to be obliterated if she were to live up to her agreement. It is not clear why Husted Harper insisted on the papers' destruction. She may have wanted to ensure that she would be the only Anthony biographer to incorporate the resources she had used. In this way, she could guarantee that no other Anthony biography could rival *The Life and Work of Susan B. Anthony*.

When the time came to burn the papers, Anthony could not do it. "The only thing for me is to wash my hands of the whole business," she said before disappearing from the scene (Anthony 1954, 475). Mary Anthony did most of the burning of the papers herself, a task that was so extensive that it could not be completed in a single day or even in a week. Constructing huge bonfires in the Anthonys' backyard day after day, Mary stood guard, armed with her shovel, as masses of letters from some of the greatest historical figures of the abolitionist, temperance, and woman suffrage movements went up in smoke.

After completing volume 4 of the *History*, Husted Harper resumed her work for NAWSA and greatly expanded her influence as a feminist journalist. She contributed prosuffrage articles, syndicated letters, and essays to major newspapers in many eastern cities and in Chicago. In 1916, when Carrie Chapman Catt returned to the presidency of NAWSA, she selected Husted Harper to lead all of NAWSA's press relations, directing her to focus on the goal of achieving national woman suffrage via a federal suffrage amendment. In so doing, Husted Harper produced voluminous quantities of highly successful NAWSA promotional and propaganda material for the press.

Beginning in 1918, Husted Harper began the arduous task of compiling and writing the final two volumes of the *History of Woman Suffrage*. They detailed the final two decades of the woman suffrage movement, from Susan B. Anthony's retirement in 1900 to the ratification of the Nineteenth Amendment in 1920. These volumes were published in 1922. During the last decade of her life, Husted Harper, then in her seventies, dedicated herself to promoting the causes of the American Association of University Women.

Related entries:
Anthony, Susan B.
The *History of Woman Suffrage*
National American Woman Suffrage Association
State Suffrage Campaigns—California
Woman Suffrage Movement

Suggestions for further reading:
Harper, Ida Husted. 1899, 1908. *The Life and Work of Susan B. Anthony*. 3 vols. Indianapolis: Bowen-Merrill (vols. 1 and 2) and Hollenbeck Press (vol. 3).
Phillips, Clifton. 1971a. "Ida A. Husted Harper." In *NAW,* 2:139–140.

The History of Woman Suffrage

*T*he six-volume *History of Woman Suffrage*, principally written and edited by Elizabeth Cady Stanton, Susan B. Anthony, Matilda Joslyn Gage, and Ida Husted Harper, remains the best single source of information about the women's rights and the woman suffrage movements in the United States. *HWS* is an extraordinary historical document because it is an unusually extensive record spanning more than six decades, created entirely by suffrage activists who were committed to preserving the history of their movement (DuBois 1991, 63).

Both Anthony and Cady Stanton felt a tremendous need to write such a history. Lucretia Coffin Mott had often prodded Cady Stanton to produce a history of women's rights. It wasn't until two weeks after Coffin Mott's death in 1880 that Cady Stanton, Anthony, and Joslyn Gage actively commenced work on *HWS,* though Cady

Stanton and Anthony had been planning and organizing the history since the mid-1870s. Cady Stanton welcomed the challenge, but Anthony dreaded it. She was fond of saying, "I love making history but hate to write it." She realized, however, that if she and Cady Stanton did not write the history of their movement, no one else would. Lucy Stone, leader of the American Woman Suffrage Association (AWSA), criticized Anthony and Cady Stanton's presumption in assuming the roles of historians of their movement. Stone wrote Cady Stanton that she preferred to place her faith in the historians of the future to document their history, but Anthony and Cady Stanton knew all too well that if future historians were anything like those of the present or the past, they would be male and interested only in recording events that involved men. "Men have been faithful in noting every heroic act of their half of the race," Anthony wrote, "and now it should be the duty, as well as the pleasure, of women to make for future generations a record of the heroic deeds of the other half" (Harper 1899, 2:919).

Anthony, Cady Stanton, and Joslyn Gage formed a contractual partnership that specified that Cady Stanton and Joslyn Gage would collect, write, and edit the history while Anthony would involve herself with the business of publication. Cady Stanton did most of the actual writing, and it is her women's rights and woman suffrage ideology that is infused into the first three volumes of *HWS*. Joslyn Gage contributed several major historical essays, but her family responsibilities prevented her from writing as much as she, Cady Stanton, and Anthony had hoped. Anthony, in addition to helping Cady Stanton reconstruct events so that she could write the history, was the business supervisor. It was her onerous task to find a publisher for *HWS* and to manage distribution. Knowing that a history of the women's rights movement would never be a bestseller, Anthony was anxious to ensure that *HWS* would reach as broad an audience as possible. She spent considerable effort raising

funds so that they could donate *HWS* to public libraries and schools. For volumes 3 and 4, Anthony invited, encouraged, and, when necessary, goaded state suffrage activists into contributing their own state suffrage histories.

Volume 1, which totaled 900 pages, was published in 1881. The second volume was published in 1882 and the third in 1886. At that point, Cady Stanton bowed out of the project, while Anthony continued to compile data for a fourth volume. She entreated Ida Husted Harper to write and edit it, and it was published in 1902. Volumes 5 and 6 were also written and edited by Harper and were published two years after ratification of the Nineteenth Amendment, the federal woman suffrage amendment, in 1922.

Anthony suffered through much of the *HWS* experience. Dredging up detailed memories of the past, particularly the Reconstruction years when she and Cady Stanton experienced estrangement, betrayal, and schism from their former abolitionist friends and colleagues, depressed her so deeply that at times she felt she would not be able to continue working on the project. The time spent living and working closely with Cady Stanton, who felt none of Anthony's angst about the past, was a balm for the resurrected trauma. Both women had to admit that in spite of their frequent arguments about dates and their interpretations of events, they worked together beautifully.

Cady Stanton made several attempts to encourage Lucy Stone to contribute to *HWS* but was refused on each occasion. Stone remained skeptical of the entire project. Behind her criticism, however, lurked her basic disinterest in the keeping and writing of history. As she explained to Cady Stanton, "I have never kept a diary, or any record of my work, so am unable to furnish you with the required dates," a habit that sharply contrasted with Anthony's custom of painstakingly collecting diaries, scrapbooks, and boxes of newspaper clippings and with Cady Stanton's copious autobiographical writings

(L. Wheeler 1981, 257). At the urging of Antoinette Brown Blackwell (Stone's sister-in-law), Stone finally submitted a few brief biographical facts. When Cady Stanton's daughter Harriot Stanton returned from Europe in 1882 and scanned the second volume of *HWS*, she took her mother to task for what she considered the blatant omission of information about the AWSA. After all, Harriot complained, her mother and Anthony had advertised *HWS* as a history of the woman suffrage movement—not a history of their National Woman Suffrage Association (NWSA). Cady Stanton then dispatched Harriot to compose a history of the AWSA, which came to a total of 60,000 words, thus creating a more complete history of the movement (Kerr 1992, 212; DuBois 1997, 49–50).

Related entries:
American Woman Suffrage Association
Anthony, Susan B.
Anthony/Cady Stanton Partnership
Gage, Matilda Joslyn
Harper, Ida Husted
National Woman Suffrage Association
Stone, Lucy
Woman Suffrage Movement

Suggestions for further reading:
Buhle, Mary Jo, and Paul Buhle, eds. 1978. *A Concise History of Woman Suffrage: Selections from the Classic Work of Stanton, Anthony, Gage, and Harper.* Urbana: University of Illinois Press.
DuBois, Ellen Carol. 1991. "Making Women's History: Activist Historians of Women's Rights, 1880–1940." *Radical History Review*, no. 49:61–84.
Griffith, Elisabeth. 1984. *In Her Own Right: The Life of Elizabeth Cady Stanton.* New York: Oxford University Press.
Lutz, Alma. 1959. *Susan B. Anthony: Rebel, Crusader, Humanitarian.* Boston: Beacon Press.

Hooker, Isabella Beecher (1822–1907)

*P*rominent New England women's rights activist and suffragist Isabella Beecher Hooker was principally active in the National Woman Suffrage Association (NWSA). A member of the famous Beecher clan, Beecher Hooker was the half-sister of the celebrated author Harriet Beecher Stowe; of conservative women's education reformer Catharine Beecher; and of the nation's most prominent clergyman, Henry Ward Beecher.

During Reconstruction, Beecher Hooker was closely aligned with New England women's rights activists and helped form the New England Woman Suffrage Association (NEWSA) in 1868. At that time, she concurred with fellow NEWSA members Lucy Stone, Julia Ward Howe, and Henry Blackwell that Susan B. Anthony and Elizabeth Cady Stanton's radicalism and their alliances with Democrats were ruining the women's rights and woman suffrage causes. Paulina Wright Davis, a member of NEWSA and also a close friend of Anthony and Cady Stanton, was deeply concerned about the unfounded prejudices and hate-mongering of New England reformers toward her friends. In Wright Davis's determination to combat these false impressions, she invited Beecher Hooker to spend several days with Anthony and Cady Stanton at her home in Providence, Rhode Island. Beecher Hooker felt immediately drawn to Cady Stanton but reported that she scrutinized Anthony's speech and behavior for several days, searching for signs to confirm the NEWSA's negative image of her. By the end of the visit, Beecher Hooker wrote:

I have studied Miss Anthony day and night for nearly a week. . . . She is a woman of incorruptible integrity and the thought of guile has no place in her heart. In unselfishness and benevolence she has scarcely an equal, and her energy and executive ability are bounded only by her physical power, which is something immense. . . . Mrs. Stanton too is a magnificent woman. . . . I hand in my allegiance to both as leaders and representatives of the great movement. (Harper 1899, 1:332)

Thus fully converted to Anthony and Cady Stanton's camp, Beecher Hooker became involved in the NWSA. At first she devoted herself to attempts to reconcile the warring factions in the woman suffrage movement. To this end, she organized a woman suffrage convention in Hartford, Connecticut, in October 1869. NEWSA members attended, as well as Anthony, Cady Stanton, and their NWSA supporters. Although this meeting failed to unite the two groups, it did establish Beecher Hooker as the leader of the new Connecticut Woman Suffrage Association (CWSA) and as a powerful force in the woman suffrage movement. After several subsequent failures to unite the American Woman Suffrage Association (AWSA, the new national suffrage organization formed by NEWSA members) and the NWSA, Beecher Hooker reluctantly abandoned this cause and concentrated instead on reforming and remolding the NWSA to her satisfaction.

Beecher Hooker funded and was principal organizer of the NWSA convention in January 1871. As she had outlined in her speech at the NWSA convention the previous year, she was convinced that the NWSA must focus solely on suffrage and not be distracted by extraneous, radical issues such as marriage and divorce reform. She believed that promoting radical causes only served to stir controversy and alienate potential new members and supporters. In general, her brand of women's rights was much more conservative than Anthony and Cady Stanton's. Beecher Hooker was also determined to add a refined, feminine gentility to all women's rights work. Cady Stanton detested Beecher Hooker and steered clear of NWSA conventions as long as she was in charge (Griffith 1984, 146). Because Anthony was traveling extensively on the lecture circuit trying to repay debts incurred in operating *The Revolution*, she tolerated Beecher Hooker. Anthony and Cady Stanton knew that they needed someone competent at the helm of the NWSA while they were absent, and they recognized that, despite their personal feelings, Beecher Hooker was an exemplary reformer and invaluable to the cause.

The NWSA convention of January 1871 was remarkable for the entrance of the extraordinary Victoria Claflin Woodhull. When Beecher Hooker, Anthony, Cady Stanton, and Wright Davis heard Claflin Woodhull speak on a new proposal concerning the Fourteenth Amendment and woman suffrage to a House judiciary committee immediately prior to the convention, they became entranced with Woodhull. Beecher Hooker and Wright Davis remained stalwart supporters of Woodhull throughout her creation of the Equal Rights Party (ERP) and her presidential candidacy in 1872, even when Anthony and others had long become disgusted by Woodhull's self-aggrandizement.

During the Beecher-Tilton Scandal, Beecher Hooker shocked her family and the reform community by publicly avowing her belief that her half-brother the Reverend Henry Ward Beecher was guilty of the adultery charge brought against him. Although she suffered ostracism from her family and her social connections and was declared insane by her famous brother, she did not waver from her position. Beecher Hooker remained actively engaged in the NWSA until the early 1890s, when she began to support Olympia Brown's Federal Suffrage Association.

Related entries:
American Woman Suffrage Association
Beecher, Henry Ward
Beecher-Tilton Scandal
Blackwell, Henry Browne
Equal Rights Party
National Woman Suffrage Association
Stone, Lucy
Woodhull, Victoria Claflin

Suggestions for further reading:
Boydston, Jeanne, Mary Kelley, and Anne Margolis. 1988. *The Limits of Sisterhood: The Beecher Sisters on Women's Rights and Women's Sphere*. Chapel Hill: University of North Carolina Press.

Rugoff, Milton. 1981. *The Beechers: An American Family in the Nineteenth Century.* New York: Harper and Row.

Tyler, Alice Felt. 1971b. "Hooker, Isabella Beecher." In *NAW,* 2:212–214.

Hovey Fund

Charles Fox Hovey (1807–1859), affluent Boston reformer and philanthropist, bequeathed $50,000 in 1859 to advance the abolitionist, women's rights, and radical religious causes. Wendell Phillips, William Lloyd Garrison, Abby Kelley Foster, and Parker Pillsbury were among the eight executors selected to oversee Hovey's bequest. Susan B. Anthony was delighted when she heard about the Hovey Fund. Donations like Hovey's and Francis Jackson's temporarily eased the burden of incessant, labor-intensive fund-raising (*see* Jackson Fund). Anthony attended one of the first meetings of the Hovey Fund committee and successfully persuaded the executors to create a central depository of abolitionist tracts, pamphlets, and other antislavery literature in Albany under the supervision of Lydia Mott.

Among the other projects that Anthony convinced the Hovey Fund committee to finance were the final months of Anthony's campaign to secure the New York Married Women's Property Law of 1860; the work of the Woman's National Loyal League (WNLL) in 1863–1864; and Anthony and Elizabeth Cady Stanton's petition drive in the fall of 1865 to support changes in the New York state constitution so that woman suffrage could be enacted.

In 1867, conflict erupted between the mostly male Hovey Fund executors and women's rights reformers concerning the fund's appropriations when Anthony, Cady Stanton, and Lucy Stone wanted money to support the American Equal Rights Association's (AERA's) woman suffrage campaign in Kansas. By 1867, Phillips and most members of the Hovey Fund committee were not in favor of using these resources to promote a cause that they believed would harm the Republican effort to obtain African-American male suffrage. The committee refused further help, agreeing to reimburse the women only for expenditures in 1866 (Harper 1899, 1:282). Stone was particularly incensed at the intransigence of the committee. To her mind and to Anthony's and Cady Stanton's, the committee ignored that Charles Hovey had strongly supported woman suffrage and that this goal was very close to being realized in Kansas. Stone wrote Anthony on May 9, 1867, while campaigning in Kansas:

> I think you should insist that all of the Hovey fund used for the Standard [the *National Anti-Slavery Standard*—organ of the American Anti-Slavery Society] and anti-slavery purposes since slavery was abolished, must be returned with interest to the three causes which by the express terms of the will were to receive *all* of the fund when slavery should be ended. . . . I have been for the last time on my knees to Phillips, Higginson or any of them. If they help now, they should ask us and not we them. (Harper 1899, 1:275)

Anthony and Cady Stanton's first volume of the *History of Woman Suffrage,* published in 1881, mentioned the Hovey and Jackson Funds but did not discuss disputes with male reformers about how the money should be channeled. After praising Charles Hovey and Francis Jackson as well as Wendell Phillips's able management of the funds, the editors focused instead on criticizing women for not having contributed more generously to the woman suffrage movement: "With the exception of $1,000 from Lydia Maria Child, we have yet to hear of a woman of wealth who has left anything for the enfranchisement of her sex. . . . it is proverbial that they never remember the Woman Suffrage movement that underlies in importance to all others" (*HWS*, 1:257–258).

Related entries:
American Equal Rights Association
Jackson Fund

Kansas Campaign of 1867
Mott, Lydia
New York Married Women's Property Law
  of 1860
Phillips, Wendell
Stone, Lucy
Woman's National Loyal League

Suggestions for further reading:
HWS, 1:257–258.

I

International Council of Women

L ong before Elizabeth Cady Stanton's trip to Europe in 1882, she had dreamed of the possibility of an international woman suffrage movement. While abroad from 1882 to 1883, she discussed the idea with European feminists. When Susan B. Anthony joined her in England in 1883, their talks with European women revealed that they were much more interested in civil and legal women's rights reform than in woman suffrage. Anthony and Cady Stanton then decided that they would call an international convocation of women to discuss the issues of women's progress throughout the world. This convention would be devoted to publicizing the broad span of women's progress—in education, women's rights legislation, the arts, the home, charitable organizations, and social reform.

While Cady Stanton remained in Europe, Anthony returned home and began preliminary preparations to hold the International Council of Women (ICW) in 1888, in celebration of the fortieth anniversary of the first woman's rights convention at Seneca Falls, New York. In 1887, at Anthony's urging, the National Woman Suffrage Association (NWSA) voted to assume full responsibility for organizing the ICW, including its financing. For several years prior to the council, NWSA suffragists Rachel Foster (Avery) and May Wright Sewall prepared for the

unprecedented event under Anthony's strict supervision.

Held at Arbaugh's Opera House in Washington, D.C., for eight days in late March 1888, the ICW proved to be the largest women's convention of its time. A total of 53 women's organizations from England, Ireland, France, Norway, India, Canada, and the United States were represented. Besides the three largest U.S. suffrage organizations (the NWSA, the American Woman Suffrage Association, and the Woman's Christian Temperance Union), trade unions, temperance groups, literary clubs, benevolent societies, professional organizations, art unions, and suffrage societies sent speakers and representatives.

The event proved to be extremely popular—the opera house was filled to capacity for each of the eight days of the convention. It also received extensive national press coverage. At the conclusion of the ICW, Anthony and Cady Stanton were walking on air—the convention experience exceeded what they had imagined would be possible. Anthony, in particular, was thrilled with the entire event, in large part because she believed it had inspired a real sense of "universal sisterhood." She believed that this spirit of unity would lead all activists toward the recognition of the central importance of the ballot for women. Although the ICW stimulated cooperation among U.S. and foreign women reformers, it did not inspire women to engage in suffrage activism as Anthony had envisioned (DuBois 1992, 177).

To Anthony's disappointment, the National Council of Women, which was the national cooperative group created from the ICW, chose not to include woman suffrage as one of its goals. This reluctance to place a priority on the struggle for the ballot was extremely common among women social and moral reformers during the late nineteenth century. Although the trend discouraged her, Anthony was convinced that once women reformers confronted their powerlessness to effect social change because they lacked the political clout of the ballot, they would rally around the suffrage movement.

Anthony attended all subsequent ICW gatherings during her lifetime—in Chicago in 1893, in London in 1899, and in Berlin in 1904. She continued to believe in the power of women's collective cooperation to improve their condition around the world. In 1902–1904, when U.S. and European suffragists realized that the ICW was moving no closer to working toward woman suffrage, they cooperated to form the International Woman Suffrage Alliance under the guiding leadership of National American Woman Suffrage Association president Carrie Lane Chapman Catt.

Related entries:
Anthony/Cady Stanton Partnership
Avery, Rachel G. Foster
Catt, Carrie Lane Chapman
Sewall, May Eliza Wright
Stanton, Elizabeth Cady
Woman Suffrage Movement

Suggestions for further reading:
Barry, Kathleen. 1988. *Susan B. Anthony: Biography of a Singular Feminist.* New York: New York University Press.
DuBois, Ellen Carol, ed. 1992. *The Elizabeth Cady Stanton–Susan B. Anthony Reader: Correspondence, Writings, Speeches.* Boston: Northeastern University Press.
HWS, 4:124–142.

J

Jackson Fund

Like fellow philanthropist Charles Fox Hovey, Francis Jackson (1789–1861), an affluent Boston businessman and antislavery reformer, was also an enthusiastic advocate of women's rights, including woman suffrage. The antislavery movement had been Jackson's primary reform interest until his daughter, Eliza Jackson Eddy, was abandoned by her husband. When he absconded, taking their two children with him to Europe, Jackson's distress over his daughter's legal powerlessness to claim her children spurred him to donate $5,000 to subsidize women's rights reform.

In the fall of 1858, Wendell Phillips informed Susan B. Anthony that he, Anthony, and Lucy Stone had been named trustees of the $5,000 fund. Anthony immediately requested and received $1,500 to support her campaign to push New York state legislators to enact the Married Women's Property Law of 1860. By the time this bill was passed in 1860, Anthony had used a total of $4,000 from both the Jackson and Hovey Funds to wage this campaign.

Although Anthony admired Phillips's astute management and reinvestment of the Jackson Fund moneys, which doubled the amount of the original donation, both she and Lucy Stone resented the occasions when he resisted funding their women's rights reforms (*HWS,* 1:257). Unlike the conflicts

concerning the Hovey Fund expenditures over which Stone and Anthony had no control, as co-trustees of the Jackson Fund they could overrule Phillips's objections as to how that money was allocated.

In the early spring of 1867, Anthony, Cady Stanton, and Stone were eager to embark on an all-out American Equal Rights Association (AERA) campaign to persuade Kansas voters to include woman suffrage in their new state constitution. Phillips protested strenuously against their using Jackson Fund moneys for this purpose. Stone and Anthony overrode his objections and allotted $1,500 for their Kansas needs. They believed that Phillips was wrong to oppose them because Francis Jackson had explicitly dictated that his fund should be spent on women's rights, and they reasoned that they, as women, should be permitted to decide which women's rights reforms were most urgent. Stone, Anthony, and Cady Stanton were convinced that woman suffrage agitation would not harm the effort to obtain the ballot for African-American males, as Phillips claimed, but would persuade the public to support universal suffrage. Why should women postpone their efforts to obtain the ballot when suffrage for all Americans was within their grasp? Unfortunately, Lucy Stone and her husband Henry Blackwell's Kansas campaign consumed the remaining Jackson Fund money before the AERA had achieved its Kansas objective, a development that

necessitated Anthony's return to the onerous, never-ending chore of fund-raising.

Related entries:
American Equal Rights Association
Hovey Fund
Kansas Campaign of 1867
New York Married Women's Property Law of
  1860
Phillips, Wendell
Reconstruction
Stone, Lucy
Women's Rights Movement

Suggestions for further reading:
HWS, 1:257–258.

Julian, George Washington
(1817–1899)

*I*ndiana abolitionist and Republican
member of Congress George Washington Julian was Susan B. Anthony and Elizabeth Cady Stanton's chief champion of
woman suffrage in the House of Representatives from 1868 to 1870. In December 1868,
several days after Republican senator Samuel
Clarke Pomeroy presented a Senate resolution in favor of a Sixteenth Amendment guaranteeing woman suffrage, Julian introduced

a similar proposal in the House of Representatives (Harper 1899, 1:310). And in
March 1869, he presented a joint resolution
to Congress in favor of a Sixteenth Amendment (*HWS*, 2:333). Also in 1869, both Julian
and Pomeroy submitted versions of the Fifteenth Amendment that would have ensured
woman suffrage in addition to suffrage for
African-American males, but their fellow Republicans refused to consider them. Although
Julian disappointed Anthony when, in a display of Republican Party unity, he temporarily shelved his pro–woman suffrage
position to back Congress's final version of
the Fifteenth Amendment, he heartily endorsed woman suffrage for the remainder of
his life.

Related entries:
Fifteenth Amendment
National Woman Suffrage Association
Pomeroy, Samuel Clarke
Reconstruction
Sixteenth Amendment Campaign
Woman Suffrage Movement

Suggestions for further reading:
DAB, 5:245–246.
Harper, Ida Husted. 1899, 1908. *The Life and Work
  of Susan B. Anthony.* 3 vols. Indianapolis:
  Bowen-Merrill (vols. 1 and 2) and Hollenbeck
  Press (vol. 3).
HWS, 2.

Kansas Campaign of 1867

*I*n March 1867, the Kansas state legislature approved two referenda to be presented to Kansas voters, one concerning African-American suffrage and the other woman suffrage. Susan B. Anthony, Elizabeth Cady Stanton, and other American Equal Rights Association (AERA) members were optimistic about the possibility of Kansas becoming the first state to enact woman suffrage. They determined that of all the states undergoing constitutional revision, Kansas, with its strong reform and antislavery history, had the best chance of voting for woman suffrage. And they realized that if the referendum succeeded, it would establish an important precedent for other states and perhaps convince their abolitionist colleagues and members of Congress that woman suffrage had the support of the public (DuBois 1978, 79). Consequently, the AERA decided to concentrate their limited resources on campaigning for woman suffrage in Kansas.

Because Anthony and Cady Stanton were deeply involved in the effort to delete the word *male* from the New York state constitution during the spring of 1867, they persuaded Lucy Stone to canvass Kansas for the AERA. For three months Stone and her husband Henry Blackwell traveled and lectured across the state. They were frequently received by audiences who were receptive to the idea of woman suffrage. Although they were ably assisted by the Equal Rights Association of Kansas, to Stone and Blackwell's consternation, their efforts were ignored by the Kansas Republican Party. Before long, Kansas Republican leaders, in their all-out campaign to secure the African-American suffrage referendum, began delivering speeches and disseminating literature that were vehemently antifeminist. They did so out of concern that the woman suffrage referendum threatened the African-American suffrage referendum. Stone was also enraged by the censorship of the male-dominated northern abolitionist and Republican press, which refused to report on the campaign in Kansas. Because of the lack of support, Stone and Blackwell were convinced that despite their campaigning, the woman suffrage message was not reaching the people.

Anthony and Cady Stanton arrived to canvass Kansas in late August 1867. Their letters home conveyed the physical hardships equal rights activists endured while campaigning on the Kansas frontier. They traveled to their "lecture halls"—schoolhouses, barns, sawmills, and cabins—in wagons. They often had to ford muddy, rain-swollen streams and rivers; sleep in rough cabins; and endure a diet of soda-raised bread, bacon, tinned meats and vegetables, and dried fruit. But the greatest torment of all, Anthony noted, was the bugs that feasted on them at night (Harper 1899, 1:284).

Anthony and Cady Stanton decided to split up and canvass different parts of the state throughout the fall. Overwhelmed by the vituperative, antifeminist Republican press, Anthony realized that the woman suffrage referendum would have a chance only if she courted as many Democratic and independent Republican votes as could be mustered. Help arrived in the form of the wealthy financier George Francis Train, who was as renowned for his Copperhead (anti–African-American, anti-Republican) views as he was for his passionate pro–woman suffrage politics. Anthony was desperate for financial and political support. She welcomed his company in spite of his positions. As they toured together, their evening speeches typically commenced with Anthony's clear, powerful endorsement of universal suffrage. She supported both referenda, although she spent most of her time endorsing woman suffrage. Train would then appeal to the audience's racial fears and prejudices to scare them into supporting woman suffrage.

You say, General, that you intend to vote for *negro suffrage* and against *woman suffrage*. In other words, not satisfied with having your mother, your wife, your sisters, your daughters, the equals politically of the negro—by giving him a vote and refusing it to woman, you wish to place your family politically still lower in the scale of citizenship and humanity. (*HWS*, 2:244)

Both referenda failed at the polls in November 1867. The Republicans in Kansas and in the North blamed Anthony, Cady Stanton, and Train for the failure of the African-American suffrage referendum. Although scholars have since determined that Train's overall impact on the Kansas campaign was slight, the popular perception persisted. Anthony found some comfort in the fact that more than 9,000 ballots were cast for the woman suffrage referendum, which was nearly one-third of the total. But in Anthony and Cady Stanton's struggle for woman suffrage, Kansas marked the end of their attempts to enlist the cooperation of Republicans and their former abolitionist colleagues. The defeat in Kansas and the Republican backlash that followed made them realize that they would have to forge new political alliances if they were to advance the cause of woman suffrage. They also realized that only an independent woman suffrage movement could achieve their goals (DuBois 1978, 81, 97).

Related entries:
American Equal Rights Association
Anthony, Susan B.
Blackwell, Henry Browne
Reconstruction
Stone, Lucy
Train, George Francis

Suggestions for further reading:
DuBois, Ellen Carol. 1978. *Feminism and Suffrage: The Emergence of an Independent Women's Movement in America 1848–1869*. Ithaca, N.Y.: Cornell University Press.
Kerr, Andrea Moore. 1992. *Lucy Stone: Speaking Out for Equality*. New Brunswick, N.J.: Rutgers University Press.
Kugler, Israel. 1987. *From Ladies to Women: The Organized Struggle for Woman's Rights in the Reconstruction Era*. Westport, Conn.: Greenwood Press.

Kansas-Nebraska Act

When Congress passed the Kansas-Nebraska Act in May 1854, Susan B. Anthony and most northern abolitionist and antislavery factions were stunned and outraged. In addition to its other provisions, the Kansas-Nebraska Act revoked a stipulation of the Missouri Compromise of 1820 that outlawed slavery in the U.S. territories north of the 36°30' parallel. It also provided that the voters of a territory were to decide if it should become a free or a slaveholding territory. Anthony and her fellow abolitionists believed that the Kansas-Nebraska Act was proof that Congress planned to uphold and proliferate the institution of slavery by extending it into the territories. Although hundreds of miles away from the homes of northern abolitionists, the problems of Kansas stirred them as no event had since Congress passed the Fugitive Slave Act of 1850.

In response to the Kansas-Nebraska Act, many northerners, including members of the New England Emigrant Aid Company, rushed to support men and women who were willing to create free-state settlements in Kansas Territory. As the months passed, conflicts between proslavery forces and free-state settlers became frequent in Kansas towns bordering Missouri. After hearing the stories of Anthony's brother, Daniel Read Anthony, who traveled with the New England Emigrant Aid Company to Kansas in 1854, and after talking with abolitionist and free-state settler John Brown at Frederick Douglass's house, Anthony's youngest brother, Jacob Merritt Anthony, joined Brown in Kansas. Merritt fought alongside Brown at Osawatomie in 1856, when free-state men overwhelmed Missouri "border ruffians." For days after the battle, the Anthony family studied the newspapers and worried about Merritt's fate. Finally a witness to the battle, who believed that Merritt had not been harmed, arrived in Rochester. Anthony then wrote to Merritt of her concern for him while also revealing her anguish over the human cost of the Kansas struggle.

How much rather would I have you at my side tonight than to think of your daring and enduring greater hardships even than our Revolutionary heroes. Words can not tell how often we think of you or how sadly we feel that the terrible crime of this nation against humanity is being avenged on the heads of our sons and brothers. (Harper 1899, 1:144–145)

Anthony's father's reflection on the event demonstrates how monumental the Kansas border struggle and the blight of slavery had become in their lives: "the hope that my son has survived brings little solace to my soul while the cause of all this terrible wrong remains untouched" (Harper 1899, 1:144–145).

Although many northern antislavery supporters welcomed the conflagration in Kansas in the hopes that it would ignite an all-out war between North and South or, at the least, alert passive northerners to take a stand against slavery, Anthony was not one of them. In a letter to a close friend who was herself to become a Kansas emigrant, she wrote of the futility and waste involved in the effort to make "poor bleeding Kansas" a free state. To Anthony, "bleeding Kansas" only proved that the South would never surrender slavery without an armed conflict and an enormous human cost.

Related entries:
Abolitionist Movement
Anthony, Daniel Read
Anthony, Jacob Merritt
Brown, John

Suggestions for further reading:
Aptheker, Herbert. 1989. *Abolitionism: A Revolutionary Movement.* Boston: Twayne Publishers.
Harper, Ida Husted. 1899. *The Life and Work of Susan B. Anthony.* Vol. 1. Indianapolis: Bowen-Merrill.

The Liberator

Among the many antislavery and abolitionist newspapers of the mid-nineteenth century, William Lloyd Garrison's *The Liberator* was unquestionably a leader. Although the paper never had more than 3,000 subscribers at any one time, it had an enormous impact on U.S. journalism and political culture while also inspiring and goading into action more than one generation of abolitionists, Susan B. Anthony among them. In *The Liberator*'s first issue, published on January 1, 1831, Garrison insisted on the immediate emancipation of the slaves, writing, "I am aware, that many object to the severity of my language; but is there not cause for severity; I will be as harsh as truth, and as uncompromising as justice. On this subject I do not wish to think, or speak, or write, with moderation" (Blassingame, Henderson, and Dunn 1980, 121).

For the next 35 years, Garrison's vehement and often scathing editorials guaranteed that the public would not only listen but react. The weekly also published national and regional news pertinent to the abolitionist movement, including horrifying accounts of slave torture, slaveowners' villainy, and slave escapes and captures as well as excerpts from both antislavery and proslavery books, speeches, and other literature. Garrison also published notices of upcoming antislavery meetings and conventions; letters from abolitionists in the field; and news of many other liberal social reform movements, including women's rights, temperance, the peace and nonresistance movements, and prison reform.

During Anthony's years of activism in the temperance, abolitionist, and women's rights movements, she provided *The Liberator* with news of her own and her colleagues' reform activities. Anthony also submitted letters to Garrison, with the understanding that he would publish them, just as she provided letters to Frederick Douglass's the *North Star*, Amelia Jenks Bloomer's the *Lily,* and Paulina Wright Davis's the *Una*. In one such letter published in *The Liberator* on February 8, 1861, she described an evening lecture during the current "winter of mobs," when she, Stephen Symonds Foster, and Aaron M. Powell attempted to speak to their audience in Rome, New York. Her letter alerted *The Liberator*'s readers to the difficult conditions abolitionists faced in the field.

> At the evening session, I placed myself . . . to take the door fee. Some thirty passed up quietly, when there came, with heavy tramp, a compact gang of forty or fifty rowdies. . . . There they stamped, and howled, and whistled, and sang "the star spangled banner"—marched on to the platform, seated themselves at the table, pulled out a pack of cards, and then took the table and threw it to the

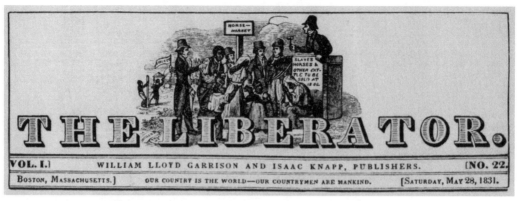

Masthead of the abolitionist newspaper **The Liberator,** *1831.*

floor with a crash. Under the circumstances, we made no attempt to speak, and soon left the hall. (*The Liberator,* February 8, 1861, in *Papers*)

After the Emancipation Proclamation in 1863, Garrison became increasingly convinced that *The Liberator*'s mission had been fulfilled. In December 1865, as ratification of the Thirteenth Amendment guaranteeing the freedom of African Americans became a reality, he terminated publication of *The Liberator.*

Related entries:
Abolitionist Movement
Garrison, William Lloyd
The *Lily*
The *North Star*
The *Una*

Suggestions for further reading:
Blassingame, John W., Mae G. Henderson, and Jessica M. Dunn, eds. 1980–1984. *Antislavery Newspapers and Periodicals.* 4 vols. Boston: G. K. Hall.
Cain, William E., ed. 1995. *William Lloyd Garrison and the Fight against Slavery.* New York: Bedford Press.

The Lily

Not long after the Ladies' Temperance Society of Seneca Falls, New York, published the first issue of its monthly jour-

nal, the *Lily,* under the direction of temperance reformer Amelia Jenks Bloomer in January 1849, it became the leading women's temperance publication in the Northeast. In its first few years of publication, the *Lily*'s editorials, news articles, prose, and poetry documented women's increasingly vocal activism in the temperance movement. By the end of its first year of publication, Jenks Bloomer had become both the sole publisher and editor. The *Lily*'s new motto, "Devoted to the Interests of Women," reflected the journal's broadening scope as it gradually began to address women's rights as well as temperance issues, a development for which leading contributor Elizabeth Cady Stanton was primarily responsible. For a journal of social reform, the *Lily* had many subscribers. From the first issue's 200–300 copies sold, it attained a circulation of more than 4,000 copies by 1853, reaching a peak of approximately 6,000 subscribers. The *Lily*'s outspoken advocacy of the Bloomer costume is most often attributed as the leading cause of the circulation boost.

Susan B. Anthony was a frequent contributor to the *Lily,* submitting letters, news, and commentary about her temperance work as she traveled and lectured throughout New York state. In a letter to *The Carson League,* another temperance paper, Anthony urged women to support the *Lily* because "it is their duty to sustain the only paper in the state owned and edited by a woman" (*HWS,* 1:489). Her involvement with the *Lily* initiated and incubated what would become a lifelong fascination with the press as a powerful instrument of vital social and political activism. In 1851, Jenks Bloomer introduced Anthony to Cady Stanton, who was already a principal contributor. Cady Stanton and Anthony's writing for the *Lily* brought them together because they frequently discussed and occasionally collaborated on pieces.

Jenks Bloomer continued publishing the *Lily* after she and her husband moved to Mount Vernon, Ohio. But when they again relocated to Council Bluffs, Iowa, in 1855, Bloomer realized that the town's lack of a suitable printing press and railroad access meant that she would have to sell the journal. Mary Birdsall of Richmond, Indiana, bought and kept the *Lily* alive for a brief time before terminating publication in 1856.

Related entries:
Bloomer, Amelia Jenks
Bloomer Costume
Daughters of Temperance
Stanton, Elizabeth Cady
Temperance
The *Una*
Women's Rights Movement

Suggestions for further reading:
Hinck, Edward A. 1991. "The *Lily*, 1849–1856: From Temperance to Women's Rights." In *A Voice of Their Own: The Woman Suffrage Press, 1840–1910,* ed. Martha M. Solomon. Tuscaloosa: University of Alabama Press.
Hoffert, Sylvia D. 1995. *When Hens Crow: The Women's Rights Movement in Antebellum America.* Bloomington: Indiana University Press.

ℳ

May, Samuel, Jr. (1810–1899)

See **American Anti-Slavery Society**

May, Samuel Joseph (1797–1871)

*U*nitarian minister, Garrisonian abolitionist, women's rights activist, and social reformer Samuel Joseph May was among the first of the American clergy to publicly support the franchise for women. Although May grew up, was educated, and received his ministerial training in the Boston area (he was uncle to Louisa May Alcott), he settled in Syracuse, New York, in 1845 and lived there until 1867.

May encouraged women to pursue equal opportunities in his congregation as early as 1823. As an abolitionist involved in the formation of the American Anti-Slavery Society (AASS) in 1833, he was committed to antislavery reform and agitation. In 1837, in the midst of a swirl of controversy and outrage about women speaking in public, May asked the abolitionists Angelina and Sarah Grimké to speak to his congregation in South Scituate, Massachusetts. Although at that time he was uncertain whether all women should have public roles, he strongly opposed the efforts of the Massachusetts clergy to censor

and silence abolitionists, particularly women antislavery activists (Yacovone 1991, 67).

As early as 1846, May wrote and published a tract entitled "The Rights and Condition of Women," which protested "this utter annihilation . . . of more than one half of the whole community." On the issue of woman suffrage, he declared:

> This entire disfranchisement of females is as unjust as the disfranchisement of the males would be; for there is nothing in their [women's] moral mental or physical nature, that disqualifies them to understand correctly the true interests of the community, or to act wisely in reference to them. (Kimmel and Mosmiller 1992, 95)

Susan B. Anthony first worked with May in the temperance movement. His experiences as an outspoken temperance activist led him to agree with her that temperance was an especially important issue for women to address. As Anthony became increasingly involved in the women's rights movement in New York state, she frequently called upon him to speak at women's rights conventions and meetings. He soon recognized her considerable talents for reform. In August 1858, he wrote to her: "I wish there were thousands more in the world like you. Some foolish old conventionalisms would be utterly routed, and the legal and social disabilities of women would not long be what they are" (Harper 1899, 1:164).

When Anthony became New York agent for the AASS in 1856, May responded to her request that he join her corps of lecturers. In the winter of 1861, during the height of antiabolitionist mob violence, May was one of Anthony's loyal band of orators. Although forewarned of the probability of violence at their meeting in Syracuse in late January, the group decided to proceed with their lectures advocating abolitionism and disunionism. When both May and Anthony tried to speak, the screams of the mob obliterated their voices. The crowd then hauled effigies of May and Anthony through the streets of Syracuse and set them afire, yelling "Constitution and Union!" (Yacovone 1991, 171).

May retained his commitment to universal suffrage after the Civil War, although he was persuaded of the need to temporarily postpone agitating for woman suffrage to gain the ballot for African-American males. In spite of this concession, May never stopped working with Elizabeth Cady Stanton and Anthony for woman suffrage, forming a branch of the American Equal Rights Association (AERA) in Syracuse to gain more support for universal suffrage. He disdained his male abolitionist colleagues' abandonment of woman suffrage and was particularly incensed by Wendell Phillips's inflexible position, which prompted May to chastise him at an AERA meeting in 1867.

Although May remained in contact with Cady Stanton and Anthony in the years immediately preceding his death in 1871, their association with George Francis Train, whom May labeled "a fool or a monomaniac," alienated him. Their alliance with Train prevented him from pursuing further close collaboration with them. Nevertheless, May spent his final years working to secure the ballot for both women and African-American males (Yacovone 1991, 180).

Related entries:
Abolitionist Movement
American Anti-Slavery Society
American Equal Rights Association
Temperance
Woman's Rights Conventions
Woman's State Temperance Society
Women's Rights Movement

Suggestions for further reading:
Kimmel, Michael S., and Thomas E. Mosmiller, eds. 1992. *Against the Tide: Pro-Feminist Men in the United States, 1776–1990: A Documentary History.* Boston: Beacon Press.
Pease, Jane H., and William H. Pease, eds. 1972. *Bound with Them in Chains: A Biographical History of the Antislavery Movement.* Westport, Conn.: Greenwood Press.
Yacovone, Donald. 1991. *Samuel Joseph May and the Dilemmas of the Liberal Persuasion, 1797–1871.* Philadelphia: Temple University Press.

McLean, Aaron M.

See **Anthony, Susan B.; McLean, Guelma Penn Anthony.**

McLean, Guelma Penn Anthony (1818–1873)

*G*uelma Penn Anthony was Daniel and Lucy Read Anthony's oldest child. Daniel named their firstborn for the wife of the late seventeenth-century Quaker leader William Penn. Guelma Anthony was born in Adams, Massachusetts, a year after her parents were married, at a time when Daniel was earning the family's living by farming and by operating a small general store in the house he built.

Guelma attended Deborah Moulson's female seminary from 1836 to 1838. Before she married, she worked as a teacher. In September 1839, she married Aaron M. McLean (1812–1896), the grandson of John McLean, Daniel Anthony's business partner. The entire Anthony family was extremely fond of

Aaron, and he was, throughout his lifetime, regarded as one of the Anthonys, as if he had been born their brother. Because Aaron was raised in the Presbyterian faith, the local Quakers withdrew Guelma's membership for "marrying out of meeting." This event saddened Daniel and all the Anthonys but did not deter Guelma from marrying Aaron.

Susan and Guelma were always very close and enjoyed spending time together. After Guelma's marriage to Aaron, the young couple lived in Battenville, New York, for a number of years before permanently relocating to Rochester, New York, in the late 1850s or early 1860s. While Susan was teaching in Canajoharie, New York, she often spent her vacations visiting Guelma and her family in Battenville. Guelma and Aaron gave birth to four children. A son died in infancy, and another son and daughter died following brief, unexpected illnesses upon reaching adulthood, Ann Eliza McLean in 1864 and Thomas King McLean in 1870. In the months of grief following Thomas's death, Guelma became ill and did not recover. Her illness, diagnosed as tuberculosis, steadily progressed, and she died in November 1873. Guelma and Aaron's daughter Margaret McLean (Baker) was their only child to survive to lead a healthy, full adult life.

Guelma dedicated herself to her family. Although there is no record that she participated in the women's rights movement or other social reforms, she was in complete sympathy with Susan's activism. In November 1872, though very ill, she left her sickbed and walked with her sisters Susan, Hannah Anthony Mosher, and Mary Anthony to the voter registration site to register to vote. Four days later, she again walked to the polls to cast her ballot. At the conclusion of Susan's trial for voting, the *United States v. Susan B. Anthony*, she spent the rest of that summer and fall of 1873 at Guelma's bedside, taking complete charge of her nursing care. By all accounts, she was a superb nurse and was determined to make

her beloved sister's final days as comfortable as possible.

Related entries:
Anthony, Susan B.
The *United States v. Susan B. Anthony*

Suggestions for further reading:
Anthony, Katharine. 1954. *Susan B. Anthony: Her Personal History and Her Era*. Garden City, N.Y.: Doubleday.
Harper, Ida Husted. 1899, 1908. *The Life and Work of Susan B. Anthony*. 3 vols. Indianapolis: Bowen-Merrill (vols. 1 and 2) and Hollenbeck Press (vol. 3).

Mosher, Hannah Lapham Anthony (1821–1877)

The third child and daughter of Daniel and Lucy Read Anthony, Hannah Lapham Anthony was born in Adams, Massachusetts, 19 months after her sister Susan B. Anthony's birth. Hannah, Susan, and their oldest sister Guelma were very close in childhood and remained so all their adult lives.

For two years Hannah attended Canajoharie Academy, where Susan would teach several years later. Like her two older sisters, Hannah taught school during the summer months and after she completed her education. Weeks before the Anthony family moved from their home in Center Falls (formerly Hardscrabble) to Rochester, New York, Hannah married Eugene Mosher, a businessman, in September 1845. The young couple settled in Mosher's hometown of Easton, 10 miles from Battenville, New York. They had five children, four of whom survived childhood. In 1863, the Moshers moved to Rochester so that Hannah could be closer to her family. They purchased the home next door to the brick house that Lucy Read Anthony would buy on Madison Street in Rochester the following year (1864). Although Susan's reform work caused her to travel for much of the year, by 1864, whenever she returned home to Rochester, she, Guelma, Hannah, and their youngest sister Mary were together once more.

Although Hannah was not involved in the women's rights or woman suffrage movements, she did eagerly answer Susan's request that she register to vote in the November 1872 elections. On Election Day, Hannah, Guelma, Susan, and a neighbor walked to the polling site in the Eighth Ward of Rochester, New York. Hannah also was with Susan on the first day of her trial in Canandaigua, New York.

When Guelma became seriously ill with tuberculosis, Hannah frequently nursed her. By the final months of Guelma's decline, it became evident that Hannah, too, had succumbed to the disease. Immediately after Guelma's death in November 1873, Susan and her brother Daniel Read (D. R.) Anthony discussed plans to send Hannah to Colorado, which was declared by many experts to be a healthier climate for tuberculosis patients. Hannah first stayed with D. R. and his family in Leavenworth, Kansas, and then spent four months in Colorado Springs. She then returned to Leavenworth, where Eugene and her youngest child joined her. But despite several rallies, Hannah was gradually overcome by her illness. In April 1877, Susan canceled her engagements and hurried to Leavenworth to nurse her sister, who died in May a few weeks later.

Following Hannah's death, Susan was desolate. She had never dreamed that she would lose the two sisters closest to her in age so soon. She felt horribly alone and for a time was unable to continue work on the *History of Woman Suffrage*. She also became preoccupied with the belief that she, too, would soon contract tuberculosis. When the opportunity to participate in the 1877 Colorado suffrage campaign presented itself, she eagerly accepted, realizing that if she did become ill, she would at least be situated in the best climate. Once she was embroiled in the hard work and arduous travel of the campaign, she discovered that she had let go of her fears of death. In the struggle to educate men and women about the nation's urgent need for woman suffrage, she regained her emotional strength and resiliency.

Related entries:
Anthony, Susan B.
McLean, Guelma Penn Anthony
The *United States v. Susan B. Anthony*

Suggestions for further reading:
Harper, Ida Husted. 1899, 1908. *The Life and Work of Susan B. Anthony*. 3 vols. Indianapolis: Bowen-Merrill (vols. 1 and 2) and Hollenbeck Press (vol. 3).
Lutz, Alma. 1959. *Susan B. Anthony: Rebel, Crusader, Humanitarian*. Boston: Beacon Press.

Mott, Lucretia Coffin (1793–1880)

Quaker minister, Garrisonian abolitionist, and feminist activist Lucretia Coffin Mott was the most universally respected woman abolitionist of the mid-nineteenth century. Her incisive analysis of issues and ideology; her unusual ability to mediate conflict; and, as Elizabeth Cady Stanton once said, her "wise sagacity" made her opinion and presence among the most sought-after in both the abolitionist and the women's rights movements.

Coffin Mott first became involved in antislavery activities in the 1820s and was instrumental in the formation of the Philadelphia Female Anti-Slavery Society. She later became a key player in both the American Anti-Slavery Society (AASS) and its auxiliary, the Pennsylvania Anti-Slavery Society. In addition to her relentless traveling and lecturing on behalf of abolitionism, she was a leader in the women's rights movement. With Cady Stanton, her sister Martha Coffin Wright, and two other Quaker women, Coffin Mott helped to organize and lead the Seneca Falls Convention of 1848. She remained actively involved in the women's rights movement and, later, the

Photograph of Lucretia Coffin Mott taken sometime between 1860 and 1880.

woman suffrage movement until her death in 1880.

Susan B. Anthony first heard Coffin Mott speak while she was a student at Deborah Moulson's female seminary in 1838 when she was 18 years old. At that time, Coffin Mott was already well known to Anthony, as she was to most Quakers. She spoke about the value of cultivating the intellect, a goal that Anthony took seriously. Years later, Anthony heard her parents and her sister rave about Coffin Mott's brilliant, gentle eloquence when they returned from attending the Rochester Woman's Rights Convention in 1848.

Yet it was not until September 1852 that Anthony had her first opportunity to talk with Coffin Mott, when she and her husband James Mott attended the Third National Woman's Rights Convention held in Syracuse, New York. From that point on, Coffin Mott was a friend and mentor to Anthony and someone whom Anthony frequently asked to speak and to preside at woman's rights conventions and meetings.

In addition to the direct influence that Coffin Mott had on Anthony's development as a feminist and reformer, Anthony was in-directly exposed to Coffin Mott's religious ideology through Cady Stanton. Cady Stanton first met Coffin Mott at the World Antislavery Convention in London in 1840 and was irresistibly drawn to her (Cady Stanton was accompanying her husband Henry Stanton, who was a delegate). The two women commiserated with each other and with the other American woman delegates when the male delegates refused to seat them, forcing them to sit out the proceedings in an adjoining gallery. After this experience and throughout the 1840s, Cady Stanton corresponded regularly with Coffin Mott, who supported Cady Stanton's burgeoning feminism and her religious soul-searching. When Anthony first met Cady Stanton in 1851, she was still enormously influenced by Coffin Mott. Through discussions with her new friend, Anthony's religious views were also shaped by Coffin Mott's liberalism and by her nondogmatic approach to religion, which encouraged Anthony to open herself to the new humanistic interpretations of the Scriptures in Quakerism and Unitarianism.

Throughout the 1850s and most of the 1860s, Coffin Mott continued to support Anthony's and Cady Stanton's feminist activism. Mott endorsed their radical, unpopular position on divorce in 1860; answered their call to participate in the Woman's National Loyal League (WNLL); and in 1866, agreed to be president of the American Equal Rights Association (AERA), the organization that Anthony and Cady Stanton formed to secure universal suffrage. And, although Coffin Mott stood steadfastly by Anthony and Cady Stanton in their efforts to add woman suffrage to the Fourteenth and Fifteenth Amendments in the late 1860s, by 1869, she found herself in the difficult position of defending two friends whose actions disturbed and disappointed her. She was particularly distressed by Cady Stanton's political posturing while asserting women's predominant claim to the ballot. Coffin Mott (and many others) perceived Cady Stanton's proclamations to be blatantly racist, something she could not tolerate, even in a good friend (Griffith 1984, 124). As a radical egalitarian, Coffin Mott could never approve of a tactic that claimed the ascendancy of one group's rights over another's. When Anthony and Cady Stanton published their ultraradical newspaper, *The Revolution*, Coffin Mott did not hide her disapproval of their association with their benefactor, George Francis Train. Soon she was trapped in the middle of the schism that tore the women's rights movement apart.

Despite her many reservations, Coffin Mott never abandoned Anthony and Cady Stanton. She also made repeated attempts to heal the breach between the New England feminists who had supported the Fifteenth Amendment and the "Negro's Hour," and Anthony and Cady Stanton, who had rejected it. None of these efforts were successful, despite Anthony's willing cooperation. That this difficult period in the three women's relationships passed is a testament to their enduring personal bond and their shared commitment to women's rights and universal suffrage. For the rest of her life, Mott was committed to Anthony and Cady Stanton's National Woman Suffrage Association (NWSA), and when her health permitted, she attended and spoke at their conventions.

Related entries:
Abolitionist Movement
American Anti-Slavery Society
American Equal Rights Association
Quakerism (Society of Friends)
Seneca Falls Convention of 1848
Stanton, Elizabeth Cady
Syracuse Woman's Rights Convention of 1852
Woman's National Loyal League
Woman's Rights Conventions
Women's Rights Movement

Suggestions for further reading:
Bacon, Margaret Hope. 1980. *Valiant Friend: The Life of Lucretia Mott.* New York: Walker.
Cromwell, Otelia. 1958. *Lucretia Mott.* Cambridge, Mass.: Harvard University Press.
Griffith, Elisabeth. 1984. *In Her Own Right: The Life of Elizabeth Cady Stanton.* New York: Oxford University Press.

Mott, Lydia (1807–1875)

Of all Susan B. Anthony's closest friends, Lydia Mott was the woman she turned to most often in crisis, confusion, and despair. Temperance reformer, abolitionist, women's rights activist, and suffragist, Mott was a dedicated reformer who, unlike Anthony, preferred to work behind the scenes where she attended to the endless minutiae of tasks that made reform campaigns possible. A cousin of James Mott, Lucretia Coffin Mott's husband, Lydia Mott was a student teacher at Deborah Moulson's Quaker boarding school when she met Anthony in 1837. Their friendship endured after both left the school. Anthony often spent her vacations from teaching at Mott's home in Albany, New York. Mott's dedicated involvement in the abolitionist movement and her and her sister Abigail Mott's self-supporting, independent lifestyle inspired and strongly influenced the young Anthony, providing her with two powerful role models of successful self-sufficiency. The Mott sisters operated a men's clothing store and managed a boarding house for New York state legislators when the state assembly was in session. Their Albany home was also a refuge for slaves traveling the Underground Railroad.

During Anthony's first years as a temperance reformer, she frequently turned to Mott for advice. When Anthony walked out of a Sons of Temperance convention in 1852 because she had been refused the opportunity to express her views on account of her gender, Mott encouraged her to form a temperance organization for women. Anthony and a loyal band of temperance reformers then established the Woman's State Temperance Society (WSTS). Mott's many contacts among New York state legislators proved an invaluable help to Anthony during her lobbying campaigns for temperance and women's rights legislation, particularly the New York Married Women's Property Law of 1860.

Unlike Anthony's intimate working partnership with Elizabeth Cady Stanton, the relationship with Mott provided Anthony with a constant flow of uncritical yet sound, levelheaded support and nurturance during Anthony's campaigns, canvasses, and reform battles. Anthony could depend on Mott to give her honest opinions on all issues and to disagree with her if her conscience so dictated. But the real balm to Anthony's battle wounds was Mott's patient, unbending conviction that even in the midst of the most disheartening setbacks and failures, positive change was always occurring.

During the Civil War, when Mott soothed Anthony in her discouragement at having to cancel the national woman's rights convention and discontinue her activism, Anthony wrote her friend:

> What a stay, counsel and comfort you have been to me, dear Lydia, ever since that eventful little temperance meeting in that cold, smoky chapel in 1852. How you have compelled me to feel myself competent to go forward when trembling with doubt and distrust. I never can express the magnitude of my indebtedness to you. (Harper 1899, 1:222)

In 1875, Anthony canceled all her engagements to spend the final weeks of Mott's life by her friend's side. When Mott died, Anthony recorded in her diary: "There passed out of my life today the one who, next to my own family, has been the nearest and dearest to me for thirty years" (Harper 1899, 1:471).

Related entries:
Abolitionist Movement
Anthony, Susan B.
Daughters of Temperance
Hovey Fund
New York Married Women's Property Law of 1860
Woman's State Temperance Society

Suggestions for further reading:
Harper, Ida Husted. 1899, 1908. *The Life and Work of Susan B. Anthony.* 3 vols. Indianapolis: Bowen-Merrill (vols. 1 and 2) and Hollenbeck Press (vol. 3).
Lutz, Alma. 1959. *Susan B. Anthony: Rebel, Crusader, Humanitarian.* Boston: Beacon Press.

National American Woman Suffrage Association

During the mid-1880s, American Woman Suffrage Association (AWSA) leader Lucy Stone's impression of the rival National Woman Suffrage Association (NWSA) changed. Instead of criticizing NWSA leaders for their statements and activities as she had in the past, she observed NWSA activities in a more favorable light and publicly acknowledged its successes and contributions. Just as Susan B. Anthony was struggling to prepare the next generation for NWSA leadership, Stone, too, was looking toward the future. As she faced the deterioration of her physical powers, she had to admit that the woman suffrage movement was very distant from its goal of national woman suffrage. As a result, she realized that monumental decisions had to be made to strengthen and advance the cause.

When Stone broached the subject of merging the two organizations into one unified society to her family, her daughter and AWSA suffragist Alice Stone Blackwell was taken aback but soon became a leading advocate for the merger. Anthony was startled by the unexpected appearance of Stone's peace offerings. Her correspondence with her closest friends and associates during the late 1880s reveals that she distrusted Stone's motives and strongly believed that Stone and her husband Henry Blackwell were not sincere in their desire to cooperate in the formation of a new organization with her and Elizabeth Cady Stanton. Despite Anthony's strong misgivings, she agreed to attend an exploratory meeting with Stone and Alice Blackwell in December 1887. With Rachel Foster (Avery) by her side, Anthony investigated the possibility of unification with her old friend and antagonist. It soon became apparent to everyone that the two younger activists, Alice Blackwell and Foster, were the most enthusiastic about pursuing union. All agreed to allow the discussions to continue. Negotiations toward the merger of the AWSA and the NWSA proceeded for more than two years before unity and the formation of the National American Woman Suffrage Association (NAWSA) were finally achieved in 1890.

Anthony encountered more resistance to the merger proposal among NWSA leaders than she had anticipated. Matilda Joslyn Gage, Olympia Brown, Lillie Devereux Blake, and some other first-generation NWSA suffragists did not want to unite with the AWSA, fearing that they would be forced to embrace their rivals' conservative ideological and religious baggage. The dissenting NWSA faction also rebelled because they believed that Anthony was being undemocratic, forcing the merger on the NWSA without consulting the wishes of its leaders. There was some truth to the charge. Once Anthony had determined that the merger was in the best interests of the woman suffrage movement, she brushed all dissent aside and determinedly pursued the union.

Stone's biggest disappointment in the process of uniting the two organizations was Anthony's refusal to honor her chief request that she, Anthony, and Cady Stanton abstain from leading the new organization. Stone believed that Anthony had assented to this demand at their initial meeting. Anthony maintained that she had not considered the initial 1887 meeting as the time to make specific requests. She asserted that the important business of that meeting had been to establish their intentions to unite their two organizations. Stone, in ill health, her power weakening, did not have the strength to persist in pressing her demand, and Anthony, wary and suspicious of Stone, Henry Blackwell, and the entire AWSA leadership, was anxious about relinquishing control of the NWSA to an unknown leader who would be elected from their joint memberships.

Cartoon drawn in 1905 by Charles Lewis Bartholomew. When former president Grover Cleveland condemned suffrage and women's club members that year, Susan B. Anthony is reported to have declared, "Ridiculous! Pure fol-de-rol!"

Anthony pushed for Cady Stanton to be elected, to the consternation of Stone, the Blackwells, and many within the NWSA who wanted Anthony to be president.

At the first convention of the NAWSA, held in Washington, D.C., in February 1890, Cady Stanton was elected president, and Anthony was elected vice president at large. Stone was chosen to serve as chair of the executive committee, Foster Avery (who married in 1888) as corresponding secretary, and Alice Blackwell as recording secretary.

Cady Stanton served as president for two years but led the NAWSA in name only. Anthony, as always, served as the executive mastermind and workhorse extraordinaire, just as she had in the NWSA. At the 1892 NAWSA convention, Anthony was elected president, a post she held until her retirement in 1900. During the 1890s, NAWSA focused most of its energies and resources on waging state suffrage campaigns in such states as South Dakota, Colorado, California, Oregon, Washington, Kansas, and New York, to name a few. Carrie Chapman Catt and Anna Howard Shaw, who had once been AWSA suffragists, became important NAWSA leaders during the 1890s. As the decade progressed, Anthony came to rely on their abilities, stamina, and insight to an increasing extent.

Following Anthony's "retirement" in 1900 (she continued to exert executive control), NAWSA presidents Chapman Catt (1900–1904 and 1916–1920) and Anna Howard Shaw (1905–1915) confronted the suffrage organization's most perplexing problems head-on—a flagging membership, insufficient funds, political strategies that were no longer effective, and a negative public image. Both women pushed NAWSA and its members to meet the challenges of a twentieth-century world. In 1898, while Chapman Catt was still leader of NAWSA's Organization Committee, she identified what she believed was the source of NAWSA's decline in the 1890s, a determination that echoed Anthony's observations

throughout the course of the woman suffrage movement.

> If I were asked to name the chief cause obstructing organization, I should not hesitate to reply. It is not to be found in the antisuffragists nor in ignorance nor in conservatism. . . . It is to be found in the hopeless, lifeless, faithless members of our own organization. . . . We find them in the state executive committees, where appalled by the magnitude of the undertaking they decide that organization is impossible because there is no money, and they make no effort to secure funds. . . . "It cannot be done" is their motto. . . . Let us banish from our vocabulary the word "can't." Let our watchword be "Organization and Union." (Peck 1944, 96–97)

As Anthony knew so well when she handpicked Chapman Catt to be her successor, the midwestern suffragist was a can-do leader who refused to accept seemingly insurmountable problems as defeats. By tightly centralizing the administration and power in the NAWSA and by careful strategizing and planning, Chapman Catt and loyal NAWSA members improved the organization's public image, dramatically boosted its membership throughout the country, and secured a sound financial base—all of which were essential if the final suffrage battles were to be won. Following Shaw's less successful presidency, Chapman Catt once again assumed her role as president. Her "Winning Plan" strategically combined state suffrage campaigns with a monumental lobbying barrage on Congress and President Woodrow Wilson. This program, along with the activism of the National Woman's Party and hundreds of other national, state, and local suffrage organizations, maneuvered the woman suffrage movement to its final victory—the ratification of the Nineteenth Amendment on August 26, 1920.

Suggestions for further reading:
Graham, Sara Hunter. 1996. *Woman Suffrage and the New Democracy.* New Haven, Conn.: Yale University Press.
Marilley, Suzanne M. 1996. *Woman Suffrage and the Origins of Liberal Feminism in the United States, 1820–1920.* Cambridge, Mass.: Harvard University Press.
Wheeler, Marjorie Spruill, ed. 1995a. *One Woman, One Vote: Rediscovering the Woman Suffrage Movement.* Troutdale, Oreg.: New Sage Press.

National Labor Union

*D*uring the late 1860s, when Susan B. Anthony and Elizabeth Cady Stanton were virtually without allies in their struggle for woman suffrage, they explored associating the suffrage movement with organized labor. Anthony and Cady Stanton were particularly impressed with the newly formed National Labor Union (NLU). Organized in 1866, the NLU was a national federation of trade unions with a membership of approximately 600,000 skilled male craftsworkers. NLU leader William H. Sylvis not only advocated the improvement of working conditions for women in the trades but was also prosuffrage.

Because the NLU platform was compatible with Anthony and Cady Stanton's goals, the two suffragists gave the NLU favorable press coverage in their women's rights newspaper, *The Revolution*. But even more important for the political future of their suffrage movement, they hoped the NLU would fulfill its aspiration to form a major political labor reform party. They hoped that such an alliance would give the suffrage movement the political power necessary to gain widespread support among legislators and the public.

In early September 1868, Anthony prepared to send to the NLU Congress its first women delegates. To do so, she organized two chapters of a new organization—the Working Women's Association (WWA)—a group of women workers that she hoped would be dedicated to improving their economic condition in the workplace. Anthony represented one chapter of the WWA at the NLU Congress, and Cady Stanton attended as a delegate of the Woman Suffrage Association of America (WSAA). Anthony also arranged for the other chapter of the WWA and one other group to send delegates. In addition to these four women, Kate Mullaney, president of the Collar Laundry Union of Troy, New York, attended the congress.

The NLU Congress accepted all the women delegates except Cady Stanton. They rejected her because she represented a suffrage organization. The male delegates feared that if they accepted her, the public and the press might construe the action as the NLU's endorsement of woman suffrage. After a prolonged debate, they permitted her to remain, but only after recording in the written proceedings that her presence in no way signified NLU's acceptance of woman suffrage.

Male NLU delegates represented white male trade unionists who were all skilled workers and the elite of the working class. In general, male trade unionists regarded women workers with distrust. They feared competition from women workers and were especially concerned that women would undercut their wages and replace male workers. But even more fundamental than these economic concerns, as a group they firmly believed that women did not belong in the trades. They were committed to the idea that a primary goal of labor should be to increase the wages of male workers so that men could sustain their families as the sole breadwinners while women remained at home. Of course, this objective neglected to consider the economic needs of single women and widows.

After the NLU Congress, Anthony and Cady Stanton were encouraged by the results of their efforts to reach out to organized labor. Anthony had been permitted to participate in debates during the congress, women (including Anthony) had been appointed to serve on committees, and Kate Mullaney was selected to high office in the NLU. During the ensuing year, Anthony continued to work on behalf of the WWA, exploring ways to expand opportunities for women in the workplace. One of her efforts, however, brought about the termination of Anthony's and Cady Stanton's connection with the NLU.

Anthony was eager to assist more women to become typesetters since this occupation's wages were much higher than other jobs open to women. She felt compelled to take remedial action because the all-male typesetters' unions did not allow women to train for the best-paying, most highly skilled jobs through their apprenticeship programs. Anthony had hoped that the new Women's Typographical Union (WTU), formed by Anthony's protégé Augusta Lewis, would reach out to women hoping to enter the printing trade, but in aligning itself with the all-male National Typographical Union (NTU), the WTU had to desist from admitting new women typesetters. As a result of these barriers, Anthony searched for some other means to enable more women workers to become typesetters. When Anthony convinced several employers to start a typesetters' school for unskilled women during a strike, NTU members accused Anthony of strikebreaking. Although she did not perceive her action in this way, there is no doubt that her action weakened the stance of organized labor in this strike.

At the NLU Congress in 1869, Anthony and Cady Stanton were deprived of their chief ally, William Sylvis, who had died in July. The delegates immediately acted to unseat Anthony. They accused her of strikebreaking and claimed that *The Revolution* was published by a nonunion printer who had recently fired Augusta Lewis for her union activities. Anthony, asserting that she had no knowledge of Lewis's fate, explained why she had acted to establish the training school. She reminded them that not only was she not a trade unionist but that the union's interests were antithetical to women's labor. Following a lengthy debate and several votes on the issue, the delegates voted to remove Anthony.

Even though Anthony and Cady Stanton's involvement in the NLU did not produce the enduring political bond they had hoped to form, both women were successful in improving working conditions for women and in making a lasting impact on labor reform. The NLU dissolved in 1872, but its record of advocacy (which Anthony and Cady Stanton helped to articulate) included the expansion of opportunities for women in the trades, the endorsement of equal pay for all workers, and the admission of women into trade unions, all precedents that were passed on to future national labor organizations. (Kugler 1987, 155).

Related entries:
The Revolution
Working Women's Association

Suggestions for further reading:
DuBois, Ellen Carol. 1978. *Feminism and Suffrage: The Emergence of an Independent Women's Movement in America 1848–1869*. Ithaca, N.Y.: Cornell University Press.
Kugler, Israel. 1987. *From Ladies to Women: The Organized Struggle for Woman's Rights in the Reconstruction Era*. Westport, Conn.: Greenwood Press.

National Woman Suffrage Association (1869–1890)

*I*n May 1869, Susan B. Anthony, Elizabeth Cady Stanton, a devout group of veteran women's rights activists (including Lucretia Coffin Mott, Paulina Wright Davis, Ernestine Potowski Rose, Matilda Joslyn Gage, Olympia Brown, Phoebe Couzins, and Martha Coffin Wright), and woman suffrage advocates from 19 states established the National Woman Suffrage Association (NWSA), which was dedicated to securing a federal woman suffrage amendment. For the next 21 years, Anthony would devote her energies to this challenge through the organization that she, more than any other person, created and sustained.

For Anthony and Cady Stanton, the years immediately preceding the formation of the NWSA (1865–1869) were filled with frustration and struggle. After the Civil War, they attempted to work toward woman suffrage through the American Equal Rights Association (AERA), an organization that focused on obtaining universal suffrage—to gain the franchise for all women as well as for African-American males. But when the majority of AERA members joined the Radical Republicans in Congress in proclaiming the emancipated slaves' urgent need of the constitutional protection of their civil and political rights, woman suffrage ceased to be a vital part of the AERA program. In 1868, as soon as Anthony, Cady Stanton, Parker Pillsbury, and a few other AERA members realized that they could no longer agitate for woman suffrage within the AERA, they began exploring the possibility of establishing an association wholly and exclusively devoted to woman suffrage.

In January 1869, Anthony and Cady Stanton formed the Woman Suffrage Association of America (WSAA), through which they investigated the prospect of creating a national woman suffrage coalition with their like-minded colleagues and friends. Keenly aware that their cause desperately needed the stalwart ranks of a woman suffrage army, they embarked on a woman suffrage lecture tour of the Midwest, traveling to Ohio, Missouri, Illinois, and Wisconsin to convert and gather women who would dedicate themselves to the labor of securing a Sixteenth Amendment guaranteeing woman suffrage.

At the May 1869 AERA convention in New York City, Anthony harbored the hope that the membership would agree to her plans for an AERA campaign to obtain a Sixteenth Amendment. In fact, she had been preparing for this convention for months. During her tour of the Midwest, she persuaded a sizable group of midwestern suffragists to attend the AERA convention and demand that the AERA support a campaign to achieve a federal woman suffrage amendment. Anthony hoped that by stacking the convention with woman suffrage supporters, they would be able to overwhelm AERA members who believed that all woman suffrage agitation should be postponed until after the Fifteenth Amendment was ratified. Her plan did not have a chance to succeed, however. As the volcanic clash of wills, egos, politics, and ideology unfolded at this historic meeting, AERA members steadfastly refused to consider even the idea of a Sixteenth Amendment, voting instead to back the Fifteenth Amendment exclusively. Although Anthony managed to assert the moral and strategic necessity of procuring woman suffrage at the same time as African-American manhood suffrage, she could not move her opponents to alter their position.

When the AERA convention disbanded, Anthony and Cady Stanton's woman suffrage contingent was bewildered and angered by the struggle they had witnessed. After all, they had journeyed to New York because Anthony had promised that they were needed to instigate an all-out campaign to achieve national woman suffrage. In this emotionally charged atmosphere, Anthony, Cady Stanton, and veteran feminists assembled their out-of-town activists and other women's rights supporters at a reception at the Women's Bureau in New York City. It was at this meeting that participants collectively organized the NWSA.

The new NWSA membership decided to welcome prosuffrage men as members but

SUSAN B. ANTHONY!
THE INVINCIBLE!
Will deliver her famous lecture entitled:

Woman wants Bread, not the Ballot

At Union Hall, Friday Evening, Oct. 12th.

This is only one chance in a life-time to hear this truly distinguished lady speak. The Press speaks of her in tones of praise wherever she has delivered this lecture.

Let everybody come and hear her. Come! Come!

ADMISSION 50 CENTS.

Poster advertising a lecture by Susan B. Anthony when she was leader of NWSA.

to bar them from leadership positions, no doubt at Anthony and Cady Stanton's assertion that no political organization or political alliance led by men could be relied upon to support the cause of women's rights. Cady Stanton was elected president, and Anthony was selected to serve on the executive committee. From the start, the NWSA was structured loosely, according to the leaders' preference for an open, grassroots model of organization, in which any prosuffrage individual who paid the $1 membership dues was entitled to attend all conventions and vote as a full-fledged member.

Months later, in November 1869, Lucy Stone, Henry Blackwell, and other New England Republicans formed the rival American Woman Suffrage Association (AWSA). Fully endorsing the Radical Republican platform, they proclaimed the AWSA the primary woman suffrage organization, protesting

that the NWSA leadership was too radical for the majority of Americans. Unlike the NWSA's federation of members, the AWSA membership and their conventions were open only to delegates from approved state suffrage organizations. The AWSA also allowed men to serve in top leadership positions and proposed gaining national woman suffrage primarily by supporting state suffrage campaigns.

The NWSA gathered all its members together at least two times each year, with at least one meeting occurring in January or February. Anthony prevailed upon the membership to hold their winter conventions in Washington, D.C., so that members could testify before Congress on the status of woman suffrage in their home states while educating and lobbying members of Congress to accept a federal suffrage amendment. This form of direct political activity distinguished the NWSA from the AWSA and reflected Anthony's core conviction that woman suffrage would never be enacted without winning over the Washington political establishment.

Anthony's organizational genius, strategic savvy, and grueling preparations in the months prior to each convention led her colleagues to acknowledge her as the principal leader of the NWSA. Yet she refused the presidency year after year, primarily because Cady Stanton presided so brilliantly at conventions. Cady Stanton was the polished, poised spokesperson who exuded the warmth and wit that Anthony believed she lacked. Anthony also relied on her partner's incisive analytical skills as a writer and rhetorician. Other prominent NWSA leaders included Matilda Joslyn Gage, Olympia Brown, Phoebe Couzins, Lillie Devereux Blake, May Wright Sewall, Sara Andrews Spencer, and Rachel Foster Avery.

In the early years of the NWSA, Anthony served as chairperson of the executive committee and as corresponding secretary.

Eventually the membership persuaded her to become vice president at large, a role that she created to encompass her gargantuan list of organizational tasks. As the years passed, Anthony assumed greater prominence on the convention platform—guiding, directing, and shaping the flow of the convention with the gavel close at hand. Since conventions were the lifeblood of the NWSA, preparations for each convention consumed months of incessant effort. Anthony, assisted by fellow suffragists, supervised the entire operation. She slaved over each detail to create stellar events that educated, energized, and invigorated beleaguered suffragists and that encouraged them to form strong suffragist networks in their home states.

During its 21-year history, the NWSA accomplished the following goals:

- Ensured that a national suffrage amendment was introduced in Congress each year beginning in 1878

Elizabeth Cady Stanton addresses a Senate Committee on the merits of the National Woman Suffrage Association's Sixteenth Amendment proposal. Wood engraving in **New York Daily Graphic,** *January 16, 1878.*

- Delivered thousands of petitions in favor of a woman suffrage amendment to Congress
- Arranged for NWSA members to lobby members of Congress annually and to testify on the state of the nationwide suffrage movement each winter
- Developed and disseminated position papers on suffrage issues and on other topics related to women's economic, legal, and political status
- Urged the major political parties to include a woman suffrage plank in their party platforms
- Presented the NWSA's *Declaration of the Rights of Woman* at the 1876 Centennial Exposition in Philadelphia
- Successfully lobbied Congress to appoint a Select Committee on Woman Suffrage, first organized in 1882
- Formed the International Council of Women, held in Washington, D.C., in 1888

During the mid- to late 1880s, a new generation of feminists, including NWSA members Rachel Foster Avery and Carrie Chapman Catt and AWSA member Alice Stone Blackwell, were convinced of the necessity of uniting the two suffrage groups' efforts. In 1890, after more than two years of negotiations, the NWSA and the AWSA merged to become the National American Woman Suffrage Association.

Susan B. Anthony was perhaps most proud of the NWSA's egalitarianism and its firm rejection of affiliation with any one political party, both of which she believed would lead to the woman suffrage movement's ultimate success. In a speech delivered in 1894, she reflected on these aspects of the NWSA's long history.

We have no political party. We have not been Democrats, we have not been Republicans, we have not cared what party anybody belonged to. We have never asked a question on this platform what anybody's religion was. All we have ever asked of anybody is simply, "Do you believe in perfect equality for women?" (Proceedings of the Twenty-sixth Annual Convention of NAWSA, February 15–20, 1894, as quoted in Sherr 1995, 89–90)

Related entries:
American Equal Rights Association
American Woman Suffrage Association
Anthony, Susan B.
Anthony/Cady Stanton Partnership
Avery, Rachel G. Foster
Blackwell, Henry Browne
Blake, Lillie Devereux
Brown, Olympia
Couzins, Phoebe Wilson
Davis, Paulina Kellogg Wright
Gage, Matilda Joslyn
Mott, Lucretia Coffin
National American Woman Suffrage Association
"New Departure" Strategy
Rose, Ernestine Louise Potowski
Sixteenth Amendment Campaign
Stanton, Elizabeth Cady
Stone, Lucy
Woman Suffrage Association of America
Woman Suffrage Movement
Wright, Martha Coffin

Suggestions for further reading:
Buhle, Mary Jo, and Paul Buhle, eds. 1978. *A Concise History of Woman Suffrage: Selections from the Classic Work of Stanton, Anthony, Gage, and Harper.* Urbana: University of Illinois Press.
DuBois, Ellen Carol, ed. 1992. *The Elizabeth Cady Stanton–Susan B. Anthony Reader: Correspondence, Writings, Speeches.* Boston: Northeastern University Press.
Sherr, Lynn. 1995. *Failure Is Impossible: Susan B. Anthony in Her Own Words.* New York: Times Books.

"New Departure" Strategy

The New Departure was the key constitutional strategy that Susan B. Anthony, Elizabeth Cady Stanton, and other National Woman Suffrage Association (NWSA) activists used to secure woman suffrage in

Photograph of Susan B. Anthony taken March 24, 1871.

waiting for them to be bestowed upon them (DuBois 1995, 86). Anthony, Cady Stanton, and NWSA leaders immediately capitalized on the New Departure theories. In 1870, in an address to a congressional committee, Cady Stanton used the New Departure ideas to back her arguments in support of a bill to enfranchise the women of the District of Columbia. Although this measure was never enacted, suffragists continued to test the New Departure theories. In January 1871, Victoria Claflin Woodhull expanded on Francis Minor's arguments to the House Judiciary Committee and later to the NWSA convention, demanding that Congress pass a declaratory act guaranteeing woman suffrage. And in 1872, the NWSA voted to accept a resolution declaring women's right to vote as established by the Fourteenth and Fifteenth Amendments, once again urging Congress to pass a declaratory act. These efforts also failed. In 1871 and in 1872, NWSA leaders encouraged and incited women throughout the country to exercise their right to vote in local political contests and in the 1872 national election. Although a few women had attempted to vote (and occasionally succeeded) even before the Minors outlined their constitutional approach, the NWSA's campaign broadcast the ideas nationwide. At least 150 women in many states voted in the 1872 presidential election, among them Anthony and the 14 women who voted with her in Rochester, New York, an act that led to Anthony's arrest and criminal trial (Harper 1899, 1:424).

The Minors tested the constitutionality of their arguments by bringing suit against a voting registrar who refused to allow Virginia Minor to vote in 1872. This official based his action on a Missouri state law that prohibited women from the franchise. When the lower courts decided against Virginia Minor, she appealed to the U.S. Supreme Court. In March 1875, in the case of *Minor v. Happersett,* the Supreme Court decided unanimously to uphold the lower courts' ruling, stating that although women are citizens of the United

the early to mid-1870s. The New Departure was based on the premise that women already possessed the right to the franchise, as guaranteed by the Fourteenth and Fifteenth Amendments. Francis and Virginia Minor of St. Louis, Missouri, were the first to delineate the legal arguments supporting the New Departure in 1869. Attorney Francis Minor interpreted the Fourteenth Amendment's first section as ensuring that all citizens are entitled to all the rights of citizenship, including the right to vote. He also argued that since the Fifteenth Amendment prohibits the states from blocking citizens' access to their rights, the states may not use the Fourteenth Amendment's second section (which directs the states to regulate suffrage) as the legal means to deny citizens their individual rights. Many states employed this practice to prevent women from voting (DuBois 1987, 852).

Anthony and Cady Stanton were exuberantly optimistic about the New Departure's potential to achieve national woman suffrage. Here at last was an opportunity for individual women to take definitive, bold action and seize their political rights instead of passively

States, it is the states that are responsible for defining "the privileges and immunities of citizens" (Harper 1899, 1:453–454). Only the states, therefore, have the power to extend the suffrage to citizens. This ruling marked the end of the New Departure strategy for suffragists. As a result of this Supreme Court decision, Anthony and Cady Stanton abandoned the New Departure to concentrate on their campaign for a federal suffrage amendment.

Related entries:
Fifteenth Amendment
Fourteenth Amendment
National Woman Suffrage Association
Sixteenth Amendment Campaign
The *United States v. Susan B. Anthony*
Woman Suffrage Movement
Woodhull, Victoria Claflin

Suggestions for future reading:
DuBois, Ellen Carol. 1987. "Outgrowing the Compact of the Fathers: Equal Rights, Woman Suffrage, and the United States Constitution, 1820–1878." *Journal of American History* 74, no. 3 (December):836–862.
———. 1995. "Taking the Law into Our Own Hands: Bradwell, Minor, and Suffrage Militance in the 1870s." In *One Woman, One Vote: Rediscovering the Woman Suffrage Movement*, ed. Marjorie Spruill Wheeler. Troutdale, Oreg.: New Sage Press.
Flexner, Eleanor. 1975. *Century of Struggle: The Woman's Rights Movement in the United States.* Cambridge, Mass.: Belknap Press of Harvard University Press.

New York Married Women's Property Law of 1860

For six years, from 1854 to 1860, Susan B. Anthony waged a massive campaign to persuade legislators to amend the Married Women's Property Law in New York state. It was her most significant contribution to the antebellum women's rights movement and is considered among the most important achievements of feminist activism in the mid-nineteenth century. She was leader, strategist, organizer, chief publicity specialist, lobbyist, principal lecturer, and relentless mover and shaker of the successful six-year campaign. No wonder social reformer and Unitarian minister William Henry Channing named her "the Napoleon of the women's rights movement."

As a young woman, Anthony was only too aware of the problems that arose when married women had no rights to their inherited property. For the first half of the nineteenth century, a married woman's property belonged to her husband. When the New York state legislature enacted the original Married Women's Property Law in 1848, Anthony's mother, Lucy Read Anthony, at long last received the title to their Rochester farm, property that had been purchased in 1845 with money she had inherited from her parents. To protect the farm from being claimed by her husband Daniel Anthony's creditors, Read Anthony's brother, Joshua Read, had superintended her inheritance, made the actual purchase of the farm, managed its payments, and held its title in his name until the law was enacted (Anthony 1954, 91; Harper 1899, 1:45–46).

Twelve years of activism preceded the passage of the 1848 property law. Both male and female reformers had been instrumental in the effort to secure its enactment. Ernestine Potowski Rose, Paulina Wright (Davis), and Elizabeth Cady Stanton, all of whom later became leaders in the women's rights movement and close colleagues of Anthony, were among the female activists who contributed to this campaign.

Although the 1848 law secured important legal rights for married women, they still did not have the right to ownership of their own wages and other income. When Anthony toured New York state in the summer and early fall of 1853 to check on temperance societies that she had helped form the previous summer, she was discouraged to discover that almost none had survived. In talking with the women she had helped organize, she found that they had disbanded because they did not possess the funds necessary to hire speakers, to engage a meeting hall, or to purchase or print their own literature. Upon reflecting on women's financial condition, particularly their lack of access to their own money, Anthony arrived at a conclusion that would transform her beliefs about women's most pressing needs.

> Thus as I passed from town to town was I made to feel the great evil of woman's entire dependency upon man, for the necessary means to aid on any & every reform movement. . . . Woman must have a *purse* of her own, & how can this be, so long as the *Wife* is denied the right to her *individual* & *joint* earnings. Reflections like these, caused me to see & really feel that there was no *true freedom* for woman without the possession of all her property rights, & that these rights could be obtained through *legislation* only, & so, the sooner the demand was made of the Legislature, the sooner would we be likely to obtain them. (1854 Diary, SBA-SL, in *Papers*)

Like most of Anthony's brainstorms, these "reflections" ignited a period of intensive strategizing followed by a course of incessant activism that redirected the focus of the women's rights movement. In November 1853, she began planning a woman's rights convention to address the property rights issue. She persuaded Elizabeth Cady Stanton to write a speech on a subject Anthony knew her friend had long been studying—women's lack of civil, legal, and political rights. Because Cady Stanton's domestic responsibilities made her homebound throughout the 1850s, Anthony gathered the facts she needed to complete the speech. Anthony then organized 60 women to circulate petitions. With them, she called on people to ask them to add their signatures to petitions demanding an expanded married women's property law and woman suffrage. The women collected a total of 10,000 signatures in a matter of

weeks, 6,000 for women's property rights and 4,000 for woman suffrage. The woman's rights convention held in Albany in February 1854 was enormously successful, and because of popular demand, the evening meetings were extended from a two-day engagement to two weeks.

True to her word, Cady Stanton delivered her address to the Senate chamber of the New York state legislature as well as to the convention. She had spent more than two months in its preparation and had consulted several legal experts to check her scholarship. Even though her domestic life prevented her from campaigning, she spared no effort in composing this manifesto. Anthony immediately recognized its value as a campaign tool and had 50,000 copies printed for distribution. After Cady Stanton delivered the speech, Potowski Rose and Channing presented the petitions to the legislators. To the disappointment of every activist involved, the legislators failed to respond to the petitions by the end of the legislative session.

Instead of letting discouragement slow her down, Anthony focused on all that had been gained. The increase in popular support and some serious press coverage had generated greater public awareness, a deeper understanding, and more discussion of the need for women's legal rights. In late 1854, she planned a one-woman canvass of 54 counties in New York state. Anthony embarked on her campaign on Christmas Day, 1854, and held her first meeting on December 26. For the next five months she was constantly on the road, holding a meeting in a different locale every other day.

Her meeting strategy demonstrated her intuitive knowledge of how to make an impact on the women and men of New York. In the afternoons, she met only with the women of a community, delivering half of the speech she would present in its entirety that evening. She then engaged the women in a discussion about their thoughts and needs concerning their property rights. In the course of the give-and-take, Anthony continually emphasized how the right to their own wages would help them with the economic problems they faced. She then closed the meeting by urging the women to return with their husbands for the evening meeting. Although the afternoon meetings were free, she charged 25 cents admission in the evening and sold all her women's property rights literature then. After the evening's speech, she responded to the audience's questions, thoughts, sarcasm, and harassment and, most important, exhorted them to sign the petition she circulated.

In this effort, as in all her women's rights, abolitionist, and suffrage campaigns, Anthony demonstrated her extraordinary ability to enlist the assistance of others in the work of the cause. This ability to draw women and men in—to spark their interest, impress them with the sound logic of her arguments and her fervent dedication, and convert some of them to embrace the cause—formed the basis of her success as a revolutionary. Nor did she seek solely to raise women's consciousness. Discussions with Lucy Stone persuaded Anthony that to effect a transformation of women's position in society, both women's *and* men's view of women and their roles would have to change (Kerr 1992, 99–100). Men and women needed to develop an expanded view of women's role—of women as active agents in the home and in society and as the directors of their own individual destinies.

In a letter to the editor of the *Woman's Advocate*, women's rights and abolitionist reformer Frances D. Gage, who briefly campaigned with Anthony, described how audiences often responded after attending an Anthony meeting and lecture.

"We have no sympathy whatever in your movement," they tell us, often, "but we are willing to give you a hearing." And then, with a patronizing smile,—"We can't do otherwise than to listen to the *ladies*." This is before our meetings. Afterward—"Why, you

have not uttered a sentiment that we do not fully endorse. That is just what we've been thinking for years. You are not as ultra [radical] as you need to be." And they sign the petition for right of suffrage, by the hundred. Now we are just as ultra, and more so, than five years ago. But they have imperceptibly had the sharp corners of their prejudices rubbed off. They have come to us, and honestly think we are going back to them. (The *Woman's Advocate*, January 26, 1856, in *Papers*)

Of course, not all responses were as salutary as those Gage described. In some communities, Anthony confronted total indifference. In others, she faced hostile, rowdy male audiences that she learned to handle by standing her ground and never retreating. After a run-in with a particularly difficult minister, Anthony wrote in a characteristic understatement, "Verily, I am embarked in an unpopular cause and must be content to row upstream" (Harper 1899, 1:120).

It is nearly impossible to fully conceive of the physical challenges her campaign presented. Winter weather in central, western, and upper New York state is legendary for its tremendous snowfall, frequent storms, and biting cold. Transportation in the mid-1850s was extremely difficult. With rail travel still in its infancy, trains were cold, uncomfortable, and unreliable. To reach the dozens of villages not connected by rail, she had to travel over the snow by sleigh, pung, and sledge in below-zero cold. Despite these hardships, New Yorkers were hardy, and Anthony frequently addressed large meetings. She attributed at least part of her popularity to the fact that many people turned out simply because they had never seen a woman speak in public before.

Although Anthony waged her campaign primarily by herself, she had the constant caring support and interest of her entire family, including her often-curmudgeonly uncle Joshua Read, who proudly defended her women's rights campaign to everyone in Canajoharie, New York. She had the nurturing friendship and helpful advice of her women friends Cady Stanton, Lucy Stone, Lydia Mott, and Antoinette Brown (Blackwell), as well as the comradeship of those who occasionally managed to help her lecture, such as Potowski Rose, Frances Gage, and Martha Coffin Wright. And she had the active assistance of many men, some of whom were abolitionist and temperance reformers, but many of whom were not.

Male legislators were impervious to Anthony's proof of popular support for an amended law. In the spring of 1856, after Anthony had been campaigning for more than three years, the chair of the Senate Judiciary Committee finally responded. The committee's report completely sidestepped every issue Anthony and Cady Stanton had presented, ignored the petitions signed by tens of thousands of their constituents, and dismissed the entire campaign with a sarcastic, demeaning humor. The chair's report stated:

> They [the legislators] have considered it [the petitions' demand] with . . . the experience married life has given them. Thus aided, they are enabled to state that the ladies always have the best place and choicest titbit at the table. They have the best seat in the cars, carriages and sleighs. . . . They have their choice on which side of the bed they will lie, front or back. . . . It has thus appeared . . . that if there is any inequality or oppression in the case, the gentlemen are the sufferers. (Harper 1899, 1:140–141)

Anthony was infuriated by the report but realized that this failure signified that there was still more work to be done. Over the next three years, she continued to tour, lecture, and gather signatures, all culminating in her six-week lobbying of legislators in Albany in the winter of 1860. Her efforts were successful, and on March 20, the day following Elizabeth Cady Stanton's address to the legislature, the bill was enacted. The amended property rights law, officially named "An Act Concerning the Rights and Liabilities of Husband and Wife," ensured that women gained the following rights: to own property separately from their husbands, to engage in business transactions, to manage their wages and other income, to sue and be sued, and to be joint guardian of their children with their husbands.

Anthony and Cady Stanton's triumph was short-lived, however. In 1862, when women's rights activists were intentionally inactive because of the Civil War, the New York legislature reversed many provisions of the 1860 law. In spite of this setback, the six-year campaign demonstrated strong public support for an expansion of legal rights for women. The law's enactment also established an important precedent that could not be reversed—that women as citizens were entitled to legal equality with men. The bill, and Anthony's six-year campaign to achieve it, also positively influenced similar property rights campaigns in many other states.

For Anthony, the success of this campaign proved that women, even when deprived of political rights, could use the right of petition to effect legislative changes that improved their lives. Large-scale petitioning was a strategy that Anthony and other women's rights and suffrage activists would continue to employ in the Woman's National Loyal League during the Civil War and in the woman suffrage campaigns of the postwar period.

Related entries:
Anthony, Susan B.
Anthony/Cady Stanton Partnership
Blackwell, Antoinette Louisa Brown
Davis, Paulina Kellogg Wright
Mott, Lydia
Rose, Ernestine Louise Potowski
Stanton, Elizabeth Cady
Stone, Lucy
Woman's National Loyal League
Woman's Rights Conventions
Women's Rights Movement

Suggestions for further reading:
Barry, Kathleen. 1988. *Susan B. Anthony: Biography of a Singular Feminist*. New York: New York University Press.
DuBois, Ellen Carol, ed. 1992. *The Elizabeth Cady Stanton–Susan B. Anthony Reader: Correspondence, Writings, Speeches*. Boston: Northeastern University Press.

The New York Tribune

Established by founding editor Horace Greeley in 1841, the *New York Tribune* was among the most widely circulated and influential newspapers of the mid-nineteenth-century press. It was one of the first "penny daily" newspapers, made possible by advances in paper manufacturing and printing technology, which enabled readers to keep abreast of all national political and social news, debate, and controversy for only a few cents a copy. Women's rights was one of the many causes Greeley championed in the *Tribune* during the decade preceding the Civil War.

Greeley's willingness to publish articles, speeches, notices, and editorials concerning women's rights and temperance issues and activities meshed with his conviction that the press has an obligation to inform readers about all sides of an issue. For women's rights activists, the *Tribune* and the other New York penny dailies afforded a unique opportunity to disseminate and popularize their views, ideology, activities, and agenda to a mass audience.

In the years immediately preceding her career as a social reformer, Susan B. Anthony relied on the *Tribune*'s weekly national edition to give her a balanced, informed picture of current political and social issues. But more important to her development as an activist, it was through the pages of the *Tribune* that Anthony was introduced to the women's rights movement. Articles, editorials, speeches, and letters to the editor acquainted her with the most influential leaders of the antislavery and women's rights movements, including William Lloyd Garrison, Lucretia Coffin Mott, Wendell Phillips, Abby Kelley Foster, Parker Pillsbury, and Lucy Stone.

Beginning in the late 1850s, Greeley began to discourage Anthony's and Elizabeth Cady Stanton's submissions of women's rights material, mostly because he wished to avoid association with their increasing radicalism. By 1860, he used the *Tribune* to oppose them on such women's rights issues as divorce and, by 1866, woman suffrage, a cause he had previously supported.

Related entries:
Greeley, Horace
Temperance
Women's Rights Movement

Suggestions for further reading:
Bovée, Warren G. 1986. "Horace Greeley and Social Responsibility." *Journalism Quarterly* 63, no. 2 (summer 1986):251–259.
Hoffert, Sylvia D. 1993. "New York City's Penny Press and the Issue of Woman's Rights, 1848–1860." *Journalism Quarterly* 70, no. 3 (autumn 1993):656–665.
———. 1995. *When Hens Crow: The Women's Rights Movement in Antebellum America*. Bloomington: Indiana University Press.

Nineteenth Amendment

See **Sixteenth Amendment Campaign; Woman Suffrage Movement**

The North Star

The *North Star*, established by Frederick Douglass in Rochester, New York, in December 1847, was one of a number of northern abolitionist newspapers published during the antebellum period. The *North Star* distinguished itself from William Lloyd Garrison's *The Liberator* and the American Anti-Slavery Society's the *National Anti-Slavery Standard* in its rousing endorsement of political solutions to slavery. *The Liberator* and the *Standard* both held to the Garrisonian view that attempts to abolish slavery by political means would necessitate compromise on the slavery issue, an outcome radical Garrisonians could not accept.

Susan B. Anthony, although committed to the Garrisonian principle of "No Compromise with Slaveholders," understood the advantage of exploiting all media outlets to inform the public about the social reforms she supported, even if she did not always agree with the publisher's opinions. Douglass, an Anthony family friend and a stalwart supporter of women's rights and woman suffrage, regularly published news items and calls for upcoming temperance and woman's rights conventions that Anthony supplied, not only to the *North Star* but to many other newspapers and journals. In 1851, Douglass changed the name of his newspaper to *Frederick Douglass's Paper,* which he continued to publish until 1863.

Related entries:
Abolitionist Movement
American Anti-Slavery Society
Douglass, Frederick
Garrison, William Lloyd
The Liberator

Suggestions for further reading:
Huggins, Nathan Irvin. 1980. *Slave and Citizen: The Life of Frederick Douglass.* Boston: Little Brown.
McFeely, William S. 1991. *Frederick Douglass.* New York: W. W. Norton.

P

Panic of 1837

The 1830s were years of prosperity for the Anthony family in Battenville, New York. Daniel Anthony's textile mills and his factory were prospering beyond his original expectations. In fact, the entire United States was reaping the benefits of an economic boom. As factories multiplied, trade continued to increase. But with the good times came the first signs of impending economic disaster—overtrading, overinvestment, and the overproduction of cotton. In 1836, President Andrew Jackson, who believed that banks were the enemies of the average citizen, unwittingly precipitated a national crisis when he interfered with the rechartering of the Bank of the United States. When the national bank closed, the nation's currency was thrown into chaos, the economy collapsed, and the United States entered a long period of depression—from 1838 to 1843.

Beginning in February 1838, Susan B. Anthony and her older sister, Guelma Penn Anthony, both students at Deborah Moulson's Quaker female seminary outside Philadelphia, learned that most of their father's business concerns had failed and that he faced bankruptcy. When they finished the term in May, Susan and Guelma returned home and discovered that the family was going to lose their beloved Battenville home. Susan was horrified to find her parents and siblings preparing an inventory of their household and personal belongings so that they could be put up for auction. At that point, Susan's uncle Joshua Read, her mother's brother, stepped in. Before the auction, he bought all the furniture and other goods that the Anthony family most wished to save. They would lose their home, but at least, thanks to Uncle Joshua, they would salvage their most treasured belongings.

In March 1839, the family moved from their Battenville home into a hotel they rented in Hardscrabble, 2 miles down the Battenkill River. To pay the rent and feed the family, they took in boarders and overnight guests. Susan attended a local school in the winter of 1839 but, upon the term's conclusion, assumed a teaching position at Eunice Kenyon's Quaker boarding school in New Rochelle, New York, to help support herself and her family.

Despite his other business losses, Daniel Anthony tried to hang on to his satinet factory and his gristmill in Hardscrabble. But no matter how hard he tried to remain in business, the depression prevented him from making a comeback in manufacturing. In 1845, he moved his family to a farm in Rochester, New York, where he vowed to make a living by farming.

Related entries:
Anthony, Daniel
Anthony, Susan B.
McLean, Guelma Penn Anthony
Read, Joshua

Suggestions for further reading:
Barry, Kathleen. 1988. *Susan B. Anthony: Biography of a Singular Feminist.* New York: New York University Press.
Lutz, Alma. 1959. *Susan B. Anthony: Rebel, Crusader, Humanitarian.* Boston: Beacon Press.

Phillips, Wendell (1811–1884)

Susan B. Anthony's relationship with Wendell Phillips was among the deepest and most complex of all her friendships with male reformers. From the early 1850s until his death in 1884, Phillips played an important role in Anthony's personal and professional life. He was Anthony's mentor, ally, and beloved leader in the world of reformers. A Garrisonian abolitionist, women's rights activist, and social reformer, Phillips's upper-class Boston Brahmin origins made him an unlikely companion for Anthony, the unsophisticated middle-class Quaker. Despite their different backgrounds, they shared the same fervid, uncompromising determination to remold society on principles of justice and equality. Yet unlike Anthony's close personal friendship with abolitionist and women's rights activist Parker Pillsbury, her relationship with Phillips was not one between equals. As a member of William Lloyd Garrison's inner circle of elite Boston reformers, Phillips's near-celebrity status elevated him above Anthony and the majority of women abolitionists and women's rights reformers.

Phillips became involved in antislavery reform in 1837 when he delivered a speech protesting the murder of the abolitionist editor Elijah Lovejoy. From that time on, he devoted himself full-time to abolition, becoming a powerful member and leader of the American Anti-Slavery Society (AASS) and a close associate of Garrison. A passionate orator, he was renowned for his intelligent and insightful, yet never pompous eloquence.

Phillips was one of the few male reformers who was very active in the antebellum women's rights movement. He attended many of the national, state, and local woman's rights conventions throughout the 1850s. He also spoke frequently on women's rights on the social reform lecture circuit. During the 1850s, he wholeheartedly supported legal, social, economic, and political equality for women. At the Second National Woman's Rights Convention held in Worcester, Massachusetts, in October 1851, he noted the significance of the women's rights movement: "I rejoice to see so large an audience gathered to consider this momentous subject, the most magnificent reform that has yet been launched upon the world. It is the first organized protest against the injustice which has brooded over the character and the destiny of one-half of the human race" (*HWS*, 1:227).

By the time Anthony became actively involved in the women's rights movement in 1852, she was already well acquainted with Phillips and admired him almost as much as she did Garrison. Anthony's enlistment as an abolitionist agent for the AASS in 1856 brought her into closer contact with Phillips. Her intrepid management of abolitionist campaigns in New York state, including her staunch refusal to be intimidated by hostile crowds during the 1861 "winter of mobs," further solidified their relationship and earned her his respect.

In May 1860, at the Tenth National Woman's Rights Convention in New York City, Phillips stunned Anthony and Elizabeth Cady Stanton when he strenuously objected to their resolutions concerning divorce reform. He insisted that their demands not only be rejected but that they be expunged from the record, a radical departure from normal convention proceedings. As he explained, a woman's rights convention had no business discussing marriage and divorce because "this Convention, if I understand it, assembles to discuss the laws that rest unequally upon women, not those that rest equally upon men and women" (*HWS*, 1:732).

Anthony immediately responded. After expressing the wish that Phillips withdraw his motion to have the resolutions deleted, she expressed her disagreement.

> Marriage has ever been a one-sided matter, resting most unequally upon the sexes. By it, man gains all— woman loses all . . . the discussion is perfectly in order, since nearly all the wrongs of which we complain grow out of the inequality, the injustice of the marriage laws, that rob the wife of the right to herself and her children— that make her the slave of the man she marries. (*HWS*, 1:735)

The divorce resolutions remained on the record, but Anthony and Cady Stanton left the convention troubled and bewildered as they groped for the meaning behind Phillips's uncharacteristic behavior. He was far too important to their women's rights work for them to shrug off his rejection. As Cady Stanton wrote later, Phillips's "words, tone, and manner came down on me like a clap of thunder" (Stanton and Blatch 1922, 2:82). Since he had supported all of their previous claims to rights for women, there had been no reason to expect that that support would not continue.

After the convention, Phillips solidified his position on the divorce issue in a letter to Anthony: "of course it is no right & no wish of mine to dictate what shall be in our platform. . . . whenever it is understood that the platform will include these questions, I shall have nothing to do with the Convention" (WP to SBA, June 5, 1860, SBA-URL, in *Papers*). But despite his own convictions, he eventually recognized Anthony and Cady Stanton's right to agitate the divorce issue. Three months after the convention, when Anthony wrote him to request money from the Hovey Fund to finance the publication of the divorce resolutions, he sent it with a genial letter (Harper 1899, 1:196).

Although many explanations have been suggested for Phillips's departure from his unquestioned support of women's rights, it is clear that by 1860 both Phillips and Garrison were increasingly chafing at Anthony and Cady Stanton's advancing radicalism and their growing power in the movement. The two men's censure of the divorce question and, seven months later, their heavy-handed attempts to curb Anthony's efforts to rescue a woman from an abusive husband indicate that their support of women's rights was not boundless and their vision of women's place in society did not jibe completely with that of Anthony and Cady Stanton (*see* Garrison, William Lloyd). As several historians have suggested, the conflicts of 1860 foreshadowed the defection of men from the women's rights movement after the Civil War.

The outbreak of war and the cessation of all women's rights activities cooled the internal conflicts in the women's rights movement. By 1863, Anthony and Cady Stanton had resumed positive, friendly working relations with Phillips. As Garrisonian abolitionists, they united with him to protest the projected postwar reconstruction policies of President Abraham Lincoln. Phillips strongly supported their Woman's National Loyal League (WNLL), and Anthony and Cady Stanton stood firmly behind his campaign for 1864 presidential candidate John C. Frémont.

In 1865, at the end of the Civil War, Anthony and Cady Stanton championed Phillips's move to assume the leadership of the AASS when Garrison stepped down. They lobbied among their abolitionist colleagues, urging them to back Phillips. "All through this struggle," Anthony wrote, "he has stood up against the tide, one of the few to hold the nation to its vital work . . . absolute justice and equality for the black man" (Harper 1899, 1:245).

Because of the closeness of Anthony and Cady Stanton's relationship with Phillips during the Civil War, the two women entered the postwar years feeling assured of his support for women's rights, particularly woman suffrage. Yet in May 1865, he announced that his reform interests were now

Wendell Phillips with Susan B. Anthony, seated, and an unnamed woman, circa 1860.

exclusively focused on achieving rights for African-American men. "While I could continue, just as heretofore, arguing for woman's rights, just as I do for temperance every day, still I would not mix the movements. . . . I think such mixture would lose for the negro far more than we should gain for the woman." Adding to Cady Stanton and Anthony's dismay, he continued, "I am now engaged in abolishing slavery in a land where abolition of slavery means conferring or recognizing citizenship, and where citizenship supposes the ballot for all men" (Stanton and Blatch 1922, 2:105).

As the new AASS leader in a chaotic, postwar world of shifting political allegiances, Phillips became immersed in exploring political avenues to achieve his reform goals, a huge departure for a former Garrisonian. As Phillips aligned the AASS with Radical Republicans in Congress, women's rights and woman suffrage became marginal, expendable issues that could not be permitted to interfere with the mission to achieve full equality for African-American males.

Although Phillips was convinced that turning away from women's rights and woman suffrage was the only feasible course of action, he had misgivings about letting Anthony and Cady Stanton down. In late 1865 and 1866, in letter after letter Anthony pressed him to continue his past support of woman suffrage. Of course, Anthony knew that he believed that this was the "negro's hour," but she believed that if she kept trying, she would be able to convince him to support universal suffrage. Phillips was too powerful and too important to the future of her cause to let him go easily. He was not to be swayed from his course, but instead of saying so directly, he evaded Anthony and did not confront the issue. His inability to say no to Anthony allowed her to maintain a false optimism about his position for many months and fueled the mutual misunderstandings that characterized their relationship at this time. Phillips's ambivalence and mystifying lack of clarity are evident in this letter to Cady Stanton, which was written in response to a letter Anthony had written him.

> I'm fully willing to ask for women's vote *now* & will never *so* ask for negro voting as to put one single obstacle in the way of *her* [women] getting it. But I shall not *do much* or go out of my way or spend money or time on it *largely*, deeming the old rule of "one thing at a time" wise—& this time is the negro's. (WP to ECS, January 14, 1866, WP-SL, in *Papers*)

Although Phillips may have hoped that this letter would make clear once and for all why he could not participate in the drive for woman suffrage, what is most succinct is his confusion and lack of resolve about his decision to withdraw from the woman suffrage struggle. No wonder Anthony and Cady Stanton were befuddled!

Phillips never became actively involved in the American Equal Rights Association (AERA), as Anthony and Cady Stanton had hoped. He was so consumed by his agitation for African-American rights that he did not participate in many of the battles that raged among abolitionists in the AERA. He frustrated Anthony, Cady Stanton, and Parker Pillsbury by refusing to continue publishing free of charge their notices and articles in the *National Anti-Slavery Standard (NASS)*, by criticizing them for campaigning for woman suffrage in Kansas, and by refusing them AASS money for the woman suffrage cause. As time passed, he became more outspoken about his revised view of women's rights.

At the Eleventh National Woman's Rights Convention in May 1866, he said that despite his support of women's rights, he did not find woman suffrage important enough to be included on an amendment. He then shocked Anthony, Cady Stanton, and Pillsbury by claiming that women already had significant power in society, particularly when compared with the absolutely powerless African Americans (Stewart 1986, 282). After turning his back on their mission, he surprised them by being deeply hurt when they refused to support him in his all-out campaign for the Fifteenth Amendment (Bartlett 1961, 377). He retaliated by attacking them repeatedly in the *NASS* in the summer of 1869: "The Women's Rights movement is essentially a selfish one; not disinterested as the Anti-Slavery cause was. It is women contending for their own rights; the Abolitionists toiled for the rights of others" ("The Fifteenth Amendment," *National Anti-Slavery Standard*, July 3, 1869). Of course, Phillips's holier-than-thou analysis neglected to consider Anthony and Cady Stanton's years of commitment to abolitionism. Not only that, the "Abolitionists" whom he described as being so self-sacrificing were primarily male and already possessed all their rights.

When the women's rights movement split in 1869, Phillips sided with the New England Republican AERA members who formed the American Woman Suffrage Association (AWSA). Following ratification of the Fifteenth Amendment and the disbanding of the AASS in 1870, Phillips turned his attention toward woman suffrage and other reforms. As the years passed, he and Anthony reconnected, although never again as closely as they had prior to Reconstruction. Even so, Anthony maintained the highest regard for Phillips throughout the rest of her life. The painful conflicts of the Reconstruction era did not diminish her overall respect and admiration for him. After his death in February 1884, Anthony was quoted as saying:

> Wendell Phillips was not an aristocrat. . . . He was a democrat in all that the fullest sense of the word implied. When a woman spoke to him she was always made to feel that he believed her to be his equal. She might herself think differently, but she would never get such an idea from Wendell Phillips. (*Cleveland Leader*, March 1, 1884, SBA Scrapbooks, LCRBD, in *Papers*)

Related entries:
Abolitionist Movement
American Anti-Slavery Society
American Equal Rights Association
Civil War
Fifteenth Amendment
Garrison, William Lloyd
Reconstruction
Thirteenth Amendment
Woman's National Loyal League
Woman's Rights Conventions
Women's Rights Movement

Suggestions for further reading:
Kimmel, Michael S., and Thomas E. Mosmiller, eds. 1992. *Against the Tide: Pro-Feminist Men in the United States, 1776–1990: A Documentary History.* Boston: Beacon Press.
Lutz, Alma. 1959. *Susan B. Anthony: Rebel, Crusader, Humanitarian.* Boston: Beacon Press.
Stewart, James Brewer. 1986. *Wendell Phillips: Liberty's Hero.* Baton Rouge: Louisiana State University Press.

Pillsbury, Parker (1809–1898)

*P*arker Pillsbury was Susan B. Anthony's closest male colleague, friend, and kindred spirit. From the early 1850s until Pillsbury's death in 1898, they remained in close contact, inspiring and encouraging each other in the sometimes overwhelming struggles that they faced in abolitionist and women's rights reform. Like many of his fellow Garrisonian abolitionists, Pillsbury not only devoted himself to the antislavery cause but was also engrossed in the work of other reform movements, including women's rights, woman suffrage, temperance, peace, and political reform.

From 1840 until 1865, Pillsbury was consumed by his travels as lecture agent for the New Hampshire, Massachusetts, and American Anti-Slavery Societies (AASS). Pillsbury's radical antislavery doctrine and his ferocious, fire-breathing oratory regularly ignited controversy both inside and outside abolitionist circles, yet the AASS leadership trusted his reports from the field and always listened carefully to his views on the mood and mind-set of the public (Robertson 1994, 131, 135, 152).

Pillsbury's early years were spent on his family's New Hampshire farm. Although his agrarian background and lack of educational opportunities prevented him from being accepted into William Lloyd Garrison and Wendell Phillips's inner circle of urban intellectuals, he was the ideal match for Anthony's simple, down-to-earth ways.

Despite Pillsbury's absorption in abolitionist reform, he was devoted to the women's rights movement. In the 1850s, he attended woman's rights conventions whenever his travel schedule permitted and wrote numerous articles supporting women's rights. Unlike many men involved in the movement, Pillsbury unstintingly and unreservedly supported complete gender equality in all areas of society. He was also unusual in that he practiced his views on women's equality in his daily life. He was known for regularly validating and publicizing the strengths of his fellow women reformers. In his working relationships with Susan B. Anthony and other women activists, he treated women as his equals to an extent not realized by other male activists (Robertson 1994, 257).

Pillsbury's friendship with Anthony was both personal and professional. He admired Anthony's intensity and indefatigable commitment to reform, a respect he sometimes communicated to her by teasing her about her "idleness." They both shared a love of poetry and literature; he once gave her a volume of Ralph Waldo Emerson's poetry. When Anthony's father died in 1862, Pillsbury's letter of condolence indicates that he was one of the few people who fully understood all that her father had meant to her. "You must be stricken sore indeed in the loss of your constant helper in the great mission to which you are devoted, your counselor, your consoler, your all that man could be, besides the endearing relation of father. What or who can supply the loss?" (Harper 1899, 1:224).

Although a compassionate friend, he was not above goading her to action when he believed she was needlessly absent from the reformers' fray. In 1865, when Anthony was working in Kansas, he chided her, "Why have you deserted the field of action at a time like this, at an hour unparalleled in almost twenty centuries? . . . wherever you are, I know you will not be idle; but New York is to revise her constitution next year, and, if you are absent, who is to make the plea for woman?" (Harper 1899, 1:244).

As coeditor of *The Revolution* from 1868 until the summer of 1869, he also understood that her decision to terminate publication in 1870 was a huge loss, much greater than most people realized. His letter of consolation reveals that he had deep insight into the reasons for the newspaper's failure that troubled her most. He knew, if even she didn't, that *The Revolution*'s financial failings were not solely her burden.

No one could do better than you have done. If any complain, ask them what they did to help you carry the paper. Suffrage is growing with the oaks. The whirling spheres will usher in the day of its triumph at just the right time, but your full meed of praise will have to be sung over your grave. (Harper 1899, 1:363)

For her part, Anthony knew that she could depend on Pillsbury to back her completely and uncomplainingly, whenever humanly feasible. He braved the mobs with her in the late 1850s when she was the AASS agent for New York state. When Anthony planned a memorial for John Brown following his execution in 1859, Pillsbury was the only abolitionist who would agree to stand up and speak with her. But it was during the early years of Reconstruction (1865–1870) that Pillsbury proved his undivided, supreme loyalty to Anthony and to women's rights.

The Reconstruction era was as trying a time for Pillsbury as it was for Anthony, Elizabeth Cady Stanton, and other ardent women's rights activists. In his unswerving commitment to women's rights after the Civil War, Pillsbury became completely and permanently

Parker Pillsbury

estranged from his former abolitionist co-workers. After he abandoned AASS president Wendell Phillips's campaigns for African-American rights through the Fourteenth and Fifteenth Amendments, his ties with abolitionism were completely severed. He was wholly committed to women's rights during Reconstruction, lecturing incessantly for universal suffrage as part of the AERA campaign to amend the New York state constitution. In fact, during Reconstruction he lectured on behalf of women's rights more than any other abolitionist (Robertson 1994, 249). He suffered, however, from the ostracism of former AASS colleagues. "My Boston correspondence has long since ceased," he wrote. "It may be fault of my own, but I could not help it. I saw an opportunity to strike a blow for woman, and to resist the conviction I felt, was not possible" (PP to Ellen Wright Garrison, May 1, 1869, GF-SSC).

After 1870, Pillsbury ceased to focus solely on women's rights. He remained loyal to the woman suffrage movement but also devoted time to other reforms. Anthony repeatedly entreated him to write a volume of his recollections of the Garrisonian abolitionist movement and "those times that tried men's

& women's souls." Although she confided to Garrison's son William Lloyd Garrison, Jr., that she feared Pillsbury would never fulfill this wish, in 1883, Pillsbury published *Acts of the Antislavery Apostles*, his memoir of the Garrisonian movement.

Very late in life, Pillsbury developed a severe paralysis that limited him and that he found difficult to accept. In a letter to Anthony in 1895, he wrote, "I am very glad to have done my very best when at my best for Woman—her Wrongs, Rights and Responsibilities—and in so doing, I have had my sufficient reward. The approval of posterity, or the estimate of the world of such service, is to me, of small account" (PP to SBA, October 9, 1895, ECS-LCMD, in *Papers*).

Related entries:
Abolitionist Movement
American Anti-Slavery Society
American Equal Rights Association
Brown, John
Fifteenth Amendment
Garrison, William Lloyd
Phillips, Wendell
Reconstruction
The Revolution
Woman's Rights Conventions
Women's Rights Movement

Suggestions for further reading:
Harper, Ida Husted. 1899, 1908. *The Life and Work of Susan B. Anthony*. 3 vols. Indianapolis: Bowen-Merrill (vols. 1 and 2) and Hollenbeck Press (vol. 3).
Oatman, Eric F. 1985. "Pillsbury, Parker." In *American Reformers*, ed. Alden Whitman. New York: H. W. Wilson.
Robertson, Stacey Marie. 1994. *Parker Pillsbury, Antislavery Apostle: Gender and Religion in Nineteenth-Century U.S. Radicalism*. Ph.D. dissertation, University of California at Santa Barbara.

Pomeroy, Samuel Clarke (1816–1891)

Samuel Clarke Pomeroy served as U.S. senator from Kansas from 1861 to 1873. Born in Massachusetts, Pomeroy emigrated to Kansas in 1854 as financial agent for the New England Emigrant Aid Company. He was elected to the U.S. Senate as a Republican in 1861, when Kansas was admitted to the union. He strongly supported Susan B. Anthony, Lucy Stone, and other women's rights activists during their campaign to gain woman suffrage in Kansas in 1867; was a *Revolution* subscriber; and, in 1868, was the first senator to propose a Sixteenth Amendment that would guarantee woman suffrage. With George Washington Julian, Republican member of Congress from Indiana, Pomeroy proposed a revised version of the Fifteenth Amendment that included woman suffrage, but his fellow senators rejected the plan. He also addressed the first woman suffrage convention in Washington, D.C., the January 1869 meeting of the Woman Suffrage Association of America.

Related entries:
Julian, George Washington
The Revolution
Sixteenth Amendment Campaign
Woman Suffrage Association of America
Woman Suffrage Movement

Suggestions for further reading:
DAB, 8:4–55.
HWS, 2:151, 324–325, 419–420.

Post, Amy Kirby (1802–1889)

Amy Kirby Post, Hicksite Quaker, abolitionist, women's rights reformer, suffragist, and leading Rochester humanitarian, was an important friend of Susan B. Anthony and the entire Anthony family from the clan's first days in Rochester, New York. Kirby Post was born on Long Island, New York, and moved to Rochester in 1836, seven years after marrying her husband Isaac Post, also a Hicksite. Kirby Post was a vital leader in the powerful network of women reformers who were an important source of inspiration and strength to Anthony throughout her career.

The Posts became zealous abolitionists after their move to Rochester. They were among the founders of the Western New York Anti-Slavery Society, an extraordinarily active and radical abolitionist organization. In the early years of her activism, Kirby Post was primarily involved in raising funds for the abolitionist cause by planning and directing antislavery fairs and bazaars. The Rochester Quaker meeting frowned upon the Posts' active engagement in abolitionist reform but most openly objected to Kirby Post's involvement, primarily because she was a woman. In 1845, the Posts and a number of other abolitionist Quakers withdrew from the Rochester Meeting to devote their attention fully to their abolitionist activities and connections.

The Posts' home was a center of abolitionist fervor. The couple frequently hosted touring abolitionist agents and lecturers, including Frederick Douglass, William Lloyd Garrison, Wendell Phillips, Abby Kelley Foster and Stephen Symonds Foster, Parker Pillsbury, and Lucretia Coffin Mott. The Posts were leaders in Rochester's Underground Railroad, and their house was a major station on the fugitive slaves' escape route to Canada.

In the summer of 1848, Kirby Post traveled to Seneca Falls, New York, to attend the first woman's rights convention. She signed the convention's *Declaration of Sentiments* and was instrumental in organizing the Rochester woman's rights convention that convened two weeks later. When Elizabeth Cady Stanton and Coffin Mott protested the Rochester women's choice to have a woman (Abigail Bush) preside over the convention, Post persuaded them that if women were able to organize a convention to assert and debate their rights, then a woman was certainly competent enough to lead a group of women wishing to press those demands.

The 1850s proved to be the zenith of Kirby Post's decades of radical reform. In addition to working energetically to advance women's political, social, and economic rights, she maintained her commitment to abolitionism, became deeply involved in spiritualism, supported the temperance movement, protested capital punishment, and traveled to abolitionist and woman's rights conventions throughout the East and West. However, despite her widespread travel, Rochester and western New York state remained the focus of her activism.

During the Civil War, Kirby Post was a hardworking member of Susan B. Anthony and Cady Stanton's Woman's National Loyal League (WNLL). She also concerned herself with the plight of the contraband slaves who escaped from bondage and gained their freedom during the war years. She assisted them by producing and organizing shipments of goods to be transported to the contraband camps. After the war, she joined wholeheartedly in the efforts of women's rights activists, including Anthony and Cady Stanton, to work toward universal suffrage through the local Rochester chapter of the American Equal Rights Association (AERA). When Anthony and Cady Stanton's efforts to forward woman suffrage through the AERA proved futile, Kirby Post supported them in the formation of the National Woman Suffrage Association (NWSA) in 1869.

In early November 1872, at the age of 70, Kirby Post joined Anthony and 50 Rochester women in registering to vote in the upcoming presidential election. Although Kirby Post was prevented from casting a ballot like most of those who registered (15 women actually voted), she never relinquished her devotion to the cause of woman suffrage. Amy Kirby Post's lifelong commitment to humanitarian reform, although never executed on the national stage, remains a sterling example of the efforts of thousands of nineteenth-century women who, within their own communities, sacrificed their time and energies to improve society.

Related entries
Anthony, Susan B.
Rochester, New York
Underground Railroad

Suggestions for further reading:
Anthony, Katharine. 1954. *Susan B. Anthony: Her Personal History and Her Era.* Garden City, N.Y.: Doubleday.
Hewitt, Nancy A. 1984a. "Amy Kirby Post." *The University of Rochester Library Bulletin* 37:4–21.
———. 1984b. *Women's Activism and Social Change: Rochester, New York, 1822–1872.* Ithaca, N.Y.: Cornell University Press.
Huth, Mary M. 1995. *Upstate New York and the Women's Rights Movement.* Online. University of Rochester Library. Available at http://www.lib.rochester.edu/rbk/women/women.htm.

Purvis, Robert (1810–1898)

Robert Purvis, one of Susan B. Anthony's most loyal male colleagues, was a wealthy African-American abolitionist and social reformer. The grandson of a slave, he was a founding member of the American Anti-Slavery Society (AASS) and of its auxiliary, the Pennsylvania Anti-Slavery Society, serving as president of the latter for five years. Purvis was most active in antislavery and pro–African-American social reform organizations centered in Philadelphia. Yet his involvement in the women's rights movement crossed those borders, and it was through this reform movement that he forged a lifelong bond with Anthony, who once called Purvis "the noblest Roman of them all."

It was during the political chaos of the late 1860s that Purvis proved his devotion to the cause of women's rights. When the majority of male abolitionists discontinued their support of woman suffrage to obtain the ballot for freed African-American males, Purvis refused to fall in line with them. In 1866, he became involved in the American Equal Rights Association (AERA). With Charles Lenox Remond, Parker Pillsbury, Samuel Joseph May, and others, he persisted in demanding universal suffrage. He declared that he could not support the Fourteenth Amendment (and later the Fifteenth Amendment) if, in the course of securing his own rights, his daughter's were excluded (Barry 1988, 287).

I am an anti-slavery man because I hate tyranny and in my nature revolt against oppression, whatever its form or character. . . . With what grace could I ask the women of this country to labor for my enfranchisement, and at the same time be unwilling to put forth a hand to remove the tyranny, in some respects greater, to which they are subjected? (Harper 1899, 1:258)

In addition to upholding woman suffrage, Purvis's stance communicated his increasing alienation from Wendell Phillips and the rest of his white male colleagues who so eagerly supported the Republican Party, which, according to Purvis, fancied itself as "the white man's party" (Sterling 1991, 323).

Following the split of the AERA into two rival factions in 1869, Purvis increasingly distanced himself from public life. He and Anthony remained in contact and, through the 1870s and 1880s, occasionally met while attending the funerals of their abolitionist comrades.

Related entries:
Abolitionist Movement
American Anti-Slavery Society
American Equal Rights Association
Fifteenth Amendment
Fourteenth Amendment
Reconstruction
Seneca Falls Convention of 1848
Woman's Rights Conventions
Women's Rights Movement

Suggestions for further reading:
Quarles, Benjamin. 1982. "Robert Purvis, Sr." In *Dictionary of American Negro Biography*, ed. Rayford W. Logan and Michael R. Winston. New York: W. W. Norton, pp. 508–510.
Ripley, C. Peter, ed. 1993. *Witness to Freedom: African American Voices on Race, Slavery, and Emancipation*. Chapel Hill: University of North Carolina Press.

Quakerism (Society of Friends)

By the time Susan B. Anthony was born in 1820, Quakers had been living in the United States for more than 150 years. English Quakers settled first in the colonies of New Jersey, Pennsylvania, Rhode Island, and North Carolina, suffering intense persecution in the American colonies. The Quakers differed from other Protestant sects because of their belief in the authority of the Inner Light, a divine presence that exists within each person regardless of gender or race. Unlike most Protestant denominations, which depend on a specially trained elite of male clergy to direct worshippers, the Quakers believe that all people have the ability and the potential to understand and communicate the word of God.

The Quakers were also unique because they permitted women to participate in church affairs—to speak at Quaker meetings, to pursue the ministry, and to voice their opinions about church government. Since the Quaker view maintained that the Inner Light resided within each person regardless of gender, they did not strictly interpret biblical scriptures that restricted or forbade women's public activity as most Protestant sects did.

It is not surprising, then, that Quaker women, who were already accustomed to speaking and acting publicly within the Quaker faith, played a vital, central role in antislavery, women's rights, woman suffrage,

temperance, and other nineteenth-century social reforms. Lucretia Coffin Mott, Angelina and Sarah Grimké, and Abby Kelley Foster were a few of the early Quaker feminists who inspired Susan B. Anthony to pursue a career as a reformer. Because of her Quaker upbringing, Anthony grew up never questioning her right to voice her opinions or her equal opportunity to assume an active public role in society.

The Anthony family had been Quakers for generations. Daniel Anthony, Susan's father, was descended from Abraham Anthony and Alice Wodell, who were among the first converts to Quakerism in Rhode Island in the late 1650s (Anthony 1954, 3). When Daniel Anthony married Lucy Read Anthony, a Baptist, in 1817, the Quaker elders censured him for "marrying out of meeting," but due to his family's stature in the community, he was dealt with leniently and was permitted to retain his membership. Read Anthony never became a Quaker, but she consented to having her children raised according to Quaker beliefs and customs.

When young Susan B. Anthony was nearly eight years old, U.S. Quakers divided into two factions as a result of the Great Separation of 1827. Those Quakers who believed in the liberal ideas of Elias Hicks, particularly his right to freely express his personal beliefs within the faith, became known as Hicksites or Hicksite Quakers. Quakers who believed in the strict authority of biblical scriptures became known as Orthodox Quakers. Like the majority of U.S. Quakers, Daniel Anthony, always a liberal freethinker, sided with the Hicksite Quakers.

Throughout her life, Susan B. Anthony considered herself first and foremost a Quaker. Yet ideologically and spiritually, she did not rigidly adhere to Quakerism. In the early 1850s, when the Rochester Society of Friends refused to condone anti-slavery reform, the Anthony family and their reform-oriented Hicksite neighbors left the Rochester Meeting, eventually attending services at a Unitarian church in Rochester. For most of her adult life, Anthony was attracted to the Unitarian commitment to social reform and activism, which stressed humanistic concerns and individual responsibility. During the 1850s, Anthony maintained contact with liberal Quakers through the reform-oriented Quaker groups known as the Congregational Friends, the Progressive Friends, and the Friends of Human Progress.

As far as Anthony's own personal religious views were concerned, she had no interest in formal theological issues but received inspiration from religious groups (Quakers and Unitarians) that emphasized the divine in all human beings as well as the individual's responsibility to improve society. She once commented on her religious orientation: "I pray every single second of my life; not on my knees but with my work. . . . Work and worship are one with me" ("Susan B. Anthony Lectures and Reminiscences," SBA-SSC, as quoted in Barry 1988, 96). Despite Anthony's ecumenical religious views, she retained her membership in the Rochester Society of Friends throughout her life.

Related entries:
Abolitionist Movement
Anthony, Daniel
Anthony, Lucy Read
Anthony, Susan B.
Foster, Abby Kelley
Mott, Lucretia Coffin

Suggestions for further reading:
Anthony, Katharine. 1954. *Susan B. Anthony: Her Personal History and Her Era.* Garden City, N.Y.: Doubleday.
Bacon, Margaret Hope. 1985. *The Quiet Rebels: The Story of the Quakers in America.* Philadelphia: New Society Publishers.
———. 1986. *Mothers of Feminism: The Story of Quaker Women in America.* San Francisco: Harper and Row.

Read, Joshua (1783–1865)

*L*ucy Read Anthony's older brother, Joshua Read, was an important figure in the Anthony family. At several critical times, Susan B. Anthony's "Uncle Joshua" rescued them financially. A resident of Palatine Bridge, near Canajoharie, New York, Read was a prosperous farmer and businessman. He was also a trustee of Canajoharie Academy. When Daniel Anthony's businesses failed after the Panic of 1837 and he was forced to put up most of his family's household furniture and goods for public auction, Read offered to buy what the Anthonys most wanted to save so that they would not be left without their most treasured furnishings. In 1845, he purchased a farm in Rochester that Daniel and Lucy had selected, using money that she had inherited from her parents. Read made the actual purchase and held the title for her because of state laws that prohibited married women from owning property in their own names. (If Daniel or Lucy had been the buyer of the farm, his creditors would have seized the property.) Also, in 1846, once the Anthonys had settled in Rochester, he helped Susan acquire an excellent teaching position at Canajoharie Academy. When the New York Married Women's Property Law of 1848 was passed, he signed the title for the farm over to Lucy.

Read did not sympathize with Daniel's abolitionist sentiments. Indeed, the entire Canajoharie area was vehemently anti-abolitionist. He did approve heartily of Susan B. Anthony's temperance activism and later her women's rights work, especially her campaign to expand the New York Married Women's Property Law of 1848. During the mid-1850s while she was lecturing in Canajoharie for the new law, townspeople tried to persuade her to resume her teaching there. Her Uncle Joshua, however, proudly insisted that there were plenty of others who could teach. Susan was needed "to go around and set people thinking about the laws" (Harper 1899, 1:121).

Related entries:
Anthony, Daniel
Anthony, Lucy Read
Panic of 1837
New York Married Women's Property Law of 1860

Suggestions for further reading:
Anthony, Katharine. 1954. *Susan B. Anthony: Her Personal History and Her Era.* Garden City, N.Y.: Doubleday.
Harper, Ida Husted. 1899, 1908. *The Life and Work of Susan B. Anthony.* 3 vols. Indianapolis: Bowen-Merrill (vols. 1 and 2) and Hollenbeck Press (vol. 3).

Reconstruction (1865–1877)

*D*uring the Reconstruction era, the nation focused on rebuilding the Union and reorganizing the South following the chaos and devastation of the Civil War. The immediate postwar period from 1865 to 1870 was a time of tremendous political upheaval, as the power in Congress shifted toward the Radical Republicans, who advocated harsh, punitive policies toward the South as well as legal and constitutional safeguards to protect the newly freed African Americans. For the first time, Garrisonian abolitionists became politically active, forging an alliance with Radical Republicans. Although abolitionists had a very limited impact on national politics before the Civil War, during Reconstruction the efforts of abolitionists ensured that the civil and political rights of African Americans became the central focus of national politics (DuBois 1978, 54, 57).

Reconstruction was also a critical time for the women's rights movement. As African-American rights took center stage, women's rights were no longer considered politically relevant. Many formerly loyal, outspoken advocates of women's rights withdrew their support because they were convinced that the political battle to enfranchise African-American males demanded an exclusive, totally concentrated effort. Activists who tried to keep woman suffrage prominent were either ignored or criticized as being disloyal to the abolitionist cause. Nevertheless, Susan B. Anthony, Elizabeth Cady Stanton, Parker Pillsbury, and a small but tenacious group of male and female abolitionists and women's rights activists struggled to keep woman suffrage as a prominent, viable political issue throughout the early years of Reconstruction.

Although Anthony's allegiance to woman suffrage caused many of her colleagues to question her sincerity as an abolitionist, she did not relinquish her advocacy of African-American rights during the first few years of Reconstruction. During the Civil War, she publicly criticized President Abraham Lincoln's projected postwar reconstruction policy, especially the lack of legal safeguards and provisions for the freed slaves. After the war, Anthony was just as vocal an opponent

of President Andrew Johnson's reconstruction plan. While in Kansas in the summer of 1865, she blasted Johnson's program in lectures, including one she gave at Ottumwa, Kansas. She demanded the ballot for freed African Americans as a means of safeguarding their liberty and their civil rights. Yet wherever and whenever she lectured, Anthony never missed an opportunity to remind audiences that African Americans were not the only disfranchised group in the United States. She encouraged her listeners to demand a government that would transform the nation into a true republic—one that would be for all the people, not just white males.

As Reconstruction progressed and many former allies of women's rights defected from the cause, Anthony, Cady Stanton, Lucy Stone, and a small, loyal group of women's rights activists organized in the belief that in this critical period of nation rebuilding and constitutional revision, they must advance women's claim to suffrage or lose an opportunity that would not reappear for decades. They formed the American Equal Rights Association (AERA) to push for suffrage for both African Americans and all women— what they called "universal suffrage."

Related entries:
Abolitionist Movement
American Anti-Slavery Society
American Equal Rights Association
Civil War
Fifteenth Amendment
Fourteenth Amendment
Kansas Campaign of 1867
Phillips, Wendell
Pillsbury, Parker
Stone, Lucy
Women's Rights Movement

Suggestions for further reading:
DuBois, Ellen Carol. 1978. *Feminism and Suffrage: The Emergence of an Independent Women's Movement in America 1848–1869.* Ithaca, N.Y.: Cornell University Press.
Foner, Eric. 1988. *Reconstruction: America's Unfinished Revolution, 1863–1877.* New York: Harper and Row.
Kugler, Israel. 1987. *From Ladies to Women: The Organized Struggle for Woman's Rights in the Reconstruction Era.* Westport, Conn.: Greenwood Press.

Remond, Charles Lenox
(1810–1873)

Charles Lenox Remond, abolitionist lecturer and brother of Sarah Parker Remond.

A prominent African-American Garrisonian abolitionist, Charles Lenox Remond was born in Salem, Massachusetts. He became involved in the Massachusetts Anti-Slavery Society in the late 1830s, and traveled widely as a lecturing agent until the Civil War. Few could rival the wild frenzy of Remond's speeches, which prompted one listener to report that he "was always in a spasm and . . . his words were as hot as if they had been steeped in a sevenfold furnace of unquenchable fire" (Porter 1985, 278).

Remond and his sister Sarah Parker Remond joined Susan B. Anthony's first cadre of lecturers who crossed New York state in late 1856 and 1857. As the agent who made all the arrangements, Anthony encountered a few of the many hardships that the Remonds regularly faced because of racial prejudice. When the Remonds were turned out of the lodging that Anthony had organized, she quickly scrambled to find people in the community to house them. Remond, who had a reputation for resisting (and detesting) the guidance of Garrison and other male abolitionist leaders, willingly submitted to Anthony's direction. At least with Anthony, he suffered none of the condescension and patronizing behavior he had to endure from Garrison and Phillips on account of his race.

In a letter to Anthony, the fiercely independent Remond inquired about the possibility of future winter lecturing opportunities with her.

> So you can depend upon me if you wish as one who is willing to be a soldier under your generalship. . . . I hope they will not allow Rochester to slumber or sleep through the winter but have the agitators in again who will torment them within an inch of

their lives. (CLR to SBA, November 26, 1857, IH-HL, in *Papers*)

Following the Civil War, Remond heartily supported universal suffrage and served as one of the vice presidents of the American Equal Rights Association (Porter 1985, 278), proclaiming: "All I ask for myself, I claim for my wife and sister. . . . No class of citizens in this country can be deprived of the ballot without injuring every other class" (Porter 1982, 521).

Related entries:
Abolitionist Movement
American Anti-Slavery Society
American Equal Rights Association
Douglass, Frederick
Garrison, William Lloyd
Remond, Sarah Parker

Suggestions for further reading:
Porter, Dorothy Burnett. 1982a. "Remond, Charles Lenox." In *Dictionary of American Negro Biography*, ed. Rayford W. Logan and Michael R. Winston. New York: W. W. Norton.
———. 1985. "The Remonds of Salem, Massachusetts: A Nineteenth-Century Family Revisited." *Proceedings of the American Antiquarian Society* 95, no. 2:259–295.
Quarles, Benjamin. 1969. *Black Abolitionists.* New York: Oxford University Press.

Remond, Sarah Parker (1826–1894)

*I*nternational African-American anti-slavery lecturer Sarah Parker Remond first lectured for the American Anti-Slavery Society (AASS) in 1856. She accompanied Susan B. Anthony and a group of Garrisonian lecturers (including her brother Charles Lenox Remond) throughout New York state in late 1856 to 1857. Fourteen years earlier, at the age of 16, Sarah Remond had delivered her first speech in Groton, Massachusetts, at a time when women speaking in public was considered an anathema. During the 1840s and 1850s, Remond actively opposed Massachusetts institutions practicing racial segregation and discrimination.

In 1859, with the financial support of several Garrisonian abolitionists and accompanied by Samuel Joseph May, Remond gained fame by lecturing about the evils of slavery throughout England, Scotland, and Ireland. Following the Civil War, she returned to the United States and, in 1866, participated in the founding of the American Equal Rights Association (AERA). Also in 1866, she joined Anthony and Elizabeth Cady Stanton in the campaign to have the words *male* and *white* expunged from the new constitution to be drawn up at the New York Constitutional Convention of 1867. Remond returned to England in 1867, eventually settling in Italy. Although little is known of her later years, it is believed that she studied and practiced medicine for a time. She remained abroad for the rest of her life.

Related entries:
Abolitionist Movement
American Anti-Slavery Society
American Equal Rights Association
May, Samuel Joseph
Remond, Charles Lenox
Women's Rights Movement

Suggestions for further reading:
Bogin, Ruth. 1974. "Sarah Parker Remond: Black Abolitionist from Salem." *Essex Institute Historical Collections* 110:2 (April).
Porter, Dorothy B. 1982b. "Remond, Sarah Parker." In *Dictionary of American Negro Biography*, ed. Rayford W. Logan and Michael R. Winston. New York: W. W. Norton.
Yee, Shirley J. 1992. *Black Women Abolitionists: A Study in Activism 1828–1860*. Knoxville: University of Tennessee Press.

The Revolution

*T*he *Revolution* was a radical, militant, women's rights journal that, for a brief time, also served as the official organ of the National Woman Suffrage Association (NWSA). In late 1867, Susan B. Anthony and Elizabeth Cady Stanton realized their dream of publishing a women's newspaper when the wealthy Democrat George Francis Train offered to finance the venture. Censorship by the all-male, pro-Republican press in the 1867 Kansas woman suffrage campaign led Anthony and Cady Stanton to realize the value and necessity of a woman suffrage paper that they could control.

On January 8, 1868, *The Revolution*'s first issue was published. As the proprietor, Anthony concentrated on advertising, promotion, and subscriptions, though she also wrote news items and editorials. Cady Stanton and fellow abolitionist and woman suffrage advocate Parker Pillsbury were the editors of the 16-page weekly, with Cady Stanton being the principal writer and editor. When Pillsbury left *The Revolution* in the summer of 1869, Cady Stanton was the only full-time editor until Paulina Wright Davis became corresponding editor in January 1870.

Many of Anthony and Cady Stanton's abolitionist colleagues were outraged by the women's association with Train, whom Republicans detested for his racist, anti-Republican views. Yet Train had vigorously supported woman suffrage in the Kansas campaign when few others had, and Anthony and Cady Stanton desperately needed his assistance to continue their work. In the pages of *The Revolution,* they defended their right to align themselves with Democrats who, unlike the Republicans who abandoned and betrayed the woman suffrage cause, honored and accepted their platform.

> The Democratic Party . . . has done all it could to keep our question [woman suffrage] alive in the State and national councils. . . . They have respectfully presented our petitions, and called attention to them in every possible way. They have franked our documents, . . . made us liberal donations, helped us to secure 9,000 votes in Kansas, and to establish a journal through which we can speak. (*The Revolution*, January 29, 1868, in *Papers*, series 1)

Train's support did not last, however. On the first day of *The Revolution*'s publication, he departed for England to fight for the Irish Fenian cause.

The Revolution was crucial to the development of the woman suffrage movement in the late 1860s. Because the women's rights movement was quiescent during the Civil War and sidelined during the postwar years of Reconstruction in the push for citizenship and suffrage for African-American men, *The Revolution* became a vital forum for Anthony, Cady Stanton, and other radical feminists to disseminate their views, theories, and propaganda regarding woman suffrage and women's rights. Central to their journalistic program was their mission "to prove the power of the ballot in elevating the character and condition of woman."

> We shall show that the ballot will secure for woman equal place and equal wages in the world of work; that it will open to her the schools, colleges, professions and all the opportunities and advantages of life. . . . We will show . . . the millions of laboring women, that their complaints, petitions, strikes and protective unions are of no avail until they hold

the ballot in their own hands; for it is the first step toward social, religious and political equality. (*The Revolution*, January 8, 1868, in *Papers*, series 1)

In addition to suffrage issues, Anthony and Cady Stanton published articles on such vital women's issues as divorce rights, dress reform, prostitution, infanticide, the deplorable conditions of working women, and women's labor unions—all taboo topics in the mid-nineteenth-century United States. Anthony was especially interested in using *The Revolution* to raise the consciousness of working women and to encourage them to organize to improve their working conditions and increase their wages.

Despite Anthony's desperate efforts to keep *The Revolution* solvent, by the spring of 1870 she realized with profound regret and a sense of failure that she would have to terminate publication. Although the paper was critically acclaimed and received widespread attention, it had never been a moneymaker.

The first issue of **The Revolution,** *January 8, 1868.*

Potential investors were wary of financing a newspaper that was constantly embroiled in controversy. When she transferred *The Revolution* to its new proprietor, Laura Curtis Bullard (who planned a literary and social journal), for $1, Anthony was left with a $10,000 debt that took her six years on the lecture circuit to repay. Cady Stanton, asserting that she was financially stressed, neglected to assume any responsibility for the debt.

Although *The Revolution* never had more than 3,000 subscribers, its influence was far-reaching. The paper's outspoken editorials publicized a radical feminist viewpoint and proved to be an effective way to popularize their views, educate the public, and gain recognition for the woman suffrage movement.

Related entries:
Anthony, Susan B.
Kansas Campaign of 1867
National Woman Suffrage Association
Pillsbury, Parker
Reconstruction
Stanton, Elizabeth Cady
Train, George Francis
Woman Suffrage Movement

Suggestions for further reading:
Mitchell, Catherine. 1993. "Historiography: A New Direction for Research on the Woman's Rights Press." *Journalism History* 19, no. 2 (summer):59–63.
Solomon, Martha M., ed. 1991. *A Voice of Their Own: The Woman Suffrage Press, 1840–1910.* Tuscaloosa: University of Alabama Press.

Rochester, New York

From the time Susan B. Anthony moved with her family to their Rochester farm in 1845 until her death in 1906, the city of Rochester, New York, was the place she called home. After Daniel Anthony's death in 1862, Susan, her mother Lucy Read Anthony, and her youngest sister Mary Anthony relocated to a smaller home closer to the city of Rochester. During Anthony's half-century of incessant traveling and campaigning, Rochester was where she returned to relax,

visit with her family, and reconnect with old friends and neighboring activists. But more than a mere resting place, Rochester was also the source of the development of Anthony's career as a reformer. The tight-knit, zealous group of radical Hicksite Quakers who inspired abolitionist Frederick Douglass to settle in Rochester and sparked Daniel Anthony's abolitionist fervor also provided his impressionable daughter with many role models of uncompromising commitment to radical social change, which helped spawn her early development as a social reformer.

Situated on the Genesee River near the southern shore of Lake Ontario in western New York state, the small village of Rochester quickly mushroomed into a booming center of commerce and trade when its access to the Erie Canal was completed in 1822. Just as the Erie Canal made thriving cities out of many of the small communities connected to it, the heavy canal trade and traffic generated explosive growth in Rochester's

Susan B. Anthony's home at 17 Madison Street, Rochester, New York.

industries, businesses, and population. But Rochester was renowned not only for its commercial success. Like other cities on the Erie Canal in the early to mid-nineteenth century, it was a center of moral and social reform. Rochester, in particular, quickly distinguished itself as a hub of ultraradical activism in the temperance, antislavery, women's rights, and spiritualist movements. Its small band of radical reformers, many of them Hicksite Quakers and Unitarians, made Rochester one of the most important lecture and convention sites for reformers of all persuasions. William Lloyd Garrison, Wendell Phillips, Abby Kelley Foster and Stephen Symonds Foster, Samuel Joseph May, and others ensured that their lecture tours included Rochester, giving them the opportunity to exchange information and ideas with like-minded activists (Hewitt 1984b, 36).

Rochester was also the site of the second woman's rights convention, coming just two weeks after the Seneca Falls Convention of 1848. The Rochester convention, the first woman's rights convention to be led by a woman (Rochester resident and Anthony family friend Abigail Bush), pronounced resolutions that demanded woman suffrage, higher wages for women, and the deletion of the word *obey* from all marriage vows (Huth 1995). During the antebellum era, Rochester was also a principal locus on the Underground Railroad. Many Rochester residents—not only Hicksite Quakers—cooperated in the effort to assist fugitive slaves on what for many was their last stop before reaching freedom in Canada.

Related entries:
Anthony, Daniel
Anthony, Mary Stafford
Anthony, Susan B.
Douglass, Frederick
Post, Amy Kirby
Quakerism (Society of Friends)

Suggestions for further reading:
DuBois, Eugene E. 1994. *The City of Frederick Douglass: Rochester's African-American People and Places.* Rochester: Landmark Society of Western New York.

Hewitt, Nancy A. 1984b. *Women's Activism and Social Change: Rochester, New York, 1822–1872.* Ithaca, N.Y.: Cornell University Press.
Huth, Mary M. 1995. *Upstate New York and the Women's Rights Movement.* Online. University of Rochester Library. Available at http://www.lib.rochester.edu/rbk/women/women.htm.

Rose, Ernestine Louise Potowski (1810–1892)

Among the first women's rights activists of the nineteenth century, Ernestine Potowski Rose was the quintessential radical reformer whose desire to serve humanity also inspired her to labor within the abolitionist, temperance, utopian socialist, free-thought, labor, and peace movements. The daughter of a rabbi, Rose was born and grew up in Poland. A fiercely independent and rebellious girl, at age 14 she repudiated Jewish teachings concerning women's inferiority to men. Two years later, she defended her right to control her own property before a Polish court. This was her first public act declaring a woman's right to her inherited property, a struggle that would one day consume decades of her activism.

After marrying in England in 1836, Potowski Rose and her husband William Rose, both disciples of the reformer Robert Owen, emigrated to the United States and settled in New York City, where they continued their radical reform activism. In the winter of 1836–1837, Potowski Rose went door-to-door gathering signatures in support of a married women's property bill that Judge Thomas Herttell presented to the New York state legislature. After five months' effort, she managed to obtain only five names on her petition. Most women told her that they already had all the rights they needed and wanted. For the next 12 years, until 1848 when the legislature finally enacted the New York Married Women's Property Law, she worked exhaustively for women's legal rights.

Susan B. Anthony first met Potowski Rose in 1852 at the Third National Woman's Rights Convention in Syracuse, New York. They first worked closely together in the spring of 1854, when Anthony accompanied her on a women's rights lecture tour of Washington, D.C., and several southern cities. Anthony had respect and admiration for Potowski Rose's intellect, knowledge, and articulate, witty eloquence. Later in 1854, Potowski Rose joined Anthony in her campaign to extend the provisions of the New York Married Women's Property Law of 1848. The two women traveled, lectured, and agitated together throughout all of New York state in 1855, both pushing themselves beyond the point of exhaustion and injuring their health. In March 1860, after six years of lecturing and thrusting petitions in the faces of state legislators, the legislature finally enacted an expanded Married Women's Property Law.

Anthony championed Potowski Rose whenever women's rights reformers protested that her ultraradical views (including atheism) would damage the movement if she were to continue holding leadership positions. Anthony's defense of her friend was based more on principle than on their personal relationship. She argued that women within the women's rights movement must be able to tolerate and support each other and work together despite differences among themselves—in religion, in political orientation, and in their ethnic backgrounds. Anthony won each time, though it was a battle she would revisit decades later on behalf of Elizabeth Cady Stanton and *The Woman's Bible*.

During the Civil War, Potowski Rose joined Anthony and Cady Stanton in lecturing and gathering petitions for the Woman's National Loyal League. After the war, in 1866, Potowski Rose firmly insisted on the necessity of working toward universal suffrage at the Eleventh National Woman's Rights Convention in New York City and as a charter member of the American Equal Rights Association (AERA). In May 1869, at the final divisive meeting of the AERA, when former Republican abolitionist allies proclaimed that women must wait for suffrage and concentrate instead on the effort to claim the ballot for African-American males through the Fifteenth Amendment, Potowski Rose became as frustrated and angry as Anthony and Cady Stanton. She echoed their arguments, even to the point of uttering racist and, oddly enough considering her own foreign birth, nativist remarks.

Congress has enacted resolutions for the suffrage of men and brothers. They don't speak of the women and sisters. . . . We might commence by calling the Chinaman a man and a brother, or the Hottentot, or the Calmuck, or the Indian, the idiot or the criminal, but where shall we stop? They will bring all these in before us, and then they will bring in the babies —the *male* babies. (Suhl 1990, 238)

With this speech, Potowski Rose voiced the frustration that came with her, Anthony's, and Cady Stanton's growing realization that no matter how exhaustively they and their colleagues had worked for the rights of African-American men and no matter how competent women were intellectually and politically, men were not ready to part with their exclusive right to the ballot. It was this fact that ignited the powerful emotions that erupted in that meeting, including the three women's outrage that the very men with whom they had worked so long in harmony would prefer to give the right to vote to any man than give women the ballot.

In 1869, exhausted, her health broken, Potowski Rose and her husband moved to England, where she lived for the rest of her life. Cady Stanton and Anthony visited her for the last time in 1883 when they were abroad arousing interest in an international woman suffrage organization. Anthony pleaded with Potowski Rose to return to the United States, where she would be near the friends who cared about her. She declined, preferring to remain in England, so that she could be buried next to her husband.

Related entries:
Abolitionist Movement
American Equal Rights Association
Davis, Paulina Kellogg Wright
Fifteenth Amendment
New York Married Women's Property Law of 1860

Reconstruction
Syracuse Woman's Rights Convention of 1852
Woman's Rights Conventions
Women's Rights Movement

Suggestions for further reading:
"Ernestine Potowski Rose." In *Women Public Speakers in the United States, 1800–1925: A Bio-Critical Sourcebook,* ed. Karlyn Kohrs Campbell. Westport, Conn.: Greenwood Press.
Suhl, Yuri. 1990, 1959. *Ernestine Rose: Women's Rights Pioneer.* 2nd ed. New York: Biblio Press.
Tyler, Alice Felt. 1971c. "Rose, Ernestine Louise Potowski." In *NAW,* 3:195–196.

S

Sargent, Aaron Augustus (1827–1887)

California Republican senator from 1873 to 1878, Aaron Augustus Sargent was one of the very few pro–woman suffrage members of the Senate during the 1870s. Born in Newburyport, Massachusetts, Sargent emigrated to California in 1849 at the height of the Gold Rush and worked as a compositor for several California newspapers before becoming owner, publisher, and editor of his own newspaper in Nevada City, California. He then studied law, became an attorney, and was soon deeply involved in California politics. He participated in the formation of the Republican Party in California and served as a representative to Congress in the 1860s and early 1870s before being elected to the Senate in 1872.

Susan B. Anthony developed a close friendship with Sargent, his wife Ellen Clark Sargent (who served as treasurer of the National Woman Suffrage Association [NWSA] in the mid-1870s), and their family in January 1872, while returning east from her whirlwind tour of California and the Pacific Northwest. Eager to be home again, Anthony was heartsick when huge snowdrifts stalled the train atop the Rocky Mountains. Thus delayed, she had the unexpected pleasure of meeting and conversing at length with the Sargents about women's rights and woman suffrage agitation. After this experience, Anthony became a frequent guest at the Sargents' home in Washington, D.C., and often stayed there when visiting the capital.

In 1877, when the Senate received the NWSA's petitions for a Sixteenth Amendment with scornful derision, Sargent was the only senator to demand that his colleagues treat the petitions with the same respectful attention they accorded all other entreaties. And in January 1878, while Anthony was detained completing a series of lecture engagements, Elizabeth Cady Stanton persuaded Sargent to propose the NWSA's new version of the Sixteenth Amendment to Congress. On January 10, Sargent presented the amendment to the Senate. It read, "The right of citizens of the United States to vote shall not be denied or abridged by the United States or by any State on account of sex."

Anthony was deeply disappointed when Sargent failed to be reelected in the 1878 election. After serving as ambassador to Germany for a brief time, he engaged in a bitter, hotly contested battle for a seat in the Senate in 1884. Following his defeat, he withdrew from politics and died three years later.

Related entries:
National Woman Suffrage Association
Sixteenth Amendment Campaign
Woman Suffrage Movement

Suggestions for further reading:
DAB, 8:353–354.
HWS, 2, 3.
Lutz, Alma. 1959. *Susan B. Anthony: Rebel, Crusader, Humanitarian.* Boston: Beacon Press.

Selden, Henry Rogers (1805–1885)

When Susan B. Anthony determined that she would cast a ballot in the 1872 presidential election, she knew that she would need the best legal assistance available. After she managed to register to vote in her home city of Rochester, New York, in early November 1872, she consulted one of the city's most distinguished and respected attorneys, Henry Rogers Selden. Once he had the opportunity to study the constitutional arguments supporting the National Woman Suffrage Association's (NWSA's) "New Departure" strategy, he agreed with Anthony that women did have the right to vote as specified by the Fourteenth and Fifteenth Amendments and vowed to represent her should the need arise.

A resident of Rochester for most of his adult life, Selden devoted his entire career to the law. In addition to his legal practice and his experience on the bench, he was active politically. An affirmed abolitionist, he participated in the formation of the Republican Party in New York state in 1856 and was elected lieutenant governor of New York in the same year. In 1862, when his older brother Samuel L. Selden stepped down as judge for the Court of Appeals, Henry Selden was appointed to fill his position, a post he held until late in 1864. And in 1865, he was selected to serve a term as a member of the New York state legislature. Following his involvement in the 1872 Republican National Convention, he decided to withdraw from political life but continued to be active in his legal practice until his retirement in 1879.

Selden and his law associate John Van Voorhis skillfully assisted Anthony from the time of her arrest in late November 1872 through the weeks of her trial in 1873. Although Judge Ward Hunt arbitrarily decided to deny Anthony, Selden, and Van Voorhis the right to have a jury deliberate and make their own decision on her case, Anthony never let her disappointment alter her exalted opinion of Selden or Van Voorhis, nor did she ever forget how hard Selden worked to champion her cause. Although she and Selden did not always agree on how to manage her case, she described him in a letter to her friend and loyal supporter Gerrit Smith as "one of the noblest and best men I have ever known" (SBA to GS, August 5, 1873, GS-SUL, in *Papers*).

Related entries:
"New Departure" Strategy
The *United States v. Susan B. Anthony*

Suggestions for further reading:
Sherr, Lynn. 1995. *Failure Is Impossible: Susan B. Anthony in Her Own Words.* New York: Times Books.

Seneca Falls Convention of 1848

In the summer of 1848, Susan B. Anthony was immersed in her teaching in Canajoharie, New York, while in Seneca Falls, Elizabeth Cady Stanton was spearheading the nation's first organized women's rights gathering. Even though women had been agitating for their rights prior to this date, the Seneca Falls Convention is widely acknowledged as the origin of the woman suffrage movement. Cady Stanton's interest in organizing a woman's rights convention can be traced as far back as 1840, when she accompanied her husband Henry Brewster Stanton to London where he was a delegate to the World Antislavery Convention. In the days following the exclusion of women delegates from the convention's proceedings, she shared her outrage about the obstacles men placed in the path of women reformers with her new friend and mentor Lucretia Coffin Mott. Throughout the 1840s, as Coffin Mott supported and nurtured Cady Stanton's developing feminism, Cady Stanton became increasingly determined to effect revolutionary, political change in the lives of women.

An occasion for action presented itself when Coffin Mott, traveling to upstate New

York to attend an annual meeting of Hicksite Quakers in July 1848, visited with Cady Stanton at the home of Hicksite reformer Jane Hunt. Also present were Coffin Mott's sister Martha Coffin Wright and another Quaker activist, Mary Ann McClintock. In the presence of sympathetic, like-minded women, Cady Stanton vented her frustrations concerning women's social and political powerlessness. When she introduced the possibility of a woman's rights convention to address these wrongs, the women were in favor and immediately began planning. Although the five women (all from Quaker backgrounds except for Cady Stanton) lacked nothing in initiative, they were stymied as to how to organize the meeting. As Cady Stanton described their quandary, they were "as helpless and hopeless as if they had been suddenly asked to construct a steam engine" (DuBois 1978, 23). Unsure of their executive abilities, they asked Coffin Mott's husband James Mott to lead the convention.

Despite their tentativeness concerning the mechanics of running a large meeting, the women were remarkably self-possessed when, following Cady Stanton's lead, they all discussed and Cady Stanton planned the convention's *Declaration of Rights and Sentiments,* which they modeled on the *Declaration of Independence.* In the weeks prior to the convention, it was Cady Stanton who wrote and finalized the *Declaration* and who composed most of the accompanying resolutions, which demanded that women be given the same civil and political rights as men, including the ballot (Flexner 1975, 75). At the convention, attended by approximately 300 people on July 19 and 20, 1848, opposition arose in response to the resolution demanding women's right to vote, yet Cady Stanton refused to withdraw it or to compromise on it. With the vehement support of Frederick Douglass, the resolution passed, though barely.

Cady Stanton expounded on women's right to the franchise in a speech she delivered two months later in September 1848 (Gordon and Miller 1997, 94). Not bothering to conceal her militancy or the enraged indignation that would propel her through the next 50 years of suffrage agitation, she declared:

> Strange as it may seem to many, we now demand our right to vote according to the declaration of the government under which we live. . . . to have drunkards, idiots, horseracing rum-selling rowdies, ignorant foreigners, and silly boys fully recognized, while we ourselves are thrust out from all the rights that belong to citizens, is too grossly insulting to be longer quietly submitted to. The right is ours. Have it we must. Use it we will. . . . the indomitable wills of many women are already pledged to secure this right. (quoted in Griffith 1984, 56)

Anthony was "amused rather than impressed" as she read news stories and editorials of the Seneca Falls Convention (Lutz 1959, 20). Two weeks later, her father, mother, and sister Mary Stafford Anthony attended the Rochester Woman's Rights Convention and were among those who signed that convention's *Declaration of Sentiments.* While Anthony vacationed at home in Rochester in August, she listened to her family's enthusiastic reports of the proceedings. Although their glowing comments stimulated her interest, she treated the entire subject with humor and lightheartedness. She was sufficiently intrigued to want to know more about women's rights, but since she was not yet involved in social reform, she did not yet see how women's rights pertained to her own life, her status as a woman, or her future goals.

Related entries:
Anthony, Susan B.
Douglass, Frederick
Mott, Lucretia Coffin
Quakerism (Society of Friends)
Stanton, Elizabeth Cady
Woman's Rights Conventions
Women's Rights Movement
Wright, Martha Coffin

Suggestions for further reading:
Flexner, Eleanor. 1975. *Century of Struggle: The Woman's Rights Movement in the United States.* Cambridge, Mass.: Belknap Press of Harvard University Press.
Griffith, Elisabeth. 1984. *In Her Own Right: The Life of Elizabeth Cady Stanton.* New York: Oxford University Press.
Gurko, Miriam. 1974. *The Ladies of Seneca Falls: The Birth of the Woman's Rights Movement.* New York: Macmillan.

Sewall, May Eliza Wright (1844–1920)

*I*nnovative and enlightened educator, suffragist, pacifist, and social reformer May Eliza Wright Sewall was one of Susan B. Anthony's most competent young lieutenants. Yet her active involvement in the woman suffrage movement was only one aspect of a multifaceted career in reform. Born in Greenfield, Wisconsin, Wright Sewall was precocious and scholarly from a young age and was attracted to the teaching profession. Following several years of teaching, she enrolled in Northwestern Female College, which later became part of Northwestern University. She received her undergraduate degree in 1866 and her master's degree in 1871. Early in her career, Wright Sewall dedicated herself to improving the education of girls. In 1882 she and her second husband, also a teacher, opened the Girls' Classical School in Indianapolis, which they soon developed into a challenging college preparatory school. Wright Sewall's program of instruction included Latin, Greek, modern languages, mathematics, and physical education, in addition to the disciplines traditionally taught to female students.

Wright Sewall first joined the woman suffrage movement by becoming a leading activist in several Indiana suffrage organizations. She served as chair of the executive committee of the National Woman Suffrage Association (NWSA) from 1882 to 1890.

Because she was an excellent administrator as well as an accomplished lecturer and writer, Anthony selected her to work alongside Rachel Foster (Avery) in planning and executing the International Council of Women (ICW) in 1888. Thanks to Wright Sewall's and Foster's laborious efforts (all under Anthony's watchful, critical eye), the ICW was a spectacular success and opened the way for women working in all fields of endeavor to communicate and work together toward common goals. Anthony never strongly considered Wright Sewall for a top leadership position in the NWSA or the National American Woman Suffrage Association (NAWSA), no doubt realizing that the Indiana activist's vast array of reform interests combined with her responsibilities as academy director would prevent her from a full-fledged commitment to suffrage activism.

In addition to her work for the suffrage movement, Wright Sewall was a leader in nearly every other reform movement she became involved in. She served as president of the National Council of Women, was the first vice president of the General Federation of Women's Clubs, was an intense activist within the American Peace Society, and was president of the Western Association of Collegiate Alumnae. She also assumed executive positions in a multitude of other social reform, cultural, and literary organizations. Wright Sewall's life passion was her conviction that all areas of professional, cultural, and artistic activity should be as open to women as to men.

Related entries:
Anthony, Susan B.
International Council of Women
Woman Suffrage Movement

Suggestions for further reading:
"Mrs. May Wright Sewall." 1893. In *A Woman of the Century*, ed. Frances E. Willard and Mary A. Livermore. Buffalo, N.Y.: Charles Wells Moulton, pp. 643–645.
Phillips, Clifton J. 1971b. "May Eliza Wright Sewall." In *NAW*, 3:269–271.

Shaw, Anna Howard
(1847–1919)

Suffrage leader, Methodist minister, physician, and compelling orator Anna Howard Shaw was the president of the National American Woman Suffrage Association (NAWSA) during the most tumultuous years of the twentieth-century woman suffrage movement. A treasured, intimate friend of Susan B. Anthony in the final years of her life, Shaw was the suffragist among Anthony's young lieutenants who most wanted to be president of NAWSA. Shaw was enormously influenced by Anthony, describing her as "an unceasing inspiration—the torch that illumined my life." As Anthony lay dying in early March 1906, Shaw sat by her bedside at her friend's request. Shaw later reflected on their powerful attachment in her autobiography *Story of a Pioneer:* "I knew that I would have given her a dozen lives had I had them, and endured a thousand times more hardship than we had borne together, for the inspiration of her companionship and the joy of her affection. They were the greatest blessings I have had in all my life" (Shaw 1915, 234–235).

Shaw's childhood required that she develop a stalwart resourcefulness at a very young age. Her family emigrated from England when Shaw was three years old to join her father Thomas Shaw, who had settled in Massachusetts months before. In 1859, he became enchanted with the idea of establishing a colony on the Michigan frontier. After building a rough-hewn cabin for his family there, he returned to Massachusetts to work. He then sent his wife, his daughters, and his oldest and youngest sons to eke out a living from the Michigan wilderness. Shaw's mother did not withstand the strain— she became mentally disabled not long after arriving on their claim. Several months later, the oldest son became so ill that he had to return to Massachusetts. As a result, 12-year-old Anna, her two older sisters, and her youngest brother were forced to struggle for their survival on the frontier for more than a year until their father finally joined them. Whatever help he provided did not last long because he enlisted in the Union army in 1861, leaving his children to fend for themselves and their mother once more.

In addition to discovering ingenious methods for coping with severe privation, as a teenager Shaw developed a strong vocation for the ministry in spite of her family's insistence that she consider another career. In 1871, after having studied debating and elocution in high school, her high school principal, a Methodist woman, encouraged her to enter the Methodist ministry. Shaw began preaching regularly in 1870 and became licensed as a clergywoman in 1871.

Her Unitarian family was distraught over her conversion to Methodism. Relatives dangled the prospect of a fully paid education at the University of Michigan before her, provided she give up her plan to become a minister, but she refused the offer. In 1873, she attended Albion College, paying her own way. After several years, she enrolled in the Boston University School of Theology, where she confronted stiff prejudice against women in the ministry. After graduating in 1879, she served as minister to several Methodist churches on Cape Cod, Massachusetts, and was ordained in the Methodist Protestant Church in 1880. As much as she enjoyed her parishioners and loved creating and delivering sermons, the work of the ministry was not the challenge she had been seeking. In 1883 she resumed her studies at Boston University, this time in quest of a medical degree. Near the end of her medical studies in 1885 (she received her degree in 1886), she was still not professionally satisfied and decided to investigate social reform as a way to make a difference in women's lives. In her autobiography, she explained this transformation in her life and the social problems she had encountered in her medical training.

For the first time women were going into industrial competition with men, and already men were intensely resenting their presence. Around me I saw women overworked and underpaid, doing men's work at half men's wages, not because their work was inferior, but because they were women. Again, too, I studied the obtrusive problems of the poor and of the women of the streets; and looking at the whole social situation from every angle, I could find but one solution for women—the removal of the stigma of disfranchisement. As man's equal before the law, woman could demand her rights, asking favors from no one. With all my heart I joined in the crusade of the men and women who were fighting for her. My real work had begun. (Shaw 1915, 151–152)

Still living in Boston, in 1885 she became involved in the Massachusetts Woman Suffrage Association (MWSA), an organization founded by Lucy Stone and Henry Blackwell that was affiliated with the American Woman Suffrage Association (AWSA). Stone soon recognized Shaw's oratorical talent and hired her as an MWSA lecturer. Through Shaw's new suffrage connections, she developed a close friendship with Frances Willard, president of the Woman's Christian Temperance Union (WCTU), and became director of its Franchise Department from 1888 to 1892. Her success as an MWSA lecturer inspired her to explore lecturing on suffrage and temperance issues as a full-time occupation, beginning in 1887.

In March 1888, Shaw attracted Anthony's attention by delivering a stunning sermon at the International Council of Women (ICW). Although there were many accomplished, talented young women in the National Woman Suffrage Association (NWSA), Anthony was well aware that the organization lacked a dynamic orator. And Anthony, who

had spent a lifetime studying and admiring eloquent oratory, knew a great talent when she saw one. She wasted no time pleading her case to Shaw. Arriving at Shaw's hotel room late one evening, Anthony spent the entire night discussing the woman suffrage movement, its needs, and her hopes for the future, Shaw's enlistment into the NWSA being one of those hopes. As they talked until dawn, Shaw was mesmerized by Anthony and her pure, single-minded devotion to the suffrage cause. She was instantly converted and, despite Shaw's strong ties to the AWSA, agreed to become a lecturer for the NWSA. Two years after the merger of the AWSA and the NWSA, when Anthony was elected president of the new NAWSA in 1892, Shaw was elected vice president, a post she filled through 1904. She herself became NAWSA's president in 1905.

Throughout the 1890s, Shaw was active in one state suffrage battle after another. In the South Dakota suffrage campaign of 1890, Shaw and Anthony campaigned together through some of the most physically grueling travel conditions Shaw had ever experienced. Anthony, beset with complaints from NAWSA and South Dakota suffragists, admired Shaw's fortitude and her determination to endure the physical hardships with an astounding stamina, good humor, and grace. In Anthony's mind, these characteristics signified the essence of a true reformer and great leader.

During Shaw's tenure as vice president, in addition to her efforts on the campaign trail, she delivered numerous addresses at NAWSA annual conventions and to annual congressional hearings for a federal suffrage amendment. Also during the 1890s, she developed a strong emotional bond with Anthony's niece, Lucy Elmina Anthony, the daughter of Anthony's youngest brother Jacob Merritt Anthony. Lucy was a tireless worker for the cause and for many years served as Anthony's secretary. She and Shaw formed a lifelong intimate friendship, eventually sharing a home together in Moylan, Pennsylvania. (In

Anna Howard Shaw

the late nineteenth century and at the turn of the century, it was not at all unusual for unmarried, middle-class social reformers and college-educated women to form close relationships and live together.)

In the furor over Elizabeth Cady Stanton's *The Woman's Bible* in December 1895 and January 1896, Shaw supported Rachel Foster Avery, Carrie Chapman Catt, Alice Stone Blackwell, and other NAWSA leaders in voting to censure *The Woman's Bible* and to disassociate NAWSA from Cady Stanton's writings. Although Shaw's participation in the censure resolution displeased and hurt Anthony, as did Foster Avery's and Chapman Catt's, Shaw believed that she had pursued the correct course. Unlike Cady Stanton, Matilda Joslyn Gage, Clara Bewick Colby, and their followers, Shaw's strong religious background and her experience as a minister convinced her that feminism and Christianity were not antithetical. Shaw wholeheartedly disagreed with Cady Stanton's position that all organized religion, churches, and the Christian clergy were opposed to the advancement of women because her experiences in the ministry had taught her otherwise. Granted, she had been discriminated against during her education and training, but she believed that Cady Stanton's sweeping indictment of Christianity in the United States was wrong and insupportable.

According to Shaw's autobiography, she desperately aspired to the presidency of NAWSA when Anthony retired in 1900. Yet she also felt strongly that she mustn't force Anthony to gratify her personal wishes. To compensate, she lavishly praised her chief rival for the position, Chapman Catt, whenever she could catch Anthony's attention. "I will admit here for the first time that in urging Mrs. Catt's fitness for the office I made the greatest sacrifice of my life," Shaw explained in *Story of a Pioneer*. "My highest ambition had been to succeed Miss Anthony" (Shaw 1915, 285). Chapman Catt, who did not want to be president, likewise lauded

Shaw whenever Anthony was within earshot. When Anthony made it clear to the membership that she had selected Chapman Catt to be her successor (a move that was moot without the approval of the majority of the NAWSA membership), Shaw was disappointed but continued to work as diligently as ever.

When Chapman Catt resigned the presidency in late 1904 due to her exhaustion and the illness of her husband, Anthony insisted that Shaw succeed her. In her autobiography, Shaw claimed that by this time she no longer wanted the position. Anthony refused to take no for an answer. Shaw recalled, "Miss Anthony actually commanded me to take the place, and there was nothing to do but obey her. She was then eighty-four, and . . . within two years of her death. It was no time for me to rebel against her wishes; but I yielded with the heaviest heart I have ever carried" (Shaw 1915, 286).

Shaw served as president of NAWSA from 1905 to 1915, through the most troublesome, chaotic years in the organization's history. Unlike Chapman Catt, Shaw was hindered by the fact that she was not as skilled an administrator, lacked the strategic insight of her predecessor, and was not as adept at managing difficult personalities or at resolving divisive disputes among warring suffragists.

Like Anthony, Cady Stanton, Chapman Catt, and other leading NAWSA suffragists, Shaw has been condemned as a racist and a nativist by some modern writers. And, like many of her fellow suffragists, U.S. social reformers, and most white Americans at the turn of the century, Shaw made statements that exposed her racial and nativist biases, all of which reflected commonly held views in American society. At a NAWSA convention in New Orleans, Louisiana, in 1903, Shaw tried to avoid broaching racial issues on NAWSA's platform. Goaded night after night by an attendee who wanted her to confront it, she finally rose to the challenge. After explaining how the South's refusal to enfranchise women made white women the political inferiors of African-American men, she stated:

> The women of the South are not alone . . . in their humiliation. All the women of America share it with them . . . in these United States American women are governed by every race of men under the light of the sun. There is not a color from white to black from red to yellow, there is not a nation from pole to pole, that does not send its contingent to govern American women. If American men are willing to leave their women in a position as degrading as this they need not be surprised when American women resolve to lift themselves out of it. (Shaw 1915, 312–313)

Although this statement clearly exhibits Shaw's racial biases (as well as those of most NAWSA suffragists), she also was strongly committed to universal suffrage for all Americans. Unlike Chapman Catt and Henry Blackwell, she was opposed to restricting the suffrage based on education or ownership of property because it meant disfranchising the poor as well as racial and ethnic minorities. In a speech delivered at a 1905 NAWSA convention, she declared:

> Whatever others may say or do . . . our Association must not accept compromises. We must guard against the reactionary spirit which marks our time and stand unflatteringly for the principle of perfect equality of rights and opportunities of all. We must refuse to restrict our demand for justice or bound it by any line of race, sex [or] creed. ("Our Ideal" Speech, DC-SL, as quoted in Graham 1996, 32)

Although this egalitarian position may appear to be in opposition to her racial and nativist biases, Shaw saw no inconsistency or conflict. Her protest concerning the social and political position of white women born in the United States never led to a demand to disfranchise African Americans, Asian Americans, Native Americans, or immigrant men.

Beginning in 1910, dissension within NAWSA led to the resignations of leading suffragists. Foster Avery, Harriet Taylor Upton, Florence Kelley, and other NAWSA leaders withdrew from the organization, in large part because of Shaw's ineffective leadership. Again in 1912 and in each year thereafter until her resignation in 1915, leaders of several factions called for Shaw to step down.

In 1912, the rise of the young New Jersey Quaker Alice Paul, veteran of British militant suffragism, further threatened to topple Shaw's leadership. At first Shaw fully endorsed Paul's efforts to pursue a federal suffrage amendment, but when Paul introduced militant tactics, Shaw reacted strongly. She declared Paul's tactics "un-American" and criticized her for promoting lawlessness. Despite Shaw's and other NAWSA leaders' vehement denouncement of Paul's methods, many NAWSA suffragists applauded the young activist's strategies and urged the leadership to agitate for suffrage more aggressively. This and other equally fractious controversies so split the NAWSA membership that by 1915 the majority wanted Shaw to resign, a decision with which Shaw concurred. As Chapman Catt resumed her presidency and struggled to knit NAWSA back together, Shaw resolved to be as active as the NAWSA leadership permitted. During the final years of the woman suffrage movement, Shaw served primarily as a NAWSA lecturer.

In 1917, as the United States entered World War I, Shaw was invited to chair the Woman's Committee of the Council of National Defense (WCCND), a federal bureau established to coordinate American women's varied war service contributions. Although Shaw reportedly was very successful in this administrative position, she found the entanglements of federal bureaucracy incredibly vexing. For her contribution, she was awarded the Distinguished Service Medal in 1919. Immediately following the war, she traveled with former Republican president William Howard Taft and the president of Harvard University. They lectured throughout the nation in support of President Woodrow Wilson's conception of the League of Nations and his version of the proposed peace treaty. During this exhausting tour, Shaw became ill with pneumonia and died in July 1919 at her home in Moylan, Pennsylvania.

Related entries:
Anthony, Susan B.
Avery, Rachel G. Foster
Catt, Carrie Lane Chapman
National American Woman Suffrage Association
National Woman Suffrage Association
Woman Suffrage Movement
The Woman's Bible

Suggestions for further reading:
Flexner, Eleanor. 1971a. "Anna Howard Shaw." In *NAW*, 3: 274–277.
Pellauer, Mary D. 1991. *Toward a Tradition of Feminist Theology: The Religious Social Thought of Elizabeth Cady Stanton, Susan B. Anthony, and Anna Howard Shaw*. Brooklyn, N.Y.: Carlson Publishing.
Shaw, Anna Howard. 1915. *Story of a Pioneer*. New York: Harper and Bros.

Sixteenth Amendment Campaign

During the Reconstruction era, when Susan B. Anthony and Elizabeth Cady Stanton failed to convince Radical Republican legislators to broaden the scope of the Fourteenth and Fifteenth Amendments to encompass woman suffrage, the two women's rights leaders proposed a Sixteenth Amendment that would guarantee the enfranchisement of all women citizens.

In December 1868, Anthony and Cady Stanton persuaded Senator Samuel Clarke Pomeroy to introduce a resolution for a Sixteenth Amendment in the Senate and Representative George Washington Julian to present a similar proposal in the House of Representatives. At that time, Anthony and Cady Stanton knew they had an uphill battle ahead of them, but they had no idea that 50 more years of constant struggle would pass before both houses of Congress accepted a federal woman suffrage amendment in 1919. Although the press and woman suffrage supporters sometimes referred to the federal woman suffrage amendment as the "Susan B. Anthony Amendment" or the "Anthony Amendment," Anthony herself shunned the term, undoubtedly in recognition of the contributions of many women and men. During her lifetime, however, she was unquestionably the supreme leader of the effort to secure a Sixteenth Amendment. In the end, however, it was not the Sixteenth Amendment that extended the franchise to American women, but the Nineteenth Amendment, which was ratified by the states in 1920.

When Anthony, Cady Stanton, and other women's rights reformers organized the National Woman Suffrage Association (NWSA) in 1869, they dedicated its work to the task of obtaining a Sixteenth Amendment. During the early years of the NWSA, however, Anthony and her fellow suffragists concentrated instead on achieving woman suffrage through the "New Departure" strategy, in the belief that the Fourteenth and Fifteenth Amendments already enfranchised women. In 1875, when the U.S. Supreme Court decision *Minor v. Happersett* eliminated the possibility that woman suffrage could be achieved according to New Departure theories, Anthony and NWSA leaders refocused their efforts on a Sixteenth Amendment campaign.

In November 1876, five months after the reading of their historic *Declaration of the Rights of Woman* at the Centennial Exposition in Philadelphia, Anthony, Cady Stanton, and Matilda Joslyn Gage appealed to NWSA members to distribute petitions in favor of a Sixteenth Amendment before the opening session of the January 1877 NWSA convention in Washington, D.C. With only a few weeks to complete the task, NWSA members from 26 states gathered over 10,000 signatures, the first of dozens of similar Sixteenth Amendment petition drives (Harper 1899, 1:484). In January, NWSA activist Sara Andrews Spencer, whose Herculean task it had been to supervise this operation, presented the petitions to the House of Representatives and the Senate, delivering them to members according to state. In the Senate, members responded to the petitions with jocularity and ridicule despite the demands of Senator Aaron Augustus Sargent, a pro–woman suffrage Republican senator from California, that they treat the petitions with the same respect they accorded all other appeals.

In January 1878, while Anthony was consumed by her lecturing in Dakota Territory and the Midwest, Cady Stanton convinced Senator Sargent to present to the Senate her newly worded version of the Sixteenth Amendment, which would remain unchanged for the next 40 years: "The right of citizens to vote shall not be denied or abridged by the United States or by any State on account of sex." Although suffragists from the NWSA, the American Woman Suffrage Association (AWSA), and, starting in 1890, the National American Woman Suffrage Association (NAWSA) brought the amendment before each successive session of Congress from 1878 through 1919, progress was discouragingly slow. In 1882, the Senate officially recognized the woman suffrage cause by establishing the Senate Select Committee on Woman Suffrage, but it proved to be no boon to the cause since its chair was filled by a succession of southern senators, all opposed to woman suffrage. Despite this disappointment, the Senate committee did respond favorably to the Sixteenth Amendment proposal several times during the 1880s.

From the late 1870s through the 1890s, Anthony supervised and participated in the NWSA's and the NAWSA's annual winter pilgrimages to Congress, when she, occasionally Cady Stanton, and many other suffragists educated members of Congress on woman suffrage, lobbied them individually, testified at congressional hearings, and initiated debate designed to promote the woman suffrage question. Although these political tactics were not as immediately successful as Anthony and her colleagues wished, there is no question that the dogged, year-by-year rousing of woman suffrage issues positively influenced members of Congress, as evidenced by the 1887 Senate vote on the amendment. At that time, champion of woman suffrage Senator Henry W. Blair of New Hampshire presented the joint resolution proposing a Sixteenth Amendment. Following a lengthy debate and the presentation of petitions listing hundreds of thousands of women's signatures, 16 senators voted in favor of the amendment and 34 against it, with 26 members absent. Although this effort failed, Anthony and her colleagues were encouraged that 16 senators approved the amendment, a considerable gain from the January day ten years before, when the entire Senate dismissed their petitions with howls of laughter.

The chief obstacle to the success of the federal woman suffrage amendment derived from the fact that the Constitution requires the approval of two-thirds of the members of both the House and Senate before an amendment can be sent to the state legislatures for ratification. Once this two-thirds majority has been achieved, three-fourths of all state legislatures must ratify the amendment for it to be adopted. Because of the unanimous opposition of southern legislators and the hostility of most border state congressmen to woman suffrage, there were not enough pro–woman suffrage senators to vote in favor of the amendment. As a result, it became clear to suffragists by the late 1880s that the Sixteenth Amendment campaign was blocked until more states entered the union or until the attitudes of southern senators changed. As far as overcoming southern prejudices was concerned, NAWSA leader Carrie Chapman Catt expressed the pessimism of her colleagues: "Senators from the

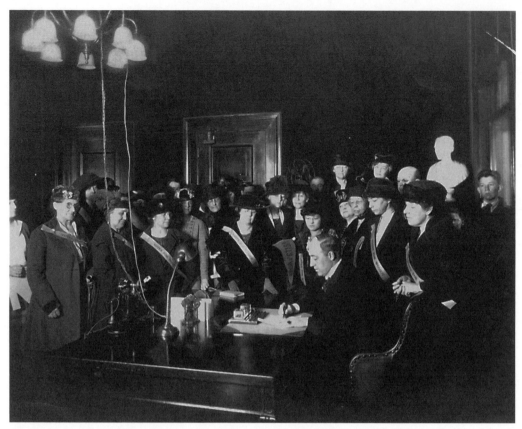

On August 26, 1920, the federal suffrage amendment was passed. Pictured is Governor Edwin P. Morrow of Kentucky signing the Nineteenth Amendment; on January 6, 1920, Kentucky became the twenty-fourth state to ratify it.

seceding States would rather have committed hari kari than vote for any federal suffrage amendment"(Catt and Shuler 1926, 230).

Given the discouraging constitutional realities facing the Sixteenth Amendment campaign, many historians have questioned why Anthony remained so stubbornly steadfast in pursuing it. AWSA leaders Lucy Stone and Henry Blackwell had always believed that it was folly to invest resources in such a struggle. They were convinced that the only viable way to achieve victory was to raise the woman suffrage question before state legislators and voters in statewide campaigns, achieving one state victory at a time. Anthony did not disagree with the efficacy of state suffrage campaigns. In fact, she endorsed and actively participated in them, but she maintained that state work was not the most expedient method of enfranchising the

nation's women. Anthony believed wholeheartedly in the political process and in the power of intensive lobbying. She was certain that it was easier to sway the hearts and minds of hundreds of congressmen than to capture the votes of millions of men, many of whom were uneducated, riddled with prejudices, unenlightened about women's capabilities, and prey to propaganda techniques exploited by antisuffragists.

In Anthony's final years of suffrage activism, NAWSA's activities were directed primarily toward winning state suffrage campaigns. Yet Anthony never relinquished her quest to see the Sixteenth Amendment become law. In 1902, she made her final appearance before the Senate Select Committee on Woman Suffrage. In her appeal, she betrayed her overwhelming sense of failure (as well as her racial and nativist prejudices) at having spent a lifetime being refused the one political right that legislators so freely and indiscriminately dispensed to any and all men.

> We have waited; we stood aside for the negro; we waited for the millions of immigrants; now we must wait till the Hawaiians, the Filipinos and the Porto Ricans [*sic*] are enfranchised; then no doubt the Cubans will have their turn. For all these ignorant, alien peoples educated American-born women have been compelled to stand aside and wait! How long will this injustice, this outrage, continue? (Harper 1908, 3:1308)

In 1913, seven years after Anthony's death, a Sixteenth Amendment instituting a federal income tax was adopted, but the most grueling suffrage battles were still to come. At first the suffrage amendment was renamed the Seventeenth Amendment. Then suffragists began referring to it as the federal suffrage amendment and the Anthony Amendment. Quaker suffragist Alice Paul, an American who came to NAWSA via the British woman suffrage movement, resuscitated the drive for the federal suffrage amendment, first through NAWSA and later through the Congressional Union, which was soon renamed the National Woman's Party. Through the dedicated efforts of NAWSA, the National Woman's Party, and suffragists in every state and territory in the union, the Nineteenth Amendment guaranteeing national woman suffrage became law on August 26, 1920.

Related entries:
American Woman Suffrage Association
Anthony, Susan B.
Catt, Carrie Lane Chapman
Julian, George Washington
National American Woman Suffrage Association
National Woman Suffrage Association
"New Departure" Strategy
Pomeroy, Samuel Clarke
Reconstruction
Woman Suffrage Movement

Suggestions for further reading:
Catt, Carrie Chapman, and Nettie Rogers Shuler. 1926. *Woman Suffrage and Politics: The Inner Story of the Suffrage Movement.* New York: Charles Scribner's Sons.
Harper, Ida Husted. 1899, 1908. *The Life and Work of Susan B. Anthony.* 3 vols. Indianapolis: Bowen-Merrill (vols. 1 and 2) and Hollenbeck Press (vol. 3).
HWS, 1–6.

Smith, Gerrit (1797–1874)

Wealthy philanthropist; politician and member of Congress; social reformer; abolitionist; advocate of women's rights, temperance, and prison reform; and accomplice to John Brown in his raid on the federal arsenal at Harpers Ferry, Virginia, Gerrit Smith funded and was actively engaged in a dizzying array of social reform causes. Eccentric and unpredictable, Smith was as generous in broadcasting his often unorthodox opinions as he was in making donations to his favorite causes. Despite his far-flung interests and idiosyncrasies, Smith's views on social and political issues were sought after and respected.

Smith had a profound early influence on his young cousin, Elizabeth Cady. As a young adult, she frequently visited Smith and his family at their home in Peterboro, New York. There she was swept up in the whirlwind of Smith's reform interests, particularly abolitionism. As a staunch believer in the necessity of finding political solutions to slavery, Smith was closely involved in the formation of the Liberty Party when it split off from the American Anti-Slavery Society (AASS) in 1840. Cady learned and absorbed much in this political environment, and it was through Smith that she met her husband-to-be, the abolitionist Henry Brewster Stanton.

Smith strongly supported the women's rights movement and attended local, state, and national conventions until 1856, when he refused further participation and donations because the women's rights movement had stopped agitating for dress reform, an issue that he believed was the key to women's emancipation (Griffith 1984, 92). By this time women's rights activists had long since abandoned the dress reform issue and were concentrating on efforts to achieve legal and civil equality. Despite Smith's stated position, Anthony appealed to him for donations regularly throughout the late 1850s, and he usually responded, although not as generously as she knew he did to other causes.

Cady Stanton and Anthony clashed with Smith during Reconstruction, when he, a loyal Republican, sided with Wendell Phillips and agreed with the Radical Republicans that women must postpone their quest for suffrage until after the enfranchisement of African-American men. Despite this position, he claimed he was never against enfranchising women, and after the ratification of the Fifteenth Amendment he again backed woman suffrage. He also publicly supported Anthony when she voted in the presidential election of 1872 and when she was arrested and put on trial in 1873.

Related entries:
Abolitionist Movement
Bloomer Costume
Fifteenth Amendment
Phillips, Wendell
Reconstruction
Stanton, Elizabeth Cady
Stanton, Henry Brewster
Woman's Rights Conventions
Women's Rights Movement

Suggestions for further reading:
Griffith, Elisabeth. 1984. *In Her Own Right: The Life of Elizabeth Cady Stanton.* New York: Oxford University Press.
Rossbach, Jeffrey. 1982. *Ambivalent Conspirators: John Brown, the Secret Six, and a Theory of Slave Violence.* Philadelphia: University of Pennsylvania Press.

Society of Friends

See **Quakerism (Society of Friends)**

Stanton, Elizabeth Cady (1815–1902)

Women's rights reformer, radical suffragist, legendary orator, nationally acclaimed writer, and leading voice of the nineteenth-century women's rights and woman suffrage movements Elizabeth Cady Stanton fought all her adult life for the political and social advancement of women. She channeled her rage about the subjugation of women in society into more than five decades of activism. As she herself acknowledged, her dynamic partnership with Susan B. Anthony, her closest colleague, impelled her to articulate and to strive to bring about her revolutionary vision of the future of women in the United States.

Born five years before Anthony in 1815, Elizabeth Cady grew up in a wealthy and prominent family in Johnstown, New York. Her father, Daniel Cady, was a judge, and her mother, Margaret Livingston Cady, was from one of New York's oldest, most distinguished families. Cady Stanton's parents valued education highly and she received the finest schooling available for a young woman of her era, yet she felt cheated that she did not receive an education that was the equal of her older brother's. Even though she attended Emma Hart Willard's Troy Female Seminary for two years, an institution that was among the first to expand the scope of a young woman's education to include mathematics and science, Cady Stanton always regretted that she did not have the opportunity to attend college.

According to Cady Stanton, the death of her oldest brother, Eleazar, in 1826 was the most significant event of her youth. It was a subject that she focused on in her speeches and her memoir. As her brother lay dying, she found her father grieving inconsolably. When she tried to comfort him, he told her, "Oh, my daughter, I wish you were a boy!" She recalled that she promised him, "I will try to be all my brother was" (Stanton 1973, 20–21). From that moment on, she strove to acquire the knowledge and the accomplishments common to educated young men—she persuaded her church pastor to teach her Greek, studied mathematics more intensely, immersed herself in the study of law and legal history, learned to play chess, and forced herself to become an accomplished equestrian.

To her disappointment and defeat, despite awards and praise in every area she attempted, her father maintained his complete lack of interest in her education and in the development of her intellect. Unlike Susan B. Anthony, whose Quaker father encouraged all his daughters (and sons) to educate themselves and who insisted that each establish an independent livelihood regardless of gender, Cady Stanton always had to be her own motivator. Even though she gained personal satisfaction from acquiring competence in areas traditionally reserved for men and boys, she never lost her anger about society's dismissal of women, a force that she later harnessed to revolutionize the roles of women in society.

After her formal education was completed in 1833, Cady Stanton spent much of her time visiting relatives and waiting until she should marry, a common occupation for women of her social position. In the home of her mother's cousin, Gerrit Smith, in Peterboro, New York, she was first introduced to the exciting whirlwind of social and moral reform. An arch-abolitionist and temperance reformer, Smith dabbled in all sorts of reforms that were the rage in the 1830s. His daughter, Elizabeth Smith (Miller), was Cady Stanton's closest lifelong friend and confidante. Together the two young women were swept up in abolitionist and temperance meetings. At an antislavery gathering at the Smith home in 1839, Cady Stanton met Henry Brewster Stanton, a prominent abolitionist and a former Garrisonian. As much as she was initially attracted to Stanton, hear-

Photograph of Elizabeth Cady Stanton with her daughter, Harriot Stanton (Blatch), who also became a leading suffragist.

ing him speak in public was what made her truly smitten. "As I had a passion for oratory," Cady Stanton recalled in her memoir, "I was deeply impressed with his power." She observed that the weeks following her first meeting with Stanton were the happiest days of her life.

I had become interested in the anti-slavery and temperance questions. . . . I felt a new inspiration in life and was enthused with new ideas of individual rights and the basic principles of government, for the anti-slavery platform was the best school the American people ever had on which to learn republican principles and ethics. (Stanton 1973, 58–59)

Their romance developed at a critical time in the abolitionist movement, when dissension within the American Anti-Slavery Society (AASS) reached the breaking point over a number of crucial issues. Henry Stanton, Smith, and James Birney were committed to the use of political means to achieve national abolition. Stanton's former mentor William

Lloyd Garrison, Wendell Phillips, and other New England abolitionists were equally convinced that political tactics must be avoided at all costs in favor of "moral suasion." AASS members were also at loggerheads as to the role women should play in the society. Garrison's group insisted that women must be allowed to voice their opinions and to participate in the AASS, whereas the political abolitionists did not want women to be involved. It is unclear what Cady Stanton's thoughts were about her future husband's resistance to the activities of women abolitionists in the AASS, but whatever they were, they did not appear to be an obstacle to their union. At the spring 1840 meeting of the AASS, the membership split and the political abolitionists separated from the AASS to form the Liberty Party.

Despite the strong opposition of Cady Stanton's parents, the couple were married on May 1, 1840. They visited among friends briefly before departing for Europe. London and the World Antislavery Convention, to which Henry Stanton was a delegate, was their first destination. There Cady Stanton met another delegate, the only female representative of the AASS and the woman who would become her principal mentor, Lucretia Coffin Mott. Cady Stanton and Coffin Mott forged a strong bond during the convention, discussed women's rights, and vowed to embark on a correspondence. According to Cady Stanton's memoir, when women delegates were prevented from being seated with their male counterparts at the convention, her husband delivered an address protesting the women's exclusion, demonstrating that he was not against women's abolitionist activity.

Throughout the 1840s, Cady Stanton was consumed by domestic responsibilities. She gave birth to the first three of her seven children in this decade. As important as raising children and creating a beautiful home were to her, she experienced an increasing discontentment and restlessness during this era and a longing to be intellectually active and productive. Her correspondence with Coffin Mott broadened her horizons, enriching her spiritually and philosophically while also stimulating her emerging feminism. In the early 1840s, when Cady Stanton's husband opened a law office in Boston, she was thrilled to meet many of the shining lights of the abolitionist and Transcendentalist movements—Theodore Parker, Ralph Waldo Emerson, Bronson Alcott, William Lloyd Garrison, Abby Kelley (Foster), Maria Weston Chapman, and Frederick Douglass, all of whom further invigorated her intellectual development.

After the Stantons moved to Seneca Falls, New York, in 1847, Cady Stanton contributed to statewide efforts to obtain property rights for women. She discussed the issue with New York state legislators and helped to gather signatures for petitions supporting a bill guaranteeing women's legal rights. In March 1848, she was greatly encouraged when the New York Married Women's Property Law was enacted. Several months later, in July 1848, her role in planning and executing the first woman's rights convention at Seneca Falls imbued her with direction, purpose, and an acute sense of what her life's work should be. It was her first opportunity to assert publicly women's social and political equality with men and to demand that laws harmful and unjust to women be erased from the books.

During the 1850s, Cady Stanton was anchored to her home and her children. Her growing sense of her own power as an intellectual and as a women's rights reformer made her painfully aware of her bondage in the traditional world of "women's sphere." In 1851, she met the woman who would help her to break free of her restraints, Susan B. Anthony.

For Cady Stanton, the disapproval of her father, her husband, and her friends was a huge obstacle to her women's rights work and one that Cady Stanton realized she had to overcome. In September 1855, she wrote to Anthony:

I passed through a terrible scourging when last at my father's. I cannot tell you how deep the iron entered my soul. I never felt more keenly the degradation of my sex. To think that all in me of which my father would have felt a proper pride had I been a man, is deeply mortifying to him because I am a woman. . . . That thought has stung me to a fierce decision—to speak as soon as I can do myself credit. . . . Henry [Stanton] sides with my friends, who oppose me in all that is dearest to my heart. They are not willing that I should write even on the woman question. But I will both write and speak. (Stanton and Blatch 1922, 2:59–60)

And write and speak she did. As she wrote to Anthony, she was going to burst if she did not. "Men and angels give me patience! I am at the boiling point! If I do not find some day the use of my tongue on this question [the oppression of women], I shall die of an intellectual repression, a woman's rights convulsion!" (Stanton and Blatch 1922, 2:41). In spite of the overwhelming responsibility of rearing seven children (she bore her seventh and last child in 1859) and feeling much of the time like a "caged lioness," Cady Stanton carefully gathered the hours she needed to become the principal rhetorician of the women's rights movement.

She read and wrote voraciously on women's rights subjects, first for the *New York Tribune* and later for the *Lily*, the *Una*, and several other newspapers. Although she could not attend national woman's rights conventions on a regular basis, she was determined to be deeply involved in the movement. She wrote lengthy letters for Anthony to read at the conventions she could not attend, penned many of Anthony's speeches for her and helped her write the rest, and corresponded with most of the leaders of the movement. Cady Stanton not only became the principal voice of the women's rights

movement but was also its most radical spokesperson.

In 1852–1853, she and Anthony founded and led the Woman's State Temperance Society. From 1854 to 1860 she participated in Anthony's campaign for the expanded New York Married Women's Property Law of 1860, delivering several speeches of pivotal importance before the New York state legislature. From her demand for woman suffrage at the Seneca Falls Convention in 1848 to her insistence on the necessity of divorce reform at the Tenth National Woman's Rights Convention in 1860, she shocked and then coaxed her fellow reformers to embrace a revolutionary vision of women's future as equal, independent, fully participating citizens in a democratic society.

In 1862, the Stanton family's move to Brooklyn, New York, brought Cady Stanton closer to the hub of reform activism and made it much easier for her to work alongside her fellow reformers. In 1863, she and Anthony created the first national women's political organization, the Woman's National Loyal League (WNLL), which fully occupied them through the summer of 1864.

During the immediate postwar years of the Reconstruction era, when all of Cady Stanton's children came of school age, she seized the opportunity to spread her wings and spend periods of time away from home. In 1866, she decided to test the legality of women running for an elected public office. In doing so, she became the first woman to run for Congress. (She received 24 votes.) Also in that year, she and Anthony helped found the American Equal Rights Association (AERA), which was dedicated to pursuing suffrage for all women and African-American males. In 1867, they campaigned for woman suffrage in New York and Kansas. When they established their newspaper, *The Revolution,* in January 1868, Cady Stanton worked long hours as its editor. Through the pages of *The Revolution*, she flexed her literary and philosophical muscles; aired all her grievances against the abolitionists who opposed her and Anthony; and stunned reformers and the general public with her editorials proposing marriage and divorce reform, coeducation, women's labor unions, and woman suffrage. She also penned protests decrying prostitution and the sexual exploitation of women.

When the final split in the women's rights movement occurred in May 1869, Cady Stanton was relieved to leave all the strife of the postwar years behind in the effort to create an independent woman suffrage organization led entirely by women. After developing and experimenting with the idea of a national woman suffrage organization during 1868 and the early months of 1869 through the Woman Suffrage Association of America, she and Anthony formed the National Woman Suffrage Association (NWSA) in May 1869. Although Anthony still felt mired in the onslaught of dissension and controversy that continued to hound them, Cady Stanton seemed to thrive on the conflicts that allowed her to publicize her position and beliefs.

Beginning in November 1869, Cady Stanton initiated an important new chapter in her life when she began lecturing on the lyceum circuit. In the post–Civil War United States, lyceum lecture companies organized popular orators to speak on diverse topics all over the country. Wendell Phillips, Anna Dickinson, Henry Ward Beecher, and eventually Anthony were just a few of Cady Stanton's friends and acquaintances who were famous lyceum lecturers. The lyceum bureaus brought entertainment to the small towns and hamlets attached to the railroads, many of them west of the Mississippi. For the lecturers, the lyceum circuit was an extremely taxing way to make a living. Only those men and women possessing the hardiest constitutions and most adventurous spirits persisted at lyceum lecturing. Cady Stanton, who had a high tolerance for physical discomfort, spoke once or twice a day while on the circuit, most often in the afternoons and evenings. She then traveled by rail the following morning to her next destination. Blizzards, floods, the miserable hovels called hotels, and the inedible food she took in stride, often asserting proudly that women lecturers endured the hardships better than the men.

Cady Stanton weathered the lyceum circuit for ten years, usually traveling eight months of the year. The experience made her completely independent financially and professionally, which gave her an enormous sense of freedom and strength. She spoke on issues of interest to women, focusing especially on women's rights. Her lectures gave her nationwide visibility and made her a household name. "The Subjection of Women," "Marriage and Divorce," "Our Girls," and "Coeducation" were a few of her most requested lecture topics. In her address "Our Girls," her most popular speech, she encouraged parents to help their daughters achieve an independent adulthood—a future in which they would not only serve others but would strive to personally fulfill themselves as individuals. Throughout most of her speeches and writings, Cady Stanton stressed the necessity of a woman's independence, including a woman's right to her own body and sexuality, a concept that she would later label "self-sovereignty." In 1879, as a result of an injury suffered from an omnibus accident and an attack of pneumonia, she decided to terminate her career as a lyceum lecturer to devote herself full-time to her writing projects.

As a result of her busy travel schedule during the 1870s, Cady Stanton could not be deeply involved in the administration of the NWSA. In any case, she had never cared for the labor of organization as Anthony did. Even though Anthony insisted that she maintain her position as president of NWSA year after year, Cady Stanton avoided its conventions whenever her schedule permitted. Despite her distance from the inner workings of the NWSA, she was not idle. She kept refining her feminist vision and broadcasting her convictions about the urgency of achieving women's civil, social, political, and sexual equality to NWSA members and the general public. And in 1878, while Anthony was in the West lecturing on the lyceum circuit, Cady Stanton led NWSA suffragists in their presentation to Congress of her newly worded version of the Sixteenth Amendment.

From 1876 until 1886, whenever Cady Stanton wasn't traveling, she was occupied with the work of compiling and then writing the first three volumes of the *History of Woman Suffrage* with Susan B. Anthony and, occasionally, Matilda Joslyn Gage. The three women worked together at Cady Stanton's home in Tenafly, New Jersey, which she had purchased in 1868 with money she had inherited from her father. Following her retirement from the lyceum circuit, Cady Stanton thoroughly enjoyed her new status as a homebody, writing in her diary, "I do not believe there ever was a woman who esteemed it such a privilege to stay at home" (Stanton and Blatch 1922, 2:179). She and Anthony spent many months together writing; for Cady Stanton the process was a thrilling challenge, for Anthony a torture beyond description.

Beginning in the late 1870s and continuing into the 1890s, Cady Stanton became increasingly concerned about the growing conservatism of the woman suffrage movement and of all American social reform. She frequently admitted that she could not comprehend the new, younger generation of women reformers—the socially and religiously conservative, educated, middle-class women—who appeared to accept women's oppression in the home and society. In this climate, Cady Stanton claimed her role as a radical visionary who openly advertised her rebellion against every institution's repression of women. As much as she tried to keep alive the radical spirit of the women's rights reformers of the antebellum and Reconstruction years, she became a lone liberal voice in a conservative wilderness. The vast majority of suffragists and women social reformers increasingly distrusted her radicalism and sought other leaders to voice their political

sentiments and aspirations—Susan B. Anthony, Frances Willard, and later, Anna Howard Shaw and Carrie Chapman Catt.

As much as Cady Stanton reveled in being rooted to one place, she did not remain at home long. In 1882, accompanied by her daughter Harriot Stanton, she ventured abroad to France to visit her son Theodore Stanton. Through her travels in France and in England, both in 1882–1883 and in 1886–1888, Cady Stanton visited with her children and grandchildren. She occasionally lectured and had long conversations with British and French reformers and feminists. During these years she envisioned an international suffrage movement but discovered that European feminists were more concerned about achieving basic civil and legal rights for women. In 1883, when Anthony joined her in England, Cady Stanton helped formulate their original conception of the International Council of Women (ICW), which she later attended and addressed in March 1888.

After the NWSA and the American Woman Suffrage Association (AWSA) merged to form the National American Woman Suffrage Association (NAWSA) in 1890, Cady Stanton allowed Anthony to talk her into serving as president for two more years. By this time, however, not only was it clear to NAWSA members that she was no longer the ideological spokesperson of the organization, but it was also obvious that her decades as the NWSA and NAWSA figurehead were at an end. Her radicalism, especially her ever-increasing attacks on the Christian clergy and theology, disturbed most suffragists. Although many reformers were willing to acknowledge the historical debt they owed to her pioneering feminism, they could not accept her leadership, especially not ideologically.

When Cady Stanton published the first volume of her work *The Woman's Bible* in 1895 at the age of 80, the majority of NAWSA suffragists rejected it even though most had never read it. It angered and

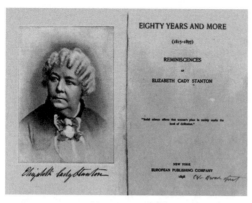

Elizabeth Cady Stanton published her memoir, **Eighty Years and More,** *in 1898, at the age of eighty-three.*

wounded her that NAWSA members believed that they had no choice but to distance themselves and NAWSA from her independent writings. It was as if they were rejecting her personally, which she found unforgivably unfair. Despite the controversy over *The Woman's Bible*, which marred the tranquillity and fulfillment of her final years, overall she was quite content with herself and her life in her old age. She had adjusted to life without her husband, who had died in 1887. She enjoyed having the leisure time to spend with her children and grandchildren, and she loved the free hours to write to her heart's content about the issues that most excited her. Although she was persona non grata among suffragists, she was, like Anthony, an extraordinarily famous national celebrity. Known as the "Grand Old Woman of America," her years on the lyceum circuit, her frequently published articles and newspaper columns, and her best-selling books *The Woman's Bible* and her 1898 memoir *Eighty Years and More: Reminiscences of Elizabeth Cady Stanton* kept her name and her ideas before the public.

When Cady Stanton died in 1902 of heart failure, she was just two weeks shy of her eighty-seventh birthday. Newspapers and magazines all over the country honored her life and legacy by publishing editorials and memorial articles reflecting on her achievements. Although nearly blind during the last few years of her life, she was mentally alert

and was still agitating for women's rights right up to the end. Just days before she died, she dictated several letters. One implored President Theodore Roosevelt to persuade Congress to approve the Sixteenth Amendment enfranchising women. She sent another letter to Edith Carow Roosevelt, the First Lady, asking her to use all her influence to pressure the president to speak for woman suffrage.

Although Anthony grieved intensely after learning of Cady Stanton's death, she consented to be interviewed by several newspaper reporters who were clamoring for her commentary on the life of her closest colleague. Although she declared that she felt wholly inadequate to express Cady Stanton's greatness, Anthony struggled to articulate her thoughts on her friend's passing. "Mrs. Stanton was a most courageous woman, a leader of thought and action," Anthony told the press.

> I have always called her the statesman
> of our movement. . . . As a speaker
> and a writer she was unsurpassed. . . .
> She combined in herself a marvelous
> trinity—reformer, philosopher,
> statesman. Had she been of the
> orthodox sex she would have been
> United States Senator or Chief Justice
> of the Supreme Court, but, belonging
> to the alleged inferior half of the
> human family, she died without
> having her opinions weighed in
> either the political or judicial scales
> of the Government. (Harper 1908,
> 3:1262–1263)

In an article for the *North American Review* published several weeks after Cady Stanton's death, Anthony wrote: "A deep feeling of regret will always prevail that the Liberator of Woman, Elizabeth Cady Stanton, could not live to see the complete triumph of her cause, as did those other great emancipators, Lincoln, Garrison and Phillips; but she died in the full knowledge that the day of its victory is clearly marked on the calendar of the near future" (Harper 1908, 3:1266). With her death, Anthony had been forced to let go of her long-cherished dream that she and Cady Stanton, standing arm in arm, would celebrate the glorious victory of national woman suffrage. Her passing and Anthony's daily reminders of her own aging and increasing frailty hammered home the tragic personal loss that she, too, would never live to see American women win the right to vote.

Related entries:
American Equal Rights Association
American Woman Suffrage Association
Anthony, Susan B.
Anthony/Cady Stanton Partnership
Beecher-Tilton Scandal
Bloomer Costume
Fifteenth Amendment
Fourteenth Amendment
Free-Love Controversy
Garrison, William Lloyd
Greeley, Horace
The *History of Woman Suffrage*
Hooker, Isabella Beecher
International Council of Women
Kansas Campaign of 1867
The *Lily*
Mott, Lucretia Coffin
National American Woman Suffrage Association
National Labor Union
National Woman Suffrage Association
New York Married Women's Property Law of 1860
The *New York Tribune*
Phillips, Wendell
Reconstruction
The Revolution
Seneca Falls Convention of 1848
Sixteenth Amendment Campaign
Smith, Gerrit
Stanton, Henry Brewster
Stone, Lucy
Thirteenth Amendment
Train, George Francis
The *Una*
Woman Suffrage Association of America
Woman Suffrage Movement
The Woman's Bible
Woman's National Loyal League
Woman's Rights Conventions
Woman's State Temperance Society
The *Woman's Tribune*
Women's Rights Movement
Woodhull, Victoria Claflin
Wright, Martha Coffin

Suggestions for further reading:
DuBois, Ellen Carol, ed. 1992. *The Elizabeth Cady Stanton–Susan B. Anthony Reader: Correspondence, Writings, Speeches.* Boston: Northeastern University Press.
Griffith, Elisabeth. 1984. *In Her Own Right: The Life of Elizabeth Cady Stanton.* New York: Oxford University Press.
Stanton, Elizabeth Cady. 1898, 1973. *Eighty Years and More: Reminiscences of Elizabeth Cady Stanton.* New York: Source Book Press.

Stanton, Henry Brewster (1805–1887)

Abolitionist, journalist, and lawyer Henry Brewster Stanton married Elizabeth Cady in May 1840, at a turning point in the history of the abolitionist movement. In Susan B. Anthony's life, Henry Stanton was nearly as distant a figure as he was to Cady Stanton. Yet despite his frequent travel and absences from the whirlwind of his wife and Anthony's activism, Henry Stanton's acute knowledge of politics, his pivotal position in abolitionist reform and history, and the sterling example of his uncompromising activism inspired Anthony during the early 1850s as she challenged herself to become a reformer. Years later, in 1862, when no abolitionist would join her in her desire to continue agitating for immediate emancipation, he encouraged her to get actively involved in spite of the naysayers. As a Washington reporter for the *New York Tribune* in the early months of the Civil War, he feared that the North was losing ground and that emancipation would never be achieved unless northerners banded together to demand the slaves' freedom. "Here then is work for you," he wrote Anthony. "Susan, put on your armor and go forth!" (Harper 1899, 1:226). And so she did—to cooperate with Cady Stanton in establishing the first women's national political organization, the Woman's National Loyal League (WNLL).

Though Henry Stanton was raised in Connecticut, he lived most of his life in New

York state, settling in Rochester as early as 1826. For a time he worked as a clerk while studying journalism and the law. He soon developed a keen interest in politics. But when he heard the renowned evangelical Protestant revivalist Charles Grandison Finney preach in 1830, Henry Stanton was immediately and overwhelmingly swept up in the revivalist frenzy. His sudden absorption in religion and the powerful influence of his friend Theodore Dwight Weld convinced Stanton that he possessed a vocation for the ministry. With Weld, he enrolled at Lane Seminary in Ohio, a center of evangelical religious reform. They stayed only until 1834, when their burgeoning commitment to abolitionism forced them and many of their like-minded fellow students to leave Lane, which was restricting their antislavery activities.

By 1835, Henry Stanton had become an agent for the American Anti-Slavery Society (AASS) and a rising protégé of William Lloyd Garrison. Stanton traveled widely for the AASS, lecturing on antislavery issues and braving violent mobs from city to city. A friend of the abolitionist Gerrit Smith, Stanton was a guest at his home when he met Smith's cousin, Elizabeth Cady, in 1839. By this time, Stanton had strong differences with Garrison and had defected from the AASS. He was exploring the possibility of forming a new political organization that would aggressively seek political solutions to achieve the emancipation of the slaves. With his colleague James Birney and others, in the spring of 1840 he helped establish the Liberty Party.

After marrying Cady Stanton and returning from their European travels and his involvement at the World Antislavery Convention in London, he realized that he needed to earn more money than the paltry income he received as an abolitionist agent. He worked as an attorney while remaining active in antislavery politics. A devout Republican from the party's inception in 1856, Stanton was a delegate to the Republican

National Conventions in 1856 and 1860. During the late 1850s and early 1860s, he eagerly sought a position in the federal government but was continually overlooked for top federal positions. Finally, in August 1861, he was appointed a deputy collector of the Customs House in New York City, part of the New York Port Authority. Stanton proved to be an ineffective administrator, perhaps in large part because he so disliked the job. In 1863, shortly after hiring his and Cady Stanton's oldest son, Daniel Cady Stanton, to work as a clerk in his office, a scandal erupted. Daniel accepted a bribe and forged his father's signature on some documents without his knowledge. When the corruption was discovered, Henry Stanton was held responsible. He lost his position as well as his reputation in government and in political circles.

Following this disastrous conclusion to Stanton's political career, he was unemployed for a time, but by 1864 he was working again as a journalist for the *New York Tribune*. From 1868 until his death in 1887, he was a writer for the *New York Sun*.

Related entries:
Abolitionist Movement
Civil War
Stanton, Elizabeth Cady
Woman's National Loyal League

Suggestions for further reading:
Gordon, Ann D., and Tamara Gaskell Miller, eds. 1997. *The Selected Papers of Elizabeth Cady Stanton and Susan B. Anthony.* Vol. 1. New Brunswick, N.J.: Rutgers University Press.
Griffith, Elisabeth. 1984. *In Her Own Right: The Life of Elizabeth Cady Stanton.* New York: Oxford University Press.

State Suffrage Campaigns

Despite the time and energy that Susan B. Anthony expended on advancing the Sixteenth Amendment, she also managed to devote herself to state suffrage campaigns. Most of the state struggles that she actively participated in or closely supervised were located

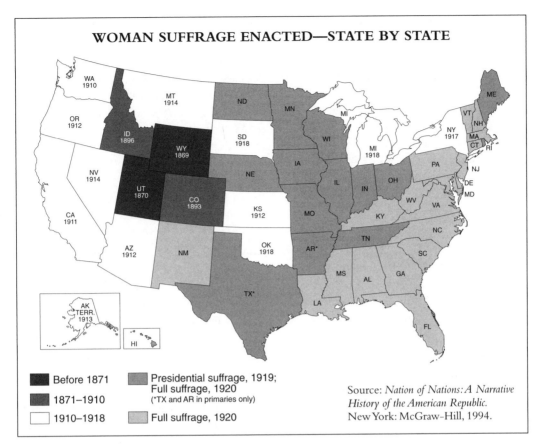

WOMAN SUFFRAGE ENACTED—STATE BY STATE

WA 1910
MT 1914
OR 1912
ID 1896
SD 1918
WY 1869
ND
MN
MI
ME
VT
NH
NY 1917
MA
CT
RI
NV 1914
UT 1870
CO 1893
NE
IA
WI
MI 1918
PA
NJ
DE
MD
CA 1911
AZ 1912
NM
KS 1912
OK 1918
MO
IL
IN
OH
WV
VA
KY
NC
TN
SC
AR*
MS
AL
GA
TX*
LA
FL

AK TERR. 1913
HI

Before 1871

1871–1910

1910–1918

Presidential suffrage, 1919;
Full suffrage, 1920
(*TX and AR in primaries only)

Full suffrage, 1920

Source: *Nation of Nations: A Narrative History of the American Republic.* New York: McGraw-Hill, 1994.

in the states and territories west of the Mississippi River. Although Anthony never ceased to be critical of the American Woman Suffrage Association's (AWSA's) state-by-state suffrage strategy, she carefully watched and tended the National Woman Suffrage Association's (NWSA's) and, after 1890, the National American Woman Suffrage Association's (NAWSA's) state campaigns.

She was especially optimistic about the possibility of suffrage victories in the West. She believed, as did other leading suffragists, that woman suffrage could be more easily and quickly attained in the West than in the East, Midwest, and South, because opposition to woman suffrage was not as well organized in the West and because she believed that western men were more receptive to the concept of women voting. But even though western women were enfranchised before women in other regions of the country, there were no easy, uncomplicated victories in the West. Each territory's and state's suffrage battle

was fraught with its own idiosyncratic issues and obstacles, which necessitated unremitting activism.

From Anthony's involvement in the Kansas campaign of 1867 through her immersion in the California suffrage campaign of 1896 nearly 30 years later, she campaigned long and hard in the West, seeking to perfect her command of state campaign strategies to overcome the often overwhelming opposition of many antisuffrage groups. Despite the frequent suffrage defeats, Anthony relished western campaigns. Although she bemoaned the discomforts and physical hardships of frontier travel, she was always invigorated by the challenge. Most of all, she was inspired by the people she met in the West. She understood their struggle for survival and respected their audacity in carving out new lives and communities from virgin land.

Anthony was wholeheartedly committed to one basic state strategy, from which all NWSA and NAWSA tactics flowed:

State Suffrage Campaigns   *197*

All we have to do is to educate a majority of the men of any state to want to have the women of their households and of everybody else's households enfranchised, and we must educate them so thoroughly that not a man of them can be influenced by the threat of the liquor men to withdraw financial or political support from them if they work for woman suffrage.

Education was the key to every state tactic that Anthony and NWSA and NAWSA activists supported. They instigated a suffrage debate in the press, conducted rallies, lectured in every town and hamlet, lobbied state legislators, and distributed suffrage literature. Anthony resented state and local suffragists who claimed that her methods and other national leaders' tactics were not appropriate for the conditions in their states. Abigail Scott Duniway, chief suffrage leader in the Pacific Northwest, complained bitterly about the destructive influence of "eastern interference" and "eastern methods" on western campaigns. Anthony had no patience with this line of reasoning. "There are no methods that are good for the East that are not equally good for the West, and there are none that are good for the West that are not equally good for the East," she declared. "I have been in nearly every State. . . . I have never seen that one place required any different tactics from every other" (SBA to CBC, February 12, 1897, CBC-HL, in *Papers*).

Anthony refused to consider the possibility that eastern suffragists' control of western state campaigns might be counterproductive. In California and in Oregon, state activists blamed their suffrage defeats on eastern suffragists' inability to listen to their ideas and input about the antisuffrage forces in their home territories. Not until after Anthony's retirement as president of NAWSA would national leaders truly value collaborating on an equal basis with state suffragists.

The following discussion of Anthony's involvement in the most visible state suffrage campaigns focuses on her experiences and her contributions. The best, all-around source of information on individual state suffrage campaigns remains the six-volume *History of Woman Suffrage*. Although *HWS* chronicles the activities of the AWSA in many states, additional information about AWSA contributions may be found in its official suffrage newspaper, the *Woman's Journal*.

NINETEENTH-CENTURY STATE SUFFRAGE VICTORIES—WYOMING, UTAH, COLORADO, AND IDAHO

At the time of Anthony's death in 1906, after more than a half-century of her woman suffrage activism, only four states had enfranchised women—Wyoming, Utah, Colorado, and Idaho. Wyoming, the first to extend the ballot to women in 1869 while it was still a territory, was symbolically important to all suffragists. As the first suffrage victory, it was the first proof that men were indeed capable of legislating and voting for woman suffrage. During the 1870s, 1880s, and 1890s, when the woman suffrage movement suffered defeat after defeat, Wyoming and Utah were the bulwarks of success that supported suffragists in the seemingly never-ending, insurmountable struggle to achieve national woman suffrage.

Wyoming

Wyoming's first territorial legislature voted to enfranchise women in 1869. Despite a number of legislative challenges over the next two decades, woman suffrage remained intact and lent credence to Wyoming residents' boasts that women's voting not only caused no problems but was a salutary, civilizing force on the political process and society. Throughout the 1870s and 1880s, national politicians and the press regarded woman suffrage in Wyoming Territory as an experiment—an aberration to be closely observed before any other state took similar action. Whenever eastern newspapers reported on the "failures" of woman suffrage in Wyoming, the Wyoming press was quick to counterattack with articles attempting to prove how favorably woman suffrage was working.

Why did Wyoming legislators enact woman suffrage, and why did they fight to keep it? Although historians have debated this question since women began voting in Wyoming, most agree on one point—legislators and business leaders wished to promote Wyoming to the nation in the hopes of attracting the attention of emigrants heading west (Beeton 1986, 4). The need to publicize Wyoming's virtues fostered the development of a societywide commitment to retaining woman suffrage that successfully resisted all encroachments. When Wyoming applied for statehood in 1889, Democrats in Congress were determined to thwart the admission of another Republican state. They used the general congressional opposition to woman suffrage as a means to deny Wyoming its statehood. Anthony, who witnessed part of this debate in Congress, was jubilant when a telegram from the Wyoming legislature arrived, declaring that Wyoming would "remain out of the Union a hundred years rather than come in without woman suffrage" (*HWS*, 4:999–1000). A vote soon followed, and the House of Representatives voted 139 to 127 to admit Wyoming as a state. The Senate delayed action but finally voted to accept Wyoming's statehood in July 1890.

Utah

Although Utah's territorial legislature voted to enfranchise women in February 1870, just two months after Wyoming, Utah's suffrage issues were completely different from Wyoming's. Utah was predominantly populated by Mormons, members of the Church of Jesus Christ of Latter-day Saints. Congress and the federal government had long been concerned with various tenets of the Mormon faith, particularly the practice of polygamy. When Utah's legislators began to debate enacting woman suffrage, the eastern political establishment and woman suffrage leaders predicted that polygamy would be abolished when Mormon women had the

power to vote. Anthony and the majority of Americans believed that the institution of polygamy, which they considered nearly as grave an evil as prostitution, oppressed and enslaved Mormon women. Utah legislators, nearly all of them Mormon men, supported woman suffrage for precisely the opposite reason. Because they knew the intensity of Mormon women's fidelity to their faith, they knew that Mormon women would never vote to curtail or eliminate polygamy and that they would support this practice against any infringement from the federal government (Iverson 1990, 8–9).

During the next 20 years, antipolygamy forces in Congress and in the nation debated how the government should handle the "Mormon problem." Included in the laws intended to subjugate Utah's Mormons and abolish polygamy were measures to disfranchise the women of Utah. None succeeded until the Edmunds-Tucker Act of 1887, when, among the bill's other provisions, all Utah women lost their right to the ballot.

During the 1870s, Anthony, Cady Stanton, and the NWSA supported Mormon women in their battle to retain suffrage. Continuing this assistance through the 1880s, however, proved to be fraught with difficulties. National and Utah antipolygamy groups grew in strength and influence during the 1880s as they infiltrated women's temperance groups and conservative religious organizations.

Anthony and NWSA leaders then faced a perplexing dilemma. How were they to support Mormon women's right to the ballot when they desperately needed the support of temperance and conservative women? Anthony's solution was to divorce the Utah women's suffrage issues from all debates concerning polygamy. According to one historian of western suffrage, this plan did not protect the NWSA from negative press coverage and unfavorable public opinion. The approach also seriously marred Anthony's and NWSA leaders' relationships with Mormon woman suffragists, who felt betrayed when their eastern sisters would not uphold the

Mormons' constitutional right to practice their religious beliefs.

A number of NWSA leaders and the leadership of the AWSA so objected to women's disfranchisement as a consequence of the Edmunds–Tucker Act that they sent a delegation to President Grover Cleveland to deliver a petition from Mormon women protesting the new law. Anthony chose not to participate. Although it is not clear why she did not join this delegation, her action is consistent with her paramount goal after the early 1870s—to steer the suffrage movement clear of political issues that might harm or detract from the cause. Anthony also must have realized that her involvement in a high-profile political maneuver would attract enormous press attention to an issue she wanted to keep out of the limelight (Iverson 1990, 12).

After Mormon leaders declared that they had abolished polygamy as part of the Woodruff Manifesto of 1890, Mormon women found it much easier to be integrated into the woman suffrage movement and the NWSA. In 1895, Utah's legislature added woman suffrage to its new constitution, and after Congress approved it, Utah was admitted as a state in January 1896.

Colorado

Although Colorado's territorial legislature began debating woman suffrage as soon as Wyoming enfranchised women in 1870, it rejected adding woman suffrage to its first state constitution because legislators feared that doing so would jeopardize Colorado's bid for statehood. After Colorado was admitted as a state in 1876, its first constitutional convention provided for a voter referendum on woman suffrage in 1877.

Anthony responded to the call of Colorado suffrage leaders in 1877 and canvassed the state even though the AWSA was also involved in the Colorado suffrage campaign. She reported that the Colorado campaign was the most arduous of her career thus far, more difficult even than the Kansas campaign of 1867 (Harper 1899, 1:490). Like Kansas in the late 1860s, most of Colorado was rough, barely settled wilderness. The mountainous terrain, sparse railroads, primitive roads, and spartan living conditions taxed this most seasoned campaigner. She spoke to voting men whenever and wherever she could encourage them to gather—in hotel dining rooms, churches, tiny schoolhouses, and saloons. As she canvassed the state, she became increasingly concerned when she discovered that many men, particularly in the mining villages, had trouble understanding what she was saying and her purpose for speaking to them. She then realized that she was pleading for her political rights with immigrant voters who spoke little or no English and lacked knowledge of the U.S. political system. And when they did understand her, they tended to be hostile to the idea of woman suffrage or, at best, indifferent to it. For these reasons, the Colorado campaign of 1877 prejudiced Anthony against the viability of state suffrage campaigns. Although she continued to participate in them, she was convinced that "begging my rights at the feet of the great unwashed rabble" was not the most effective means of achieving national woman suffrage (*The New Northwest*, January 11, 1878, in *Papers*).

Despite an organized, albeit grossly underfinanced campaign, woman suffrage was overwhelmingly defeated. Henry Blackwell, who directed the AWSA effort with Lucy Stone, declared that the combined forces of the various antisuffrage liquor interests were instrumental in defeating the referendum (Marilley 1996, 96).

After a lull of 16 years, the Colorado state legislature again put woman suffrage to a referendum in 1893. Colorado suffragists were much more highly organized than they had been in 1877, and with the enthusiastic endorsement of the extremely popular Populist Party and the support of all the Republican factions and the Prohibition Party, woman suffrage was assured. Anthony did not travel to Colorado for this campaign but kept in constant communication with

Women at the polls in Denver, first appearing in **Harper's** **Weekly,** *1894.*

her trusted, top-notch organizer par excellence, NAWSA suffragist Carrie Chapman Catt, who worked in concert with Colorado suffragists and Woman's Christian Temperance Union (WCTU) reformers. Anthony insisted that the education of male voters be the focus of the campaign. She also ordered all groups involved to walk the political tightrope—to obtain political party endorsements while remaining solidly independent of them. "Don't be Democrats, nor Republicans, nor Populists—don't be Prohibitionists nor Saloonists. Don't be religionist or agnostic—just be nothing but woman and her disenfranchised" (SBA to Ellis Meredith, July 16, 1893, EM-CHS, in *Papers*). The key to success, Anthony always told state workers, was to keep the focus solely on obtaining the ballot for women. This time the referendum passed with a 55 percent majority, and Colorado became the first state to win suffrage by a popular referendum.

Idaho

The Idaho territorial legislature voted on a woman suffrage measure as early as 1871, but when that failed, the issue did not receive serious attention again until 1889, during Idaho's first state constitutional convention. Idaho legislators were concerned that enfranchising the state's women would disproportionately enhance the voting power of the state's Mormon population (approximately 25 percent of the total) and cause more Mormons to settle in Idaho. The state's liquor interests also feared that the female vote would enact prohibition (Beeton 1986, 119).

When Congress admitted Idaho as a state in 1890, the state constitution did not include woman suffrage, nor did it permit Mormon men to vote. During the next six years, Idaho suffragists, Oregon suffrage activist Abigail Scott Duniway, and NAWSA leaders lobbied the legislators and appealed to voters. In 1896 the Idaho legislature voted to submit a woman suffrage amendment to the electorate, and a vigorous suffrage campaign was initiated. Anthony did not campaign in Idaho because she was immersed in the California suffrage campaign, but she remained in constant correspondence with NAWSA leaders and Idaho suffragists. As in the Colorado suffrage campaign of 1893, she advised Idaho activists to focus their efforts and resources on educating the legislators and the public—through party newspapers, the press, public suffrage meetings, and lectures.

Despite Scott Duniway's 20 years of activism on behalf of Idaho woman suffrage and her wish to lead the 1896 campaign, Anthony found she had to make the difficult decision to urge her old friend to stand aside. NAWSA leaders, particularly Carrie Chapman Catt, distrusted and disliked Scott Duniway, who insisted on her independence and refused to cooperate with the NAWSA Idaho suffrage team.

During the Idaho campaign, NAWSA and Idaho suffrage leaders resorted to racist and nativist arguments to sway the public. They emphasized that since uneducated, "uncivilized" African-American and Chinese men and, in some states, "savage" Native American men were permitted to vote, shouldn't educated, white, morally upright women be extended the same privilege? (Beeton 1986, 127).

By the time of the election, the Idaho press and all political parties—Populists, Democrats, and both wings of the Republican Party—supported woman suffrage. Even though the amendment passed by almost a two-to-one margin, suffragists were aghast when the state's board of canvassers asserted that it had been defeated. The board officials based this determination on the fact that a majority of the *total* voters in the election had not cast ballots in favor of the referendum, only a majority of those who voted on the actual amendment. Suffragists nationwide held their breath as the Idaho state supreme court reviewed the issue. When the court decided that the amendment indeed had become law, Anthony was ecstatic, if for no

other reason than that a court of law had finally decided in favor of woman suffrage, after nearly 30 years of unfavorable judicial review of woman suffrage measures (Harper, 3:918–919).

THE PACIFIC STATES

California

In the early years of the woman suffrage movement, Anthony and Cady Stanton embarked on a lecture tour of California in the hopes of rousing woman suffrage sentiment in the Far West and to help Anthony repay *The Revolution* debt. As much as they both reveled in viewing the magnificent western scenery and spending long, uninterrupted periods of time together, their 1871 California tour was completely marred for Anthony by the stormy aftermath to a lecture she gave in San Francisco. Near the conclusion of this speech, Anthony emphasized that society's institutions and leaders, contrary to the popular perception, do not and cannot protect women. She declared that women must be enfranchised so that they have the power to influence legislators to pass laws that will enable them to receive wages that are on a par with men's so that they can be economically self-sufficient. The audience became enraged when Anthony asserted that Laura Fair, a notorious prostitute convicted of the murder of her lover, would not be in jail if it were true that men successfully protected the economic needs of women. To Anthony, the mere existence of prostitution disproved this notion. While the crowd tried to hiss and boo her off the stage, she held her ground, as she did in the days when she was an abolitionist. She kept repeating her statements until the audience, perhaps admiring her courage, cheered. The press, however, lambasted her in every newspaper the next day. They misconstrued her message as an endorsement of Laura Fair's lifestyle and crime. As a result of the massive press pillorying, Anthony had to abandon those lectures that were not canceled outright, although she did manage to speak a few times before concluding this disappointing introduction to California.

Anthony returned to California with NAWSA suffragist Anna Howard Shaw in 1895 on a lecture and convention tour that proved to be an entirely different experience from her 1871 trip. The California legislature had recently voted in favor of submitting a woman suffrage amendment to the electorate in 1896. Before Anthony and Howard Shaw returned east, they assisted California suffrage leaders in planning and organizing their 1896 campaign. Following their mutual recoveries from serious illness, both women returned to California in early March 1896, to supervise and participate in the campaign.

For its time, the 1896 California campaign was the largest, longest, and most extensively organized woman suffrage campaign (Flexner 1975, 230). Anthony insisted that she would not remain active in the campaign unless multiple political party endorsements were secured. Within months of her arrival, the Populists, the Republicans, the Prohibitionists, and the Socialist Labor and National Labor Parties sanctioned the woman suffrage amendment, though the Republicans later withdrew their support. At the age of 76, Anthony maintained an exhausting schedule for eight months with no apparent ill effect. She lectured at least once a day, and often as many as three times a day, to political rallies,

> church conventions of every denomination, Spiritualist and Freethinkers' gatherings, Salvation Army meetings, African societies; Socialists, all kinds of labor organizations, granges, Army and Navy Leagues, Soldier's Homes and military encampments, women's clubs and men's clubs; farmers' picnics on the mountain tops . . . and in poolrooms where there was printed on the blackboard, "Welcome to Susan B. Anthony." (*HWS*, 4:490)

Anthony and NAWSA suffragist Ida Husted Harper visited the editors of dozens of newspapers to enlist their support for the amendment. Only a fraction of the hundreds of newspapers consulted did not advocate the amendment. On top of this grueling schedule, Anthony managed to write a 1,600-word

At the age of 75, Susan B. Anthony (center) rode through Yosemite Valley with her faithful suffrage "lieutenants," just before launching an enormous campaign in California for woman suffrage.

column for the *San Francisco Examiner* every week for seven months.

In California, the extensive organization and teamwork between national and state suffragists, the total cooperation of the WCTU, and the financial contributions from every stratum of society added a new dimension to this state suffrage campaign, but when the November election day arrived, the amendment was resoundingly defeated. Oddly enough, votes against the amendment were concentrated in a small, extremely conservative area of the state—in San Francisco, Oakland, and Alameda. The morning after the election, Anthony said, "I don't care for myself, I am used to defeat, but these dear California Women who have worked so hard, how can they bear it?" (Harper 1899, 2:891). Anthony would not live to see California women enfranchised in 1911, when the suffrage campaign of that year at long last managed to break the grasp of the liquor interests. The woman suffrage referendum passed by only 3,587 votes.

Oregon

Anthony left Cady Stanton in California at the conclusion of their 1871 tour to answer the invitation of Oregon suffragist Abigail Scott Duniway to accompany her on a tour of Oregon and Washington Territory. Anthony, whose earnings from lecturing in California fell short of her expectations, felt drawn to the challenge and to Scott Duniway's promise that Pacific Northwest suffragists were eager to see and hear her. As a major historian of the Pacific Northwest suffrage movement has asserted, Anthony's 1871 tour made an enduring impact on this region and greatly influenced the development of Oregon's and Washington's suffrage movements (Edwards 1990, 9).

Anthony enjoyed Scott Duniway's company and admired the younger woman's stamina and fervor for the suffrage cause. For the next three months the two women toured together. Scott Duniway assumed the role of manager, planning all the travel arrangements,

speaking engagements, lodgings, and meals. In return, Anthony agreed to give Scott Duniway half the proceeds from her speeches. Anthony was excited to see the blossoming of a dynamic suffrage leader in Scott Duniway and instructed her in the ideology, methods, and strategies of NWSA suffragists. She felt inspired as she did whenever she saw an opportunity to educate women and men receptive to her suffrage message. She loved setting the reform work in motion, the sense of being in on the ground floor to shape and influence a fledgling movement. Throughout her travels, she encouraged Oregon women to establish local and state suffrage societies as the key organizing element necessary to obtaining the franchise. Through these organizations, she counseled them, they could organize meetings and lectures, print and distribute suffrage literature, and urge women to vote at upcoming elections as a test of the NWSA's "New Departure" strategy (Edwards 1990, 115).

Although Anthony did not impress everyone connected with the press, on the whole, she received favorable reviews from many editors and reporters. Even those who objected to her message gave her views prominent coverage. Throughout this tour, Anthony relied on her "The Power of the Ballot" speech, which emphasized the harsh, discriminatory economic realities oppressing disfranchised women. Even her most outspoken critics had to admit that her meetings and lectures awakened Oregon citizens to an unfamiliar subject—the deplorable economic condition of women. Following Anthony's return east, Scott Duniway became the principal suffrage leader of the Pacific Northwest, although her success in the national suffrage movement would be extremely limited and her relationship with Anthony and NWSA and NAWSA suffragists would be stormy at best.

Oregon endured six separate suffrage campaigns before finally achieving woman suffrage in 1912. The first woman suffrage referendum was defeated in 1884. Scott

Duniway blamed the NWSA for not sending sufficient funds, and she accused the liquor and business interests for manipulating the "ignorant, beer-guzzling" immigrants into voting against woman suffrage.

When the next referendum was submitted to the voters in 1900, the Oregon suffrage leader insisted on using a tactic that ignited a battle with Anthony and NAWSA leaders—the "still hunt" stratagem. Through her still hunt method, she quietly prevailed upon prominent citizens, legislators, top public officials, and business and civic leaders to support woman suffrage. By neglecting the education of the electorate through public rallies, canvassing, speeches, and the press as Anthony and NAWSA leaders advised, she hoped to avoid triggering the virulent antisuffrage tactics of the liquor industry. Although woman suffrage nearly passed, capturing 48 percent of the vote, the defeat forever alienated Scott Duniway from Anthony and NAWSA leaders, who believed that her still hunt method lost the campaign by failing to involve apathetic women and to educate male voters.

In preparation for the next referendum in 1906, NAWSA held its 1905 convention in Portland. Anthony, now 85 years old, made the cross-country trek against medical advice. "Oh, these doctors," she remarked to a reporter. "They said I couldn't make the trip and live, . . . and I sat and watched myself all the time expecting to die every minute; but I didn't" (June 27, 1905, *Oregon Journal*, as quoted in Edwards 1990, 214). Scott Duniway soon regretted having invited the NAWSA convention to meet in Portland when its leaders closed her out of the leadership of her own state's campaign. The Oregon 1906 campaign was in full swing as Anthony lay dying at her home in Rochester, New York. With NAWSA president Anna Howard Shaw at her side, Anthony regretted being absent from the Oregon suffrage struggle she had initiated 35 years earlier. This campaign, too, failed, as did the 1908 and 1910 contests. In 1912, the referendum succeeded in a campaign devoid of any still hunt tactics, a fitting tribute to the efficacy of Anthony's political campaign strategies.

Washington

When Anthony and Abigail Scott Duniway arrived in Olympia, Washington Territory, in 1871 after a 48-hour bone-wracking stagecoach journey from Oregon, ardent Washington suffragists offered an enthusiastic welcome that lifted Anthony's exhaustion. As in Oregon, Anthony hoped to open the question of woman suffrage and stimulate debate among legislators, the press, and the general public while also urging the organization of territorial and local suffrage societies. She so successfully agitated the issue that Washington activists clamored for the territorial legislature to enact woman suffrage. In 1883, the legislature extended the franchise to Washington women, but the territory's supreme court dismissed it three years later. Following Washington's admission as a state in 1889, a woman suffrage referendum failed overwhelmingly. Scott Duniway's and Washington suffragists' best efforts were no match for the liquor industry's well-financed, extensive campaign.

The victorious 1910 Washington suffrage campaign, though it came four years after Anthony's death, bore the unmistakable marks of her influence. Experienced NAWSA campaigner and new Tacoma, Washington, resident Emma Smith De Voe managed an artful combination of Duniway's still hunt tactics and Anthony's NAWSA program of education, agitation, speeches, and rallies (Edwards 1990, 298). The referendum passed easily and triggered a string of western states and Alaska Territory to also enact woman suffrage.

OTHER NOTABLE NAWSA SUFFRAGE CAMPAIGNS

South Dakota

The Dakota territorial legislature nearly enfranchised women in 1872, when a law that would have extended the suffrage to women was defeated by a single vote. In 1879, it granted women "school suffrage," enabling women to cast ballots at school committee meetings throughout the territory. But when Dakota entered the union as the states of South Dakota and North Dakota in 1889, both new state legislatures did not continue to grant women this right.

South Dakota's first state legislature agreed to submit a woman suffrage amendment to the voters in November 1890. Anthony, as was her policy, had no intention of campaigning in South Dakota unless woman suffrage received the endorsement of at least two major political parties. When representatives from the South Dakota Farmers' Alliance and the Knights of Labor promised their undying support for the amendment, Anthony prepared for a long campaign and arrived in Huron, South Dakota, in early May 1890. She canvassed the state along with Henry Blackwell and a host of NAWSA suffragists—Clara Bewick Colby, Olympia Brown, Anna Howard Shaw, Carrie Chapman Catt, and Emma Smith De Voe. When the Farmers' Alliance and the Knights of Labor united to create a third independent party, their advocacy of the amendment evaporated. Then the Republican Party, the Democrats, and the Prohibition Party refused to endorse woman suffrage. Without any political party support, Anthony, Blackwell, and the NAWSA team knew they faced failure. Yet, they did not pull out of the campaign but continued to canvass the sprawling prairie in a summer that set all-time records for its scorching heat.

Anthony declared in a letter to friends back east that she "never felt so buoyed up with the love and sympathy and confidence of the good people everywhere." She sympathized with the tribulations of the South Dakota homesteaders who had suffered two seasons of searing drought. Destruction from raging prairie fires had decimated many homesteads. These pioneers faced financial ruin, and now, she wrote, "starvation stares them in the face" (Harper 1899, 2:688–690).

At a vigorous age 70, Anthony did not appear to suffer from being deprived of regular, edible meals or rest, asserting that with seven state suffrage campaigns behind her, she was better inured to these hardships than her younger colleagues. NAWSA vice president Shaw campaigned with Anthony in South Dakota. Years later, in her autobiography *Story of a Pioneer*, she portrayed a startlingly clear picture of the physical hardships they faced.

> That South Dakota campaign was one of the most difficult we ever made. . . . The sand was like powder, so deep that the wheels of the wagons in which we rode "across country" sank half-way to the hubs; . . . Many days, and in all kinds of weather, we rode forty and fifty miles in uncovered wagons. Many nights we shared a one-room cabin with all the members of the [a] family. But the greatest hardship we suffered was the lack of water. There was very little good water in the state, and the purest water was so brackish that we could hardly drink it. The more we drank the thirstier we became, and when the water was made into tea it tasted worse than when it was clear. A bath was the rarest of luxuries. The only available fuel was buffalo manure, of which the odor permeated all our food. (Shaw 1915, 200–201)

Facing the opposition of both the liquor interests and the Prohibitionists as well as both foreign and American-born men presented extraordinary challenges to Anthony and her fellow suffragists. They found it almost impossible to navigate the complex political scene without offending someone. As Anthony wrote fellow South Dakota campaigner and close friend Olympia Brown:

> So I try to keep my talk on general principles—the bettering of women's

chances for work & wages, tyrany of taxation & c—But it is hardly possible to say anything that will not hurt somebody—so each of us must be governed by our own true inwardness—as to what & how to present our claims. (SBA to OB, September 3, 1890, OB-SL, in *Papers*)

She also cautioned Brown about a recurrent problem in the campaign—the tendency of suffragists (especially Brown) to alienate foreigners with their nativist comments and arguments, a risky strategy in a state where the foreign vote composed nearly half of the electorate.

Mr Blackwell writes back that each & all of us female missionaries must be very careful to speak of the foreigners only in the most respectful manner— It took him an hour to re-convert a Norwegian who had been repelled from voting by one of our women. (SBA to OB, September 3, 1890, OB-SL, in *Papers*)

In September, Chapman Catt offered one of her characteristically shrewd analyses of the political situation.

We have not a ghost of a show for success. With the exception of the work of a few women, nothing is being done. We have opposed to us the most powerful elements in the politics of the state. . . . Ours is a cold, lonesome little movement, which will make our hearts ache about November 5. (Harper 1899, 2:693–694)

As Anthony, Chapman Catt, and Blackwell predicted, the amendment went down to an overwhelming defeat. Less than a third of the votes cast were in favor of woman suffrage. South Dakota would not attempt to enfranchise its women for nearly 30 years; it finally granted women the ballot in 1918.

Kansas

One of the first states to legislate municipal suffrage for women (1887), the Kansas state legislature voted in 1893 to submit a woman suffrage amendment to the electorate in 1894. Since there was widespread public sentiment for woman suffrage throughout the state, Anthony was hopeful that the 1894 Kansas campaign would be vastly different from the discouraging defeat that the American Equal Rights Association (AERA) suffered during the Kansas campaign of 1867. Although the Kansas Republican Party had pledged its support for woman suffrage, its fear of the growing power of the state's Populist Party caused Kansas Republicans to align with the state's Democrats. This action necessitated that the Republicans abandon woman suffrage. Anthony was infuriated; seeing Kansas Republicans court and then discard woman suffrage was doubly horrifying to her because she was seeing the history of the disastrous 1867 campaign repeat itself. She, NAWSA leaders, and a legion of state suffragists lobbied for the Populist Party's endorsement and won it after a long battle. Henry Blackwell, an ever-loyal Republican and fellow NAWSA leader, cautioned Anthony to steer clear of any close alignment with the Populists. In her retort to Blackwell, Anthony summed up the essence of her convictions about the necessity of enlisting the support of multiple political parties while remaining stubbornly nonpartisan.

No, I shall not praise the Republicans of Kansas, or wish or work for their success, when I know by their own confessions to me that the rights of the women of their State have been traded by them in cold blood for the votes of the lager beer foreigners and whiskey Democrats. . . . I have not allied and shall not ally myself to any party or any measure save the one of justice and equality for woman. . . . I never, in my whole forty years' work, so utterly repudiated any set of

Susan B. Anthony and her sister Mary Stafford Anthony (left) shared their commitment to woman suffrage.

politicians as I do those Republicans of Kansas. . . . no self-respecting woman should wish or work for the success of a party which ignores her political rights. (Harper 1899, 2:794)

Still, as Anthony had been well aware from the moment of the Republicans' defection, Populist support was not sufficient to pass the amendment. Kansas women would have to wait another 18 years until 1912, when the harsh partisan politics of the past were long forgotten and Kansas voters approved the woman suffrage referendum.

New York

Not all of Anthony's hard-fought struggles were in the West. Delegates to the New York Constitutional Convention rejected revising the state constitution to enfranchise women in 1867. After decades of struggle, in 1893, New York suffragists initiated a campaign to demand that the 1894 constitutional conven-

tion consider the issue again. Offering her Rochester home as a central campaign office, Anthony and her sister Mary Anthony worked incessantly and in cooperation with state suffrage leaders—circulating petitions, distributing suffrage literature, and organizing speakers and lecture engagements. Anthony was determined to win woman suffrage in her home state. From January through April 1894, at the age of seventy-four, she traveled statewide, speaking in each of New York's 60 counties. She wrote a friend, "I am in the midst of as severe a treadmill as I ever experienced, travelling from fifty to one hundred miles a day and speaking five or six nights a week" (Harper 1899, 2:763).

Although suffragists collected petitions containing over 600,000 signatures, spoke to enthusiastic audiences, and received mostly favorable press coverage, the constitutional convention rejected submitting a woman suffrage amendment to the voters by a vote of 98 (against) to 58 (in favor). This defeat,

Anthony's biographer noted, "was the bitterest disappointment of her life," although with another huge suffrage battle waiting in Kansas, she had neither the time nor the energy to dwell upon it (Harper 1899, 2:772–773).

Future state suffrage battles after Anthony's death in 1906, of which there would be many, consumed another generation of suffragists. In 1917, 11 years after Anthony's death, New York became the first eastern state to enfranchise its women, bringing to a close a mission that had begun in the small New York village of Seneca Falls, site of the first woman's rights convention in 1848, nearly 70 years before.

Related entries:
American Woman Suffrage Association
Anthony, Susan B.
Blackwell, Henry Browne
Brown, Olympia
Catt, Carrie Lane Chapman
Duniway, Abigail Scott
Kansas Campaign of 1867
National American Woman Suffrage Association
National Woman Suffrage Association
Woman Suffrage Movement

Suggestions for further reading:
Beeton, Beverly. 1986. *Women Vote in the West: The Woman Suffrage Movement 1869–1896.* New York: Garland Publishing.
———. 1991. "How the West Was Won for Woman Suffrage." In *One Woman, One Vote: Rediscovering the Woman Suffrage Movement,* ed. Marjorie Spruill Wheeler. Troutdale, Oreg.: New Sage Press.
Catt, Carrie Chapman, and Nettie Rogers Shuler. 1926. *Woman Suffrage and Politics: The Inner Story of the Suffrage Movement.* New York: Charles Scribner's Sons.
Edwards, G. Thomas. 1990. *Sowing Good Seeds: The Northwest Suffrage Campaigns of Susan B. Anthony.* Portland, Oreg.: Oregon Historical Society Press.
Iverson, Joan. 1990. "The Mormon-Suffrage Relationship: Personal and Political Quandaries." *Frontiers* 12, nos. 2–3:8–16.

Stone, Lucy (1818–1893)

As one of the earliest pioneers of the women's rights movement, acknowledged leader of the American Woman Suffrage Association (AWSA), publisher of the most illustrious and longest-lived women's rights journal (the *Woman's Journal*), and inexhaustible campaigner for woman suffrage for more than 40 years, Lucy Stone is recognized along with Susan B. Anthony and Elizabeth Cady Stanton as one of the three most preeminent of nineteenth-century American suffragists. The ups and downs of Stone's long and exceedingly complex relationship with Anthony, ranging from their close, sisterly friendship of the 1850s to the bitter and resentful feuding from the late 1860s on, help illuminate the deep, bitter conflicts driving the split in the woman suffrage movement, a division that lasted from 1869 until 1890.

The daughter of a Massachusetts farmer, Stone struggled to receive an education against the wishes of her father. After completing her public schooling, Stone earned all the money for her higher education by teaching. Determined to attend college, Stone waited nine years before she had acquired the money to enroll at Oberlin College in Ohio. Inspired by abolitionists Sarah and Angelina Grimké and Abby Kelley Foster, Stone decided to become an antislavery and women's rights activist after her 1847 graduation from Oberlin. She was the first Massachusetts woman to obtain a college degree.

Stone commenced her career in reform in 1848 as a lecturing agent for the American Anti-Slavery Society (AASS). She was soon conquering the societal restriction barring women from speaking in public by delivering antislavery lectures throughout the Northeast. Her natural, unstudied, commonsense eloquence charmed audiences. Contemporary critics marveled over the extraordinary quality of her voice. In a field in which most great lecturers were men spouting fiery oratory, Stone's remarkably soothing, musical voice was a valuable asset, especially when speaking before hostile, proslavery audiences (Kerr 1992, 54). She soon became one of the AASS's most popular lecturers, occasionally sharing equal billing with two of the abolitionist movement's most powerful orators, Wendell Phillips and William Lloyd Garrison.

Stone could not resist mingling women's rights issues and themes with her antislavery message. To her and to fellow feminist abolitionists Lucretia Coffin Mott and Kelley Foster, it was nearly impossible to differentiate the issues of political and social domination that enslaved African Americans from those that subjugated and oppressed women. At the insistence of the AASS leadership, Stone agreed to address women's rights concerns and abolitionist issues in separate lectures. Thus began Stone's extremely successful, lucrative career as a women's rights lecturer. She also devoted herself to organizing and executing a leadership role in the early national woman's rights conventions.

Anthony attributed her conversion to the cause of women's rights to Stone's speech at the First National Woman's Rights Convention held in Worcester, Massachusetts, in 1850, which Anthony later read in the *New York Tribune*. After reading it, she longed to meet Stone and other key luminaries of the women's rights movement. In 1851, at the home of Cady Stanton, Anthony was first introduced to Stone at a meeting to brainstorm ideas for a People's College, a coeducational venture (Harper 1899, 1:64). From that point on, Stone and Anthony frequently corresponded. Their early letters reflect their opinions, determination, fears, and problems concerning their wearing of the controversial Bloomer costume. As the more seasoned activist, Stone's letters to Anthony were filled with friendly advice and encouragement, often countermanding Anthony's image of herself as an inadequate lecturer and reformer. Their later letters illustrate their mutual passion for women's rights reform as well as their increasing personal closeness, their exchange of deeply personal feelings, and their warm affection. Anthony greatly admired Stone's breadth of knowledge about abolitionism, her oratorical prowess, her thriving career, and her impassioned devotion to women's rights. For all these reasons, Anthony was extremely

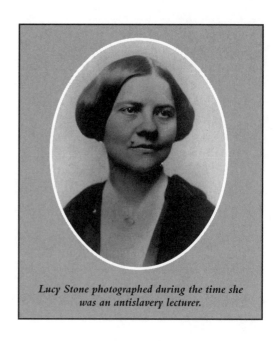

Lucy Stone photographed during the time she was an antislavery lecturer.

optimistic about their future together as women's rights crusaders.

Anthony was shocked and devastated when she learned that both Stone and another close friend and fellow activist, Antoinette Brown, intended to marry. In 1855, Stone became engaged to Cincinnati abolitionist and businessman Henry Blackwell, and not long afterward, Brown promised to marry Samuel Blackwell, Henry's brother. Anthony could not believe that Stone, who had so vehemently sworn herself to a life of single independence, could so easily give up her reform career. Despite Stone's and Brown's protestations to the contrary, Anthony perceived marriage as the death knell of a woman's activism. She knew from her married sisters' and Cady Stanton's experiences that the demands of marriage, the management of a household, and the bearing and raising of children severely limited a woman's freedom to travel and would obliterate their ability to participate in arduous women's rights campaigns. Anthony interpreted Stone's decision to marry as betrayal and abandonment—leaving Anthony to fight the women's rights battle alone. Stone was hurt and bewildered by Anthony's resentment and at first tried to prove that she was as committed to women's rights as ever. Although marriage would not reduce Stone's ardor or her allegiance to women's rights, the 1857 birth of her daughter, Alice Stone Blackwell, did prevent her from active involvement in the movement until 1866.

Anthony, perhaps overwhelmed by the demands of leading the campaign for the New York Married Women's Property Law and her commitments as New York agent of the AASS, wrote stern letters to Stone, nagging and disapproving of her decision to retire temporarily to raise her daughter. Anthony's words wounded Stone, who was already struggling with her new roles as wife and mother and with her isolation from her reform colleagues. Although she was in desperate need of understanding from old friends, she would not find support for her domestic life from Anthony. Both women's unresolved anger and pain seriously eroded their bond. Yet despite the slowly festering resentment on both sides, Stone and Anthony continued to correspond—Stone to encourage and applaud Anthony's achievements, Anthony to inform Stone of developments in her and others' women's rights campaigns. In 1863, Stone consented to Anthony's request that she preside at the convention that formed the Woman's National Loyal League (WNLL). Although Anthony hoped that leading the meeting would push Stone back into the vanguard of reform, Stone remained firm about her exclusive commitment to her family.

Following the Civil War, as Stone's school-age daughter needed her less, she rejoiced at having more time for women's rights work. She was actively involved in helping Anthony and Cady Stanton organize and execute the Eleventh National Woman's Rights Convention in 1866, at which the American Equal Rights Association (AERA) was formed. Stone and Henry Blackwell were leaders of the AERA, along with Anthony, Cady Stanton, Parker Pillsbury, Frederick Douglass, and other former abolitionists. In 1866 and 1867, Stone and Henry Blackwell worked closely with Anthony and Cady Stanton to counter efforts by Phillips, Douglass, and other predominantly male Republican AERA members who determined that obtaining civil and political rights for African-American males must take priority over woman suffrage. In the spring of 1867, Stone responded to Anthony's pleas that she lead an AERA woman suffrage campaign in Kansas. In November, Kansans were to vote on two suffrage referenda—to enfranchise African-American males and all women.

In the fall of 1867, months after she and Blackwell returned from Kansas, Stone was enraged to discover that Anthony had teamed up with the anti–African-American Democrat George Francis Train in the final months of the Kansas campaign. Stone could not fathom how Anthony could have reneged on her principles and her years of dedication to African-American rights to join forces with a racist. But what was even more heinous in Stone's view was the fact that Anthony used equal rights money to pay for the Train campaign without consulting her or any other AERA members. When Anthony returned east, Stone, Blackwell, and other members of the AERA executive committee harshly confronted her at a private AERA meeting, berating her for her alliance with Train and the resultant misuse of AERA funds (Barry 1988, 186). According to Stone, Anthony retorted, "I AM the Equal Rights Association. Not one of you amounts to shucks except for me" (Kerr 1992, 130). This response, perhaps the result of being called on the carpet by members who had not devoted every waking minute to woman suffrage and African-American rights as she had for the last 13 years, only confirmed Stone and Blackwell's opinion of Anthony's despotic tendencies and unwillingness to share leadership.

By 1868, Stone and Blackwell had joined forces with Phillips and New England Republican AERA members who postponed agitating for woman suffrage to push through the Fifteenth Amendment. Stone and Blackwell then established the pro-Republican,

Boston-based New England Woman Suffrage Association (NEWSA). Its first goal was to secure the franchise for African-American men through the Fifteenth Amendment. Meanwhile, Anthony and Cady Stanton's anti-Republican, pro-Democratic rhetoric and radical feminism as broadcast in their newspaper *The Revolution*, along with Stone and Blackwell's anti-Anthony and anti-*Revolution* protests, intensified the divisiveness among AERA members and women's rights reformers, causing the once-united group to split into two factions.

Stone and Blackwell were enraged by Anthony and Cady Stanton's formation of the National Woman Suffrage Association (NWSA) in May 1869 and by what they perceived as their purposeful exclusion from it. Stone immediately initiated plans for a separate national suffrage organization for conservative and moderate female and male suffragists who supported the Fifteenth Amendment and were either offended by *The Revolution* or estranged from Anthony and Cady Stanton because of it (Kerr 1992, 142). Although *The Revolution's* radicalism distressed her, Stone was more opposed to what she perceived as its anti–African-American agenda and its endorsement of the Democratic Party. To rally a membership for their new organization, soon to be named the American Woman Suffrage Association (AWSA), Stone and Blackwell appealed to all women's rights activists, including many who were longtime friends and allies of Anthony and Cady Stanton.

Like Anthony, Stone recognized the ability of the press to influence and educate the public. She also began preparations to launch a women's rights newspaper that would rival *The Revolution* and provide an alternative publication for more moderate and conservative women's rights activists. The *Woman's Journal* was first published in Boston on January 8, 1870, two years to the day after the first publication of *The Revolution*.

None of the reconciliation attempts of the early 1870s tempted Stone, undoubtedly be-cause none tackled the thorniest issues that had compelled her to form a separate organization. In addition to their considerable ideological differences, Stone was convinced that she could not trust Anthony or Cady Stanton. She was also opposed to most of their radical stands on women's rights issues such as marriage and divorce reform, the unionization of labor, labor reform, and prostitution. Stone had always been highly critical of Cady Stanton's work on divorce reform. Since Cady Stanton had first proposed massive changes in marriage and divorce law in 1860, Stone had agreed with Phillips that divorce reform was not women's rights. As the years passed and throughout Stone's decades of leadership in the AWSA, she struggled to keep the AWSA focused only on woman suffrage. She pushed aside what she considered to be marginal, radical women's rights issues that alienated moderate and conservative Americans from woman suffrage. Consequently, Stone wasted no time worrying about unification with the NWSA, instead focusing her energies on developing a vital national organization.

In 1872, Anthony, Cady Stanton, and the NWSA backed the Republican Party presidential candidate, Ulysses S. Grant. Since ever-loyal Republicans Stone and Henry Blackwell were also supporting him, Anthony wrote to Stone inviting her to consider a joint campaign. When Stone refused, Anthony was dejected. It was her last personal attempt to move closer to Stone.

Although the NWSA's and the AWSA's separate goals and areas of emphasis kept them from colliding in the field for the most part, the leaders of both organizations were acutely aware of the competitive rivalry between them. Both NWSA and AWSA leaders accused their rivals of deliberately undermining them, but in reality each organization tried to "steal" or drum up membership in the other's backyard, and each was guilty of exaggerating its achievements while neglecting to mention its competitors' contributions. Oddly enough, Anthony and Cady

Stanton as well as Stone and Blackwell interpreted these political maneuvers as personal affronts and insults—a pattern that underscores the intensity of their interpersonal relationships and the traumatic nature of the original split.

By 1886, Stone found herself approving of and praising the achievements of NWSA leaders, who she believed were finally beginning to help the cause of woman suffrage. Factions in both the AWSA and NWSA were eager to explore the possibilities of cooperating on campaigns and projects and coordinating a merger. In December 1887, with the prodding and impetus provided by the younger generation of suffragists in both organizations, Stone and Anthony attended a meeting to discuss unification. More than two years of negotiation later, the woman suffrage movement was united under the banner of the new National American Woman Suffrage Association (NAWSA).

Stone was gravely disappointed by Cady Stanton's assumption of the presidency of the NAWSA. Throughout the negotiations, Stone had been adamant about one issue—that she, Anthony, and Cady Stanton abstain from the leadership of the new organization. But when the new NAWSA membership kept clamoring for either Cady Stanton or Anthony to be president, Anthony took advantage of the opportunity to maneuver Cady Stanton into the presidency, thus maintaining her (Anthony's) primary role and the NWSA's top leadership structure.

Stone chose not to confront Anthony directly concerning the NAWSA leadership issue. She maintained an externally positive, laudatory public attitude toward the NWSA, but inwardly she was seething. Stone's and Anthony's pattern of avoiding rather than mediating areas of interpersonal turmoil, first established in the late 1850s, not only characterized their 35-year relationship but also contributed to the divergent natures, functions, and agendas of the AWSA and the NWSA.

As far as Stone and Anthony's relationship was concerned, not much had changed by the time of the merger. From the late 1860s until Stone's death in 1893, each woman regularly confided to friends that she was repeatedly hurt by the other's words and actions. Biographies of Stone and Anthony abound with anecdotes of both women being stunned by the nasty comments their friends had supposedly overheard each woman say about the other. Neither Stone nor Anthony appears to have confronted the other directly about the veracity of such rumors, nor did either woman approach the other about the possibility of resolving their differences. They both chose instead to rage in private and vent their angst to their friends.

Despite the intensity of their conflicts, Stone and Anthony shared one striking characteristic—their single-minded, wholehearted passion and undivided devotion to the cause of women's rights and woman suffrage. In a letter to Alice Blackwell in 1887, Stone explained to her daughter: "Its [the cause's] success and prosperity have always been more to me, than any personal feeling, and any damage to IT far more than any personal ill will, or misunderstanding of myself, so I could always rejoice in good work no matter who did it" (LS to ASB, April 12, 1887, quoted in Wheeler 1981, 304).

Stone opted not to actively participate in the NAWSA. In addition to her sense of defeat because the AWSA's identity and decades of achievement had been swallowed whole by the NWSA, Stone's health was deteriorating rapidly in the early 1890s. She decided to direct her energies toward continuing the publication of the *Woman's Journal* and involving herself more deeply in her New England and Massachusetts causes, including the Massachusetts Woman Suffrage Association (which Stone and Henry Blackwell had founded), the Working Girls' Clubs, the New England Press Association, the Association of Collegiate Alumnae, and the New England Women's Club (Kerr 1992, 232).

Related entries:
Abolitionist Movement
American Anti-Slavery Society

Suggestions for further reading:

Blackwell, Alice Stone. 1930. *Lucy Stone: Pioneer of Women's Rights*. Boston: Little Brown.

Hays, Elinor Rice. 1961. *Morning Star: A Biography of Lucy Stone 1818–1893*. New York: Harcourt, Brace and World.

Kerr, Andrea Moore. 1992. *Lucy Stone: Speaking Out for Equality.* New Brunswick, N.J.: Rutgers University Press.

Syracuse Woman's Rights Convention of 1852

The Third National Woman's Rights Convention, held in Syracuse, New York, in September 1852, was the first women's rights gathering Susan B. Anthony attended. By this time Anthony was an acknowledged leader of women's temperance reform in New York state; her temperance work led directly to her new interest in women's rights. In 1848, when her parents and her sister attended the Rochester Woman's Rights Convention, Anthony lightheartedly questioned their enthusiasm for the new women's rights movement. But as her involvement in temperance reform deepened and particularly as she sought legislative solutions to intemperance, she realized how women's powerlessness in society prevented them from solving many of their problems. These realizations and her new friendship with feminist Elizabeth Cady Stanton provided the impetus that drove her to investigate the women's rights movement.

The Syracuse convention proved to be a crucial landmark in Anthony's development as a feminist activist. It was at this gathering of 2,000 women and men (many of the women wearing the new Bloomer costume) that Anthony first met women's rights activists who would soon become her lifelong friends, mentors, and colleagues. Among the invaluable connections that she made at this convention were those with Lucretia Coffin Mott and her husband James Mott, Paulina Wright Davis, Martha Coffin Wright, Ernestine Potowski Rose, Antoinette Brown, Matilda Joslyn Gage, and Gerrit Smith.

Anthony was selected to be a member of the nominating committee and was elected secretary. She was inspired by the free and open exchange of ideas at this convention, the commitment and intelligence of the activists, and the discussion of the key women's rights issues of the day: women's property rights, personal rights, and, most intriguing to Anthony, women's right to the ballot. Women's rights reformer Gerrit Smith, also a congressman from New York, emphasized women's need for the vote. "The right of suffrage," he asserted, "is the right that guarantees all others," and Anthony was indeed persuaded (Harper 1899, 1:77).

Related entries:
Blackwell, Antoinette Louisa Brown
Bloomer Costume
Davis, Paulina Kellogg Wright
Mott, Lucretia Coffin
Rose, Ernestine Louise Potowski
Seneca Falls Convention of 1848
Woman's Rights Conventions
Women's Rights Movement
Wright, Martha Coffin

Suggestions for further reading:

Lutz, Alma. 1959. *Susan B. Anthony: Rebel, Crusader, Humanitarian*. Boston: Beacon Press.
HWS, 1:517–545.

Teachers' Conventions

Throughout most of the 1850s, while Susan B. Anthony was thoroughly engaged in her temperance, women's rights, and antislavery activism, she also found the time to concern herself with problems in public education. Anthony's teaching experience had laid the foundation for her lifelong interest in improving the economic condition of women. During her teaching career, she had been disturbed and angered by the gulf between male and female teachers' salaries. It had mortified her that whenever she successfully replaced an incompetent male teacher, she received only a quarter of his salary (Harper 1899, 1:45).

Anthony's interest in becoming a labor agitator at the New York state annual teachers' conventions began in the summer of 1852, when she stopped in at a teacher's convention in Elmira, New York, while there on temperance business. She endured a speech given by Charles Anthony (a distant relative) on "The Divine Ordinance of Corporal Punishment." As much as she opposed the premise and conclusions of this speech, she was more concerned that the audience, three-quarters of them women, did not voice any opposition or criticism. Not only that, but throughout the entire convention, no woman spoke, voted, or was named to a committee. It was as if they were not present at all. Anthony vowed that at future conventions, she would find a way to encourage women to expand their role and power within their profession (Harper 1899, 1:71–72).

The next August, in 1853, Anthony attended the state teachers convention in Rochester. After two days of keen attention to the proceedings, Anthony stood up and indicated that she wanted to add to the debate at hand a discussion of the reasons why teachers were not as respected as other professionals. Though inwardly quaking, Anthony waited while the astounded male members tried to decide if they should permit her to speak. Finally, the men voted and agreed to hear her. Anthony said:

> It seems to me you fail to comprehend the cause of the disrespect of which you complain. Do you not see that so long as society says woman has not brains enough to be a doctor, lawyer or minister, but has plenty to be a teacher, every man of you who condescends to teach, tacitly admits before all Israel and the sun that he has no more brains than a woman? (Harper 1899, 1:99)

Although Ida Husted Harper's biography of Anthony portrays her as being too overwhelmed to continue speaking beyond this point, the *History of Woman Suffrage* contains Anthony's version of the conclusion to this speech.

> And this, too, is the reason that teaching is a less lucrative profession, as here men must compete with the cheap labor of woman. Would you exalt your profession, exalt those who labor with you. Would you make it more lucrative, increase the salaries of the women. (*HWS,* 1:514)

Afterward, Anthony was disheartened by the women teachers' negative responses to her efforts to help them. Most were horrified at her audacity to speak publicly, and some told her that they were ashamed that she had spoken so freely. Yet a few women reassured her that they appreciated what she was trying to do for them.

To Anthony's delighted surprise, at the next day's meetings, a woman teacher from Rochester presented two resolutions—one demanding the right of female teachers to an equal role in the conventions and another demanding the right to equal pay (Harper 1899, 1:99–100). The president tried to ignore them, but the teacher insisted that they be read. Once addressed, Anthony spoke strongly in favor of the resolutions, and both passed unanimously.

Encouraged by her success, Anthony returned each summer to the teachers' conventions until 1862, urging male and female teachers to struggle for equal wages and equal opportunities in education. In 1857, she shocked the convention by presenting a group of resolutions that protested New York state's policies toward African-American students and teachers. One of her resolutions stated that "the exclusion of colored youth from our public schools, academies, colleges and universities is the result of a wicked prejudice" (Harper 1899, 1:155). These resolutions were all accepted. Of all her proposals at teachers' conventions over the years, it was her attempt to encourage

the convention to accept the value of coeducation that met with the most heated resistance (Barry 1988, 113).

Related entries:
Woman's Rights Conventions
Women's Rights Movement

Suggestions for further reading:
Barry, Kathleen. 1988. *Susan B. Anthony: Biography of a Singular Feminist.* New York: New York University Press.
HWS, 1.

Temperance

*T*he temperance movement was Susan B. Anthony's first active involvement in social reform. Temperance activists, working in organized societies, sought to reduce or eliminate alcohol consumption in society. Throughout the nineteenth century, they believed that intemperance, especially among men, was seriously undermining the quality of American society by causing unemployment, poverty, and domestic violence. Alcohol abuse was indeed a serious problem in this era. Statistics show that the 1840 per capita alcohol consumption was three times greater than in 1940 (Giele 1995, 3).

In the early nineteenth century, temperance organizations were composed almost entirely of men, but by the early 1830s, a few women-led societies had emerged (Blocker 1989, 3). From the 1840s through the early 1850s, women's involvement in temperance greatly increased, their membership numbering in the tens of thousands. Women's role in temperance reform proved to be one of the sources of the women's rights movement because it highlighted the causes of some of women's most difficult economic and social problems while also providing the means for women to seek solutions outside the home.

In 1848, Susan B. Anthony, then in her late twenties, had become bored with the routine of teaching in Canajoharie, New York, and was searching for a cause to which she

Lithograph entitled "Woman's Holy War: Grand Charge on the Enemy's Works," published in 1874 during the Women's Temperance Crusade by Currier & Ives.

could dedicate herself. No doubt influenced by her father Daniel Anthony's temperance activities, she was attracted to the movement. In a letter to her mother, Anthony wrote of her longing to be an active participant in the quest to make the world a better place. "I am tired of theory. I want to hear how we must act to have a happier & more glorious world," she wrote. "Oh this Canajoharie is a hot bed of vice & drunkenness[;] reform, reform needs to be the watch word. And somebody much [must] preach it" (SBA to LRA, October 15, 1848, SBA-SL, in *Papers*).

In temperance, Anthony believed she had found the cause she was seeking. She joined the Daughters of Temperance in Canajoharie in 1848, and in Rochester in 1849, after she left teaching and returned home. In 1852 she organized the Woman's State Temperance Society (WSTS). Like other women temperance and antislavery activists, Anthony was continually frustrated by the obstacles male reformers placed in the path of women reformers. She and other women demanded to be equal activists with men. In this struggle for equality, women temperance workers had the support of a number of influential men, including *New York Tribune* editor Horace Greeley and the abolitionists William Henry Channing, Samuel Joseph May, Thomas Wentworth Higginson, Gerrit Smith, Wendell Phillips, and William Lloyd Garrison.

By 1851, Anthony had begun to discover that the temperance solution to society's problems—achieving men's total abstinence from alcohol—would not affect what she believed was women's fundamental problem, their powerlessness in society and the home. In a letter to temperance reformer Amelia Jenks Bloomer that was published in the *Lily*, Anthony wrote: "if women may do nothing toward removing the Cause of drunkenness, then she is indeed powerless—then may she well sit down, and with folded hands weep over the ills that be" (The *Lily*, September 1852, in *Papers*). She soon recognized that legal and political solutions were essential to

reversing women's subservient position in society. "The redress of our Legal Wrongs can only come through legislation," she wrote her friend Elizabeth Cady Stanton, "and our Legislators will not be likely to act upon them, before we are wide enough awake to ask them to do so" (SBA to ECS, November 11, 1853, ECS-LCMD, in *Papers*). Because Anthony was well aware that these concerns far exceeded the boundaries of temperance, she transferred her activism to the women's rights movement.

Alcohol consumption, which had decreased in the 1850s due to antialcohol legislation, rose again sharply after the Civil War. This increase resulted partly from an increase in the number of saloons and other retail liquor outlets. Women, especially in the Midwest, rallied together in 1873–1874 to take action against liquor retailers. Groups of desperate women, known as the Women's Temperance Crusade, prayed on saloon doorsteps; pleaded with saloon owners, local officials, and legislators; and occasionally resorted to violence to put an end to the sale of liquor and the explosion of alcohol-related problems in their homes and communities.

Although she strongly disagreed with their methods, Anthony was sympathetic to the temperance crusaders. In 1874, when a group of crusaders in Rochester, New York, asked her to assist them in forming an organization, she agreed willingly. Later, when they asked her to address them, Anthony seized the opportunity to point them in a more political direction. "Now my good women," she told them, "the best thing this organization will do for you will be to show you how utterly powerless you are to put down the liquor traffic. . . . You never will be able to lessen this evil until you have votes" (Harper 1899, 1:457).

As if in response to Anthony's message "to pray with their ballots," Frances Willard, leader of the Woman's Christian Temperance Union from 1879 to 1898, steered the women's temperance movement toward suffrage activism. Largely through her efforts, WCTU women became a preponderant force in the woman suffrage movement.

Related entries:
Bloomer, Amelia Jenks
Daughters of Temperance
Greeley, Horace
The *Lily*
May, Samuel Joseph
The *New York Tribune*
Willard, Frances Elizabeth Caroline
Woman Suffrage Movement
Woman's Christian Temperance Union
Woman's State Temperance Society

Suggestions for further reading:
Blocker, Jack S., Jr. 1989. *American Temperance Movements: Cycles of Reform.* Boston: Twayne Publishers.
Giele, Janet Zollinger. 1995. *Two Paths to Women's Equality: Temperance, Suffrage, and the Origins of Modern Feminism.* New York: Twayne Publishers.

Terrell, Mary Eliza Church (1863–1954)

As a suffragist, a leader of the African-American women's club movement, and a crusader for equal rights, Mary Eliza Church Terrell dedicated herself to the social, economic, and political advancement of all African Americans. From her early days exploring the woman suffrage movement, Susan B. Anthony welcomed her to the National American Woman Suffrage Association (NAWSA) and quickly recognized her multifaceted talents. On several occasions, Anthony encouraged Church Terrell to speak at NAWSA conventions and to the members of some of Anthony's other favorite organizations, including the Political Equality Club in Rochester, New York. Church Terrell idolized Anthony and never neglected an opportunity to publicly express her admiration for Anthony's contributions to the quest for racial equality and justice.

Mary Eliza Church was born in Memphis, Tennessee, the daughter of former slaves. Her father Robert Reed Church, a successful entrepreneur, was the son of a wealthy white businessman who also had been his owner. Church was a shrewd investor and is reported to have been the first African-American millionaire in the South. Church Terrell's mother, Louisa Ayers Church, also prospered in business. When she was freed from slavery, she established a lucrative Memphis hair salon. Even though the Churches gave their daughter a privileged, comfortable childhood, by the time Church Terrell was a teenager she was keenly aware of the effects of racial discrimination, prejudice, and violence. As a very young woman, she focused on preparing herself to help African Americans elevate their degraded position in society. She attended high school in Oberlin, Ohio, in preparation for her studies at Oberlin College. Gifted in languages, at Oberlin she insisted on taking the more difficult "gentlemen's" collegiate course rather than the women's curriculum or the "literary course."

After her graduation in 1884, her father expected her to settle in his household and wait for marriage. But Church Terrell had other ideas. She became a teacher at Wilberforce University in Ohio. After a year there, she moved to Washington, D.C., to teach at a high school, where she met her future husband, the Harvard scholar Robert H. Terrell. In 1888, instead of marrying right away, she departed for Europe and spent two years studying French, German, and Italian. She contemplated remaining in Europe because she so enjoyed living where race was not an issue, but in 1890 she returned to her teaching job in Washington and to an even closer relationship with Terrell, whom she married in 1891.

Following her marriage and throughout the 1890s, Church Terrell explored community activism. When she became a member of the District of Columbia Board of Education, she became the first African-American woman in the United States to serve on a school board. In 1896, the Colored Women's League of Washington, an organization she helped establish, joined other African-American women's clubs to unite as the National Association of Colored Women (NACW). Church Terrell became the NACW's first president, a post she filled for five years. The work of the NACW occupied her throughout the late 1890s and through the first decade of the next century. She used the organization to improve the lives of African-American women and their families by advocating the development of community programs—nurseries, kindergartens, mothers' groups, schools of domestic science, evening schools, and nursing programs, to name a few. When Church Terrell and NACW members identified a need in the African-American community, they sought to address it. In 1909–1910, the focus of her activism shifted as she became engrossed in the founding of the National Association for the Advancement of Colored People (NAACP). As an NAACP leader for many years, she became deeply involved in the effort to achieve complete equality in all areas of public life.

Church Terrell's involvement in the woman suffrage movement ran parallel to her women's club work. She stated in her autobiography, *A Colored Woman in a White World,* that she was vigorously pro–woman suffrage from the time of her youth. While living in Washington, D.C., she rarely missed an opportunity to attend NAWSA conventions. She attended her first national women's rights meeting in 1888, when at the International Council of Women, she was among the very few who rose from their seats to declare their support for woman suffrage.

At the 1898 NAWSA convention, before she was a NAWSA member, Church Terrell boldly suggested that the organization issue a resolution protesting the rampant racial discrimination and prejudice afflicting African Americans. Anthony urged her to approach the platform to record this resolution and later encouraged her to deliver a speech to NAWSA members. In "The Progress and Problems of Colored Women," Church Terrell implored NAWSA suffragists to help Afri-

Mary Church Terrell

can Americans destroy the stranglehold of the nation's Jim Crow laws, which denied them their civil and political rights and prevented them from living full lives as citizens. Church Terrell's delivery was so moving and eloquent that NAWSA suffragists were completely won over. In spite of the accolades they showered on her, NAWSA's predominantly conservative members were fearful of alienating their southern white colleagues. They never actively responded to Church Terrell's pleas for racial justice. Although she was disappointed that the NAWSA did not take a stand on racial issues, she continued to be a NAWSA member and a devoted follower of Anthony.

Late in life, during the 1940s, Church Terrell's activism became much more militant when she participated in demonstrations for the abolishment of racial discrimination and segregation. In 1950, at age 86, she relentlessly agitated to abolish racial segregation in restaurants and other eateries in the nation's capital. Finally, on June 8, 1953, a year before her death in Washington, D.C., laws upholding the segregation of restaurants and diners were declared unconstitutional.

Related entry:
Woman Suffrage Movement

Suggestions for further reading:
Jones, Beverly. 1993. "Mary Eliza Church Terrell."
    In *Black Women in America: An Historical
    Encyclopedia,* ed. Darlene Clark Hine, Elsa
    Barkley Brown, and Rosalyn Terborg-Penn.
    Brooklyn, N.Y.: Carlson Publishing, 2:1157–
    1159.
Sterling, Dorothy. 1988b. "Mary Church Terrell."
    In *Black Foremothers: Three Lives.* New York:
    Feminist Press.
Terrell, Mary Church. 1940. *A Colored Woman in a
    White World.* Washington, D.C.: Ransdell.

Thirteenth Amendment

Emancipation of the slaves occupied Anthony's thoughts throughout the Civil War. Following Lincoln's Emancipation Proclamation of January 1, 1863, Anthony and other prominent abolitionists realized that only an amendment to the Constitution would guarantee the freed slaves' liberty. Anthony discussed her concerns first with Elizabeth Cady Stanton, Horace Greeley, Theodore Tilton, Henry Ward Beecher, and Robert Dale Owen, who had been recently named director of the Freedmen's Inquiry Commission. Anthony and Cady Stanton then formed the Woman's National Loyal League (WNLL), which was dedicated to gathering signatures on petitions demanding a Thirteenth Amendment.

The work of the WNLL was an enormous success. Anthony and Cady Stanton, with the cooperation of women from many states, managed to collect 400,000 signatures, which were presented to Congress. In April 1864, the Thirteenth Amendment was approved by the Senate, in January 1865, by the House of Representatives, and by December 1865, it was finally ratified by the states. It read, "Neither slavery nor involuntary servitude, except as a punishment for crime whereof the party shall have been duly convicted, shall exist within the United States, or any place subject to their jurisdiction."

Related entries:
Emancipation Proclamation of 1863
Woman's National Loyal League

Suggestions for further reading:
Foner, Eric. 1988. *Reconstruction: America's
    Unfinished Revolution, 1863–1877.* New York:
    Harper and Row.
Venet, Wendy Hamand. 1991. *Neither Ballots nor
    Bullets: Women Abolitionists and the Civil War.*
    Charlottesville: University Press of Virginia.

Tilton, Theodore (1835–1907)

Influential editor and abolitionist Theodore Tilton had a powerful impact on the women's rights and woman suffrage movements from 1866 through the early 1870s. His career in journalism began at the *New York Tribune* in the early 1850s and was followed by a stint at the *New York Observer*, a Presbyterian newspaper. While at the *Observer*, Tilton regularly recorded the sermons of the nationally renowned liberal Congregational minister Henry Ward Beecher. Tilton quickly became a disciple of Beecher and a devotee of Beecher's "Gospel of Love." In 1856, Tilton was named managing editor of the liberal Congregational newspaper the *Independent.* His journalistic prowess and his penchant for attracting celebrity literary talent to the *Independent* were instrumental in making it a leading national journal with an extensive circulation. In 1861, when Beecher became editor in chief of the *Independent,* Tilton, who had been Beecher's ghostwriter from 1856 to 1860, assumed the post of assistant editor and became Beecher's closest friend. Through Beecher, Tilton gained access to the world of social reformers, particularly Garrisonian abolitionists and women's rights activists. It was at this time, during the Civil War years, that he became good friends with Susan B. Anthony and Elizabeth Cady Stanton and a strong supporter of the Woman's National Loyal League (WNLL).

In 1866, Tilton became an enthusiastic activist in the women's rights movement. He suggested that the women's rights cause and the American Anti-Slavery Society (AASS) merge to form one powerful organization dedicated to obtaining the franchise for all women and African-American men. Although this idea did not materialize, Tilton joined Anthony, Cady Stanton, Parker Pillsbury, Lucy Stone, and other women's rights reformers in pursuing the American Equal Rights Association's (AERA's) mission to obtain universal suffrage. Although Tilton was strongly pro–woman suffrage in 1866–1867, by 1869 he had discontinued promoting the ballot for women and had aligned himself with Wendell Phillips, Lucy Stone, Henry Blackwell, Beecher, and New England Republican AERA members to work solely to secure the ballot for African-American males through the Fifteenth Amendment.

Unlike Anthony and Cady Stanton, Tilton did not consider this move an abandonment of women's rights. After the May 1869 AERA convention caused the women's rights movement to split, Tilton became increasingly distressed that the suffrage movement was weakening itself by dividing its forces, thereby needlessly delaying the attainment of national woman suffrage.

In 1870, he developed an ambitious plan to unite Anthony and Cady Stanton's National Woman Suffrage Association (NWSA) and Lucy Stone and Blackwell's American Woman Suffrage Association (AWSA). He called a meeting for April 1870 and invited three delegates each from the NWSA, the AWSA, and the Union Woman Suffrage Association (UWSA)—the newly proposed merger unit that he had created to bring about the unification. Anthony and Cady Stanton, on tour in the West, cabled Tilton to assure him of their support for the merger. They believed that in spite of their personal misgivings about a reconciliation with Stone and Blackwell, they had no choice but to accept Tilton's overture. They were convinced that they had to demonstrate to their rivals and to the public that NWSA leaders were not the divisive element in the rupture (Griffith 1984, 145).

At the May 1870 NWSA convention, with Anthony and Cady Stanton's approval, members were persuaded to vote to accept the merger and Tilton as president (Griffith 1984, 142). In the end, however, the AWSA rejected Tilton's plan, and the UWSA dissolved.

In the midst of the 1870 unification effort, a crisis erupted in Tilton's personal life that ultimately exploded into the Beecher-Tilton Scandal, a debacle that had long-lasting repercussions for the woman suffrage movement, nineteenth-century social reform, and the lives of many social reformers, including Anthony and Cady Stanton. The crisis erupted when Tilton's wife Elizabeth Richards Tilton confessed to her husband that she had been engaged in an extramarital relationship with Beecher. Not only were Tilton's two most important relationships destroyed, but the scandal and the subsequent courtroom trial wrecked Tilton's reputation, ruined his career, and consumed his financial resources. In 1883, he emigrated to Europe, eventually settling in Paris, where he eked out a poor livelihood selling his prose and poetry.

Related entries:
American Equal Rights Association
American Woman Suffrage Association
Beecher, Henry Ward
Beecher-Tilton Scandal
Fifteenth Amendment
Free-Love Controversy
National Woman Suffrage Association
Reconstruction
Woman Suffrage Movement
Woman's National Loyal League
Woodhull, Victoria Claflin

Suggestions for further reading:
DAB, 9:551–553.
Waller, Altina L. 1982. *Reverend Beecher and Mrs. Tilton: Sex and Class in Victorian America.* Amherst: University of Massachusetts Press.

Train, George Francis (1829–1904)

Wealthy, eccentric financier, Democrat, and flamboyant advocate of woman suffrage George Francis Train played a key role in the American Equal Rights Association's (AERA's) Kansas campaign of 1867 and in launching Susan B. Anthony and Elizabeth Cady Stanton's radical newspaper *The Revolution* in 1868. Train traveled and lectured with Anthony during the final months of the Kansas campaign in a last-ditch attempt to persuade voters to cast ballots for the woman suffrage referendum. Train's exuberant support came at a critical time when Republicans had all turned their backs on the woman suffrage referendum in an effort to save the African-American suffrage referendum. With no allies and no money to back the AERA mission, Anthony perceived Train's financial and physical assistance as a godsend.

Unfortunately for Anthony and Cady Stanton, their association with Train created problems that had long-lasting repercussions for them personally and politically. Although Train ardently supported women's economic, social, civil, and political rights, he just as strongly opposed rights for African Americans. Already infamous for his racist stands on issues, Train's strategy of encouraging audiences to support women's rights as a means of combating the ascendancy of African Americans appalled Anthony and Cady Stanton's friends and northern Republicans (DuBois 1978, 94).

Out of political necessity, Anthony and Cady Santon chose to overlook Train's racism because of his unparalleled advocacy of all women's rights issues. Their alliance with Train is a testament to the profound depth of their alienation and estrangement from their former abolitionist allies and the Republican Party. Northern abolitionists detested Train just as vociferously as he hated them, and in this fact may lie at least a small part of his attraction for Anthony and Cady Stanton. Train offered his help when the Republicans refused all, and Cady Stanton expressed her reaction this way: "It seems to me it would be right and wise to accept aid even from the devil himself, provided he did not tempt us to lower our standard" (Stanton and Blatch 1922, 2:119–120).

Although all AERA Republican abolitionists were shocked by Anthony and Cady

George Francis Train

Stanton's partnership with Train, Lucy Stone was particularly flummoxed. In fact, when she read about it in the newspaper, she was convinced that the report was a "monstrous hoax" (Kugler 1987, 59). Upon discovering that the report was true, she was furious. She could not conceive how Anthony could have enlisted a racist demagogue on a mission for the AERA, an organization devoted to promoting both African-American and woman suffrage. The resulting breach between Stone and Anthony over this issue was so extensive that it eventually contributed to the split in the women's rights movement in 1869.

True to the promise he made during the Kansas campaign, Train made it financially possible for Anthony and Cady Stanton to begin publication of *The Revolution* in January 1868. Yet his support proved to be short-lived. On the day that the first issue of *The Revolution* appeared, Train informed Anthony that he was leaving for Europe to fight for the Fenian cause. Although financial support continued for a short time, soon Train was no longer involved in their affairs.

Related entries:
American Equal Rights Association
Blackwell, Henry Browne
Kansas Campaign of 1867

Reconstruction
The Revolution
Stone, Lucy

Suggestions for further reading:
DAB, 9:626–627.
DuBois, Ellen Carol. 1978. *Feminism and Suffrage: The Emergence of an Independent Women's Movement in America 1848–1869*. Ithaca, N.Y.: Cornell University Press.
Kugler, Israel. 1987. *From Ladies to Women: The Organized Struggle for Woman's Rights in the Reconstruction Era*. Westport, Conn.: Greenwood Press.

Truth, Sojourner (ca. 1797–1883)

African-American preacher, abolitionist, and women's rights activist Sojourner Truth was a dynamic, frequent presence on the social reform lecture circuit in the Northeast and Midwest from the early 1850s through the 1870s. At birth Truth was given the name Isabella. She was a slave until 1827, when New York state granted freedom to all its enslaved inhabitants. She gave herself the name Sojourner Truth in 1843 when she set out to become an itinerant preacher. A deeply spiritual woman, Truth gained a considerable following among Methodists as she traveled from one religious revival meeting to the next.

Truth discovered Garrisonian abolitionism when she visited the utopian community of the Northampton Association in Massachusetts. Through her contact with many social reformers, including William Lloyd Garrison, Truth was moved to embrace the work of abolitionism and the cause of women's rights. Among the well-educated, primarily white, middle-class reformers with whom she began lecturing and traveling in the 1850s, Truth was an oddity. Uneducated and determinedly illiterate, a self-possessed and an arresting though homespun speaker, Truth made an enormous impact on white audiences. Her power as an orator derived from the fact that she alone successfully embodied the enslaved African American for white northerners, a persona she and white reformers intentionally cultivated (Painter 1994, 140, 153–154). Her fellow African-American feminist-abolitionist colleagues, the well-educated and erudite Sarah Parker Remond and Frances Ellen Watkins Harper, interested audiences but never achieved Truth's popularity, although Remond later became a sensation among European audiences.

Truth attended woman's rights conventions during the 1850s. At the Fourth National Woman's Rights Convention in 1853 in New York City, she impressed Susan B. Anthony, who recorded excerpts of Truth's speech in the *History of Woman Suffrage*. As Anthony saw it, Truth was captivating because she

> combined in herself, as an individual, the two most hated elements of humanity. She was black, and she was a woman, and all the insults that could be cast upon color and sex were together hurled at her; but there she stood, calm and dignified, a grand, wise woman, who could neither read nor write, and yet with deep insight could penetrate the very soul of the universe about her. (*HWS*, 1:567)

During the crisis among Garrisonians in the late 1860s, Sojourner Truth, a member of the American Equal Rights Association (AERA), is recorded as standing firmly beside Susan B. Anthony and Elizabeth Cady Stanton in demanding that the AERA continue to support universal suffrage. Yet unlike Anthony and Cady Stanton, Truth never intended votes for women to assume priority over votes for black men (Painter 1996, 226). Eventually, she became more closely aligned with the American Woman Suffrage Association (AWSA), relinquishing her connection with Anthony and Cady Stanton's National Woman Suffrage Association (NWSA).

I SELL THE SHADOW TO SUPPORT THE SUBSTANCE.

SOJOURNER TRUTH.

Sojourner Truth

Related entries:
Abolitionist Movement
American Equal Rights Association
American Woman Suffrage Association
National Woman Suffrage Association
Woman's Rights Conventions
Women's Rights Movement

Suggestions for further reading:
Painter, Nell Irvin. 1994. "Difference, Slavery, and Memory: Sojourner Truth in Feminist Abolitionism." In *The Abolitionist Sisterhood: Women's Political Culture in Antebellum America*, ed. Jean Fagan Yellin and John C. Van Horne. Ithaca, N.Y.: Cornell University Press.
———. 1996. *Sojourner Truth: A Life, a Symbol.* New York: W. W. Norton.
Sterling, Dorothy. 1984. *We Are Your Sisters: Black Women in the Nineteenth Century.* New York: W. W. Norton.
Yee, Shirley J. 1992. *Black Women Abolitionists: A Study in Activism 1828–1860.* Knoxville: University of Tennessee Press.

𝒰

The Una

Paulina Wright Davis, leading women's rights activist and social reformer, initiated publication of her women's rights periodical the *Una* ("signifying Truth") in February 1853. As its masthead proclaimed, the *Una* was "A Paper Devoted to the Elevation of Woman." In a letter to Elizabeth Cady Stanton, Wright Davis explained her motivations for establishing a women's rights publication.

> I am anxious beyond measure to get this paper started we need it so much. Almost every paper is misrepresenting the movement or else shutting us out. . . . I am determined to do my utmost to remove the idea that all the womens rights women are horrid old frights with beards and mustaches who want to smoke and swear. (Paulina Wright Davis to ECS, February 9, 1852, ECS-LCMD, in *Papers*)

Published in Providence, Rhode Island, and funded almost entirely by Wright Davis, the *Una* attracted some of the best and most distinguished writers devoted to women's rights and woman suffrage. Lucy Stone, Ernestine Potowski Rose, Antoinette Brown (Blackwell), Thomas Wentworth Higginson, William Henry Channing, Elizabeth Cady Stanton, and Susan B. Anthony were among those who contributed to the monthly journal, which promised "to discuss the rights, duties, sphere, and destiny of woman fully and fearlessly" (*HWS*, 1:246). Cady Stanton, by her own admission writing in concert with Anthony, was a regular contributor to the *Una*. Through the *Una*, Wright Davis strove to satisfy both the intellectual and practical needs of women whose interests included politics, the arts, and foreign affairs as well as women's rights and domestic concerns.

Related entries:
Davis, Paulina Kellogg Wright
The *Lily*
Rose, Ernestine Louise Potowski
Stanton, Elizabeth Cady
Stone, Lucy
Women's Rights Movement

Suggestions for further reading:
Hoffert, Sylvia D. 1995. *When Hens Crow: The Women's Rights Movement in Antebellum America*. Bloomington: Indiana University Press.
Solomon, Martha M., ed. 1991. *A Voice of Their Own: The Woman Suffrage Press, 1840–1910*. Tuscaloosa: University of Alabama Press.

Underground Railroad

Susan B. Anthony's home city of Rochester, New York, was an important link on the Underground Railroad and, for many slaves escaping to freedom, was their last stop before reaching safe haven in Canada. Following the passage of the Fugitive Slave Act of 1850, Anthony, like many of her antislavery colleagues, assisted fugitives on their flight north. Her friend and fellow abolitionist Frederick Douglass was intensely involved in harboring escaped slaves. Amy Kirby Post, another Rochester participant and also a friend of Anthony's and Douglass's, estimated that approximately 150 slaves traveled through Rochester each year during this era (Barry 1988, 63).

By 1857, Anthony realized that, for her, extending more effort to help African Americans to flee the United States was not the most productive or efficient use of her energies and talents. She felt compelled to strike at the heart of the institution of slavery, to destroy it once and for all, and she believed she could best achieve this as an agent and lecturer for the American Anti-Slavery Society (AASS). Even so, she did not ignore the plight of runaway slaves but used her political acumen to take action. In 1860, Anthony lobbied the New York legislature to pass a "personal liberty bill," a law similar to those passed in a number of northern states that attempted to override the Fugitive Slave Act of 1850 and that guaranteed the freedom of both fugitive and freed slaves.

Related entries:
Abolitionist Movement
Douglass, Frederick
Dred Scott Decision
Rochester, New York

Suggestions for further reading:
Blockson, Charles L. 1987. *The Underground Railroad*. New York: Prentice Hall.
Buckmaster, Henrietta. 1941, 1992. *Let My People Go*. Columbia: University of South Carolina Press.
Rosenberg-Naparsteck, Ruth. 1984. "A Growing Agitation: Rochester Before, During, and After the Civil War." *Rochester History* 46, nos. 1–2:1–39.

Unitarianism

The American Unitarian Association, a liberal Protestant denomination, was founded in 1825 as a result of dissension in New England Congregationalism in the late eighteenth and early nineteenth centuries. During this period, many Congregational ministers diverged from the rigidly orthodox Calvinism that permeated U.S. Protestantism. William Ellery Channing, the pioneering leader of Unitarianism, espoused the views of many eastern Massachusetts Congregationalists who preferred to "emphasize God's benevolence, humankind's free will, and the dignity rather than the depravity of human nature" (Robinson 1985, 4). U.S. Unitarians also rejected the concept of the trinity and questioned the deity of Jesus Christ, though they considered themselves Christians. From its beginnings, U.S. Unitarianism (known today as the Unitarian Universalist Association) has been distinguished by its lack of religious orthodoxy and complex theology. Unitarians have traditionally valued the freedom of the individual to worship according to his or her personal beliefs.

During the antebellum period, Unitarians were in the vanguard of many social and moral reform movements, especially the abolitionist movement. Humanitarian concern and social activism have always been an integral part of the Unitarian experience. Susan B. Anthony first became closely acquainted with Unitarianism when her father Daniel Anthony and their radical Hicksite Quaker neighbors withdrew from the Rochester Society of Friends because its members refused to tolerate their antislavery convictions and their desire to be involved in concerted abolitionist reform. Many of the Rochester antislavery Quakers began attending services at the Unitarian Church in Rochester. One of the more inspiring ministers who welcomed Rochester Quakers was the temperance, women's rights, and abolitionist reformer William Henry Channing, the nephew of William Ellery Channing. The younger Channing's passionate commitment to social change profoundly influenced the young Anthony. Although she joined the Rochester Society of Friends in 1853 and remained a lifelong member of that Quaker meeting, she continued to attend Unitarian church services for the rest of her life. She never perceived this duality as a conflict. The religious freedom, social conscience, and institutional support for social reform that Anthony found in Unitarianism dovetailed perfectly with her Quaker beliefs.

Related entries:
Anthony, Susan B.
May, Samuel Joseph
Quakerism (Society of Friends)

Suggestions for further reading:
Robinson, David. 1985. *The Unitarians and the Universalists.* Westport, Conn.: Greenwood Press.
Stange, Douglas C. 1977. *Patterns of Antislavery among American Unitarians, 1831–1860.* Cranbury, N.J.: Associated University Presses.

The United States v. Susan B. Anthony

On November 5, 1872, Susan B. Anthony cast her ballot for Republican presidential candidate Ulysses S. Grant and two members of Congress. This single act of voting, although duplicated by more than 150 women nationwide on this election day, formed the basis of the case known as the *United States v. Susan B. Anthony.* Anthony's first occasion voting, her arrest, and her subsequent trial dominated newspaper headlines for months. The case embroiled the nation in a debate over the constitutional issues concerning woman suffrage and the "New Departure" strategy. It also resulted in widespread condemnation of the federal judicial system's failure to recognize Anthony's legal rights as a U.S. citizen.

Anthony had been eagerly waiting for a chance to test the New Departure strategy, which held that women, as citizens of the United States, have the right to vote as specified by the Fourteenth and Fifteenth Amendments. Anthony, as a leader of the National Woman Suffrage Association (NWSA), had urged women nationwide to register to vote in this and in other elections. Four days prior to election day, 1872, Anthony; her three sisters Guelma Anthony McLean, Hannah Anthony Mosher, and Mary Anthony; and her friend Rhoda De Garmo walked to the barbershop that was the voter registration site for the Eighth Ward in Anthony's home of Rochester, New York. After Anthony read aloud the Fourteenth Amendment and explained how it supported woman suffrage, two of the three officials registered the women to vote. Having cleared that hurdle, Anthony then went door-to-door urging her female neighbors and friends to register. A total of 50 Rochester women successfully registered, although on election day only those from the Eighth Ward were permitted to cast ballots.

After Anthony registered, she consulted Henry Rogers Selden, respected Rochester attorney and a former appeals court judge. He agreed to scrutinize the constitutional analyses supporting woman suffrage that she presented, including Francis Minor's legal argument that the Fourteenth and Fifteenth Amendments enfranchised women. A day later, Selden informed Anthony that he had concluded that the Fourteenth Amendment did indeed enfranchise women. He also promised to support her legally in her effort to claim her right to the ballot.

On election day, Anthony was invigorated by her first voting experience. She immediately wrote to Cady Stanton of her elation at finally having taken direct action to achieve suffrage: "Well, I have been and gone and done it! Positively voted the Republican ticket—straight—this A.M. at seven o'clock . . . Not a jeer, not a word, not a look disrespectful has met a single woman" (*HWS,* 2:934–935). Following a bitter outcry from a Rochester newspaper that Anthony and her fellow women voters had violated federal law, federal officials eventually responded. More than two weeks after election day, a U.S. marshal arrived at Anthony's Rochester

Copy of the front page of the courtroom proceedings of the trial of the United States v. Susan B. Anthony.

home to arrest her for violating the Enforcement Act, a law that held, among its other provisions, that "any person . . . who shall vote without having a legal right to vote; or do any unlawful act to secure . . . an opportunity to vote for himself or any other person, shall be deemed guilty of a crime" (Sherr 1995, 108). The Enforcement Act, however, had not been enacted to ensnare suffragists; it had been intended to safeguard the voting rights of African Americans in the reconstructed South. Anthony had been expecting the government to react to the suffragists who voted on election day, but she never imagined that she could be arrested on a criminal offense merely for casting a ballot!

Selden defended Anthony by asserting that because she believed that she possessed the constitutional right to vote, she could not be criminally convicted of voting. At the hearing of all the Rochester women voters on December 23, 1872, Selden and his associate John Van Voorhis ably presented the constitutional arguments supporting the women's right to vote. The commissioner then declared the women and the registrars guilty and set bail at $500 each.

Anthony was the only person accused who did not post bail. She instead requested a writ of habeas corpus, which, if granted, would confirm that she had been arrested unlawfully and would free her from all charges. In January 1873, the U.S. district judge refused the writ and summarily reestablished her bail at $1,000. Because Selden was becoming more and more anxious that Anthony might be subjected to the indignity of incarceration, he paid the bond, thereby depriving Anthony of the opportunity to have her case presented before a higher court. Although Anthony understood that Selden had acted out of a paternal sense of protectiveness, she was enormously frustrated when he caved in on this point. In fact, she never completely forgave him for abandoning her cause at this most crucial moment (Lutz 1959, 202). Nevertheless, she never ceased to respect and honor his legal assistance. In a letter to her friend Gerrit Smith, who publicly supported her throughout her trial, she described Selden as "one of the noblest and best men I have ever known" (SBA to GS, August 5, 1873, GS-SUL, in *Papers*).

In January 1873, Anthony was indicted by a grand jury and then waited for her trial date to be announced. Not wasting any time in idle speculation or worry, Anthony departed on a lecture tour of the Midwest, returning home in March to be the only woman voter to cast a ballot in the Rochester municipal elections (Barry 1988, 253). Once her trial date was set for May 1873, Anthony immediately commenced a dizzyingly complete canvass of Monroe County,

New York (in which Rochester is located), to inform the public about the constitutional issues in her case.

> I stand before you under indictment for the alleged crime of having voted at the last presidential election, without having a lawful right to vote. It shall be my work this evening to prove to you that in thus doing, I not only committed no crime, but instead simply exercised my citizen's right, guaranteed to me and all United States citizens by the National Constitution. (Harper 1899, 2:977)

Then, after reading aloud the preamble to the Constitution, she declared:

> It was we, the people, not we the white male citizens, nor we, the male citizens; but we, the whole people, who formed this Union. We formed it not to give the blessings of liberty but to secure them; not to the half of ourselves and the half of our posterity, but to the whole people—women as well as men. (Harper 1899, 2:978. See the Documents section for the full text of this speech.)

This lecture campaign publicized her case but, more importantly, clearly delineated the constitutional arguments supporting women's claim to the ballot. When her speeches significantly influenced public opinion in her favor, federal officials decided to relocate the trial venue to the small town of Canandaigua, in Ontario County, New York, on June 17, 1873. Not to be dissuaded, Anthony and her close friend and fellow suffragist Matilda Joslyn Gage then proceeded to canvass Ontario County. Anthony gave the lecture, "Is It a Crime for a United States Citizen to Vote?" and Gage delivered the address, "The United States on Trial, Not Susan B. Anthony" (Harper 1899, 1:436).

Whatever Anthony expected in the way of a trial, she never anticipated the brand of justice she received at the U.S. District Court in Canandaigua. Former president Millard Fillmore, two U.S. senators, a jury of 12 white men, and many supporters and curious onlookers filled the jam-packed courtroom. Since Ward Hunt, the judge assigned, was hearing his first criminal case and because he had been appointed by a well-known opponent of woman suffrage, Anthony was not optimistic about the outcome of her trial. But she was in no way prepared to be denied the right to defend herself and the right to a trial by jury. Judge Hunt declared that Anthony would not be permitted to defend herself because, being female, she was not competent as a witness in her own behalf.

After Anthony's attorneys, Selden and Van Voorhis, delivered their arguments, Judge Hunt read his opinions on the case, which he had obviously formulated prior to the day's proceedings. He maintained that the states, through their state constitutions, bestow the right to vote on their citizens, not the federal government. He added that neither the Fourteenth nor the Fifteenth Amendment grants women the right to the franchise. Lastly, Judge Hunt determined that since Anthony had been fully aware of her actions and the law concerning woman suffrage at the time that she voted, she had acted illegally. He then surprised everyone in the courtroom when he ordered the jurors to yield a guilty verdict without allowing them any deliberation. Anthony was infuriated by this travesty of justice, calling it "the greatest judicial outrage ever recorded" (Harper 1899, 1:441). When Judge Hunt gave Anthony the opportunity to speak the next day, she was prepared to expose the trial for the mockery it was.

> Yes, your honor, I have many things to say; for in your ordered verdict of guilty, you have trampled underfoot every vital principle of our government. My natural rights, my civil

rights, my political rights, my judicial rights, are all alike ignored. Robbed of the fundamental privilege of citizenship, I am degraded from the status of a citizen to that of a subject; and not only myself individually but all of my sex, are, by your honor's verdict, doomed to political subjection under this so-called republican government. (*HWS,* 2:687. See the Documents section for Anthony's remarks at her trial.)

Judge Hunt fined her $100, which Anthony openly vowed she would never pay. Although established procedure dictated that she be jailed until her fine was paid, Judge Hunt did not extend this order, undoubtedly realizing that if he confined her, Anthony would have the right to have her case reviewed by the U.S. Supreme Court under a writ of habeas corpus. Again thwarted in her quest to reach a higher court, Anthony, acting on Selden and Van Voorhis's advice, submitted a request to Congress to have the fine remitted, which would render Judge Hunt's verdict illegal. This attempt also failed, leaving Anthony scrambling to obtain pardons from President Ulysses S. Grant for the three jailed voting officials who had accepted the Rochester women's ballots. He granted the pardons, perhaps realizing that although they had unwittingly violated federal law, the registrars had helped women to cast ballots for his presidency.

For Anthony, one consolation was the prominent attention her trial received in the national press. From coast to coast, many newspaper editors criticized the government's actions in her case, though a few supported Hunt's arbitrary ruling. From Anthony's point of view, regardless of the range of editorial opinions on the case, the publicity generated from the press coverage of the trial promulgated the constitutional issues involved and broadcast the court's blatantly discriminatory abridgment of justice. To further disseminate the issues and to emphasize the institution-alization of women's powerlessness before the courts, she printed and distributed 3,000 copies of the courtroom proceedings. And, for years to come, she incorporated the experience into her women's rights and suffrage lectures.

Related entries:
Anthony, Susan B.
Fifteenth Amendment
Fourteenth Amendment
National Woman Suffrage Association
"New Departure" Strategy
Selden, Henry Rogers
Woman Suffrage Movement

Suggestions for further reading:
DuBois, Ellen Carol. 1987. "Outgrowing the Compact of the Fathers: Equal Rights, Woman Suffrage, and the United States Constitution, 1820–1878." *Journal of American History* 74, no. 3 (December):836–862.
Sherr, Lynn. 1995. *Failure Is Impossible: Susan B. Anthony in Her Own Words.* New York: Times Books.
HWS, 2: 647–716.

University of Rochester

*E*ven before Susan B. Anthony entered the women's rights movement in the early 1850s, achieving equal educational opportunities for women was critically important to her. Her own education and her teaching experiences underscored her conviction that women urgently needed to expand their limited access to education. Although Anthony left the teaching profession in 1849, her advocacy of equality in education continued throughout her lifetime. Anthony agreed wholeheartedly with Elizabeth Cady Stanton and Lucy Stone that coeducation, especially in higher education, would be an excellent means of improving women's education. As early as 1851, Anthony was meeting with Cady Stanton and Stone to discuss the feasibility of coeducational colleges.

From the time the University of Rochester expanded its curriculum to become a liberal arts college, Anthony had longed for it to open its doors to young women. Beginning in 1890, discussion within the Rochester community became action when a group of Rochester's women's organizations dedicated themselves to the goal of seeing women enrolled alongside men in collegiate programs at the University of Rochester. Their initial inquiries and requests led to a decision by the university's board of trustees that women could not be admitted unless $200,000 were raised. The trustees argued that this sum was necessary to expand and renovate university facilities to accommodate female students. Throughout the 1890s, Anthony and her sister Mary Stafford Anthony joined civic-minded Rochester women to raise the necessary funds.

In 1898, the board of trustees announced that women would be welcome to enroll at the university if a sum of $100,000 could be raised within a one-year period. Given this more attainable goal, Rochester women revitalized their fund-raising forces. Despite their previous success raising $40,000, they had difficulty obtaining much more because they encountered stiff resistance among university alumni and opponents of co-education and higher education for women. In the summer of 1899, acknowledging that the fund-raising committee was still far from its goal, the trustees decided that if it could offer the university $50,000 by the first week of September 1900, women would be admitted.

The years 1899 and 1900 were exceedingly busy ones for the 80-year-old Anthony. As she prepared to turn the reins of the National American Woman Suffrage Association (NAWSA) over to the next generation of suffrage leaders, she was preoccupied with NAWSA business while she also compiled material for the fourth volume of the *History of Woman Suffrage*. Then, in late August 1900, she and Mary entertained the entire executive board of NAWSA for three long, exhausting days and nights of business meetings. After the NAWSA "Cabinet" departed, Anthony realized that she was more than fa-

tigued; she was very weak and completely drained of all energy. She vowed to rest.

Several days later on the evening of September 4, after a sweltering day in a week of scorching heat, Anthony received a telephone call from Fannie Bigelow, secretary of the fund-raising committee. She informed Anthony that the deadline to raise the $50,000 fell on the following day and that the fund was $8,000 short. On top of that, all the fund's leaders were out of town.

What Bigelow expected an 80-year-old woman to do about the problem the night before the money was due is not clear. But Anthony, being Anthony, and even being as deathly tired as she was, could not bear to let the deadline drop. All of her life, time and time again, she had wrestled and conquered the fund-raising dragon. She was determined to do it once more if she could.

The next morning she convinced Mary to donate the $2,000 she had planned to give to the university on her death. Then, in the oppressive heat, Anthony and Bigelow traveled by carriage all over Rochester, visiting Anthony's old friends and wealthy benefactors. They met with many refusals, but her dear friends the Unitarian minister William Gannett and his wife Mary T. Lewis Gannett gave $2,000, and another friend, Sarah Willis, also donated $2,000. The elderly, ever-generous philanthropist Samuel Wilder promised another $2,000. With the pledges, Anthony and Bigelow hurried to the meeting of the trustees.

After the trustees considered the pledges and the funds the women had already raised, they refused to accept Samuel Wilder's donation, claiming that he might die before he could fulfill his promise. Anthony was nonplused but refused to accept the rejection as an obstacle. She explained that she would back Wilder's pledge with her $2,000 life insurance policy, which she had established in 1855. The trustees were finally satisfied, and Anthony and Bigelow left the meeting, knowing that women students would be permitted to enroll immediately. Finally

Susan B. Anthony at her desk in Rochester. Photo by Francis Benjamin Johnson, 1900, the year of her retirement as president of the National American Woman Suffrage Association.

Anthony could return home to collapse in exhaustion.

The next day Anthony suffered a stroke, although she did not know it at first. She reported in her diary that evening that she had felt peculiar all day, as if there were something wrong with her tongue and her speech. The next day when she awoke, she was unable to speak at all, an affliction that lasted a week. Although her doctor feared she would never speak again, in time she was able to converse normally. She spent weeks recovering. When at last she was strong enough to ride in a carriage, she insisted on going first to the University of Rochester where at last she could see her dream of women students and coeducation realized (Harper 1908, 3:1221–1225).

Related entry:
Anthony, Susan B.

Suggestions for further reading:
Harper, Ida Husted. 1908. *The Life and Work of Susan B. Anthony.* Vol. 3. Indianapolis: Hollenbeck Press.
Kovnat, Denise Bolger. 1995. "Dear, Blessed Susan B." *University of Rochester Review* (fall):16–22.

Upton, Harriet Taylor (1853–1945)

Suffragist, Republican political activist, and historian Harriet Taylor Upton was an indispensable leader of the National American Woman Suffrage Association (NAWSA) from 1890 to 1910. Although officially recognized as treasurer of the organization, she was integrally involved in the daily administration of NAWSA, working full-time to carry out its daily business. All accounts of Taylor Upton's life emphasize her remarkable personality, which did much to ease tensions among warring factions within NAWSA. Her jovial, easygoing nature and her wit made her beloved by all who knew her. Because of these qualities, her industriousness, and her unparalleled involvement in Republican politics, Anthony regarded Taylor Upton as a key NAWSA leader and a potential future president.

Harriet Taylor was born and grew up in Ohio, her family eventually settling in the community of Warren. Her father, Ezra Booth Taylor, an attorney and judge, served as Republican congressman from Ohio for 13 years beginning in 1880. She was fascinated by politics at a young age and in her young adulthood enjoyed accompanying her father on his political campaign tours throughout northern Ohio. Although her father provided her with an eye-opening education in politics, he refused to consider the possibility of a college education for his daughter.

In the late 1870s, Harriet Taylor heard Susan B. Anthony when she lectured in Warren, but at this time and until the late 1880s, Taylor was a committed antisuffragist. She objected to the woman suffrage movement because she believed that suffragists promoted the erroneous view that men treated women unjustly. During the 1880s, Taylor married George Whitman Upton, an attorney who became her father's law partner.

Sometime after the International Council of Women in 1888, while Taylor Upton was researching an antisuffrage article, she became completely alienated from antisuffragism and found herself drawn to the woman suffrage movement. In 1890, she attended the first NAWSA convention and became a member, offering her considerable Republican political connections and knowledge to NAWSA. During the first decade of

the new century, she was extremely active. Besides serving as treasurer, she engaged in fund-raising activities, handled press inquiries, testified before Congress, directed the distribution of suffrage literature, edited *Progress* (a monthly suffrage newspaper that eventually served as the chief press organ of NAWSA), traveled and lectured for woman suffrage, and wrote suffrage articles for the press.

Taylor Upton was also deeply engrossed in the Ohio state suffrage struggle. From 1899 to 1908 she was president of the Ohio Woman Suffrage Association (OWSA). After she resigned from NAWSA in 1910 in protest over Anna Howard Shaw's ineffective leadership, she again served as OWSA president from 1911 until ratification of the Nineteenth Amendment in 1920.

Once women were in possession of the ballot, Taylor Upton remained active in Republican politics. In 1920, the year Warren G. Harding of Ohio was elected president of the United States, she was selected to serve as vice chair of the Republican National Executive Committee, a post she held for four years. In 1924, she decided to run for her father's former congressional seat, but she lost in the initial primaries. From 1928 until her retirement from public life in 1931, she was dedicated to social reform while serving as a member of Ohio Republican governor Myers Cooper's staff.

Related entries:
National American Woman Suffrage Association
Woman Suffrage Movement

Suggestions for further reading:
Lutz, Alma. 1959. *Susan B. Anthony: Rebel, Crusader, Humanitarian.* Boston: Beacon Press.
Shriver, Phillip R. "Harriet Taylor Upton." In *NAW,* 3:501–502.
Wrench, Susan Bleiweis. "Upton, Harriet Taylor." 1985. In *American Reformers,* ed. Alden Whitman. New York: H. W. Wilson, pp. 820–821.

Wells-Barnett, Ida Bell (1862–1931)

Throughout her life, Ida Wells-Barnett concentrated all her reform efforts on securing the civil and political rights of African Americans. As part of this quest, she worked as a teacher, an investigative journalist, a suffragist, a social reformer, and a women's club leader. In the early 1890s, as Wells-Barnett's interest in the woman suffrage movement grew, she became close friends with Susan B. Anthony, a relationship that endured until Anthony's death in 1906.

Ida Bell Wells was born in Mississippi, the daughter of former slaves. From a young age, Wells was a fighter. In 1878, when her parents and a brother died from yellow fever, she took charge of her younger brothers and sisters and their household, although she was only 16 years old. She obtained a teaching job to support her family by persuading her employers that she was 18 years old. Years later, in 1884, after having relocated with several of her siblings to Memphis, Tennessee, she boarded a train but refused to sit in the car set aside for African Americans. When the conductor forced her off, she consulted attorneys who helped her win a lawsuit against the rail company. This success was short-lived, however, because the state supreme court overturned the original decision.

During the 1880s, she wrote articles for newspapers and was eventually hired as a newspaper editor. In 1892, when three Memphis African-American grocery store owners were lynched, all men whom Wells knew, her outrage catapulted her into a career as an investigative journalist and full-time antilynching activist. She traveled widely, tracking down the facts involved in lynching cases throughout the South. She then publicized them in her articles. Through her writing, lectures, and formation of antilynching societies, she tried to awaken northerners to the emergency posed by the explosion of lynching incidents in the South. In 1895, her incessant travel and organizing were interrupted when she married Ferdinand Barnett, a Chicago attorney and publisher of *The Conservator*, the first African-American weekly newspaper in Chicago.

While on a lecture tour in the 1890s, Wells-Barnett delivered a speech in Rochester, New York, the home of Susan B. Anthony. After her address (which Anthony attended), Wells-Barnett recalled that a man in the audience, a theological student from Texas, asked:

"If the colored people were so badly treated in the South, why was it that more of them didn't come North?" Before I could answer, Miss Anthony sprang to her feet and said, "I'll answer that question. It is because we, here in the North, do not treat the Negroes any better than they do in the South, comparatively speaking." (Wells-Barnett 1970, 227)

Several Rochester residents later objected to Anthony's statement. Northern racial prejudice and segregation practices were realities that many northerners preferred to ignore or to deny existed. But on this one subject, Wells-Barnett and Anthony were in complete agreement. They both knew from experience that the North, although it prided itself on its just, humane, and liberal treatment of African Americans, was in reality a closed society, steeped in racial prejudice and discrimination. In fact, Anthony had protested northerners' treatment of African Americans as early as the 1850s, while she was an abolitionist.

Wells-Barnett nurtured an intense admiration for Anthony in the 1890s. "Those were precious days in which I sat at the feet of this pioneer and veteran in the work of women's suffrage," she wrote. And Anthony was in awe of Wells-Barnett's abilities, telling her: "I know of no one in all this country better fitted to do the work you had in hand than yourself" (Wells-Barnett 1970, 255). As much as they respected and liked each other, however, they disagreed on many key racial issues. Time and again Anthony tried to explain to Wells-Barnett why she could not make racial issues a focus of NAWSA's activism, and why she had to do whatever was necessary to obtain the support of southern white suffragists and southern white male voters. Wells-Barnett understood Anthony's position but spoke out against it. She did not allow Anthony to forget that her policy of excluding racial issues from NAWSA's agenda retarded the effort to achieve equality for African Americans.

Wells-Barnett recalled in her autobiography, *Crusade for Justice,* that Anthony had a habit of sweeping aside racial injustice and other societal problems by saying, "Well, now when women get the ballot all that will be changed." On one occasion Wells-Barnett openly challenged her friend's inflated confidence in the ballot, declaring, "Knowing women as I do, and their petty outlook on life, . . . I do not believe that the exercise of the vote is going to change women's nature nor the political situation." According to Wells-Barnett, "Miss Anthony seemed a bit startled, but she did not make any contention on that point" (Wells-Barnett 1970, 230).

Wells-Barnett's confidence in the potential of the woman suffrage movement to improve the lives of African-American men and women increased during the first decade of the twentieth century. She came to believe that achieving voting rights for all African Americans was the prerequisite to social, economic, and political equality. Toward this goal, she formed the Alpha Suffrage Club (ASC) in Chicago, the first African-American woman suffrage society in Illinois. Yet she discovered that organizing African Americans to agitate for suffrage proved to be far easier than having them join forces with white suffragists. To the detriment of the woman suffrage movement, uniting African-American and white suffragists' efforts was never achieved due to the latter's exclusionary policies. Nevertheless, Wells-Barnett, like many courageous African-American suffragists, struggled to integrate the movement. She attended NAWSA's Suffrage Parade in Washington, D.C., in March 1913 as the delegate from the ASC. When white Illinois delegates objected to her attempt to join them at the parade site, she adamantly refused to march at the back of the parade with other African-American suffragists. Instead she disappeared into the crowd. When the white Illinois suffragists strode by, she slipped in among them and completed the march, having successfully integrated the parade.

Following the ratification of the Nineteenth Amendment and throughout the 1920s, Wells-Barnett continued her full-fledged civil rights activism—lecturing, campaigning, writing articles and books, and unyieldingly pressing the agenda of African-American equality.

Related entries:
Anthony, Susan B.
Woman Suffrage Movement

Suggestions for further reading:
Sterling, Dorothy. 1988a. "Ida B. Wells." *Black Foremothers: Three Lives.* New York: Feminist Press.
Wells-Barnett, Ida B. 1970. *Crusade for Justice: The Autobiography of Ida B. Wells*, ed. Alfreda M. Duster. Chicago: University of Chicago Press.
Wheeler, Marjorie Spruill, ed. 1995a. *One Woman, One Vote: Rediscovering the Woman Suffrage Movement.* Troutdale, Oreg.: New Sage Press.

Willard, Frances Elizabeth Caroline (1839–1898)

Temperance activist, suffragist, social reformer, and friend of Susan B. Anthony, Frances Willard encouraged more women to engage in political activity than any other nineteenth-century reformer. Because of her dynamic, charismatic leadership of the Woman's Christian Temperance Union (WCTU), hundreds of thousands of women joined her crusade to protect themselves, their children, their homes, and their communities from intemperance by actively campaigning for the ballot through the woman suffrage movement.

Willard was raised principally in Ohio and Wisconsin Territory. She spent her young adulthood as a teacher, became president of Evanston College for Ladies, and later served as dean of the Woman's College of Northwestern University. In 1874, she left education to dedicate herself to the temperance movement. As the leader of a group of Chicago temperance women, she attended the Cleveland convention that formed the WCTU in 1874 and was selected corresponding secretary of the new organization.

In her autobiography, Willard described a spiritual experience that changed the direction of her reform career. In 1876 she believed that she received a message from God instructing her "to speak for woman's ballot as a weapon of protection" that would safeguard the home and the family from "the tyranny of drink" (Willard 1892, 351). From this moment on, Willard committed herself to achieving woman suffrage. Her two years of temperance activism had proven to her that women needed the political power of the ballot to completely protect themselves from the abuses wrought by alcohol. Once enfranchised, Willard realized, women would have the power to pressure legislators to enact sweeping antialcohol legislation in local, municipal, state, and national elections.

The WCTU's conservative leadership did not agree with Willard's suffrage ideas, but this did not deter her from her mission. During the late 1870s she lectured widely on temperance and woman suffrage and published her views in *Our Union*, the WCTU's official journal. In 1878, when she was elected president of the Illinois WCTU, she led a monumental petition campaign demanding that the state legislature enfranchise women. Although Illinois legislators refused to respond, the signatures of more than 100,000 women proved to Willard, Illinois politicians, and WCTU activists that women supported woman suffrage as a means of attaining prohibition legislation. In 1879, Willard was elected WCTU national president, further endorsement of WCTU members' support for the ballot for women. In the early years of the 1880s, Willard transformed the WCTU into a political machine pushing for what she called the "Home Protection Ballot."

Anthony, who first met Willard when she lectured in Rochester, New York, in 1875, was elated by the temperance leader's turn toward suffrage activism and by her election to the top leadership position of the WCTU. Always in awe of Willard's outstanding strength as a leader, Anthony reflected on the nature of the temperance leader's charismatic power. "She was a bunch of magnetism possessing this occult force," Anthony observed. "I never approached her but what I felt my nerves tingle from this magnetism" (Washington, D.C., *Evening Star*, February 18, 1898, SBA Scrapbooks, LCRBD, in *Papers*). The two women were extremely fond of each other and enjoyed long visits at each other's homes.

In the suffrage struggle, they tried to cooperate whenever possible but always respected the fact that they possessed entirely opposing views on many issues. Anthony was disappointed that Willard preferred the American Woman Suffrage Association's (AWSA's) state-by-state strategy to the NWSA's methods. Another major disagreement concerned the role political parties should play in the suffrage movement. Willard did not agree with Anthony's staunch nonpartisan policy toward political parties. During the 1880s, when Willard forged an alliance between the WCTU and the Prohibition Party (which she had helped form in 1882), she longed for Anthony and the NWSA to join them. Anthony refused each overture from Willard on this issue, explaining that she could not endorse one party because that would mean turning her back on members of other political parties who had supported woman suffrage. As the years passed, Anthony became even more firmly committed to a nonpartisan policy. In 1896, Willard, too, adopted a nonpartisan policy to preserve WCTU unity.

Like Anthony, Willard explored the possibility of forming an international women's movement in the early 1880s. Her efforts culminated in the formation of the World's Woman's Christian Temperance Union in 1883. In 1888, Willard joined Anthony in leading the International Council of Women (ICW), and in 1890, Willard became the first president of its national body, the National Council of Women. In the early 1890s, she attempted to unify the WCTU, the Prohibition Party, and the new Populist Party into one united reform party that would fully endorse woman suffrage and national prohibition. When these efforts failed, the exhausted and discouraged Willard spent long periods of time in England with her close

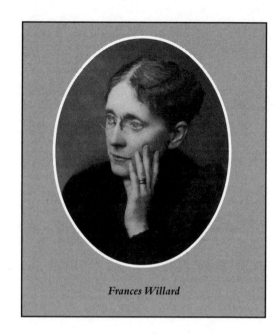

Frances Willard

friend Lady Henry Somerset, president of the British Women's Temperance Association. Despite her frequent absences during the 1890s, Willard managed to retain the presidency of the WCTU. Later in the decade, Willard's health began to fail, and in February 1898, she died at the age of 58.

Related entries:
American Woman Suffrage Association
National Woman Suffrage Association
Temperance
Woman Suffrage Movement
Woman's Christian Temperance Union

Suggestions for further reading:
Bordin, Ruth. 1986. *Frances Willard: A Biography.* Chapel Hill: University of North Carolina Press.
Dillon, Mary Earhart. "Frances Elizabeth Caroline Willard." In *NAW*, 3:613–619.
Earhart, Mary. 1944. *Frances Willard: From Prayers to Politics.* Chicago: University of Chicago Press.

Woman Suffrage Association of America

E lizabeth Cady Stanton and Susan B. Anthony conceived of the plan to form the Woman Suffrage Association of America

(WSAA) in October 1868, at a time when they realized that they could no longer work effectively for woman suffrage within the American Equal Rights Association (AERA). Women delegates from 20 state suffrage associations attended the organizational meeting of the WSAA in January 1869 in New York City. Other prominent women leaders included Elizabeth Smith Miller (daughter of Gerrit Smith and cousin of Cady Stanton), Abigail Hopper Gibbons, and Mary Cheney Greeley (wife of Horace Greeley). At this meeting, Cady Stanton demanded that a Sixteenth Amendment guaranteeing woman suffrage be initiated in Congress (Griffith 1984, 135).

The WSAA had a very loose organizational structure that acted as an umbrella encompassing Anthony and Cady Stanton's widely varying suffrage activities. Among these was their tour of Ohio, Illinois, Wisconsin, and Missouri, in which they not only agitated on the woman suffrage question but concentrated on recruiting new women to the movement, especially those who had had no prior antislavery connections. Anthony and Cady Stanton were well aware that with the strong Republican support of the Fifteenth Amendment, antislavery women would be less likely to support woman suffrage during "the negro's hour."

The final meeting of the WSAA was held in January 1870. Members resolved to dismantle the WSAA to make way for Anthony and Cady Stanton's new suffrage organization, the National Woman Suffrage Association (NWSA), formed in the spring of 1869.

Related entries:
American Equal Rights Association
Fifteenth Amendment
National Woman Suffrage Association
Reconstruction
Sixteenth Amendment Campaign

Suggestions for further reading:
Griffith, Elisabeth. 1984. *In Her Own Right: The Life of Elizabeth Cady Stanton*. New York: Oxford University Press.
HWS, 2:341–377.

Woman Suffrage Movement

The woman suffrage movement was among the largest, the longest-lived, and the most politically significant mass reform movements in U.S. history. Although traditional historians continue to ignore its central importance to U.S. history and culture, it cannot be denied that the woman suffrage movement was a vibrant, integral, influential, and ever-present part of American life. It had an impact on the life of every American, regardless of race, nationality, creed, age, or gender. The woman suffrage movement demanded that the U.S. population consider the most fundamental issue of a democracy—who shall be entitled to enjoy all the rights and privileges of a democratic society and who shall be excluded.

For late-twentieth-century Americans living in a culture marked by voter apathy, in which millions of Americans never register to vote or neglect to cast ballots in election after election, it is difficult to understand why nineteenth- and early-twentieth-century Americans were so obsessed by the issue of suffrage. Why did some women desire the ballot so desperately? And what was it about women's quest for the ballot that ignited and sustained such heated debate and controversy? Radical Republican leader Senator Charles Sumner encapsulated the unbridled enthusiasm and optimism of nineteenth-century reformers for the ballot in his 1866 address to Congress.

> To him who has the ballot all other things shall be given—protection, opportunity, education, a homestead. The ballot is like the Horn of Abundance, out of which overflow rights of every kind, with corn, cotton, rice, and all the fruits of the earth. . . . "Give me the ballot, and I can move the world." (*HWS*, 2:168)

Although he was promoting the ballot for the newly freed African Americans, women abolitionists and suffragists, Susan B. Anthony, Elizabeth Cady Stanton, and Lucy Stone among them, embraced this same passion for the vote.

From the time that the first woman suffrage amendment was proposed in Congress in 1868 until the ratification of the Nineteenth Amendment in 1920, more than 50 years of ceaseless agitation ensued. Although Susan B. Anthony's death in 1906 prevented her from experiencing the culmination of her more than five decades' dedication to women's rights, she was aware at the end of her career that national woman suffrage ultimately would be realized. Leading National American Woman Suffrage Association (NAWSA) suffragist Carrie Chapman Catt, writing in the early 1920s, totaled the monumental labors that led to the passage of the Nineteenth Amendment:

- 56 separate woman suffrage referenda submitted to male voters
- 480 campaigns to persuade state legislatures to present suffrage amendments to voters
- 47 efforts to urge state constitutional conventions to add woman suffrage to their constitutions
- 277 campaigns to persuade state political party conventions to include woman suffrage planks in their party platforms
- 30 campaigns to urge national political party conventions to incorporate woman suffrage planks
- 19 presentations of a federal woman suffrage amendment to 19 successive Congresses from 1878 to 1896 (Catt and Shuler 1926, 107)

These efforts, waged by the National Woman Suffrage Association (NWSA) and the American Woman Suffrage Association (AWSA) from 1869 to 1890, the NAWSA from 1890 to 1920, the Congressional Union and the National Woman's Party from 1913 to 1920, the Woman's Christian Temperance Union (WCTU) from 1879 to 1920, and hundreds of state and local suffrage societies, demonstrate the direct political involvement of hundreds of thousands of women activists.

American women's first demands for the right to the franchise predated the 1868 woman suffrage amendment proposal by 20 years. In 1848, at the first woman's rights convention in Seneca Falls, New York, Elizabeth Cady Stanton asserted women's right to vote. At the time, her suffrage resolution was so controversial that it was the one demand that the convention nearly did not accept. The ensuing antebellum women's rights movement of the 1850s continued to articulate women's demand for the ballot but did not focus solely on winning the franchise because it also concentrated on achieving many other civil and legal reforms for women.

Following the Civil War, during the early years of Reconstruction, northern Radical Republicans struggled to obtain constitutional protection of African-American civil and political rights. Since the political climate seemed to favor sweeping constitutional revision, Anthony, Cady Stanton, Lucretia Coffin Mott, Lucy Stone, and other women's rights activists realized that Congress might be induced to bestow the suffrage on women as well as on African-American men. When the Fourteenth and Fifteenth Amendments granted political rights to African-American men only, women's rights reformers responded by founding national organizations dedicated solely to achieving woman suffrage, the NWSA and the AWSA.

ANTHONY'S ROLE IN THE SUFFRAGE MOVEMENT

Anthony's crusade for the ballot was unusual, considering that she was raised in a culture that prohibited voting. Quaker men, Anthony's father Daniel included, abstained from voting because they believed they must not uphold a government that engaged in warfare or other violence. Daniel Anthony cast his first ballot in 1860 for Abraham Lincoln when his fervent abolitionism proved stronger than his Quaker convictions. Anthony was first struck by the potential power of the ballot during her years as a temperance reformer, when she realized that it was the most expedient means for women to influence the government to remedy their economic and social problems. This awakening, sparked by discoveries that emerged in dialogue with the pioneering suffragist Elizabeth Cady Stanton, led her directly into the women's rights movement and into demands for woman suffrage.

As the "Napoleon" of the women's rights movement and the acknowledged "General" of the NWSA and the NAWSA, Anthony believed that her primary task was to educate society—legislators, government officials, the national male electorate, and, most of all, disfranchised women—to an understanding of the crucial importance of the ballot for all citizens in a democracy. "There can be but one possible way for women to be freed from the degradation of disfranchisement," she once said, "and that is through the slow processes of agitation and education, until the vast majority of women themselves desire freedom" (Harper 1899, 2:918). She strove to educate women and men through her sweeping cross-country lecture tours, her responsiveness to members of the press, her extensive lobbying of state legislators and members of Congress, as well as through petition drives, speeches at congressional hearings, state suffrage campaigns, and the dialogue that she cultivated with scores of national and state suffragists. She was less concerned about converting nonbelievers, the antisuffragists, than she was in rousing the vast majority of American women and men to an awareness of what she believed was the most crucial issue facing society—woman suffrage.

Of all the dozens of male and female reformers who shaped Anthony's career, Cady Stanton was undoubtedly the most influential in molding Anthony into an incomparable suffragist. Cady Stanton's role in the woman

This marble sculpture in the Capitol Rotunda in Washington, D.C., is by Adelaide Johnson and portrays (left to right) Elizabeth Cady Stanton, Susan B. Anthony, and Lucretia Coffin Mott.

suffrage movement has been overshadowed by Anthony's contributions because Cady Stanton was not as visible or as active a participant in the day-to-day ministrations of the NWSA and NAWSA or of their suffrage campaigns. Cady Stanton disliked the organizational details of reform that Anthony so successfully commandeered. Nor did Cady Stanton relish the repetitive ritual or the hoopla of conventions, though she attended and often presided, at Anthony's insistence. Until her death, however, Cady Stanton sustained her role as the radical spokeswoman and philosopher of the movement. Hers was the principal voice of suffrage activism, through her speeches, newspaper articles, essays, and other writing, but she was never won over to Anthony's conviction that the ballot was the all-important goal to be pursued to the exclusion of other women's rights issues. Throughout her career, Cady Stanton championed divorce reform, a woman's right to reproductive freedom, the international women's rights movement, and protests against organized religion and Christian theology. Anthony regretted Cady Stanton's reluctance to be a reformer battling on the front lines of the suffrage movement because, to her mind, Cady Stanton had long proved that she was more than equal to the challenge.

ANTHONY'S SUFFRAGE IDEOLOGY

Unlike her friend and closest partner Cady Stanton, Anthony was neither a philosopher nor a rhetorician. Her views on suffrage, the basic beliefs that propelled and inspired her activism, were strikingly uncomplex. Her suffrage ideology was streamlined for her audience's immediate consumption. She repeated her core suffrage beliefs over and over from speech to speech, the imagery and examples changing to mesh with her audience's environment and experience. First and foremost, she emphasized that the ballot was the "open sesame" to all other rights and privileges in society—economic sustenance and independence, respect and harmony in the home, and the solution for all the problems facing women and men in society. Described by Anthony as "the badge of freedom, of independence, of sovereignty," the ballot would enable women to create a better, more just society. "When women vote," she insisted, "they will make a new balance of power that must be weighed and measured and calculated in its effect upon every social and moral question. . . ." Anthony had the highest expectations for a world made perfect by women's votes. She especially looked forward to the day when women would share government with men. "Who can doubt that when the representative women of thought and culture . . . sit in counsel with the best men of the country, higher conditions will be the result?" (Harper 1899, 2:1002).

In each suffrage speech, Anthony made sure that her audience comprehended the disgrace and humiliation of disfranchisement. She argued that convicted criminals, the mentally incompetent, and the mentally ill were the only other individuals with whom women shared the degradation of political powerlessness. "Disfranchisement is the symbol of weakness, of dependence, of incompetence political, social, and intellectual," she protested (*Monticello Express*, March 20–21, 1875, SBA Scrapbooks, LCRBD, in *Papers*). And in another speech, she argued, "My purpose tonight is to demonstrate . . . that disfranchisement is not only political degradation, but also moral, social, educational and industrial degradation. . . . Disfranchisement means inability to make, shape or control one's own circumstances" (Harper 1899, 2:996).

THE IMPACT OF THE ANTISUFFRAGISTS

From the inception of the woman suffrage movement through the ratification of the Nineteenth Amendment in 1920, there were women and men who vigorously opposed it. Antisuffrage individuals and groups obstructed the enfranchisement of women for a multitude of reasons. Early antisuffragists of the late 1860s and 1870s were primarily concerned that the ballot would disrupt women's domestic and maternal roles and create disharmony in the family. Horace Greeley, one of the most influential antisuffragists of this era, asserted that the vast majority of women had no interest in voting or in politics. In 1871, conservative domestic authority Catharine Beecher and the wives of General William Sherman and Admiral John Dahlgren delivered to Congress a petition containing 1,000 women's signatures pleading with Congress to desist from enacting a law enfranchising women. Beecher, in her book *Woman Suffrage and Woman's Profession,* proclaimed that if women were given the vote, most would consider it an overwhelming burden that would cause them to shortchange their domestic duties (Sherr 1995, 181).

Other early arguments that persisted throughout the woman suffrage movement included the following:

- Women have all the rights they need already;

- The ballot will degrade women by causing them to mingle in the "dirty," corrupt world of politics;
- Women don't need the vote because their husbands already vote for what is in women's best interests; and
- Women don't vote when they have the right to do so (an argument based on the occasional low voter turnouts in some municipal elections in states where women already had the vote).

Beginning in the 1880s, female and male antisuffragists became more organized, especially in the East. The antisuffrage movement was particularly strong in Massachusetts, where a number of antisuffrage groups gained prominence and spread their influence into other states. They wrote, published, and disseminated antisuffrage literature wherever state woman suffrage referenda or other suffrage measures were pending.

In the West and Midwest, the liquor industry and liquor interest groups (including the owners and managers of hotels, restaurants, billiard halls, saloons, bars, and other sites where liquor was sold) opposed woman suffrage vigorously, primarily because they feared that the female vote would legislate prohibition. The well-financed, highly organized liquor groups created a negative outcome for woman suffrage measures in many states. Their antisuffrage tactics included courting and then bribing the press to publicize their antisuffrage arguments, lobbying and occasionally buying votes from legislators, persuading saloon workers to cajole their customers into voting against woman suffrage, and instructing illiterate and immigrant men in marking their ballots to vote against woman suffrage. Late in the woman suffrage movement, large corporations and business interests cooperated to oppose woman suffrage, in the belief that women, because of

Many men were attracted to the arguments of the antisuffragists.

their close affiliation and approval of many social reforms, would vote to regulate industry and legislate labor and social welfare restrictions on businesses.

In the South, opposition to woman suffrage was rampant among many factions in society. A principal concern among white southerners was their fear of enfranchising African-American women and the impact that would have on the South's efforts to retain white political supremacy.

During the 1880s and 1890s, a number of well-educated, prominent, female social reformers and workers in benevolent organizations believed that the vote would hamper women's effectiveness in creating social change. Political involvement, they reasoned, would force them to seek alliances with unscrupulous politicians and would necessitate their involvement in political activities, thereby squandering valuable resources that could be better expended on social reform.

Although Anthony's speeches were filled with skilled refutations of antisuffragists' arguments, she did not spend much time or energy responding directly to them. Her distaste and anger occasionally emerged, however. "When a so-called educated woman is . . . found protesting against the enfranchisement of her sex, she will invariably be found to be a shallow and thoroughly selfish woman. There are unhappily, millions of such women in this republic" (*New York Daily News*, December 10, 1894, SBA Scrapbooks, LCRBD, in *Papers*). But most of her bluster was reserved for the many millions of other women who were apathetic about suffrage issues. More than any other goal, Anthony wanted to blast them into awareness. Indeed, they were the major reason that she pushed herself to travel and broadcast her suffrage message from coast to coast.

THE ROLE OF AFRICAN-AMERICAN AND OTHER MINORITY WOMEN

From the earliest days of the women's rights movement through the Reconstruction years

of crisis in the American Equal Rights Association (AERA) and through the struggle for ratification of the Nineteenth Amendment, African-American women were actively engaged in the woman suffrage movement. Following the split in the women's rights movement in 1869 and the demise of the AERA, most of the few African-American suffragists joined the Boston-based AWSA, which dedicated itself first and foremost to securing the political rights of African-American men through the Fifteenth Amendment.

Harriet Forten Purvis, her daughter Hattie Purvis, and Mary Ann Shadd Cary (who resented the Fourteenth Amendment's inclusion of the word *male*) were three African-American activists who were affiliated with Anthony and Cady Stanton's NWSA. Sojourner Truth occasionally attended NWSA conventions but was primarily attached to the AWSA (Terborg-Penn, in Wheeler 1995a, 142).

In general, few African-American women were involved in the national suffrage movement in the 1870s and 1880s, but by the end of the nineteenth and early twentieth centuries, many more middle-class, educated African-American women became suffrage activists. The southern states' systematic disfranchisement of African-American men during the late 1880s and 1890s alerted African-American women to the necessity of the ballot as the prerequisite to the protection of all other civil and political rights.

In 1893, the U.S. Supreme Court's reversal of the Civil Rights Act of 1875 and the concomitant increase in lynchings throughout the South also pushed African-American women toward political activism. Many turn-of-the-century African-American women suffragists became active through their membership in the African-American women's clubs. Through these organizations, women educated one another about suffrage and related political issues, and collaborated to find solutions to the severe social and economic problems afflicting African Americans in their communities.

African-American suffragists urgently wanted to participate in the national effort to obtain the ballot but were continually frustrated by white suffragists' exclusionary policies. Beginning in the early 1890s, NAWSA leaders believed that to achieve national woman suffrage, whether by federal suffrage amendment or by the state-by-state strategy, they had to acquire the support of southern legislators and southern male voters, who were overwhelmingly opposed to the suffrage movement. To accomplish this feat, NAWSA leaders were convinced that they needed to court southern white suffragists while appearing to support the South's intention to reinstate white political supremacy. With this priority paramount, NAWSA leaders realized that they could neither reach out to the growing ranks of African-American suffragists nor could they, as an institution, welcome those who wished inclusion. Anthony fully cooperated with this NAWSA policy, though she did not originate it.

In a conversation with her African-American friend and fellow reformer Ida Wells in 1894, Anthony indicated that she had been obliged to reject the request of a group of African-American women who wanted to organize their own suffrage society as a chapter of NAWSA, something that groups of white suffragists had done for many years. According to Wells-Barnett, writing in her book *Crusade for Justice: The Autobiography of Ida B. Wells*, Anthony explained to her that she had refused this group's admission because she had not wanted to antagonize southern white women whose support was pivotal to the cause. "And you think I was wrong in so doing?" Anthony asked. Wells recalled, "I answered uncompromisingly yes, for I felt that although she may have made gains for suffrage, she had also confirmed white women in their attitude of segregation" (Wells-Barnett 1970, 230).

African-American suffragists refused to be deterred by the actions of white suffragists.

Through the leadership of African-American suffrage activists Mary Church Terrell, Wells-Barnett, Adella Hunt Logan, and others, African-American involvement in the woman suffrage movement vastly increased. Hunt Logan, a lifetime member of NAWSA and a devotee of Anthony, lectured on woman suffrage throughout the South. She persuaded African-American women who were lukewarm about suffrage to consider the reasons why white women were so insistent upon obtaining the ballot. Hunt Logan emphasized that if white women, endowed with all the privileges of their race, believed they needed the ballot, then oppressed African-American women needed the vote even more urgently to obtain and protect their rights (Adele Logan Alexander, in Wheeler, 1995b, 90).

Anthony greatly admired the efforts of Church Terrell, the first president of the National Association of Colored Women (NACW), who organized African-American women to work toward woman suffrage. Both Church Terrell and Wells-Barnett, another NACW suffrage leader, attended and occasionally addressed NAWSA conventions in the years before Anthony's death, despite their awareness that many NAWSA suffragists preferred that they remain segregated in their own organizations.

Although much has been written about NAWSA's exclusion of African-American women, they were not the only minority group unwelcome in national suffrage organizations. White suffragists' anti-Catholic and nativist, or anti-immigrant, rhetoric repelled Catholic women, Jewish women, and those of many ethnic minorities. Throughout their careers in suffrage, however, Anthony and Cady Stanton frequently defended the inclusion of all groups in the movement before their more conservative fellow reformers. In the 1870s, Anthony endorsed the inclusion of Mormon women against a tide of criticism both inside and outside the movement. In 1890, Cady Stanton, sensing the conservative shift in the new, younger generation of suffragists, warned NAWSA members about the dangers of exclusion.

> We must manifest a broad catholic spirit for all shades of opinion in which we may differ and recognize the equal rights of all parties, sects and races, tribes and colors. Colored women, Indian women, Mormon women and women from every quarter of the globe have been heard in these Washington conventions and I trust they always will be. (ECS, February 1890, "Address to the Founding Convention of the NAWSA," in DuBois 1992, 226)

Once the Nineteenth Amendment was ratified in 1920, African-American women still had a long struggle to obtain woman suffrage. In Alabama, Tennessee, and many other states in the South, state laws prohibited African-American women (and men) from voting because of mandated property requirements, literacy tests, and other voting restrictions. Not until after the civil rights movement and the passage of the federal Voting Rights Act of 1965 would African-American women and men be fully enfranchised.

RACISM AND NATIVISM AMONG SUFFRAGISTS

In the late nineteenth century, the massive influx of immigrants from Europe intensified the nativism of Americans that had already increased in strength following the tide of Irish immigration in the late 1840s and 1850s. Social Darwinism—the theory that the educated, financially successful upper and middle classes are the "fittest" and most superior members of society—and other racialist theories further stimulated nativist as well as racial biases. Suffragists, frequently clashing with immigrants during their state suffrage campaigns, used nativist arguments to express their frustrations about hostile immigrant audiences and defeats in state campaigns.

A woman's suffrage parade in New York City, 1913.

Although NAWSA leaders Henry Black-well and Chapman Catt, beginning in the 1880s, refined and promoted "educated suffrage" proposals that would require voters to be literate and to own property, Anthony never pursued such a strategy. For one thing, despite her castigations of immigrant men on the campaign trail, she never relinquished her belief in universal suffrage. She asserted that she believed in "universal suffrage without either property or educational qualification. I hold that every citizen has a right to a voice in the government under which he lives . . . a man may be unable to read but may attend political meetings, talk with his neighbors and form intelligent opinions" (Harper 1899, 2:899). She also pointed out that enfranchising only educated and propertied women "would antagonize not only every man who had neither property nor education but also every one whose wife had neither, and all such would vote against the enfranchisement of rich and educated women" (Harper 1899, 2:922).

Yet Anthony often did contrast the unsuitability of "ignorant" immigrant men to be informed voters with the superiority of millions of educated American-born women, leading many to conclude that she was against the foreign vote. Though she did not oppose the right of immigrants or African Americans to vote, she was vehemently against the legislators and government officials who denied women—half of the U.S. population—the right to vote. Her real outrage was directed at the men in power who repeatedly and consistently denied her the ballot while they freely bestowed it on every male foreigner after only a few months' residence in the United States. Anthony was further inflamed when she encountered foreign-born men who told her that she had no right to demand the vote. As was the case with her occasional belittling comments about African-American male voters, Anthony's angry, sometimes ugly comments about immigrant men unwittingly and unmistakably fueled prejudices.

Most NAWSA leaders (Anthony, Cady Stanton, Rachel Foster Avery, Chapman Catt, Henry Blackwell, Anna Howard Shaw, and others) made statements that exposed their racial and nativist biases, all of which reflected commonly held views in American society. It is essential to understand the origins of these prejudices, not for the purpose of condoning them but to comprehend the forces that fueled them. White suffragists frequently referred to the fact that their lack of political rights painfully degraded and humiliated them. But why did they feel so debased? Quite simply, their perception of their degradation stemmed from the fact that the vast majority of white, American-born men and women believed that African Americans, Native Americans, Asian Americans, and all immigrants were their political and social inferiors. As a result, when politicians and the majority of male voters refused to extend the vote to white women but lavished it on men whom they believed were inferior, white suffragists howled their objections. In their speeches and their writings, they became obsessed with the mission to correct what they believed was a preposterous illogic and a heinous misjudgment. How could white American men persist in disfranchising white women when this decision made their wives, mothers, and daughters the basest members of society?

By the 1890s, Anthony was determined that no political or social issue would share space with woman suffrage on the NAWSA platform, and that policy included racial issues. The ballot for women must come first, or woman suffrage would never be achieved. Many twentieth-century historians and observers have criticized her neglect of the disfranchisement of African-American men in the South and her refusal to become involved in that struggle. Although she did speak out against their disfranchisement, the explosion of lynching incidents in the South, and northern racial prejudice, she refused to lead or participate in a campaign for African-American political rights in the South or North.

Rosalyn Terborg-Penn, widely acclaimed as the foremost historian of African-American suffragists, notes that Anthony "chose expedience over loyalty and justice" when she urged Frederick Douglass to avoid the 1895 NAWSA Convention in Atlanta, Georgia, because, in wooing southern suffragists, she dared not risk offending any (Terborg-Penn, in Wheeler 1995a, 148). Anthony deliberately "chose expedience" because she fervently believed that no worthwhile social, economic, political, or moral change would occur in society until women had the power to vote. According to her worldview, when women were enfranchised, they would use their political power to ensure that justice and loyalty prevail.

I am as deeply and keenly interested in the many reforms in city, state & National government as any one can possibly be—but knowing that no right solution of any great question can be reached until the whole people have a voice in it—I give all of myself to the getting the whole people inside the body politic. (SBA to Thomas Bowman, September 7, 1894, AFC-HL, in *Papers*)

THE ROLE OF MEN IN THE WOMAN SUFFRAGE MOVEMENT

Although men did not play as integral a role in the woman suffrage movement as they did in the women's rights movement of the 1850s, a very small percentage of men were active supporters of the ballot for women, although for the most part they were external to the actual administration of the movement. In general, men of the late nineteenth and early twentieth centuries were much more likely to be involved in the leadership of antisuffrage organizations than they were to be dedicated suffragists.

Frederick Douglass, William Lloyd Garrison, Thomas Wentworth Higginson, Henry Ward Beecher, Wendell Phillips, and Henry Blackwell were among the male women's rights activists from the 1850s who became involved in the woman suffrage movement. For the most part, these men attended national conventions and wrote prosuffrage articles and editorials, but with the exception of Blackwell and a few others, most men tended to support woman suffrage from a position outside the movement's leadership.

Male prosuffrage legislators in Congress and in the state and territorial legislatures were extremely important in influencing the majority of their antisuffrage colleagues to consider woman suffrage measures and referenda. Besides Senator Samuel Clarke Pomeroy of Kansas and Representative George Washington Julian of Indiana, who introduced the first suffrage amendments to Congress in 1868, Senators Aaron Augustus Sargent of California, Thomas W. Palmer of Michigan, Henry W. Blair of New Hampshire, George Frisbe Hoar and Benjamin Butler of Massachusetts, and Benjamin Wade of Ohio were among the respected congressional leaders who swayed the opinions of their colleagues in a way that nonlegislators could not.

In the state suffrage campaigns from coast to coast, the participation of men was crucial to suffragists' success. Men knew which suffrage arguments were most likely to win the support of their gender. Male politicians' intimate knowledge of state political machines and key political players made their advice and assistance invaluable to women suffragists. Activists purposefully cultivated strong relationships with male, prosuffrage newspaper editors and reporters who proved essential to state suffrage campaigns. Carrie Chapman Catt, who directed many a state suffrage campaign, demanded that female suffragists elicit men's active involvement. In the successful 1893 Colorado campaign, she instructed state suffragists to enlist a man in every precinct to be in charge of campaigns to nominate delegates to the state political conventions, an essential task if suffragists were to attain the all-important political party endorsements of woman suffrage.

Confronting the Challenges of the Twentieth Century

The year 1900, when Anthony stepped down as president of NAWSA, marked an important turning point in the history of the woman suffrage movement. Beginning in that year and increasing steadily through the next two decades, woman suffrage truly became a mass political movement. Just as hundreds of thousands of WCTU reformers had transformed the national suffrage movement in the late nineteenth century, so the influx of twentieth-century Progressive-era social reformers, college-educated women, and female trade unionists broadened and radically altered the way the woman suffrage movement pressed its agenda. As Anthony had predicted so astutely in 1900, social reformers who had rejected seeking a political solution to the nation's social problems in the late nineteenth century reconsidered their position during the Progressive era (1900–1914). Once they realized how ineffectual they were as nonvoters persuading legislators to back their reform proposals in education and social welfare, they flocked to support the woman suffrage movement.

In 1902, the NAWSA was still a vital part of Anthony's activism, even though she was no longer president. By this time she had realized that she would not live to see national woman suffrage achieved, a fact she frequently lamented.

> If I could only live another century! I do so want to see the fruition of the work for women in the past century. There is so much yet to be done, I see so many things I would like to do and say, but I must leave it for the younger generation. . . . The young blood, fresh with enthusiasm and with all the enlightenment of the twentieth century must carry on the work.
> (Rochester *Democrat and Chronicle*, August 28, 1902, SBA Scrapbooks, LCRBD, in *Papers*)

In her final years, not only was Anthony intensely aware of her celebrity status, but she actively cultivated it to publicize the cause. Even so, she could not have predicted the public outpouring of emotion that followed her death, a phenomenon that NAWSA leaders quickly harnessed to benefit the movement. Following on the heels of Anthony's funeral in March 1906, at which 10,000 admirers had gathered to mourn her, NAWSA leaders succeeded in convincing NAWSA-affiliated suffrage societies throughout the country to hold memorial services dedicated to her memory. This effort and the NAWSA's overall program to immortalize Anthony helped solve two of the organization's most perplexing problems—low membership and inadequate funding. Indeed, NAWSA membership boomed from a meager 12,000 members in 1906 to a total of over 117,000 in 1910 (Graham 1996, 52).

What made the NAWSA program to exalt Anthony so successful was that it focused on those of Anthony's extraordinary characteristics that the NAWSA most urgently needed its members to emulate—ceaseless, self-sacrificing labor, single-minded dedication to the cause of woman suffrage, and an uncompromising commitment to the ideal of women's political and social equality—all essential to propel the movement to its final victory. Of course, the fact of the NAWSA's deliberate "canonization" of Anthony, as some historians have chosen to label it, can never diminish her truly monumental contribution to the women's rights and woman suffrage movements.

Related entries:
American Equal Rights Association
American Woman Suffrage Association
Anthony, Susan B.
Anthony/Cady Stanton Partnership
Avery, Rachel G. Foster
Catt, Carrie Lane Chapman
Kansas Campaign of 1867
National American Woman Suffrage Association

Suggestions for further reading:

Buhle, Mary Jo, and Paul Buhle, eds. 1978. *A Concise History of Woman Suffrage: Selections from the Classic Work of Stanton, Anthony, Gage, and Harper.* Urbana: University of Illinois Press.

Flexner, Eleanor. 1975. *Century of Struggle: The Woman's Rights Movement in the United States.* Cambridge, Mass.: Belknap Press of Harvard University Press.

Graham, Sara Hunter. 1996. *Woman Suffrage and the New Democracy.* New Haven, Conn.: Yale University Press.

Marilley, Suzanne M. 1996. *Woman Suffrage and the Origins of Liberal Feminism in the United States, 1820–1920.* Cambridge, Mass.: Harvard University Press.

Wheeler, Marjorie Spruill, ed. 1995a. *One Woman, One Vote: Rediscovering the Woman Suffrage Movement.* Troutdale, Oreg.: New Sage Press.

The Woman's Bible

*E*lizabeth Cady Stanton's lifelong concern with organized religion's oppression of women assumed its fullest expression in her publication of *The Woman's Bible* in 1895 when she was 80 years old. Its radical message rocked the woman suffrage movement and had widespread repercussions for the National American Woman Suffrage Association (NAWSA), for Cady Stanton's position of leadership in the movement, and for her relationship with Susan B. Anthony.

Following the publication of *The Woman's Bible*, Cady Stanton was no longer as revered an icon in the woman suffrage movement. Although she had not been in a position of administrative power, until the publication of *The Woman's Bible* she had been the undisputed figurehead and ideological leader of the woman suffrage movement.

For decades, Cady Stanton had blasted the clergy for their biblical interpretations that served to confine women to the domestic world of "women's sphere" and to restrict their public activity. Beginning in the 1880s, after years of research, reading, and thinking about the subject of the Bible's treatment of women, she began to plan a comprehensive treatise that would correct biblical passages demeaning to women by suggesting alternative interpretations. Cady Stanton was careful never to question the legitimacy of the Bible as holy writ. She focused her wrath on the centuries of male biblical writers and clergymen who tried to impose their prejudices onto the word of God, and she demanded that a reinterpretation or a corrective voice be issued.

In the 1880s, Cady Stanton encouraged a number of women to assist her in the project, and although they made some headway in this decade, it was not until the 1890s that she fully reinvested herself in the project and decided to publish it. Cady Stanton wanted Anthony's cooperation and participation, but she refused to be involved in any way. Anthony firmly believed in Cady Stanton's right to publish as she saw fit, declaring, "I think women have just as good a right to interpret and twist the Bible to their own advantage as men always have twisted and turned it to theirs . . . ," but it disappointed her that Cady Stanton chose to invest all her energies in religious reform rather than in suffrage activism (Harper 1899, 2:856).

When *The Woman's Bible* was published in 1895, it became an immediate best-seller. It also instigated enormous controversy, to the delight of Cady Stanton. At last her lifelong views on religion and theology were receiving serious attention and provoking widespread public debate. Many conservative men and women proclaimed the volume blasphemous and Cady Stanton a heretic, outcomes that she had anticipated. But what she had not expected was the reaction of the younger, more conservative generation of NAWSA suffragists, many of whom were outraged that their leader would jeopardize the cause of woman suffrage by publicizing radical views that would alienate millions of Americans from woman suffrage. Prior to publication of *The Woman's Bible*, Anthony had tried to persuade Cady Stanton not to publish it because of its ramifications for the movement. Carrie Chapman Catt, in a meeting with Cady Stanton and Anthony, stated her conviction that its publication would cause irreparable harm to NAWSA. But Cady Stanton would not be swayed from her course.

At a NAWSA board meeting at the January 1896 national convention, the organization's leading suffragists voted 53 to 41 to approve a resolution to censure *The Woman's Bible*. The resolution read, "This association is non-sectarian, being composed of persons of all shades of religious opinions, and has no official connection with the so-called *Woman's Bible*, or any theological publication to maintain the allegiance of its conservative majority." Although the resolution's wording appears to be merely an attempt to distance NAWSA from Cady Stanton's radical religious thought, the move was unprecedented in NWSA and NAWSA history. At no time had the leadership or its members thought it necessary to issue a formal statement against another member's independent writings for any reason. Many of Anthony's most trusted coworkers voted for the resolution, including Chapman Catt, Rachel Foster Avery, Anna Howard Shaw, Alice Stone Blackwell, and Henry Blackwell.

Anthony was deeply disturbed by the entire proceedings, which she believed were bigoted, unjust, and contrary to the principles of justice on which the woman suffrage movement was based. Prior to the vote on the resolution, Anthony made one final plea for broad-mindedness. "The one distinct feature of our association has been the right of individual opinion for every member," she declared. "I shall be pained beyond expression if the delegates here are so narrow and illiberal as to adopt this resolution. . . . I pray you vote for religious liberty, without censorship or inquisition." Anthony also pointed out an important potential danger of such a move for the entire membership. "This year it is Mrs. Stanton; next year it may be I or one of yourselves, who will be the victim" (Harper 1899, 2:853–854).

When Anthony conveyed the news to her old friend, Cady Stanton was distraught. She had expected a hue and cry from the NAWSA leadership but never a total repudiation and rejection. She insisted that both she and Anthony resign from NAWSA, a demand that put Anthony into a torturous bind. To be loyal to Cady Stanton and to Anthony's belief in religious freedom and free speech meant abandoning her life's work. It proved to be a sacrifice that Anthony could not make.

Cady Stanton was immensely disappointed and hurt by Anthony's refusal to resign but responded only by persisting on her course to publish the second volume of *The Woman's Bible*. She refused to resign from NAWSA and in her radical, outspoken lectures and articles continued to proclaim her beliefs.

Cady Stanton and Anthony continued to disagree on the subject of religious oppression and *The Woman's Bible*. Of course, Anthony never denied the existence of religious oppression of women, and although she believed that Cady Stanton's crusade was a waste of effort, she supported her friend's choice and right to do it. As Anthony explained in a letter to Cady Stanton, "You say . . . 'Get rid of religious bigotry and then get political rights,' while I shall keep pegging away saying, 'Get political rights first and religious bigotry will melt like dew before the morning sun;' and each will continue still to believe in and defend the other" (Harper 1899, 2:857).

In addition to the difficulties *The Woman's Bible* posed for Anthony in her relationship with Cady Stanton, the actions of her colleagues who voted to censure the volume disrupted relationships within NAWSA. Anthony was incensed and deeply hurt by the vote, and she reserved her strongest anger for her friends and closest colleagues who supported the resolution, especially Foster Avery, Chapman Catt, and Shaw. Anthony could not comprehend how her friends could be so disloyal to Cady Stanton, whom she believed they had revered. What Anthony did not understand was that her young lieutenants' fealty was strictly reserved for her, and did not carry over automatically to Cady Stanton. After all, they had never worked closely with Cady Stanton and, for the most part, knew her only from a distance. She was the respected but also very distant pioneer of the women's rights and woman suffrage movements. Cady Stanton's isolation from the day-to-day administration of NWSA and NAWSA and her radical religious theologies seriously affected how suffragists viewed her and strongly influenced the minimization of her contributions in the early histories of the suffrage movement.

Related entries:
Anthony/Cady Stanton Partnership
Avery, Rachel G. Foster
Catt, Carrie Lane Chapman
National American Woman Suffrage Association
Shaw, Anna Howard
Stanton, Elizabeth Cady

Suggestions for further reading:
Barry, Kathleen. 1988. *Susan B. Anthony: Biography of a Singular Feminist*. New York: New York University Press.
Griffith, Elisabeth. 1984. *In Her Own Right: The Life of Elizabeth Cady Stanton*. New York: Oxford University Press.

Woman's Christian Temperance Union

*I*n November 1874, the Woman's Christian Temperance Union (WCTU) was formed in Cleveland, Ohio, at a convention called by women temperance activists. This massive organization, attaining a membership of 245,000 by 1911, was by far the largest and most powerful women's organization of its time (Giele 1995, 159). The WCTU's pledge to join the struggle for women's enfranchisement gave the woman suffrage movement the large constituency it needed to prove to the public that woman suffrage had broad support among women.

The women's temperance movement, active in the 1840s and 1850s, was quiescent during the Civil War. After the war, in response to a proliferation of saloons and a national increase in alcohol consumption, women participated in the Women's Temperance Crusade of 1873–1874. The crusaders' tactics—praying, singing, and beseeching saloon owners and liquor dealers to stop selling alcohol—were successful in a few locales but a dismal failure in many others. In response to these defeats, some midwestern women banded together to form temperance groups that would create more organized protests. One such organization was the WCTU, which was formed in 1874 under the leadership of Annie Wittenmyer to coordinate a women's movement that would institute prohibition nationwide and eradicate alcohol consumption.

In 1879, temperance activist and newly elected WCTU president Frances Willard transformed the WCTU around the quest for the "Home Protection Ballot." Willard persuaded her followers that woman suffrage was the best "weapon" for women to acquire if they were serious about protecting their families and their homes from the ravages of intemperance. With the vote, she argued, women would have the political clout they needed to pressure legislators to enact antialcohol legislation and prohibition. Willard's leadership and her temperance mission for woman suffrage caused the WCTU's membership to explode from a mere 27,000 in the early 1880s to 150,000 members by 1890—making the WCTU not only the largest temperance organization but the largest mass political movement of women (Bordin 1986, 112; Marilley 1996, 101).

Susan B. Anthony was enormously pleased by the growth of the WCTU. An admirer and friend of Willard, Anthony was encouraged by the vast numbers of temperance women who were committed to woman suffrage. She reasoned that the WCTU's addition to the ranks of national suffrage organizations could only hasten the political changes women were seeking. But as Anthony moved closer to cooperation with the WCTU, her fellow National Woman Suffrage Association (NWSA) leaders Elizabeth Cady Stanton, Matilda Joslyn Gage, Clara Bewick Colby, and others protested. They were concerned that collaboration with the WCTU would overwhelm the small NWSA. They also feared that an influx of conservative, evangelical temperance women would replace the NWSA's radical suffrage activism with a conservative, religious agenda.

Anthony, however, persisted in pursuing a course of cooperation with the WCTU. She knew that national woman suffrage could not be achieved without a huge constituency to impress its demands on legislators and the public. With the NAWSA membership numbering only 13,000 in 1890, she knew the woman suffrage movement desperately needed more suffragists to swell its ranks.

In state suffrage campaigns, Anthony and NWSA activists soon learned that as helpful as WCTU workers were in the field, their presence intensified the antisuffrage activities of the prohibition-wary liquor industry. Whenever possible, WCTU and national suffrage leaders worked together to minimize the damage. In the California suffrage campaign of 1896, at Anthony's request, Willard relocated the national WCTU convention from California to another state to avoid stimulating the state's liquor industry's antisuffrage campaign. Despite national suffrage activists' initial skepticism, they successfully cooperated with WCTU reformers in many state suffrage campaigns.

Although the WCTU's mission to achieve local and municipal suffrage was its primary and most urgent temperance goal, members also dedicated themselves to a variety of other social and moral reforms. WCTU members were involved in establishing kindergartens, reforming prisons, assisting the disabled and the chronically ill, combating prostitution, and providing support to mothers and their children. Although most of its members were white, Protestant, conservative, midwestern, middle-class women, the WCTU was more effective in including African-American women than were the national suffrage organizations.

After Willard's death in 1898, the WCTU's new president, Lillian Stevens, reestablished national prohibition as the organization's chief priority. Despite the change, WCTU women continued to be an important force in the woman suffrage movement, particularly in state suffrage campaigns.

Related entries:
National American Woman Suffrage Association
National Woman Suffrage Association
Temperance
Willard, Frances Elizabeth Caroline
Woman Suffrage Movement

Suggestions for further reading:
Bordin, Ruth. 1981. *Woman and Temperance: The Quest for Power and Liberty, 1873–1900.* Philadelphia: Temple University Press.
Gifford, Carolyn De Swarte. 1995. "Frances Willard and the Woman's Christian Temperance Union's Conversion to Woman Suffrage." In *One Woman, One Vote: Rediscovering the Woman Suffrage Movement,* ed. Marjorie Spruill Wheeler. Troutdale, Oreg.: New Sage Press.
Marilley, Suzanne M. 1996. *Woman Suffrage and the Origins of Liberal Feminism in the United States, 1820–1920.* Cambridge, Mass.: Harvard University Press.

The Woman's Journal

*O*f the more than 30 late-nineteenth- and early-twentieth-century women's rights and woman suffrage periodicals in the United States, the *Woman's Journal* was the most prominent, the most widely circulated, and the longest-lived. From 1870 to 1917, the weekly "Torchbearer of the Woman Suffrage Cause" was published in Boston,

Massachusetts, under the strong executive direction of leading suffragist Lucy Stone, who managed the publication until her death in 1893. She was ably assisted by her husband, the reformer Henry Blackwell, and beginning in 1881, by their daughter Alice Stone Blackwell, who eventually succeeded her parents as manager and editor. Through the *Woman's Journal*, Stone and her extraordinarily talented editorial staff not only informed activists about issues and events pertaining to the woman suffrage movement but also presented the most comprehensive and objective coverage of the struggle to improve the status of women in education, government, politics, the arts, and the professions.

In 1869, Stone enticed former New Englander Mary Ashton Livermore, publisher and editor of the Chicago suffrage newspaper *The Agitator*, to come to Boston to merge her publication with the journal Stone was envisioning and to serve as its editor in chief. First published on January 8, 1870, the *Woman's Journal* soon exceeded the circulation of its first rival, Susan B. Anthony's and Elizabeth Cady Stanton's newspaper, *The Revolution*. In addition to the *Woman's Journal* having a stronger financial base, it appealed to a broader audience than the more radical *Revolution*—attracting moderate and conservative reform-minded women and men. The *Woman's Journal*'s success was also due to Stone's ability to attract some of the most talented and popular writers of the era. Louisa May Alcott, Harriet Beecher Stowe, Lydia Maria Child, and Elizabeth Cady Stanton were just a few of the *Woman's Journal*'s most celebrated literati. The journal's editorial staff consisted of equally well-known and respected writers and reformers—Julia Ward Howe, William Lloyd Garrison, Thomas Wentworth Higginson, and Henry Blackwell.

Despite its broad, middle-class appeal, the *Woman's Journal* was first and foremost an invaluable resource for dedicated suffrage activists. It published all the proceedings and notices of the American Woman Suffrage Association (AWSA); the New England Woman Suffrage Association (NEWSA); and much later, the National American Woman Suffrage Association (NAWSA). It also reported on many of the activities of its rival, the National Woman Suffrage Association (NWSA), and state and regional suffrage societies from coast to coast. Anthony was a loyal reader of the *Woman's Journal*, although not without mixed feelings. In addition to the regret she must have experienced at having failed to make *The Revolution* as thriving a publication as Stone had managed to do, Anthony was often disappointed when Stone neglected to report or to recognize sufficiently the efforts and achievements of the NWSA and its leaders. Nevertheless, Anthony depended upon the *Woman's Journal* for suffrage news and for its rational coverage of national and state legislative developments.

Anthony's favorable opinion of Stone's newspaper, however, did not prevent her from trying to supplant the *Woman's Journal* as the official organ of the soon-to-be-formed NAWSA at merger negotiation meetings. Anthony suggested that her protégé Clara Bewick Colby's publication, the *Woman's Tribune,* become the official publication of the postmerger organization. Anthony probably knew that this attempt would be unsuccessful; still, she could not relinquish the opportunity to try to have some control over the mouthpiece of the new organization (Wheeler 1981, 311).

Throughout Stone's 23 years as publisher of the *Woman's Journal*, her most pressing goal was to create and maintain the publication's close relationship with its readers. She determinedly molded the *Woman's Journal* into a vehicle that served as a recruiting beacon for new and established women activists—encouraging, supporting, and exhorting women (and men) to fully dedicate themselves to improving women's status in all areas of society. New subscribers soon discovered that Stone and her staff demanded that their readership be much more than a passive audience. Through regular columns, articles, and editorials, readers were urged to organize suffrage societies; add their signatures to petitions demanding a Sixteenth Amendment for woman suffrage; distribute suffrage literature in their communities; attend various state and national legislative committee hearings; raise funds for the AWSA and NEWSA; support the editors' choice for president; and, perhaps most important, assume an active, participatory role in the overall improvement of society (Huxman 1991, 99, 107).

In 1917, by which time the *Woman's Journal* had attained its peak circulation of 27,000 and was distributed to 48 states and 39 countries, Alice Stone Blackwell retired as editor and publisher at the age of 60. The newspaper was then merged with two other suffrage periodicals to become the *Woman Citizen,* which continued publication until after the ratification of the Nineteenth Amendment in 1920.

Related entries:
American Woman Suffrage Association
Blackwell, Alice Stone
Blackwell, Henry Browne
National American Woman Suffrage Association
The Revolution
Stone, Lucy
Woman Suffrage Movement

Suggestions for further reading:
Blackwell, Alice Stone. 1930. *Lucy Stone: Pioneer of Women's Rights.* Boston: Little Brown.
Huxman, Susan Schultz. 1991. "The *Woman's Journal,* 1870–1890: The Torchbearer for Suffrage." In *A Voice of Their Own: The Woman Suffrage Press, 1840–1910,* ed. Martha M. Solomon. Tuscaloosa: University of Alabama Press.
Kerr, Andrea Moore. 1992. *Lucy Stone: Speaking Out for Equality.* New Brunswick, N.J.: Rutgers University Press.

*Woman's National Loyal League**

*I*n late February 1863, Susan B. Anthony and Elizabeth Cady Stanton conceived of a new role for women in wartime—participation in the first national women's political organization, which would petition

Congress to approve a constitutional amendment guaranteeing the freedom of African Americans. In 1863–1864, the Woman's National Loyal League (WNLL) executed the most successful petition campaign of the abolitionist movement (Venet 1991, 1). As Anthony had demonstrated in the campaign for the New York Married Women's Property Law during the 1850s, the massive petitioning of legislators (the only political avenue open to mid-nineteenth-century women) was a dynamic, effective political strategy.

During the late winter of 1863, with their idea still in the fledgling stage, Anthony and Cady Stanton conferred with trusted, politically astute male advisers and colleagues such as Horace Greeley, William Lloyd Garrison, newly appointed chief of the Freedmen's Inquiry Commission Robert Dale Owen, Theodore Tilton, and Henry Ward Beecher (Lutz 1968, 284). They confirmed what Anthony and Cady Stanton had estimated—that a constitutional amendment was necessary to secure the liberty of African Americans and that a large-scale petitioning of Congress would help persuade legislators to act upon it.

When Anthony and Cady Stanton composed their "Call for a Meeting of the Loyal Women of the Nation," they especially wanted to invoke women to dedicate themselves to shaping the future of the nation. They also wanted to prove to women that becoming involved in the political process was as much women's concern as men's.

> In this crisis of our country's destiny, it is the duty of every citizen to consider the peculiar blessings of a republican form of government. . . . At this hour, the best word and work of every man

*Historians have not been consistent in the name they use to refer to the WNLL. National Woman's Loyal League and National Loyal Women's League are two common variants. Anthony and Cady Stanton were by no means consistent in their usage. The name Woman's National Loyal League appears on their original organization documents; hence the use of that name in this volume (*HWS,* 2:50).

and woman are imperatively demanded. . . . Woman is equally interested and responsible with man in the final settlement of this problem of self-government; therefore let none stand idle spectators now. (*HWS*, 2:53)

An enormous crowd, composed mostly of women, filled the Church of the Puritans in New York City on May 14, 1863, for the organizational meeting of the new, soon-to-be-named WNLL. Many noted feminist abolitionists participated, including pioneers Lucretia Coffin Mott, Angelina Grimké Weld, Lucy Stone, Ernestine Potowski Rose, and Paulina Wright Davis. The speeches and resolutions lauded Lincoln for issuing the Emancipation Proclamation and demanded that the government enact total emancipation.

Anthony and Cady Stanton's efforts to interweave women's rights issues into the proceedings immediately spawned controversy. Many women objected to the resolution that stated, "There never can be a true peace in this Republic until the civil and political rights of all citizens of African descent and all women are practically established." A Mrs. E. O. Sampson Hoyt from Wisconsin pointed out the potential hazard in interjecting women's rights issues into a patriotic agenda.

We all know that Woman's Rights as an *ism* has not been received with entire favor by the women of the country, and I know that there are thousands of earnest, loyal, and able women who will not go into any movement of this kind, if this idea is made prominent. (*HWS*, 2:59–60)

But Potowski Rose, Stone, and the other leaders, one by one, resoundingly supported the inclusion of women's rights, and the majority voted to carry the resolution. Although the decision ultimately would limit the number of women willing to be members of the WNLL, the leaders realized that

women's rights were of central importance to the entire mission and could not be deleted.

The women set the WNLL's goal at securing a million signatures in favor of a Thirteenth Amendment and presenting them to Congress. Once the effort was launched, Anthony immediately began fund-raising and had petitions printed for distribution to members throughout the country. As the principal organizer and publicist, she took charge of all political strategy and finances (Venet 1991, 110). Cady Stanton served as president, chief rhetorician, and writer. Many of their friends also contributed their skills and labor to the effort. In a matter of months, in a colossal feat of organization, 5,000 women members from Maine to California gathered signatures on petitions. In February 1864, Anthony and Cady Stanton packed petitions bearing 100,000 signatures into a trunk and sent it to Senator Charles Sumner, the Massachusetts Republican driving the congressional campaign for the Thirteenth Amendment. He then exhibited them on the floor of the Senate. The Senate, responding to a groundswell of support from the public as well as to the petitions, passed the Thirteenth Amendment on April 8, 1864. As Anthony and Cady Stanton encouraged WNLL members to obtain more and more signatures, Sumner kept the pressure on Congress by regularly displaying petitions, proving the public's support for the amendment.

By the first anniversary meeting of the WNLL in May 1864 in New York City, more than 265,000 signatures had been collected, and by August, a total of 400,000. Although this total fell far short of the projected 1,000,000 signatures, it surpassed that of any petition previously presented to Congress. The House of Representatives voted in favor of the Thirteenth Amendment in January 1865, and by year's end it had been ratified by the states.

In addition to achieving a much-needed political goal, Anthony, Cady Stanton, and other leaders and members of the WNLL proved to themselves and to society that a national organization of women could indeed make a deep and lasting impact on the political process and on the goals of justice, equality, and freedom, a precedent that would support them in the struggle for woman suffrage.

Related entries:
Abolitionist Movement
Beecher, Henry Ward
Civil War
Emancipation Proclamation of 1863
Garrison, William Lloyd
Greeley, Horace
New York Married Women's Property Law of 1860
Rose, Ernestine Louise Potowski
Stanton, Elizabeth Cady
Stone, Lucy
Tilton, Theodore
Thirteenth Amendment
Women's Rights Movement

Suggestions for further reading:
Lutz, Alma. 1968. *Crusade for Freedom: Women in the Antislavery Movement.* Boston: Beacon Press.
Venet, Wendy Hamand. 1991. *Neither Ballots nor Bullets: Women Abolitionists and the Civil War.* Charlottesville: University Press of Virginia.

Woman's Rights Conventions

Americans of the mid-nineteenth century were fascinated by the social, moral, religious, and intellectual reform movements that emerged in this era. Among the array of causes that attracted Americans were the temperance, abolitionist, women's rights, evangelical, free-thought, peace, non-resistance, social utopian, and Transcendentalist movements, to name only a few. Intrigued and mesmerized by new ideas, the general public relished attending the conventions organized by the proponents of these movements. Yet as popular a pastime as conventioneering was for the public, conventions were also an excellent means for leaders of reform movements to publicize their beliefs, missions, and agendas.

Woman's rights conventions, originating with the Seneca Falls Convention of 1848, were largely a phenomenon of the Northeast and Midwest during the 1850s. They were organized, executed, and attended by leaders and supporters of the women's rights movement. Not only were these local, state, regional, and national meetings open to all, but the public was also welcome to voice its opinions and engage in discussions and debates. Most of the early leadership were feminist abolitionists—Paulina Wright Davis, Ernestine Potowski Rose, Lucy Stone, Abby Kelley Foster, Lucretia Coffin Mott, and Elizabeth Cady Stanton. Lively and frequently raucous debate was a familiar feature of woman's rights conventions. Among the issues hotly contested were the following:

- Women's lack of civil and legal rights, especially property rights
- Women's right to suffrage
- Women's right to divorce
- Women's right to serve as a member of Congress or as president of the United States
- Women's intellectual equality with men
- Women's claim to moral superiority
- The need for expanded educational opportunities for women, including higher education and professional training
- The need to enlarge "women's sphere" beyond the realm of home and family to include public activity
- The need for increased opportunities for women in the professions

National woman's rights conventions gathered activists from many northern, eastern, and midwestern states and were held annually from 1850 to 1860, with the exception of 1857. Since many women's rights reformers were also antislavery activists, national meetings were often scheduled so that they met during the same week and in the same city as annual meetings of the American Anti-Slavery Society (AASS). National meetings afforded women's rights leaders the opportunity to share ideas and strategies, report on the progress of activism in their own states and regions, and discuss issues. Yet as well and as faithfully attended as these meetings were by both female and male reformers, women's rights leaders of the 1850s did not see the need to formally organize an ongoing national organization. It was not until the Civil War and the formation of the Woman's National Loyal League (WNLL) in 1863 that women's rights leaders began to appreciate the political advantages of a central, national organization.

To Susan B. Anthony, woman's rights conventions were an ideal forum for educating the public about women's rights issues and for recruiting women and men to the cause. She became involved in organizing woman's rights conventions at the local, state, and national levels after attending her first national convention in Syracuse, New York, in 1852. Starting in 1856, she became the principal organizer of national conventions. With the exception of 1857, when the best leaders and speakers were unavailable because they were either bearing or raising children, she planned and executed an annual national gathering each year through 1860. In the spring of 1861, when the southern states began to secede from the Union and the Civil War began, Anthony's fellow male and female reformers persuaded her to cancel the upcoming convention, against her better judgment. She knew it was a mistake for women's rights activists to disband, and she accurately predicted that the male political establishment would chisel away at their hard-won achievements as soon as women's rights activists disappeared from view. But, as she explained in a letter to her close friend and colleague Lydia Mott, "I am sick at heart, but I can not carry the world against the wish and the will of our best friends" (*HWS,* 1:749).

In May 1866, after five years with no national convention, Anthony and Cady Stanton organized the Eleventh National Woman's Rights Convention in New York City. Unlike all previous national meetings, this post–Civil War gathering exemplified the tremendous change that had occurred in the

women's rights movement, especially among its leadership. Instead of debating many women's rights issues as had been done at antebellum national conventions, Cady Stanton opened this postbellum meeting with the announcement that the women's rights movement now had a single focus and purpose—to obtain national woman suffrage (*HWS,* 2:153–154). Over the next four years, the women's rights activists unsuccessfully labored to gain universal suffrage through meetings and conventions of the American Equal Rights Association (AERA). This failure led Anthony and Cady Stanton to reforge the women's rights movement into an exclusively female-led woman suffrage movement under the aegis of the National Woman Suffrage Association (NWSA).

Related entries:
American Equal Rights Association
Anthony, Susan B.
Anthony/Cady Stanton Partnership
Davis, Paulina Kellogg Wright
Mott, Lucretia Coffin
National Woman Suffrage Association
Rose, Ernestine Louise Potowski
Seneca Falls Convention of 1848
Stanton, Elizabeth Cady
Stone, Lucy
Syracuse Woman's Rights Convention of 1852
Woman's National Loyal League
Women's Rights Movement

Suggestions for further reading:
Buhle, Mary Jo, and Paul Buhle, eds. 1978. *A Concise History of Woman Suffrage: Selections from the Classic Work of Stanton, Anthony, Gage, and Harper.* Urbana: University of Illinois Press.
Davis, Paulina W. 1871. *A History of the National Woman's Rights Movement for Twenty Years.* Republished 1970. New York: Source Book Press.
HWS, 1.

Woman's State Temperance Society

Though short-lived, the Woman's State Temperance Society (WSTS) marked a crucial milestone in Susan B. Anthony's development as a feminist activist. Through the rhetoric of the WSTS, Anthony and Elizabeth Cady Stanton promoted a feminist advocacy based on women's fundamental right to control her destiny. They urged women to use whatever means necessary to protect themselves and their children from the poverty, discord, and violence wrought by intemperate husbands. For women willing to dedicate themselves to activism in the WSTS, taking control meant "wage[ing] a war of extermination against the Liquor Traffic"— organizing at the grassroots level, forming auxiliary societies, speaking publicly on behalf of temperance, distributing temperance newspapers and tracts, circulating petitions and lobbying legislators for new antiliquor laws, and proclaiming the right to divorce drunkard husbands.

Susan B. Anthony and several other women and men formed the WSTS in January 1852, when Anthony was refused the right to speak at a Sons of Temperance statewide convention in Albany because she was a woman (see Daughters of Temperance). Acting upon seasoned reformer Lydia Mott's advice, the group decided to form their own independent temperance organization.

At their first organizational meeting in the winter of 1852, Anthony was selected to be chair of a committee to organize a Woman's State Temperance Convention to be held in Rochester in April. For the next few months, supported by the advice of Cady Stanton, Horace Greeley, and Samuel Joseph May, Anthony threw herself into organizing the convention, executing the preconvention multitude of tasks that would become her stock-in-trade—writing hundreds of letters, traveling statewide to publicize the convention, enlisting speakers, and sending notices to newspapers.

In April, the majority of the 500 women attending the first meeting of this convention decided to admit men as members but exclude them from holding office. This decision, unusual among temperance organizations, was designed to encourage women to seek executive office and give them the opportunity to control the treasury. In a speech in May 1852, Anthony explained to prospective WSTS members that "women have long paid their dollars into the various [temperance] societies . . . and had them all expended in such manner as the men chose" ("Speech in Batavia, New York," May 24, 1852, SBA-LCMD, in *Papers*). Like most women engaged in social reform, Anthony, Cady Stanton, and other women temperance reformers were frustrated by the obstacles men placed in the path of their good works. They longed to be full-fledged participants in temperance reform and resisted men's attempts to marginalize their efforts and to control the money women contributed and raised in their own societies. The male-dominated press reacted negatively to Anthony's rhetoric and, as would become a typical pattern throughout her career, discredited her message by creating an image of her as an ugly, shockingly improper, ignorant, sexually unfulfilled "maiden." A reporter writing in the Utica, New York, *Evening Telegraph* declared:

> Personally repulsive, she seems to be laboring under feelings of strong hatred towards male men, the effect we presume, of jealousy and neglect. . . . With a degree of impiety which was both startling and disgusting, this shrewish maiden counseled the numerous wives and mothers present to separate from their husbands whenever they become intemperate, *and particularly not to allow the said husbands to add another child to the family.*
> (*Evening Telegraph*, April 28, 1853, SBA Scrapbooks, LCRBD, in *Papers*)

At the first convention of the WSTS in Rochester, Cady Stanton was elected president, and Anthony and Amelia Jenks Bloomer were elected to serve as secretaries. Cady Stanton, dressed in the Bloomer costume, shocked the women with a speech in which she demanded that women be given the right to divorce drunkard husbands. In her address she also spoke in derogatory terms of the clergy's and the church's ineffectual efforts to control vice and help the poor. Her radical, prodivorce, and anticlerical message antagonized many conservative women and men in attendance and sowed the seeds of future dissension.

The most ambitious project of the WSTS was its campaign in the summer of 1852 to obtain signatures for a petition demanding that the Maine law be adopted in the state of New York. The Maine law prohibited the sale of alcohol except in vast quantities and was intended to eliminate saloons and bars. Anthony and three other women traveled throughout the state, acquiring 28,000 signatures, which they presented to the New York state legislature (Harper 1899, 1:82).

At the first anniversary gathering of the WSTS in 1853, with 2,000 members in attendance, Cady Stanton and Anthony caved in to pressure to allow men the opportunity to vote at conventions. The conservative element, composed of both women and men, was disturbed and angered by Cady Stanton's speech, in which she continued to link women's rights issues with temperance. She further alienated the membership when she insisted on women's right to divorce and denounced the clergy for thwarting women's efforts to effect positive change in society. The membership then reorganized and refused to reelect her as president. They voted instead to permit men to run for office, changed the name of the society to the People's League, and by the end of the convention, took control of the society.

Outraged and grief-stricken even though she was reelected, Anthony resigned her post and withdrew with Cady Stanton. Although Anthony supported her colleague's radical agenda, she deeply regretted the outcome of the convention. It marked the end of her career as a temperance reformer before she had had a chance to achieve all she had planned. A few weeks after the convention,

in response to a despairing letter from Anthony, Cady Stanton responded:

> You ask me if I am not plunged in grief at my defeat at the recent convention for the presidency of our society. Not at all. I accomplished at Rochester all I desired by having the divorce question brought up. . . . Now Susan, I do beg of you to let the past be past, and to waste no powder on the Woman's State Temperance Society. We have other and bigger fish to fry. (ECS to SBA, in Stanton and Blatch 1922, 2:50–52)

In this letter, Cady Stanton seems to have lacked all awareness of what Anthony lost at the 1853 WSTS convention. She also appears to have overlooked that it had been Anthony's relentless labor, not Cady Stanton's, that had been the driving force behind the WSTS. Cady Stanton was able to move on to the next project because she had neither created the society nor dedicated 18 months of her life to it as Anthony had. In any event, Anthony's depression soon lifted as she refocused her energies toward the women's rights movement.

Related entries:
Bloomer, Amelia Jenks
Bloomer Costume
Daughters of Temperance
Greeley, Horace
May, Samuel Joseph
Stanton, Elizabeth Cady
Temperance

Suggestions for further reading:
Barry, Kathleen. 1988. *Susan B. Anthony: Biography of a Singular Feminist.* New York: New York University Press.
HWS, 1:493–499.

The Woman's Tribune

*T*he *Woman's Tribune* was a woman suffrage newspaper published and edited by leading Nebraska suffragist Clara Bewick

Colby from 1883 to 1909. It was also the principal voice of the National Woman Suffrage Association (NWSA) in the 1880s, though it never became its official organ. In December 1889, Bewick Colby transferred publication of the *Woman's Tribune* from her hometown of Beatrice, Nebraska, to Washington, D.C., when her husband Leonard Wright Colby assumed the post of assistant attorney general in President Benjamin Harrison's administration. This move came on the heels of her most successful publishing venture—printing a widely circulated daily issue of the *Woman's Tribune* throughout the duration of the historic International Council of Women meeting and the NWSA convention in 1888. Based on this success, Bewick Colby took advantage of her opportunity to publish in the nation's capital, where she could be closer to the source of congressional and governmental news relating to woman suffrage and become more actively involved in NWSA affairs. As soon as Congress adjourned its legislative session in April each year, Bewick Colby transferred publication from Washington, D.C., to Beatrice until the next congressional session convened in November. This schedule enabled her to maintain close ties with the rank and file of midwestern and western suffragists. Although the *Woman's Tribune* was highly acclaimed and widely read by NWSA activists, it did not surpass the circulation or the literary excellence of the American Woman Suffrage Association's (AWSA's) publication, the *Woman's Journal.*

Bewick Colby directed the *Woman's Tribune* primarily toward an audience of suffragists who were not in the vanguard of the movement. As president of the Nebraska Woman Suffrage Association from 1885 to 1898, Bewick Colby was well acquainted with the information needs of western women reformers who, despite their devotion to woman suffrage, were isolated from the hub of suffrage activism for most of the year. With this audience always uppermost in her mind, Bewick Colby constructed her

reports of suffrage meetings, conventions, and campaigns so that readers could experience the occasions visually, as if they had been present. Susan B. Anthony, who greatly admired Bewick Colby's writing acumen, did not share her vision of the *Woman's Tribune's* ideal target audience. Although Anthony appreciated Bewick Colby's willingness to publish her (Anthony's) views and news of NWSA business, she regularly criticized Bewick Colby for publishing articles on topics that were not germane to the mainstream suffrage community. Despite Bewick Colby's allegiance to the NWSA, however, she remained steadfast to her commitment to meet the diverse information needs of the women she perceived as her readership (Jerry 1991, 117–118).

The *Woman's Tribune* published many speeches and other writings of Elizabeth Cady Stanton, a close friend and mentor of Bewick Colby's. Anthony's speeches were also published, but not as frequently as Cady Stanton's. Despite Bewick Colby's coverage of Anthony's activities and the inclusion of her columns, articles, and speeches, it was clear that from an ideological standpoint, the Nebraska suffragist more closely sympathized with Cady Stanton's philosophies. Bewick Colby was one of the very few in the younger generation of suffragists who actively promoted Cady Stanton's campaign for complete religious freedom. She also published portions of Cady Stanton's controversial *The Woman's Bible*, which was heavily criticized by most NAWSA suffragists.

Of all the suffrage newspapers, the *Woman's Tribune* is the best source of information about NWSA history from the mid-1880s until its merger with the AWSA in 1890, at which time the Boston-based AWSA publication, the *Woman's Journal,* became the official newspaper of the newly formed National American Woman Suffrage Association (NAWSA). Bewick Colby continued publication of the *Woman's Tribune* after 1890 despite competition from the *Woman's Journal.* In 1904, Bewick Colby moved her newspaper to

Portland, Oregon, where it competed with Abigail Scott Duniway's journal *The New Northwest*. Suffragists in the Pacific Northwest did not respond favorably to the *Woman's Tribune*, and in 1909, Bewick Colby was forced to terminate publication for financial reasons.

Related entries:
Anthony, Susan B.
Colby, Clara Dorothy Bewick
Duniway, Abigail Jane Scott
National Woman Suffrage Association
Stanton, Elizabeth Cady
The Woman's Bible
The *Woman's Journal*

Suggestions for further reading:
Brown, Olympia. 1917. *Democratic Ideals: A Memorial Sketch of Clara B. Colby.* n.p. A Federal Suffrage Association Publication.
Green, Norma Kidd. 1971. "Colby, Clara Dorothy Bewick." In *NAW*, 1:355–357.
Jerry, E. Claire. 1991. "Clara Bewick Colby and the *Woman's Tribune*, 1883–1909." In *A Voice of Their Own: The Woman Suffrage Press, 1840–1910*, ed. Martha M. Solomon. Tuscaloosa: University of Alabama Press.

Women's Rights Movement

*W*omen's rights movement is the term used most frequently to encompass women's rights activity from the time of the Seneca Falls Convention of 1848 until the formation of national woman suffrage organizations in 1869. Although adherents were predominantly white middle-class residents of the Northeast and Midwest, both white and African-American women's rights activists strove to obtain civil, legal, and political equality with men. Prior to the Seneca Falls Convention, women's rights activism included efforts to expand women's educational opportunities; scattered attempts to attain their legal rights; and demands to actively engage in the work of benevolent societies, religious organizations, and social and moral reform movements such as temperance and abolitionism. Women reformers initiated their struggle for inclusion with the demand to be free to speak publicly. This goal challenged entrenched societal taboos about women's activity in the public sphere.

What is fascinating about the Seneca Falls Convention's *Declaration of Rights and Sentiments* and its *Resolutions* is that they embraced nearly every women's rights claim for equality that would be made in the nineteenth century—equal rights for women in the home; the workplace; and in education, religion, and public and political life (DuBois 1978, 23). Women's claim to the franchise was the most radical demand made at Seneca Falls, as it would continue to be for the rest of the century. It was the one right that nineteenth-century men would refuse to surrender and one that would eventually become the central focus of women's rights activists. The struggle for suffrage was rooted in the prevalent nineteenth-century conviction that the ballot was the embodiment and the symbol of the U.S. citizen's social, economic, and political power (DuBois 1978, 42).

The origins of the women's rights movement are embedded in the antislavery and abolitionist movements. Although historians do not agree precisely how abolition affected and influenced the growth of the women's rights movement, there is no question that female abolitionists provided much of its leadership. Yet not all women antislavery reformers became involved. A large sector of white conservative antislavery activists determinedly distanced themselves from what they perceived to be the radicalism of women's rights reformers. Although African-American women abolitionists were always in the minority, most became engaged in the women's rights movement, including Sojourner Truth, Sarah Parker Remond, Frances Ellen Watkins Harper, Sarah Mapps Douglass, Harriet Forten Purvis, and Margaretta Forten.

Women's rights activists recycled abolitionist methods and strategies to advance their agenda. Conventions, the mass production and dissemination of propaganda pamphlets, the women's rights press, and the lecture circuit were all reform strategies that women reformers borrowed from Garrisonian abolitionism. From the political antislavery activists, women's rights reformers absorbed such political strategies as petition campaigns and the lobbying of legislators.

Unlike the majority of women's rights leaders, Susan B. Anthony did not come to the women's rights movement through abolitionist activism but through her involvement in temperance reform. (Her years in Garrisonian abolitionism postdated her first women's rights activities by four years.) Anthony's letters, speeches, newspaper articles, and other writings of the early 1850s reveal that her growing awareness of women's social and economic powerlessness, as discovered through her temperance activism, led directly to her political awakening.

Anthony's close relationship with Elizabeth Cady Stanton was crucially important to all her future women's rights and woman suffrage activism. Cady Stanton was the principal ideologist, rhetorician, and intellectual of the women's rights movement and, as such, had an enormous influence on Anthony. As the primary organizer of the Seneca Falls Convention and the creative force behind its *Declaration of Rights and Sentiments* and its *Resolutions*, Cady Stanton articulated the clearest, sharpest presentation of women's rights philosophy and issues. Although she rarely attended conventions in the 1850s, through her published writing and voluminous correspondence with other women's rights activists, she became a recognized leader of the movement. Her intensely busy family life and her concomitant reluctance to leave home gave her the opportunity to think, study, and write newspaper articles and speeches. Through her close relationships with political abolitionists Gerrit Smith and her husband Henry Brewster Stanton, Cady Stanton honed her political astuteness, a strength she passed on to Anthony. Cady Stanton helped Anthony compose her speeches and, in fact, wrote many for her. She also provided essential guidance as An-

thony learned to analyze the social, political, and philosophical issues involved in each women's rights battle.

Many other women's rights activists of this era also educated, inspired, and were personally connected with Anthony. Women's rights pioneers Ernestine Potowski Rose, Paulina Wright Davis, Lucretia Coffin Mott, Lucy Stone, Lydia Mott, Antoinette Brown (Blackwell), Martha Coffin Wright, and Matilda Joslyn Gage were among those whom Anthony met at woman's rights conventions and with whom she developed strong working relationships and warm, lifelong friendships.

THE ROLE OF MEN

The antebellum women's rights movement was not a women-only movement. Men were encouraged to attend and participate in conventions. Among the profeminist men who strongly supported women's rights and woman suffrage in the 1850s were African-American abolitionists Frederick Douglass and Robert Purvis and white reformers Samuel Joseph May, Gerrit Smith, William Lloyd Garrison, Wendell Phillips, and Parker Pillsbury, all colleagues and friends of Anthony, and all Garrisonians except for Smith, who was a political antislavery activist. Men also contributed money to sustain the fledgling movement. Garrison, Douglass, and Horace Greeley, through their respective newspapers *The Liberator*, the *North Star*, and the *New York Tribune*, published women's rights notices and articles, editorials, and letters favorable to women's rights. Garrison, Douglass, Pillsbury, and Phillips often agreed to lecture on women's rights.

The active support of men was crucial to the women's rights movement at this early stage. In the eyes of a skeptical public, the presence of men added credibility and legitimacy and also helped to attract larger crowds at conventions and greater press attention. Yet the men who supported the women's rights movement suffered for their commitment. They were ridiculed and harassed in the press, and their masculinity was frequently called into question. They also endured scathing name-calling, including taunts of "Aunt Nancy men" and "miss-Nancys" (Kimmel and Mosmiller 1992, 6).

It was not until 1860 that Anthony and Cady Stanton began to realize that as much as their male colleagues supported women's rights, they did not share every women's rights belief or aspiration. At the Tenth National Woman's Rights Convention in 1860, Phillips and Garrison strongly opposed Cady Stanton's resolution asserting the right of women to divorce. To Anthony and Cady Stanton, the men's arguments revealed that they opposed divorce because they did not comprehend the fundamentals of women's legal and economic powerlessness in the marriage relationship, even when the dynamics were explained to them. This miscomprehension proved to be a harbinger of further, more serious and divisive conflicts between male and female reformers, which eventually contributed to the exclusion of men from leadership positions in future women's rights and woman suffrage organizations.

ANTHONY'S CONTRIBUTIONS TO THE WOMEN'S RIGHTS MOVEMENT

To Anthony, women's rights reform was about education—exposing women and men to the ideology of the women's rights movement; expanding the public's awareness of the limitations of traditional gender roles; and emphasizing that men and women are equal in their need to explore, develop, and exercise the fulfillment of their own individual potentials. Anthony's speech "The True Woman," written during the years 1857–1859 and delivered in the late 1850s as she campaigned throughout New York, crystallized her vision of the ideal modern woman. Anthony's "true woman" was a free agent and the architect of her own destiny. She would inherit the society that women's rights reformers were struggling to achieve—a world based on complete gender equality.

Years of temperance, women's rights, and abolitionist campaign travel exposed Anthony to the life situations and living conditions of thousands of women in the Northeast. As she struggled to raise their political consciousness, she became intimately familiar with women's imprisonment within "women's sphere." This term refers to the predominant nineteenth-century cultural notion that the supreme role and function of women is to cultivate the domestic world of home and family. Until her reform campaign travel, Anthony had not been fully aware of the crippling effects of "women's sphere." Because her Quaker upbringing had encouraged her to develop her intellect and to be active outside the home, she had been protected, in a sense, from such cultural indoctrination. Anthony was convinced that any woman could become a "true woman," once she recognized that there is more to life than total absorption in the domestic realm. In her speech "The True Woman," Anthony protested that young women are

> educated to the idea that their sole aim should be to reign supreme in the *domestic affections*;—that the one proud goal of all their attainments is the *happy home*;—that to be the centre of attraction to husband, children and friends, is the *highest*, and *only* legitimate aspiration of their whole lives.

Anthony believed that women suffered because they had no individual "life-purpose," no personal goals to attain, and no stimulation to develop their intellects. "The true woman will not be the exponent of another," Anthony declared, "or allow another to be such for her. She will be her own individual self, do her own individual work, stand or fall by her own individual wisdom and strength" ("The True Woman" Speech, SBA-LCMD, in *Papers*).

Anthony's keen awareness of the need to awaken women to their own individual power fueled the passion behind her grassroots work. In all of her campaigns of the 1850s (her canvasses of New York state for temperance legislation and for the 1860 Married Women's Property Law), she invited the women she met to talk about their problems. She explained to them that their inability to find solutions to their most pressing concerns was rooted in their social, economic, and political powerlessness. She then offered them the opportunity to participate in her present campaign as a means of gaining the power they needed to improve their lives.

From Anthony's early days in the temperance movement and throughout her lifelong career in activism, she skillfully used the press to educate the public and to agitate reform issues. Cady Stanton did not introduce Anthony to the advantages of being media-savvy, but she was instrumental in helping Anthony to expand her repertoire of ways to boldly use the press to advance the women's rights agenda. Throughout the 1850s, Anthony sought to increase her press contacts, sending news of women's rights events and issues to dozens of small newspapers throughout New York state as well as to the *New York Tribune;* to the abolitionist newspapers *The Liberator,* the *North Star,* and the *National Anti-Slavery Standard;* and to the women's rights publications the *Lily* and the *Una.* Her skillful use of the press in the 1850s laid the groundwork for the development of her phenomenally acute ability to manipulate and exploit the press to promote the cause of women's rights and woman suffrage.

To Anthony's consternation, the outbreak of the Civil War made it necessary for her to discontinue women's rights work. But by 1863, she and Cady Stanton had managed to conceive of an organization that would be dedicated to a patriotic, political mission while simultaneously advancing the cause of women's rights. This new organization, the Woman's National Loyal League (WNLL), formed a bridge between the women's rights movement of the 1850s and the postwar women's rights and woman suffrage organizations, including the American Equal Rights

Association (AERA), the National Woman Suffrage Association (NWSA), and the American Woman Suffrage Association (AWSA).

Related entries:
Abolitionist Movement
American Equal Rights Association
Blackwell, Antoinette Louisa Brown
Civil War
Davis, Paulina Kellogg Wright
Douglass, Frederick
Garrison, William Lloyd
The Liberator
The *Lily*
May, Samuel Joseph
Mott, Lucretia Coffin
Mott, Lydia
New York Married Women's Property Law of 1860
The *New York Tribune*
The *North Star*
Phillips, Wendell
Pillsbury, Parker
Purvis, Robert
Rose, Ernestine Louise Potowski
Stone, Lucy
The *Una*
Woman's Rights Conventions

Suggestions for further reading:
Buhle, Mary Jo, and Paul Buhle, eds. 1978. *A Concise History of Woman Suffrage: Selections from the Classic Work of Stanton, Anthony, Gage, and Harper.* Urbana: University of Illinois Press.
DuBois, Ellen Carol. 1978. *Feminism and Suffrage: The Emergence of an Independent Women's Movement in America 1848–1869.* Ithaca, N.Y.: Cornell University Press.
Sterling, Dorothy. 1984. *We Are Your Sisters: Black Women in the Nineteenth Century.* New York: W. W. Norton.

Woodhull, Victoria Claflin (1838–1927)

*I*n the early 1870s, Victoria Claflin Woodhull took the woman suffrage movement by storm. In a few short months, seemingly out of nowhere, she rose to sit side by side with the leadership of the National Woman Suffrage Association (NWSA). She disappeared just as swiftly from its ranks, but not before creating a destructive maelstrom that had serious, long-lasting repercussions for both branches of the woman suffrage movement—the NWSA and the American Woman Suffrage Association (AWSA) as well as the entire community of nineteenth-century reformers.

Claflin Woodhull was a newspaper publisher and editor, the first woman stockbroker, the first woman to run for president, and a social reformer. She emerged from an impoverished, obscure background in Ohio with the help of her second husband, Colonel James Harvey Blood (she used the name of her first husband, Dr. Canning Woodhull) and Commodore Cornelius Vanderbilt, the New York railroad magnate.

Anthony was well aware of the multifaceted talents of Claflin Woodhull before she met her. In early 1870, Anthony had tried to interview her for *The Revolution* concerning her rise to fortune in the stock market. Instead, she had been obliged to interview her sister Tennessee Claflin, who comanaged the stock brokerage firm with Claflin Woodhull. Shortly thereafter, the two sisters began publishing *Woodhull and Claflin's Weekly,* a newspaper devoted to the open discussion of free love, greenbackism, spiritualism, legalized prostitution, and other radical causes.

In January 1871, Susan B. Anthony, Elizabeth Cady Stanton, Isabella Beecher Hooker, Paulina Wright Davis, and several other NWSA activists flocked to hear Claflin Woodhull present her memorial to the House Judiciary Committee. In this address, she asserted that women, as citizens of the United States, could not be barred from voting because the Constitution upheld their right to do so through the Fourteenth and the Fifteenth Amendments. She was not the first person to use the "New Departure" arguments, but she was the first to demand that Congress legislate this right by enacting a declaratory act that would guarantee the franchise for all citizens (DuBois 1987, 854). She expressed her views so persuasively, brilliantly, and modestly that Anthony immediately recognized her potential as a political "evangel" for the woman suffrage movement. Anthony's

enthusiasm was shared equally by the rest of the suffragists who attended. They persuaded the charismatic Claflin Woodhull to repeat her speech at the soon-to-be-convened NWSA convention.

From the moment Claflin Woodhull became associated with the NWSA, rumors about her family background, her dedication to her free-love beliefs, and her marital status and supposedly scandalous living arrangements multiplied. A mounting stream of anti-Woodhull criticism became rampant in both wings of the suffrage movement and in the press, distracting suffragists, legislators, and the public from her powerful constitutional arguments. Claflin Woodhull, who despised hypocrisy, responded by openly attesting to her free-love convictions. "Yes, I am a free lover! . . . I have an inalienable, constitutional, and natural right to love whom I may, to love as long or as short a period as I can, to change that love every day if I please!" (quoted in Arling 1928, 135). Anthony upheld Claflin Woodhull's right to speak her mind, though she wished the young reformer would keep her free-love sentiments separate from her women's rights work. What most concerned Anthony was the need for the woman suffrage movement to capitalize on Claflin Woodhull's aptitude as a powerful political activist.

Anthony first became concerned about Claflin Woodhull's effect on the NWSA when the press labeled the May 1871 NWSA meeting a "Woodhull Convention." The *New York Tribune* and other newspapers falsely reported that Woodhull had instigated a free-love revolution among suffragists. These press reports and editorials about Claflin Woodhull's views repelled many suffragists and other women who had been leaning toward the woman suffrage cause. Worst of all from Anthony's point of view, the relentless negative press about Claflin Woodhull and her free-love ideas obliterated public interest in the real work of the NWSA—the campaign for woman suffrage. But whenever Anthony expressed her misgivings to her closest col-

Standing (center right), Victoria Claflin Woodhull reads her memorial upholding women's right to vote before the Judiciary Committee of the House of Representatives, January 11, 1871. Seated behind her is Elizabeth Cady Stanton. Wood engraving in Frank Leslie's **Illustrated** *Newspaper, February 4, 1871.*

leagues, they all assured her that Claflin Woodhull was a "true woman" and vital to the movement (Lutz 1959, 185).

In the months following the January 1872 NWSA convention in Washington, D.C., Anthony's sense of foreboding about Claflin Woodhull intensified when the young woman urged NWSA members to join her in establishing an equal rights party. She also asked them to support her as that party's presidential candidate. Although Anthony managed to refocus the membership's attention on its upcoming plans to achieve woman suffrage based on their Fourteenth and Fifteenth Amendment claims, she began to realize that Claflin Woodhull was more concerned with advancing her own political career than she was with winning the battle for woman suffrage.

During the spring of 1872, while Anthony was lecturing in the Great Plains states and territories, Cady Stanton and Beecher Hooker cooperated with Claflin Woodhull's plans for a national convention that would sponsor her presidential candidacy, against Anthony's stern warnings to the contrary. When Anthony discovered that her name had been listed on the call for this meeting, she was enraged at Cady Stanton because she had demanded that her name be omitted. She had warned Cady Stanton that, despite her personal affection and sympathy for Claflin Woodhull's philosophies and plans, she must keep Claflin Woodhull removed from any connection with the NWSA. By this time Anthony was convinced that Claflin Woodhull's continued association with the NWSA would come at the expense of the struggle for woman suffrage.

Anthony hastened to New York City for the May 1872 NWSA convention, prepared to assume absolute control of the association. Just as she had feared, Claflin Woodhull made two attempts to take over the convention and its membership for what she called the "People's Convention." Anthony successfully thwarted her on each occasion, although the second time she was able to do so only by extinguishing the lights in the convention hall. Afterward, although Anthony was relieved that she had saved the NWSA, her relationships with Cady Stanton, Beecher Hooker, and Wright Davis were in urgent need of repair. Cady Stanton was so disturbed by Anthony's dictatorial leadership that she resigned as president. The membership then elected Anthony in her place. Cady Stanton, Beecher Hooker, Wright Davis, and a number of other NWSA members proceeded to attend the People's Convention at another hall in the city. This meeting then formed the Equal Rights Party (ERP) and nominated Claflin Woodhull for president.

The Equal Rights Party (ERP) began to disintegrate in the weeks following its May 1872 convention. Claflin Woodhull, realizing that her political career was faltering because of the ceaseless barrage of negative press, contrived a plan to retaliate against the most vehement of her critics. She selected AWSA members as her principal targets, although she also blackmailed a number of NWSA members. She threatened to expose those who "preach against free love openly, [yet] practice it secretly" (Kerr 1992, 165). By this avowal, she meant that she intended to publicize the illicit affair between one of her most ardent naysayers, Henry Ward Beecher (president of the AWSA and brother to two of Claflin Woodhull's most persistent critics, Harriet Beecher Stowe and Catharine Beecher), and Elizabeth Richards Tilton, the wife of NWSA leader Theodore Tilton, Beecher's best friend. By igniting the Beecher-Tilton Scandal, Claflin Woodhull unleashed a series of events that seriously harmed the woman suffrage movement and caused her complete downfall. By the November 1872 election, she was in jail for violating a new law prohibiting the mailing of obscene materials, the result of her publication of another sexually explicit exposé. Although she was eventually acquitted, her political career and reputation were already destroyed. Financially ruined, she retreated from the political arena. In 1877, Claflin

Woodhull and her sister relocated to England, and both eventually married British subjects.

Related entries:
American Woman Suffrage Association
Anthony/Cady Stanton Partnership
Beecher, Henry Ward
Beecher-Tilton Scandal
Equal Rights Party
Free-Love Controversy
Hooker, Isabella Beecher
National Woman Suffrage Association
"New Departure" Strategy
Tilton, Theodore

Suggestions for further reading:
Arling, Emanie Sachs. 1928. *"The Terrible Siren": Victoria Woodhull (1838–1927)*. New York: Harper and Bros.
Barry, Kathleen. 1988. *Susan B. Anthony: Biography of a Singular Feminist*. New York: New York University Press.
Underhill, Lois Beachy. 1995. *The Woman Who Ran for President: The Many Lives of Victoria Woodhull*. Bridgehampton, N.Y.: Bridge Works Publishing.

Working Women's Association

When Susan B. Anthony established the Working Women's Association (WWA) in September 1868, she realized a long-cherished dream to be directly involved in helping women improve their inferior economic status in the workplace. She hoped to encourage women to explore ways to increase their wages and to expand their opportunities for advancement in the trades. Equally important, she wanted working women to realize that obtaining the ballot was the key to achieving equality with men. Anthony was also eager to form the WWA so that she and other women could participate in the National Labor Union (NLU) Congress in September 1868. Both she and Elizabeth Cady Stanton were optimistic that a strong alliance with the NLU would eventually add the political power that the suffrage movement needed to secure the franchise.

Most of the original WWA members were typesetters in the printing trade. Women typesetters were vastly outnumbered by men and faced universal discrimination. Because the all-male unions denied women union membership, women were also prevented from participation in union apprenticeship programs. Without the training they needed to obtain the best jobs, women typesetters were relegated to low-paying printing jobs that required less skill. Women typesetters and other working women who joined the WWA were mostly interested in improving their economic condition. They were resistant to Anthony's emphasis on the importance of securing the ballot as the best means to achieve their economic objectives. WWA member Aurora S. Phelps articulated the perspective of many WWA members.

> The poor working-women do not, most of them, want the ballot. . . . I say we want bread and clothes and *homes* first, and after we caught as good pay for our work as the men do for theirs . . . it will be time enough for you to talk to us about wanting the ballot. (*New York World*, May 22, 1869, as quoted in Kugler 1987, 135)

Although Phelps and other women kept trying to communicate to Anthony their most pressing concerns, she was not swayed from her agenda. She continued to try to persuade them of the preeminence of the ballot. This conflict intensified until many working women abandoned the WWA because they believed the leadership was not serious about addressing their needs.

In spite of this conflict, WWA members managed to collaborate on their goals for a number of months. Encouraged by Anthony, Augusta Lewis organized the Women's Typographical Union (WTU) to overcome the discriminatory practices that the all-male National Typographical Union (NTU) used to keep women typesetters out of the trade. The NTU leadership immediately responded. Because NTU members feared the potential of a women's union to undercut men's wages and the NTU's power as a bargaining unit, they invited the WTU membership to join them as equal members in the NTU, as long as the WTU did not accept any new members. The NTU also vowed to secure equal pay for WTU members. This was an immense victory, and as Anthony told WTU members, "you have taken a great, a momentous step forward in the path to success" ("Women's Typographical Union," *The Revolution*, October 15, 1868, in *Papers*, series 1).

Anthony also formed a second chapter of the WWA, which comprised women working in the sewing trade. With the addition of new middle-class members, the WWA investigated the deplorable working conditions of ragpickers in New York City and also provided assistance to Hester Vaughan, an immigrant and domestic servant unjustly charged with infanticide. But when, during a strike, Anthony managed to persuade an association of book printing employers to establish a typesetting school for unskilled women, she deeply alienated many WWA members and trade unionists in the NTU and the NLU. Her efforts, which were interpreted as strikebreaking, harmed the NTU's bargaining position as it attempted to reach a favorable settlement during the strike.

This event caused Anthony to be unseated at the 1869 NLU Congress and contributed to the demise of the WWA. The WTU struggled to carry on under the leadership of Augusta Lewis. But by 1871, the NTU no longer made efforts to eliminate discrimination, and women typesetters eventually lost the few gains they had achieved. Because Anthony and Cady Stanton's alliance with organized labor and their attempts to organize working women did not produce the suffrage constituency they were seeking, they abandoned these efforts and focused instead on developing stronger connections with middle-class women (DuBois 1978, 160–161).

Related entries:
National Labor Union
Reconstruction

Suggestions for further reading:
DuBois, Ellen Carol. 1978. *Feminism and Suffrage: The Emergence of an Independent Women's Movement in America 1848–1869.* Ithaca, N.Y.: Cornell University Press.
Kugler, Israel. 1987. *From Ladies to Women: The Organized Struggle for Woman's Rights in the Reconstruction Era.* Westport, Conn.: Greenwood Press.

Wright, Martha Coffin (1806–1875)

One of Susan B. Anthony's closest and most devoted friends and advisers, Martha Coffin Wright was a principal activist in the women's rights movement and in the early period of the woman suffrage movement. The youngest sister of the Quaker Lucretia Coffin Mott, Coffin Wright was permanently ejected from membership in the Society of Friends when she "married out of meeting" at age 17, wedding a non-Quaker without the approval of Quaker elders. She grew to adulthood purposefully unattached to any organized religion and became recognized for her independent, freethinking views on religion and on social and moral reform issues. In addition to women's rights, she participated in the abolitionist movement, briefly joining Anthony's troupe of lecturers during the 1861 "winter of mobs" tour in New York state.

Coffin Wright, in concert with Elizabeth Cady Stanton, Coffin Mott, and two other Quaker women, helped organize the Seneca Falls Convention of 1848. Anthony first met Coffin Wright at the Third National Woman's Rights Convention in Syracuse, New York, in 1852. At that convention, as at nearly all the national woman's rights conventions, Coffin Wright consistently assumed top ex-ecutive positions. Beginning in the 1850s and lasting until her death in 1875, she was a close adviser to Anthony and Cady Stanton in every convention, campaign, and battle waged for women's rights and woman suffrage. Coffin Wright always could be relied upon to analyze problems shrewdly and to give her uncensored, honest opinions.

After the Civil War, Coffin Wright was active in the American Equal Rights Association (AERA). When the women's rights movement split into two factions, she stood steadfastly beside Anthony and Cady Stanton and helped them form the National Woman Suffrage Association (NWSA) in 1869. Active in this organization until her death, she served as its president in 1874. She died unexpectedly in January 1875, leaving Anthony bereft of her support and counsel in the midst of the trauma of the Beecher-Tilton Scandal. Upon hearing of Coffin Wright's death, Anthony wrote in her diary:

> … clear-sighted, true and steadfast almost beyond all other women! Her home was my home, always so restful and refreshing, her friendship never failed; the darker the hour, the brighter were her words of encouragement, the stronger and closer her support. I can not be reconciled. (Harper 1899, 1:467)

Related entries:
American Equal Rights Association
Mott, Lucretia Coffin
National Woman Suffrage Association
Quakerism (Society of Friends)
Seneca Falls Convention of 1848
Syracuse Woman's Rights Convention of 1852
Woman's Rights Conventions
Women's Rights Movement

Suggestions for further reading:
Bacon, Margaret Hope. 1986. *Mothers of Feminism: The Story of Quaker Women in America.* San Francisco: Harper and Row.
Gurko, Miriam. 1974. *The Ladies of Seneca Falls: The Birth of the Woman's Rights Movement.* New York: Macmillan.

DOCUMENTS

DAUGHTERS OF TEMPERANCE SPEECH
CANAJOHARIE, NEW YORK, MARCH 1849

Susan B. Anthony delivered this, her first speech, in March 1849. This edited version appears in volume 1 of Ida Husted Harper's biography *The Life and Work of Susan B. Anthony*. Although Anthony's women's rights activism was years in her future, this speech clearly demonstrates her awareness that women must collectively organize and seize the power to improve their lives, their environment, and the well-being of their friends and family (see Harper 1899, 1:53–55).

Welcome, Gentlemen and Ladies, to this, our Hall of Temperance. We feel that the cause we have espoused is a common cause, in which you, with us, are deeply interested. We would that some means were devised, by which our Brothers and Sons shall no longer be allured from the *right* by the corrupting influence of the fashionable sippings of wine and brandy, those sure destroyers of Mental and Moral Worth, and by which our Sisters and Daughters shall no longer be exposed to the vile arts of the gentlemanly-appearing, gallant, but really half-inebriated seducer. Our motive is to ask of you counsel in the formation, and co-operation in the carrying-out of plans which may produce a radical change in our Moral Atmosphere. . . .

But to the question, what good our Union has done? Though our Order has been strongly opposed by ladies professing a desire to see the Moral condition of our race elevated, and though we still behold some of our thoughtless female friends whirling in the giddy dance, with intoxicated partners at their side and, more than this, see them accompany their reeling companions to some secluded nook and there quaff with them from that Virtue-destroying cup, yet may we not hope that an influence, though now unseen, unfelt, has gone forth, which shall tell upon the future, which shall convince us that our weekly resort to these meetings has not been in vain, and which shall cause the friends of humanity to admire and respect—nay, venerate—this now-despised little band of Daughters of Temperance?

We count it no waste of time to go forth through our streets, thus proclaiming our desire for the advancement of our great cause. You, with us, no doubt, feel that Intemperance is the blighting mildew of all our social connections; you would be most happy to speed on the time when no Wife shall watch with trembling heart and tearful eye the slow, but sure descent of her idolized Companion down to the loathsome haunts of drunkenness; you would hasten the day when no Mother shall have to mourn over a darling son as she sees him launch his bark on the circling waves of the mighty whirlpool.

How is this great change to be wrought, who are to urge on this vast work of reform? Shall it not be women, who are most aggrieved by the foul destroyer's inroads? Most certainly. Then arises the question, how are we to accomplish the end desired? I answer, not by confining our influence to our own home circle, not by centering all our benevolent feelings upon our own kindred, not by caring naught for the culture of any minds, save those of our own darlings. No, no; the gratification of the *selfish* impulses *alone*, can never produce a desirable change in the Moral aspect of Society.

It is generally conceded that it is our sex that fashions the Social and Moral State of Society. We do not presume that females possess unbounded power in abolishing the evil customs of the day; but we do believe that were they en masse to discountenance the use of wine and brandy as beverages at both their public and private parties, not one of the opposite Sex, who has any claim to the title of gentleman, would so insult them as to come into their presence after having quaffed of that foul destroyer of all true delicacy and refinement.

I am not aware that we have any inebriate females among us, but have we not those, who are fallen from *Virtue*, and who claim our efforts for their reform, equally with the inebriate? And while we feel it our duty to extend the hand of sympathy and love to those who are wanderers from the path of Temperance, should we not also be zealous in reclaiming those poor, deluded ones, who have been robbed of their most precious Gem, Virtue, and whom we blush to think belong to our Sex?

Now, Ladies, all we would do is to do all in our power, both individually and collectively, to harmonize and happify our Social system. We ask of you candidly and seriously to investigate the Matter, and decide for yourselves whether the object of our Union be not on the side of right, and if it be, then one and all, for the sake of erring humanity, come forward and *speed* on the right. If you come to the conclusion that the end we wish to attain is right, but are not satisfied with the plan adopted, then I ask of you to devise means by which this great good may be more speedily accomplished, and you shall find us ready with both heart and hand to co-operate with you. In my humble opinion, all that is needed to produce a complete Temperance and Social reform in this age of Moral Suasion, is for our Sex to cast their United influences into the balance.

Ladies! there is no Neutral position for us to assume. If we sustain not this noble enterprise, both by precept and example, then is our influence on the side of Intemperance. If we say we love the Cause, and then sit down at our ease, surely does our action speak the lie. And now permit me once more to beg of you to lend your aid to this great Cause, the Cause of God and all Mankind.

SUSAN B. ANTHONY CONFRONTS SLAVERY
BALTIMORE, APRIL 1854

Although Anthony was well acquainted with abolitionism before her 1854 journey to the South and the border states with women's rights reformer and abolitionist Ernestine Potowski Rose, this trip fully awakened her to the evils of slavery and brought her to the doorstep of her determination to become an antislavery activist (see *The Liberator*, April 14, 1854, in *Papers*).

Dear Mr. Garrison:
From the land of slavery I write. There is no mistaking the fact. The saddening, hateful evidences are on every side. Pro-slavery people, both of the North and the South, have often said to me, "Just go South, and see slavery as it really is, and you

will cease to speak of it as you now do." How strangely blind must that person be, who hates slavery less, by coming in closer contact with its degrading influences! How wanting in true nobility of soul must he be, who can hear a human being speak of himself as being the property of another, without evincing the least discontent! How unworthy the boon of freedom is the man who sees himself surrounded, for the first time, with beings wearing the human form from whose faces slavery has blotted out almost every token of that Divine spark within, that aspires to a higher, a nobler life, that scorns to be a thing,—and from the very depths of his soul, hates not slavery more than it were possible for him ever to have done before! I hate slavery less? Heaven forbid!

I have been travelling in company with Ernestine Rose the past three weeks, during which time Mrs. Rose has lectured on Woman's Rights, in Washington, Alexandria [Virginia], and Baltimore. Her meetings have all been but thinly attended, compared with our Northern meetings. Still, the people here call the audiences large, and quite equal to the number who usually attend literary or scientific lectures. But few people here seem to be in the least interested in any subject of reform. The only thing that in any way alarms them is the fear that some word shall be uttered which shall endanger their "pet institution." In making application for a hall in this city, the proprietor said to me, "You know we are a sensitive people, and don't like to allow persons to speak in our halls, who will introduce topics foreign to those they announce." I said, "I suppose you refer to the topic of slavery?" He answered, "Yes." "Well, sir, I wish you to understand that Mrs. Rose is an out and out abolitionist. She is here now to speak on Woman's Rights, and wishes the hall for that purpose; but if she should feel disposed, as I hope she will, to give an anti-slavery lecture, she will duly inform all parties

concerned of her intentions." Thus is it with the editors, and thus is it with the people. All are afraid of us; if we don't say any thing, our very presence seems to arouse their suspicions. Still, notwithstanding this ever-present apprehension lest a word shall be dropped touching the tender subject, all the editors, in the different cities we have visited, have been very respectful in their notices of Mrs. Rose, both before and after her meetings.

Mrs. Rose's third lecture in Washington was on the "Nebraska Question, as Deduced from Human Rights." The only paper that reported anything of her speech was the *Washington Globe*, which, though it spoke most highly of her as a lecturer, misrepresented her, by ascribing to her the arguments of the South. She did not say that "she was aware that it was almost an utter impossibility, in the present state of society, to bring about the abolition of slavery." Nor did she say that "the slaveholder could no more be expected to relinquish his hold on his slaves, than the Northern capitalist to relinquish his grasp upon his bag of hard-earned dollars;" but that she knew such were the arguments of the South. Mrs. Rose's whole speech was marked with bold denunciation of the institution that robs man of his first inalienable right—the right to himself. She said there was no possible argument that could have a feather's weight in the balance against human freedom, and that, though no advocate of disunion, still, if she were convinced that slavery could be abolished by a dissolution of the Union, she would rather see, not only the North separate from the South, but State from State and city from city, than that the curse of slavery should longer continue.

While Mrs. R. could see some reasons why the South should desire an acquisition of slave territory, in the well-known fact that their lands are impoverished by slave labor, there was no excuse for the North. She could feel pity and commiseration for some men of the South, while for Northern recreants she felt the most utter contempt. She said the introduction of the Nebraska bill [Kansas-Nebraska Act], and its consequent agitation throughout the Union, would be productive of great good to the cause of freedom, it mattered not whether it was passed or not. She commented severely on [Stephen] Douglas, and consigned him to the fate of John Mitchel, and all others before him, who have attempted to get to themselves place or power, by pandering to the prejudices of the South.

Strange as it may seem the *National Era*, the only paper in Washington that makes any professions of being on the side of human freedom, took no notice of the fact of Mrs. Rose having spoken in that city on the subject of slavery. Can it be possible that its editor's love for the poor downtrodden slave is so weak as to allow the prejudices of sect or sex to hold it in abeyance? Can it be that he panders to the narrow, mean, bigotted sectarianism, that recognizes no anti-slavery save that bounded by "time-worn creeds," no divine right of utterance, save that of man alone? . . .

May the day soon come when justice and equality shall be fully established between all mankind, without distinction of sex or color!

Susan B. Anthony

"WHAT IS AMERICAN SLAVERY?"
NEW YORK STATE, 1857–1861

Anthony delivered this speech, written in 1857, while she was New York agent for the American Anti-Slavery Society (AASS). As a general agent, her job was to direct groups of AASS field lecturers from city to city as they crossed New York state. In addition, she wrote and gave her own speeches. Months spent in the company of Charles Lenox Remond, Parker Pillsbury, Abby Kelley Foster, and Wendell Phillips soon breathed fire into her oratory (see "What

Is American Slavery?" Speech, 1857, SBA Papers, LCMD, in *Papers*).

What is American Slavery? The question of all questions, that is now agitating our entire country? The one vexed question that intrudes itself upon our every thought, that is spoken of in all our newspapers and magazines, that gives fertile theme to the moralist and novelist, that startles, nay, appals the political economist, that is discussed at the family fireside, at the public dinner, on the railroad car, at the corners of the streets, and wherever men and women do congregate?

What is American Slavery? The one disturbing question that thrusts itself into every gathering of the people, that is the "apple of discord" in all our literary, political, and religious organizations, that causes angry divisions and subdivisions in our Churches, General Assemblies, General Conferences, and Associations, that has turned our American Congress into one great national debating club, and all our State Legislatures into schools, where declamations, both pro and con, are always in order?

What is this question of American Slavery, that has thus the power to shake this mighty nation from centre to circumference, and from circumference back to centre again? The one blot on our nation's escutcheon, that shames the fact of every true American, and astonishes the whole civilized world, the one "pet institution," that makes our professedly Christian, Democratic, Republican America, a lie,—a hissing and a by-word in the mouth of all Europe, and an offense in the sight of High Heaven!

What is American Slavery? It is the Legalized Systematized robbery of the bodies and souls of nearly four millions of men, women and children. It is the Legalized traffic in God's Image; It is the buying and selling of Jesus Christ himself on the auction block, as Merchandise, as chattel property, in the person of the outraged slave, For the Divine Jesus said, "Inasmuch as ye do it unto one of the least of these, my brethren, ye do it unto me."

What is American Slavery? It is the depriving of four millions of native born citizens of these United States, of their inalienable right to life, liberty, and the pursuit of happiness. It is the robbing of every sixth man, woman and child, of this glorious republic, of their God-given right—the ownership and control of their own persons, to the earning of their own hands and brains, to the exercise of their own consciences and wills, to the possession and enjoyment of their own homes. It is the sundering of what God has joined together, the divorcing of husbands and wives, parents and children, brothers and sisters. It is the robbery of every comfort, and every possession, sacred to a child of earth and an heir of Heaven. American Slavery? It is a wholesale system of wrong and outrage perpetrated on the bodies and souls of these millions of God's children. Its the legalized prostitution of nearly two millions of the daughters of this proud republic; it is the blotting out from the soul of womanhood, the divine spark of purity, the god of her inheritance. It is the abomination of desolation spoken of by the prophet Daniel, engrafted into the very heart of the American government, it is all and every villainy . . . consolidated into one. It is theft, robbery, piracy, murder. It is avarice, covetousness, lust, licentiousness, concubinage, polygamy; it is atheism, blasphemy, and sin against the Holy Ghost.

SUSAN B. ANTHONY VOTES IN THE 1872 PRESIDENTIAL ELECTION
ROCHESTER, NEW YORK, NOVEMBER 5, 1872

Anthony dashed this letter off to her friend and partner Elizabeth Cady Stanton after she successfully cast her ballot for the Re-publican presidential candidate Ulysses S. Grant and two members of Congress in the 1872 presidential election (see *HWS*, 2:934–935).

Dear Mrs. Stanton:

Well, I have been and gone and done it! Positively voted the Republican ticket— straight—this A.M. at seven o-clock and *swore my vote in, at that*; was registered on Friday and fifteen other women followed suit in this ward, then in sundry other wards some twenty or thirty women tried to register, but all save two were refused. [Although Anthony did not know it at the time she wrote this letter, a total of 50 Rochester women registered to vote, though only 15 successfully cast ballots on Election Day.] All my three sisters voted— Rhoda De Garmo, too. Amy Post was rejected, and she will immediately bring action against the registrars; then another woman who was registered, but vote refused, will bring action for that. . . . Hon. Henry R. Selden will be our counsel; he has read up the law and all of our arguments, and is satisfied that we are right, and ditto Judge Samuel Selden, his elder brother. So we are in for a fine agitation in Rochester on this question.

I hope the morning telegrams will tell of many women all over the country trying to vote. It is splendid that without any concert of action so many should have moved here. . . .

Haven't we wedged ourselves into the work pretty fairly and fully, and now that the Republicans have taken our votes—for it is the Republican members of the board; the Democratic paper is out against us strong, and that scared the Democrats on the registry boards.

How I wish you were here to write up the funny things said and done. Rhoda De Garmo told them [the officers of the voter registry board] she wouldn't swear nor affirm, "but would tell them the truth," and they accepted that. When the Democrats said that my vote should not go in the box, one Republican said to the other, "What do you say, Marsh?" "I say put it in." "So do I," said Jones, "and we'll fight it out on this line if it takes all winter." Mary Hallowell was just here. She and Sarah Willis tried to register, but were refused; also Mrs. Mann, the Unitarian minister's wife, and Mary Curtis, sister of Catharine Stebbins. Not a jeer, not a word, not a look disrespectful has met a single woman.

If only now all the Woman Suffrage women would work to this end of enforcing the existing Constitutional supremacy of National law over State law, what strides we might make this very winter! But I'm awfully tired; for five days I have been on the constant run, but to splendid purpose; so all right. I hope you voted too.

Affectionately,

Susan B. Anthony

"IS IT A CRIME FOR A UNITED STATES CITIZEN TO VOTE?" [EXCERPTS]

MONROE AND ONTARIO COUNTIES, NEW YORK, SPRING 1873

While waiting for her trial in the case *United States v. Susan B. Anthony*, Anthony delivered this speech throughout Monroe and Ontario Counties in New York during the spring of 1873 to gain public support for her constitutional position and the NWSA's "New Departure" strategy. Ida Husted Harper edited this speech for inclusion in Anthony's biography, *The Life and Work of Susan B. Anthony* (see Harper 1899, 2:977–992).

Friends and Fellow Citizens: I stand before you under indictment for the alleged crime of having voted at the last presidential election, without having a lawful right to vote. It shall be my work this evening to prove to you that in thus doing, I not only committed no crime, but instead simply exercised my citizen's right, guaranteed to me and all United States citizens by the

National Constitution beyond the power of any State to deny.

Our democratic-republican government is based on the idea of the natural right of every individual member thereof to a voice and a vote in making and executing the laws. We assert the province of government to be to secure the people in the enjoyment of their inalienable rights. We throw to the winds the old dogma that government can give rights. No one denies that before governments were organized each individual possessed the right to protect his own life, liberty, and property. When 100 or 1,000,000 people enter into a free government, they do not barter away their natural rights; they simply pledge themselves to protect each other in the enjoyment of them through prescribed judicial and legislative tribunals. They agree to abandon the methods of brute force in the adjustment of their differences and adopt those of civilization. Nor can you find a word in any of the grand documents left us by the fathers which assumes for government the power to create or to confer rights. The Declaration of Independence, the United States Constitution, the constitutions of the several States and the organic laws of the Territories, all alike propose to *protect* the people in the exercise of their God-given rights. Not one of them pretends to bestow rights.

> All men are created equal, and endowed by their Creator with certain inalienable rights. Among these are life, liberty and the pursuit of happiness. To secure these, governments are instituted among men, deriving their just powers from the consent of the governed.

Here is no shadow of government authority over rights, or exclusion of any class from their full and equal enjoyment. Here is pronounced the right of all men, and "consequently," as the Quaker preacher said, "of all women," to a voice in the government. And here, in this first paragraph of the Declaration *[Declaration of Independence],* is the assertion of the natural right of all to the ballot; for how can "the consent of the governed" be given, if the right to vote be denied? Again:

> Whenever any form of government becomes destructive of these ends, it is the right of the people to alter or abolish it, and to institute a new government, laying its foundations on such principles, and organizing its powers in such form, as to them shall seem most likely to effect their safety and happiness.

Surely the right of the whole people to vote is here clearly implied; for however destructive to their happiness this government might become, a disfranchised class could neither alter nor abolish it, nor institute a new one, except by the old brute force method of insurrection and rebellion. One-half of the people of this nation today are utterly powerless to blot from the statute books an unjust law, or to write there a new and a just one. The women, dissatisfied as they are with this form of government, that enforces taxation without representation—that compels them to obey laws to which they never have given their consent—that imprisons and hangs them without a trial by a jury of their peers—that robs them, in marriage, of the custody of their own persons, wages and children—are this half of the people who are left wholly at the mercy of the other half, in direct violation of the spirit and letter of the declarations of the framers of this government, every one of which was based on the immutable principle of equal rights to all. By these declarations, kings, popes, priests, aristocrats, all were alike dethroned and placed on a common level, politically, with the lowliest born subject or serf. By them, too, men, as such, were deprived of their divine right to rule

and placed on a political level with women. By the practice of these declarations all class and caste distinctions would be abolished, and slave, serf, plebeian, wife, woman, all alike rise from their subject position to the broader platform of equality.

The preamble of the Federal Constitution says:

> We, the people of the United States, in order to form a more perfect union, establish justice, insure domestic tranquility, provide for the common defence, promote the general welfare and secure the blessings of liberty to ourselves and our posterity, do ordain and establish this Constitution for the United States of America.

It was we, the people, not we, the white male citizens, nor we, the male citizens; but we, the whole people, who formed this Union. We formed it not to give the blessings of liberty but to secure them; not to the half of ourselves and the half of our posterity, but to the whole people— women as well as men. It is downright mockery to talk to women of their enjoyment of the blessings of liberty while they are denied the only means of securing them provided by this democratic-republican government—the ballot.

The early journals of Congress show that, when the committee reported to that body the original articles of confederation, the very first one which became the subject of discussion was that respecting equality of suffrage. Article IV said:

> The better to secure and perpetuate mutual friendship and intercourse between the people of the different States of this Union, the free inhabitants of each of the States (paupers, vagabonds and fugitives from justice excepted) shall be entitled to all the privileges and immunities of the free citizens of the several States.

Thus, at the very beginning, did the fathers see the necessity of the universal application of the great principle of equal rights to all, in order to produce the desired result—a harmonious union and a homogeneous people.

Luther Martin, attorney-general of Maryland, in his report to the legislature of that State of the convention which framed the United States Constitution, said:

> Those who advocated the equality of suffrage took the matter up on the original principles of government: that the reason why each individual man in forming a State government should have an equal vote, is because each individual, before he enters into government, is equally free and equally independent.

James Madison said:

> Under every view of the subject, it seems indispensable that the mass of the citizens should not be without a voice in making the laws which they are to obey, and in choosing the magistrates who are to administer them. . . . Let it be remembered, finally, that it has ever been the pride and the boast of America that the rights for which she contended were the rights of human nature.

These assertions by the framers of the United States Constitution of the equal and natural right of all the people to a voice in the government, have been affirmed and reaffirmed by the leading statesmen of the nation throughout the entire history of our government. Thaddeus Stevens, of Pennsylvania, said in 1866: "I have made up my mind that the elective franchise is one of the inalienable rights meant to be secured by the *Declaration of Independence*." B. Gratz Brown, of Missouri, in the three days' discussion in the United States Senate in 1866, on Senator Cowan's motion to strike "male" from the District of Columbia suffrage bill, said:

> Mr. President, I say here on the floor of the American Senate, I stand for universal suffrage; and as a matter of fundamental principle, do not recognize the right of society to limit it on any ground of race or sex. I will go farther and say that I recognize the right of franchise as being intrinsically a natural right. I do not believe that society is authorized to impose any limitations upon it that do not spring out of the necessities of the social state itself. Sir, I have been shocked, in the course of this debate, to hear senators declare this right only a conventional and political arrangement, a privilege yielded to you and me and others; not a right in any sense, only a concession! Mr. President, I do not hold my liberties by any such tenure. On the contrary, I believe that whenever you establish that doctrine, whenever you crystallize that idea in the public mind of this country, you ring the death-knell of American liberties.

Charles Sumner, in his brave protests against the Fourteenth and Fifteenth Amendments, insisted that so soon as by the Thirteenth Amendment the slaves became free men, the original powers of the United States Constitution guaranteed to them equal rights—the right to vote and to be voted for. In closing one of his great speeches he said:

> I do not hesitate to say that when the slaves of our country became "citizens" they took their place in the body politic as a component part of the "people," entitled to equal rights and under the protection of these two guardian principles: First, that all just governments stand on the consent of

the governed; and second, that taxation without representation is tyranny; and these rights it is the duty of Congress to guarantee as essential to the idea of a republic.

The preamble of the constitution of the State of New York declares the same purpose. It says: "We, the people of the State of New York, grateful to Almighty God for our freedom, in order to secure its blessings, do establish this constitution." Here is not the slightest intimation either of receiving freedom from the United States Constitution, or of the State's conferring the blessings of liberty upon the people; and the same is true of every other State constitution. Each and all declare rights God-given, and that to secure the people in the enjoyment of their inalienable rights is their one and only object in ordaining and establishing government. All of the State constitutions are equally emphatic in their recognition of the ballot as the means of securing the people in the enjoyment of these rights. Article I of the New York State constitution says:

No member of this State shall be disfranchised or deprived of the rights or privileges secured to any citizen thereof, unless by the law of the land, or the judgment of his peers.

So carefully guarded is the citizen's right to vote, that the constitution makes special mention of all who may be excluded. It says: "Laws may be passed excluding from the right of suffrage all persons who have been or may be convicted of bribery, larceny or any infamous crime."

In naming the various employments which shall not affect the residence of voters, Section 3, Article II, says "that neither being kept in any almshouse, or other asylum, at public expense, nor being confined in any public prison, shall deprive a person of his residence," and hence of his

vote. Thus is the right of voting most sacredly hedged about. The only seeming permission in the New York State constitution for the disfranchisement of women is in Section 1, Article II, which says: "Every male citizen of the age of twenty-one years, etc., shall be entitled to vote."

But I submit that in view of the explicit assertions of the equal right of the whole people, both in the preamble and previous article of the constitution, this omission of the adjective "female" should not be construed into a denial; but instead should be considered as of no effect. Mark the direct prohibition, "No member of this State shall be disfranchised, unless by the law of the land, or the judgment of his peers." "The law of the land" is the United States Constitution; and there is no provision in that document which can be fairly construed into a permission to the States to deprive any class of citizens of their right to vote. Hence New York can get no power from that source to disfranchise one entire half of her members. Nor has "the judgment of their peers" been pronounced against women exercising their right to vote; no disfranchised person is allowed to be judge or juror—and none but disfranchised persons can be women's peers. Nor has the legislature passed laws excluding women as a class on account of idiocy or lunacy; nor have the courts convicted them of bribery, larceny or any infamous crime. Clearly, then, there is no constitutional ground for the exclusion of women from the ballot-box in the State of New York. No barriers whatever stand today between women and the exercise of their right to vote save those of precedent and prejudice, which refuse to expunge the word "male" from the constitution.

The clauses of the United States Constitution cited by our opponents as giving power to the States to disfranchise any classes of citizens they please, are contained in Sections 2 and 4, Article I. The second says:

The House of Representatives shall be composed of members chosen every second year by the people of the several States; and the electors in each State shall have the qualifications requisite for electors of the most numerous branch of the State legislature.

This can not be construed into a concession to the States of the power to destroy the right to become an elector, but simply to prescribe what shall be the qualifications, such as competency of intellect, maturity of age, length of residence, that shall be deemed necessary to enable them to make an intelligent choice of candidates. If, as our opponents assert, it is the duty of the United States to protect citizens in the several States against higher or different qualifications for electors for representatives in Congress than for members of the Assembly, then it must be equally imperative for the national government to interfere with the States, and forbid them from arbitrarily cutting off the right of one-half the people to become electors altogether. Section 4 says:

The times, places and manner of holding elections for senators and representatives shall be prescribed in each State by the legislature thereof; but Congress may at any time, by law, make or alter such regulations, except as to the places of choosing senators.

Here is conceded to the States only the power to prescribe times, places and manner of holding the elections; and even with these Congress may interfere in all excepting the mere place of choosing senators. Thus, you see, there is not the slightest permission for the States to discriminate against the right of any class of citizens to vote. Surely, to regulate can not be to annihilate; to qualify can not be wholly to deprive. To this principle every true Democrat and Republican said amen, when applied to black men by Senator Sumner in his great speeches from 1865 to 1869 for equal rights to all; and when, in 1871, I asked that senator to declare the power of the United States Constitution to protect women in their right to vote—as he had done for black men—he handed me a copy of all his speeches during that reconstruction period, and said:

Put "sex" where I have "race" or "color," and you have here the best and strongest argument I can make for woman. There is not a doubt but women have the constitutional right to vote, and I will never vote for a Sixteenth Amendment to guarantee it to them. I voted for both the Fourteenth and Fifteenth under protest; would never have done it but for the pressing emergency of that hour; would have insisted that the power of the original Constitution to protect all citizens in the equal enjoyment of their rights should have been vindicated through the courts. But the newly-made freedmen had neither the intelligence, wealth nor time to await that slow process. Women do possess all these in an eminent degree, and I insist that they shall appeal to the courts, and through them establish the powers of our American magna charta [carta] to protect every citizen of the republic.

But, friends, when in accordance with Senator Sumner's counsel I went to the ballot-box last November, and exercised my citizen's right to vote, the courts did not wait for me to appeal to them—they appealed to me, and indicted me on the charge of having voted illegally. Putting sex where he did color, Senator Sumner would have said:

Qualifications can not be in their nature permanent or insurmountable.

Sex can not be a qualification any more than size, race, color or previous condition of servitude. A permanent or insurmountable qualification is equivalent to a deprivation of the suffrage. In other words, it is the tyranny of taxation without representation, against which our Revolutionary mothers, as well as fathers, rebelled.

For any State to make sex a qualification, which must ever result in the disfranchisement of one entire half of the people, is to pass a bill of attainder, an ex post facto law, and is therefore a violation of the supreme law of the land. By it the blessings of liberty are forever withheld from women and their female posterity. For them, this government has no just powers derived from the consent of the governed. For them this government is not a democracy; it is not a republic. It is the most odious aristocracy ever established on the face of the globe. An oligarchy of wealth, where the rich govern the poor; an oligarchy of learning, where the educated govern the ignorant; or even an oligarchy of race, where the Saxon rules the African, might be endured; but this oligarchy of sex which makes father, brothers, husband, sons, the oligarchs over the mother and sisters, the wife and daughters of every household; which ordains all men sovereigns, all women subjects—carries discord and rebellion into every home of the nation. This most odious aristocracy exists, too, in the face of Section 4, Article IV, which says: "The United States shall guarantee to every State in the Union a republican form of government."

What, I ask you, is the distinctive difference between the inhabitants of a monarchical and those of a republican form of government, save that in the monarchical the people are subjects, helpless, powerless, bound to obey laws made by political superiors; while in the republican the people are citizens, individual sovereigns, all clothed with equal power to make and unmake both their laws and law-makers? The moment you deprive a person of his right to a voice in the government, you degrade him from the status of a citizen of the republic to that of a subject. It matters very little to him whether his monarch be an individual tyrant, as is the Czar of Russia, or a 15,000,000 headed monster, as here in the United States; he is a powerless subject, serf or slave; not in any sense a free or independent citizen.

It is urged that the use of the masculine pronouns *he*, *his* and *him* in all the constitutions and laws, is proof that only men were meant to be included in their provisions. If you insist on this version of the letter of the law, we shall insist that you be consistent and accept the other horn of the dilemma, which would compel you to exempt women from taxation for the support of the government and from penalties for the violation of laws. There is no *she* or *her* or *hers* in the tax laws, and this is equally true of all the criminal laws.

Take for example the civil rights law which I am charged with having violated; not only are all the pronouns in it masculine, but everybody knows that it was intended expressly to hinder the rebel men from voting. It reads, "If any person shall knowingly vote without *his* having a lawful right." It was precisely so with all the papers served on me—the United States marshal's warrant, the bail-bond, the petition for habeas corpus, the bill of indictment—not one of them had a feminine pronoun; but to make them applicable to me, the clerk of the court prefixed an "s" to the "he" and made "her" out of "his" and "him;" and I insist that if government officials may thus manipulate the pronouns to tax, fine, imprison and hang women, it is their duty to thus change them in order to protect us in our right to vote. . . .

Though the words persons, people, inhabitants, electors, citizens, are all used indiscriminately in the national and State constitutions, there was always a conflict of opinion, prior to the war, as to whether they were synonymous terms, but whatever room there was for doubt, under the old regime, the adoption of the Fourteenth Amendment settled that question forever in its first sentence:

All persons born or naturalized in the United States, and subject to the jurisdiction thereof are citizens of the United States, and of the State where-in they reside.

The second [sentence] settles the equal status of all citizens:

No state shall make or enforce any law which shall abridge the privileges or immunities of citizens of the United States; nor shall any State deprive any person of life, liberty or property without due process of law, or deny to any person within its jurisdiction the equal protection of the laws.

The only question left to be settled now is: Are women persons? I scarcely believe any of our opponents will have the hardi-hood to say they are not. Being persons, then, women are citizens, and no State has a right to make any law, or to enforce any old law, which shall abridge their privileges or immunities. Hence, every discrimination against women in the constitutions and laws of the several States is today null and void, precisely as is every one against negroes.

Is the right to vote one of the privileges or immunities of citizens? I think the dis-franchised ex-rebels and ex-State prisoners all will agree that it is not only one of them, but the one without which all the others are nothing. Seek first the kingdom of the ballot and all things else shall be added, is the political injunction. . . .

If once we establish the false principle that United States citizenship does not carry with it the right to vote in every State in this Union, there is no end to the petty tricks and cunning devices which will be attempted to exclude one and another class of citizens from the right of suffrage. It will not always be the men combining to disfranchise all women; native born men combining to abridge the rights of all naturalized citizens, as in Rhode Island. It will not always be the rich and educated who may combine to cut off the poor and ignorant; but we may live to see the hard-working, uncultivated day laborers, foreign and native born, learning the power of the ballot and their vast majority of numbers, combine and amend State constitutions so as to disfranchise the Vanderbilts, the Stewarts, . . . It is a poor rule that won't work more ways than one. Establish this precedent, admit the State's right to deny suffrage, and there is no limit to the confusion, discord and disruption that may await us. There is and can be but one safe principle of government—equal rights to all. Discrimination against any class on account of color, race, nativity, sex, property, culture, can but embitter and disaffect that class, and thereby endanger the safety of the whole people. Clearly, then, the national government not only must define the rights of citizens, but must stretch out its powerful hand and protect them in every state of the Union.

Benjamin F. Butler, in a recent letter to me, said: "I do not believe anybody in Congress doubts that the Constitution authorizes the right of women to vote, precisely as it authorizes trial by jury and many other like rights guaranteed to citizens."

It is upon this just interpretation of the United States Constitution that our National Woman Suffrage Association, which celebrates the twenty-fifth anniversary of the woman's rights movement next May in New York City, has based all its arguments and action since the passage of these amendments. We no longer petition legislature or Congress to give us the right to vote, but appeal to women everywhere to exercise their too long neglected "citizen's right." We appeal to the inspectors of election to receive the votes of all United States citizens, as it is their duty to do. We appeal to United States commissioners and marshals to arrest, as is their duty, the inspectors who reject the votes of United States citizens, and leave alone those who perform their duties and accept these votes. We ask the juries to return verdicts of "not guilty" in the cases of law-abiding United States citizens who cast their votes, and inspectors of election who receive and count them.

We ask the judges to render unprejudiced opinions of the law, and wherever there is room for doubt to give the benefit to the side of liberty and equal rights for women, remembering that, as Sumner says, "The true rule of interpretation under our National Constitution, especially since its amendments, is that anything *for* human rights is constitutional, everything *against* human rights is unconstitutional." It is on this line that we propose to fight our battle for the ballot—peaceably but nevertheless persistently—until we achieve complete triumph and all United States citizens, men and women alike are recognized as equals in the government.

EXCERPTS FROM SUSAN B. ANTHONY'S TRIAL—UNITED STATES V. SUSAN B. ANTHONY
U.S. DISTRICT COURT, CANANDAIGUA, NEW YORK, 1873

At the conclusion of Anthony's trial, after Judge Ward Hunt refused her attorney Henry Rogers Selden's motion for a new trial, Anthony was asked if she would like to speak.

The following is a transcript of her remarks as recorded in the *History of Woman Suffrage* (2:687–689).

The Court: The prisoner will stand up. Has the prisoner anything to say why sentence shall not be pronounced?

Miss Anthony: Yes, your honor, I have many things to say; for in your ordered verdict of guilty, you have trampled underfoot every vital principle of our government. My natural rights, my civil rights, my political rights, are all alike ignored. Robbed of the fundamental privilege of citizenship, I am degraded from the status of a citizen to that of a subject; and not only myself individually, but all of my sex, are, by your honor's verdict, doomed to political subjection under this so-called republican government.

Judge Hunt: The Court can not listen to a rehearsal of arguments the prisoner's counsel has already consumed three hours in presenting.

Miss Anthony: May it please your honor, I am not arguing the question, but simply stating the reasons why sentence can not, in justice, be pronounced against me. Your denial of my citizen's right to vote is the denial of my right of consent as one of the governed, the denial of my right of representation as one of the taxed, the denial of my right to a trial by a jury of my peers as an offender against law, therefore, the denial of my sacred rights to life, liberty, property, and—

Judge Hunt: The Court can not allow the prisoner to go on.

Miss Anthony: But your honor will not deny me this one and only poor privilege of protest against this high-handed outrage upon my citizen's rights. May it please the Court to remember that since the day of my arrest last November, this is the first time that either myself or any person of my disfranchised class has been allowed a word of defense before judge or jury—

Judge Hunt: The prisoner must sit down. The Court can not allow it.

Miss Anthony: All my prosecutors, from the Eighth Ward corner grocery politician, who entered the complaint, to the United States Marshal, Commissioner, District Attorney, District Judge, your honor on the bench, not one is my peer, but each and all are my political sovereigns; and had your honor submitted my case to the jury, as was clearly your duty, even then I should have had just cause of protest, for not one of those men was my peer; but, native or foreign, white or black, rich or poor, educated or ignorant, awake or asleep, sober or drunk, each and every man of them was my political superior; hence, in no sense, my peer. Even, under such circumstances, a commoner of England, tried before a jury of lords, would have far less cause to complain than should I, a woman, tried before a jury of men. Even my counsel, the Hon. Henry R. Selden, who has argued my cause so ably, so earnestly, so unanswerably before your honor, is my political sovereign. Precisely as no disfranchised person is entitled to sit upon a jury, and no woman is entitled to the franchise, so, none but a regularly admitted lawyer is allowed to practice in the courts, and no woman can gain admission to the bar—hence, jury, judge, counsel, must all be of the superior class.

Judge Hunt: The Court must insist—the prisoner has been tried according to the established forms of law.

Miss Anthony: Yes, your honor, but by forms of law all made by men, interpreted by men, administered by men, in favor of men, and against women; and hence, your honor's ordered verdict of guilty, against a United States citizen for the exercise of "that citizen's right to vote," simply because that citizen was a woman and not a man. But, yesterday, the same man-made forms of law declared it a crime punishable with $1,000 fine and six months' imprisonment, for you, or me, or any of us, to give a cup of cold water, a crust of bread, or a night's shelter to a panting fugitive as he was tracking his way to Canada. And every man or woman in whose veins coursed a drop of human sympathy violated that wicked law, reckless of consequences, and was justified in so doing. As then the slaves who got their freedom must take it over, or under, or through the unjust forms of law, precisely so now must women, to get their right to a voice in this Government, take it; and I have taken mine, and mean to take it at every opportunity.

Judge Hunt: The Court orders the prisoner to sit down. It will not allow another word.

Miss Anthony: When I was brought before your honor for trial, I hoped for a broad and liberal interpretation of the Constitution and its recent amendments, that should declare all United States citizens under its protecting aegis—that should declare equality of rights the national guarantee of all persons born or naturalized in the United States. But failing to get this justice—failing, even, to get a trial by a jury *not* of my peers—I ask not leniency at your hands—but rather the full rigors of the law.

Judge Hunt: The Court must insist—
(Here the prisoner sat down.)

Judge Hunt: The prisoner will stand up. (Here Miss Anthony rose again.) The sentence of the Court is that you pay a fine of one hundred dollars and the costs of the prosecution.

Miss Anthony: May it please your honor, I shall never pay a dollar of your unjust penalty. All the stock in trade I possess is a $10,000 debt, incurred by publishing my paper—*The Revolution*—four years ago, the sole object of which was to educate all women to do precisely as I have done, rebel against your man-made unjust, unconstitutional forms of law, that tax, fine, imprison, and hang women, while they deny them the right of representation in the Government; and I shall work on with might and main to pay every dollar of that honest debt, but not a penny shall go to this unjust claim. And I shall earnestly and persistently continue to urge all women to the practical recognition of the old revolutionary maxim, that "Resistance to tyranny is obedience to God."

Judge Hunt: Madam, the Court will not order you committed until the fine is paid.

DECLARATION OF THE RIGHTS OF WOMAN
PHILADELPHIA, JULY 4, 1876

Susan B. Anthony, Elizabeth Cady Stanton, and Matilda Joslyn Gage, representing the National Woman Suffrage Association (NWSA), composed this manifesto, which Anthony read aloud at the nation's Centennial Exposition on July 4, 1876, outside Independence Hall in Philadelphia. The *Declaration* was signed by many leaders of the women's rights and woman suffrage movements, among them Lucretia Coffin Mott, Ernestine Potowski Rose, Olympia Brown, Phoebe Couzins, Lillie Devereux Blake, Abigail Scott Duniway, and Isabella Beecher Hooker, in addition to its authors (see *HWS*, 3:31–34).

While the nation is buoyant with patriotism, and all hearts are attuned to praise, it is with sorrow we come to strike the one discordant note, on this one-hundredth anniversary of our country's birth. When subjects of kings, emperors, and czars, from the old world join in our national jubilee, shall the women of the republic refuse to lay their hands with benedictions on the nation's head? Surveying America's exposition, surpassing in magnificence those of London, Paris, and Vienna, shall we not rejoice at the success of the youngest rival among the nations of the earth? May not our hearts, in unison with all, swell with pride at our great achievements as a people; our free speech, free press, free schools, free

church, and the rapid progress we have made in material wealth, trade, commerce and the inventive arts? And we do rejoice in the success, thus far, of our experiment of self-government. Our faith is firm and unwavering in the broad principles of human rights proclaimed in 1776, not only as abstract truths, but as the corner stones of a republic. Yet we cannot forget, even in this glad hour, that while all men of every race, and clime, and condition, have been invested with the full rights of citizenship under our hospitable flag, all women still suffer the degradation of disfranchisement.

The history of our country the past hundred years has been a series of assumptions and usurpations of power over woman, in direct opposition to the principles of just government, acknowledged by the United States as its foundation, which are:

First—The natural rights of each individual.
Second—The equality of these rights.
Third—That rights not delegated are retained by the individual.
Fourth—That no person can exercise the rights of others without delegated authority.
Fifth—That the non-use of rights does not destroy them.

And for the violation of these fundamental principles of our government, we arraign our rulers on this Fourth day of July, 1876,—and these are our articles of impeachment:

Bills of attainder have been passed by the introduction of the word "male" into all the State constitutions, denying to women the right of suffrage, and thereby making sex a crime—an exercise of power clearly forbidden in Article 1, Section 9, 10 of the United States Constitution.

The writ of habeas corpus, the only protection against *lettres de cachet* and all forms of unjust imprisonment, which the

Constitution declares "shall not be suspended, except when in cases of rebellion or invasion the public safety demands it," is held inoperative in every State of the Union, in case of a married woman against her husband—the marital rights of the husband being in all cases primary, and the rights of the wife secondary.

The right of trial by a jury of one's peers was so jealously guarded that States refused to ratify the original Constitution until it was guaranteed by the Sixth Amendment. And yet the women of this nation have never been allowed a jury of their peers—being tried in all cases by men, native and foreign, educated and ignorant, virtuous and vicious. Young girls have been arraigned in our courts for the crime of infanticide; tried, convicted, hanged—victims, perchance, of judge, jurors, advocates—while no woman's voice could be heard in their defense. And not only are women denied a jury of their peers, but in some cases, jury trial altogether. During the war, a woman was tried and hanged by military law, in defiance of the Fifth Amendment, which specifically declares, "no person shall be held to answer for a capital or otherwise infamous crime, unless on a presentment or indictment of a grand jury, except in cases . . . of persons in actual service in time of war." During the last presidential campaign, a woman, arrested for voting, was denied the protection of a jury, tried, convicted, and sentenced to a fine and costs of prosecution, by the absolute power of a judge of the Supreme Court of the United States.

Taxation without representation, the immediate cause of the rebellion of the colonies against Great Britain, is one of the grievous wrongs the women of this country have suffered during the century. Deploring war, with all the demoralization that follows in its train, we have been taxed to support standing armies, with their waste of life and wealth. Believing in temperance, we have been taxed to support the vice, crime and pauperism of the liquor traffic. While we suffer its wrongs and abuses infinitely more than man, we have no power to protect our sons against this giant evil. During the temperance crusade, mothers were arrested, fined, imprisoned, for even praying and singing in the streets, while men blockade the sidewalks with impunity, even on Sunday, with their military parades and political processions. Believing in honesty, we are taxed to support a dangerous army of civilians, buying and selling the offices of government and sacrificing the best interests of the people. And, moreover, we are taxed to support the very legislators and judges who make laws, and render decisions adverse to woman. And for refusing to pay such unjust taxation, the houses, lands, bonds, and stock of women have been seized and sold within the present year, thus proving Lord Coke's assertion, that "The very act of taxing a man's property without his consent is, in effect, disfranchising him of every civil right."

Unequal codes for men and women. Held by law a perpetual minor, deemed incapable of self-protection, even in the industries of the world, woman is denied equality of rights. The fact of sex, not the quantity or quality of work, in most cases, decides the pay and position; and because of this injustice, thousands of fatherless girls are compelled to choose between a life of shame and starvation. Laws catering to man's vices have created two codes of morals in which penalties are graded according to the political status of the offender. Under such laws, women are fined and imprisoned if found alone in the streets, or in public places of resort, at certain hours. Under the pretense of regulating public morals, police officers seizing the occupants of disreputable houses, march the women in platoons to prison, while the men, partners in their guilt, go free. While making a show of virtue in forbidding the importation of

Chinese women on the Pacific coast for immoral purposes, our rulers, in many States, and even under the shadow of the national capitol, are now proposing to legalize the sale of American womanhood for the same vile purposes.

Special legislation for woman has placed us in a most anomalous position. Women invested with the rights of citizens in one section—voters, jurors, office-holders— crossing an imaginary line, are subjects in the next. In some States, a married woman may hold property and transact business in her own name; in others, her earnings belong to her husband. In some States, a woman may testify against her husband, sue and be sued in the courts; in others, she has no redress in case of damage to person, property or character. In case of divorce on account of adultery in the husband, the innocent wife is held to possess no right to children or property, unless by special decree of the court. But in no State of the Union has the wife the right to her own person, or to any part of the joint earning of the co-partnership during the life of her husband. In some States women may enter the law schools and practice in the courts; in others they are forbidden. In some universities girls enjoy equal educational advantages with boys, while many of the proudest institutions in the land deny them admittance, though the sons of China, Japan, and Africa are welcomed there. But the privileges already granted in the several States are by no means secure. The right of suffrage once exercised by women in certain States and territories has been denied by subsequent legislation. A bill is now pending in Congress to disfranchise the women of Utah, thus interfering to deprive United States citizens of the same rights which the Supreme Court has declared the national government power-less to protect anywhere. Laws passed after years of untiring effort, guaranteeing married women certain rights of property, and mothers the custody of their children,

have been repealed in States where we supposed all was safe. Thus have our most sacred rights been made the football of legislative caprice, proving that a power which grants as a privilege what by nature is a right, may withhold the same as a penalty when deeming it necessary for its own perpetuation.

Representation of woman has had no place in the nation's thought. Since the incorporation of the thirteen original States, twenty-four have been admitted to the Union, not one of which has recognized woman's right of self-government. On this birthday of our national liberties, July Fourth, 1876, Colorado, like all her elder sisters, comes into the Union with the invidious word "male" in her constitution.

Universal manhood suffrage, by establishing an aristocracy of sex, imposes upon the women of this nation a more absolute and cruel despotism than monarchy; in that, woman finds a political master in her father, husband, brother, son. The aristocracies of the old world are based upon birth, wealth, refinement, education, nobility, braved deeds of chivalry; in this nation, on sex alone; exalting brute force above moral power, vice above virtue, ignorance above education, and the son above the mother who bore him.

The judiciary above the nation has proved itself but the echo of the party in power, by upholding and enforcing laws that are opposed to the spirit and letter of the Constitution. When the slave power was dominant, the Supreme Court decided that a black man was not a citizen, because he had not the right to vote; and when the Constitution was so amended as to make all persons citizens, the same high tribunal decided that a woman, though a citizen, had not the right to vote. Such vacillating interpretations of constitutional law unsettle our faith in judicial authority, and undermine the liberties of the whole people.

These articles of impeachment against our rulers we now submit to the impartial judgment of the people. To all these wrongs and oppressions woman has not submitted in silence and resignation. From the beginning of the century, when Abigail Adams, the wife of one president and mother of another, said, "We will not hold ourselves bound to obey laws in which we have no voice or representation," until now, woman's discontent has been steadily increasing, culminating nearly thirty years ago in a simultaneous movement among the women of the nation, demanding the right of suffrage. In making our just demands, a higher motive than the pride of sex inspires us; we feel that national safety and stability depend on the complete recognition of the broad principles of our government. Woman's degraded, helpless position is the weak point in our institutions today; a disturbing force everywhere, severing family ties, filling our asylums with the deaf, the dumb, the blind; our prisons with criminals, our cities with drunkenness and prostitution; our homes with disease and death. It was the boast of the founders of the republic, that the rights for which they contended were the rights of human nature. If these rights are ignored in the case of one-half the people, the nation is surely preparing for its downfall. Governments try themselves. The recognition of a governing and a governed class is incompatible with the first principles of freedom. Woman has not been a heedless spectator of the events of this century, nor a dull listener to the grand arguments for the equal rights of humanity. From the earliest history of our country woman has shown equal devotion with man to the cause of freedom, and has stood firmly by his side in its defense. Together, they have made this country what it is. Woman's wealth, thought and labor have cemented the stones of every monument man has reared to liberty.

And now, at the close of a hundred years, as the hour-hand of the great clock that marks the centuries points to 1876, we declare our faith in the principles of self-government; our full equality with man in natural rights; that woman was made first for her own happiness, with the absolute right to herself—to all the opportunities and advantages life affords for her complete development; and we deny that dogma of the centuries, incorporated in the codes of all nations—that woman was made for man—her best interests, in all cases, to be sacrificed to his will. We ask of our rulers, at this hour, no special favors, no special privileges, no special legislation. We ask justice, we ask equality, we ask that all the civil and political rights that belong to citizens of the United States, be guaranteed to us and our daughters forever.

THE COLORADO SUFFRAGE CAMPAIGN OF 1877
LAKE CITY, COLORADO, SEPTEMBER 21, 1877

Anthony's letter to the editor of the *Ballot Box*, written while traveling through Colorado, colorfully illustrates life on the woman suffrage campaign trail. Anthony's spellings of place names were often recorded phonetically and may be inaccurate (*Ballot Box*, November 1877, in *Papers*).

Dear *Ballot Box*:
My meeting at this place last night surpassed all before it in numbers and enthusiasm. Their largest audience chamber would not begin to hold the people. So I took my stand on a dry goods box on the courthouse steps, and the ten or fifteen hundred people, mainly men, took theirs on the ground; and there with these grand old Rocky mountains for our four walls, the blue heavens for our roof, the full moon and twinkling stars for our light, we stood and talked and listened full an hour and a half. It was a magnificent sight. No man-made temple ever contained a more attentive and respectful audience; and at the close at

least three-fourths of the men shouted "Aye." Only one woman voted "No."

I am bound here to-day, because my appointment for to-night at Ouras is fifty miles across the mountain, on "buroo" back, by a frightfully dangerous trail, which no mountaineer would attempt in to-day's rain and hail—and at the top of the pass snow; and 125 miles around by private carriage, which would take three days, and camping out o'nights. Ouras is an important mining point, but it is simply impossible for me to reach it. Tomorrow at 6 a.m. I am to take stage—no, Buck-board—for Saguache, 100 miles—a two days' journey and over the Chetope pass. My next is to be at South Arkansas, fifty miles "buck-board," and over the Puncho pass into the valley of the Arkansas river. But to give you a slight glimpse of our Colorado woman suffrage canvass experience, let me tell you: I left my home, Rochester, New York, on September 4th; spoke that night at Somerset, sixty miles distant, to a large audience of Niagara county farmers, all jubilant with their luscious peach harvest. At 7 o'clock next morning took stage and rode seventeen miles to Lockport, spoke to a large audience, and at midnight took the train for Detroit and thence to Toledo [Ohio], arriving at 6 p.m. Lecturing to an immense assemblage of working men on their "strikes," and hearing them vote a solid "aye" in favor of giving to working women equal chances with themselves. At 12 o'clock took the train for Leavenworth, Kansas, via Chicago and the Rock Island railroad. Spent Sunday with my brother, D. R. Anthony, and Monday morning via the Santa Fe railroad was speeding westward over the rich and rolling prairies of Kansas. Fifty years hence, when beautiful farm houses with their green blinds, their shade trees, their orchards and gardens shall dot every quarter section; when vast wheat and corn fields, interspersed with towering forests shall break the monotony of that boundless expanse, Kansas will indeed be the farmers' paradise. And even now one is delighted at every step with the wonderful progress made in its settlement and the well-to-do look of its settlers all along the line of the railroad, which passes through the very heart of the State, and is, by the way, the very best of all the western roads.

My first point was Granada, September 11th, where nobody knew that anybody there believed in Woman Suffrage. There was no hotel, no church, no schoolhouse, so I spoke in the railroad depot to a dozen men, as many women and double the number of children and babies. There are only forty voters in the precinct, and a majority of those Mexicans. The 12th at Los Animas—fine audience, among them a good representation from Fort Lyon. At Pueblo, the 13th, where I arrived at 4 p.m., no notice of my coming had been given, therefore I had to begin at the foundation of things, hire a hall, get [illegible] printed and distributed, etc. At last, bethinking me that the State Committee might possibly have addressed a letter to me, to somebody's care, I rushed to the post office, and sure enough they had; but then there was a hunt to be installed after said persons, and by 7:30 you can imagine my inclination was of rather a sharp order; but their largest hall was packed; men standing in every available spot, and when, at the close of my speech, an [illegible] majority of that curious crowd voted "aye," I felt better natured and right well paid for all my worry and hard work.

[Much of the following paragraph of the original is indecipherable.]

The 15th I reached El [illegible], and after the passengers had eaten their suppers the tables were cleared and I spoke in the hotel dining room to a goodly number. The 16th, Sunday, I lectured at Trinidad, where I for the first time stopped at a private house and luxuriated in a "Christian" cup of coffee, to say nothing of enjoying the society of cultivated New Yorkers.

The 17th I started at 6 a.m. for Garland, over the La Veta pass—the highest point yet reached by any railroad in this country—9,300 feet above the level of the sea. It is simply appalling as the narrow gauge steam-horse puffs, puffs, up, up, the heavy grades of the zig-zag road, to look to the depths below you. At 8 p.m. we reached the hardly three months old city, and at 8:30 I had eaten supper, arrayed myself, and was speaking to a crowd of men, women and children, packed into the dining room of a hotel, the first nail of which was driven not over thirty days before. The 18th, was again up, breakfast eaten and aboard the stage for Del Norte at 6 o'clock. We at once struck across the San Louis valley, 65 miles wide and 200 long, surrounded on all sides by high mountain ranges—evidently the bed of an immense inland sea—through alkali dust, such as only the stage line from Walula to Walla Walla, in Washington Territory, could possibly overtop. All that day, as we sped westward at the rate of eight miles an hour, the bald head of Sierra Blanca, the highest peak of the Sangre De Christo range, up and around which the railroad had wound me the day before, seemed hardly to recede from us; and when at last we had compassed the sixty-five miles its hoary head towered high above all its fellows. Del Norte is on the west side of the Rio Grande river. Here again good fortune gave me a home in a private family and I was in clover; but, oh how weary, how dusty, how utterly forlorn I entered that home—spoke in a new large M.E. church, crowded to its utmost, and again at the close a solid "aye" vote of both men and women.

At 7 p.m. of the 19th I took the stage for this city, a distance of eighty-four miles; rode all that night and all the next day to 1 p.m. over the mountains and through their various passes, crossing the divide between the waters that flow into the Atlantic and Pacific—at its highest point over 11,000 feet. And the ride down that mountain pass, "Slum Gullion" they call it, was the most fearful rough and tumble I ever experienced, though I returned overland from Oregon to California—nearly 400 miles—in 1871; and though[t] I knew all in that line. And even here, in this deep ravine, just wide enough for the Gunnison river and one street on its bank, the height is still 8,500 feet. All that fearfully long, but beautiful, frosty night, the moon shone brightly and on scenery most magnificent. At midnight I alighted at Wagon Wheel Gap, and with tin cup in hand trudged through the sand to the Rio Grande bank, bound to drink fresh from the pure, cold waters from the snow peaks above. It was here, where the mountains crowd up to the river's edge so closely, that Frémont, in his early survey, was compelled to leave his wagons, hence the name. The rock bound sides are not only perpendicular but actually overhanging the river thousands of feet below.

Here, too, I am in luck in the delightful home of Mr. and Mrs. Olney, of the "Silver World," both in full sympathy with our movement.

The friends everywhere are very hopeful of the vote on the 2nd of October, and I too might be had I not before me Michigan and Kansas; or could I imagine that the stock-men and miner, the ranch-men and mountain men of Colorado would vote any better than did the farmers of those States, but no one will be more rejoiced if they should than would

Susan B. Anthony

"WOMAN WANTS BREAD, NOT THE BALLOT!"
1870–1880

Anthony used this address countless times as she toured the United States between 1870 and 1880. It encapsulates almost all of the major tenets of her suffrage ideology. According to Ida Husted Harper, this speech was never written down in its entirety. She compiled and edited this version from a collection of Anthony's scattered notes and newspaper reports of her speeches (Harper 1899, 2:996–1003).

My purpose tonight is to demonstrate the great historical fact that disfranchisement is not only political degradation, but also moral, social, educational and industrial degradation; and that it does not matter whether the disfranchised class live under a monarchial or a republican form of government, or whether it be white workingmen of England, negroes on our southern plantations, serfs of Russia, Chinamen on our Pacific coast, or native born, tax-paying women of this republic. Wherever, on the face of the globe or on the page of history, you show me a disfranchised class, I will show you a degraded class of labor. Disfranchisement means inability to make, shape or control one's own circumstances. The disfranchised must always do the work, accept the wages, occupy the position the enfranchised assign to them. The disfranchised are in the position of the pauper. You remember the old adage, "Beggars must not be choosers"; they must take what they can get or nothing! That is exactly the position of women in the world of work today; they can not choose. If they could, do you for a moment believe they would take the subordinate places and the inferior pay? Nor is it a "new thing under the sun" for the disfranchised, the inferior classes weighed down with wrongs, to declare they "do not want to vote." The rank and file are not philosophers, they are not educated to think for themselves, but simply to accept, unquestioned, whatever comes.

Years ago in England when the workingmen, starving in the mines and factories, gathered in mobs and took bread wherever they could get it, their friends tried to educate them into a knowledge of the causes of their poverty and degradation. At one of these "monster bread meetings,"

held in Manchester, John Bright said to them, "Workingmen, what you need to bring to you cheap bread and plenty of it, is the franchise;" but those ignorant men shouted back to Mr. Bright, precisely as the women of America do to us to-day, "It is not the vote we want, it is bread"; and they broke up the meeting, refusing to allow him, their best friend, to explain to them the powers of the franchise. The condition of those workingmen was very little above that of slavery. Some of you may remember when George Thompson came over to this country and rebuked us for our crime and our curse of slavery, how the slaveholders and their abettors shouted back to Mr. Thompson. "Look at home, look into your mines and your factories, you have slavery in England."

You recollect a book published at that time entitled, "The Glory and Shame of England." Her glory was the emancipation of slaves in the British West Indies, and her shame the degraded and outraged condition of those very miners and factory men. In their desperation, they organized trade unions, went on strike, fought terrible battles, often destroying property and sometimes even killing their employers. Those who have read Charles Reade's novel, "Put Yourself in his Place," have not forgotten the terrible scenes depicted. While those starving men sometimes bettered their condition financially, they never made a ripple on the surface of political thought. No member ever championed their cause on the floor of Parliament. If spoken of at all, it was as our politicians used to speak of the negroes before the war, or as they speak of the Chinese today—as nuisances that ought to be suppressed.

But at length, through the persistent demands of a little handful of reformers, there was introduced into the British Parliament the "household suffrage" bill of 1867. [Anthony is referring to the British law, the Reform Act of 1867.] John Stuart

Mill not only championed that bill as it was presented, but moved an amendment to strike out the word "man" and substitute therefore the word "person," so that the bill should read, "every person who shall pay a seven-pound rental per annum shall be entitled to the franchise." You will see that Mr. Mill's motive was to extend the suffrage to women as well as men. But when the vote [on the amendment] was taken, only seventy-four, out of the nearly seven hundred members of the British Parliament, voted in its favor.

During the discussion of the original bill, the opposition was championed by Robert Lowe, who presented all the stock objections to the extension of the franchise to "those ignorant, degraded workingmen," as he called them, that ever were presented in this country against giving the ballot to the negroes, and that are today being urged against the enfranchisement of women. Is it not a little remarkable that no matter who the class may be that it is proposed to enfranchise, the objections are always the same? "The ballot in the hands of this new class will make their condition worse than before, and the introduction of this new class into the political arena will degrade politics to a lower level." But notwithstanding Mr. Lowe's persistent opposition, the bill became a law; and before the session closed, that same individual moved that Parliament, having enfranchised these men, should now make an appropriation for the establishment and support of schools for the education of them and their sons. Now, mark you his reason why! "Unless they are educated," said he, "they will be the means of overturning the throne of England." So long as these poor men in the mines and factories had not the right to vote, the power to make and unmake the laws and lawmakers, to help or hurt the government, no measure ever had been proposed for their benefit although they were ground under the heel of the capitalist to a condition of abject slavery. But the moment this power is placed in their hands, before they have used it even once, this bitterest enemy to their possessing it is the first man to spring to his feet and make this motion for the most beneficent measure possible in their behalf—public schools for the education of themselves and their children.

From that day to this, there never has been a session of the British Parliament that has not had before it some measure for the benefit of the working classes. Parliament has enacted laws compelling employers to cut down the number of hours for a day's work, to pay better wages, to build decent houses for their employees, and has prohibited the employment of very young children in the mines and factories. The history of those olden times records that not infrequently children were born in the mines and passed their lives there, scarcely seeing the sunlight from the day of their birth to the day of their death.

Sad as is the condition of the workingmen of England today, it is infinitely better than it was twenty years ago. At first the votes of the workingmen were given to the Liberal party, because it was the leaders of that party who secured their enfranchisement; but soon the leaders of the Conservative party, seeing the power the workingmen had, began to vie with the Liberals by going into their meetings and pledging that if they would vote the Tory ticket and bring that party into control, it would give them more and better laws even than the Liberals. In 1874 enough working men did go over to bring that party to the front, with Disraeli at its head, where it stood till 1880 when the rank and file of the working men of England, dissatisfied with Disraeli's policy, both domestic and foreign, turned and again voted the Liberal ticket, putting that party in power with Gladstone as its leader. This is the way in which the ballot in the hands of the masses of wage-earners, even under a monarchial form of government, makes of them a tremendous balance of power whose wants and wishes the instinct of self-interest compels the political leaders to study and obey.

The great distinctive advantage possessed by the working men of this republic is that the son of the humblest citizen, black or white, has equal chances with the son of the richest in the land if he takes advantage of the public schools, the colleges and the many opportunities freely offered. It is this equality of rights which makes our nation a home for the oppressed of all the monarchies of the old world.

And yet, notwithstanding the declaration of our Revolutionary fathers, "all men created equal," "governments derive their just powers from the consent of the governed," "taxation and representation inseparable"—notwithstanding all these grand enunciations, our government was founded upon the blood and bones of half a million human beings, bought and sold as chattels in the market. Nearly all the original thirteen States had property qualifications which disfranchised poor white men as well as women and negroes. Thomas Jefferson, at the head of the old Democratic party, took the lead in advocating the removal of all property qualifications, as so many violations of the fundamental principle of our government—"the right of consent." In New York the qualification was $250. Martin Van Buren, the chief of the Democracy, was a member of the Constitutional Convention held in Buffalo in 1821, which wiped out that qualification so far as white men were concerned. He declared, "The poor man has as good a right to a voice in the government as the rich man, and a vastly greater need to possess it as a means of protection to himself and his family." It was because the Democrats enfranchised poor white men, both native and foreign, that that strong old party held absolute sway in this country for almost forty years, with only now and then a one-term Whig administration.

In those olden days Horace Greeley, at the head of the Whig party and his glorious *New York Tribune*, used to write long editorials showing the workingmen that they had a mistaken idea about the Democratic party; that it was not so much the friend of the poor man as was the Whig, and if they would but vote the Whig ticket and put that party in power, they would find that it would give them better laws than the Democrats had done. At length, after many, many years of such education and persuasion, the workingmen's vote, native and foreign, was divided, and in 1860 there came to the front a new party which, though not called Whig, was largely made up of the old Whig elements. In its turn this new party enfranchised another degraded class of labor. Because the Republicans gave the ballot to negroes, they have been allied to that party and have held it solid in power from the ratification of the Fifteenth Amendment, in 1870, to the present day. Until the Democrats convince them that they will do more and better for them than the Republicans are doing, there will be no appreciable division of the negro vote.

The vast numbers of wage-earning men coming from Europe to this country, where manhood suffrage prevails with no limitations, find themselves invested at once with immense political power. They organize their trade unions, but not being able to use the franchise intelligently, they continue to strike and to fight their battles with the capitalists just as they did in the old countries. Neither press nor politicians dare to condemn these strikes or to demand their suppression because the workingmen hold the balance of power and can use it for the success or defeat of either party. . . .

It is said women do not need the ballot for their protection because they are supported by men. Statistics show that there are 3,000,000 women in this nation supporting themselves. In the crowded cities of the East they are compelled to work in shops, stores and factories for the merest pittance. In New York alone, there are over 50,000 of these women receiving less than fifty cents a day. Women wage-earners in different occupations have organized themselves into trade unions, from time to time, and made their strikes to get justice at the hands of their employers just as men have done, but I have yet to learn of a successful strike of any body of women. The best organized one I ever knew was that of the collar laundry women of the city of Troy, New York, the great emporium for the manufacture of shirts, collars and cuffs. They formed a trade union of several hundred members and demanded an increase of wages. It was refused. So one May morning in May 1867, each woman threw down her scissors and her needle, her starch-pan and flat-iron, and for three long months not one returned to the factories. At the end of that time they were literally starved out, and the majority of them were compelled to go back, but not at their old wages, for their employers cut them down to even a lower figure.

In the winter following I met the president of this union, a bright young Irish girl, and asked her, "Do you not think if you had been 500 carpenters or 500 masons, you would have succeeded?" "Certainly," she said, and then she told me of 200 bricklayers who had the year before been on strike and gained every point with their employers. "What could have made the difference? Their 200 were but a fraction of that trade, while your 500 absolutely controlled yours." Finally she said, "It was because the editors ridiculed and denounced us." "Did they ridicule and denounce the bricklayers?" "No." "What did they say about you?" "Why, that our wages were good enough now, better than those of any other workingwomen except teachers; and if we weren't satisfied, we had better go and get married." "What then do you think made this difference?" After

studying over the question awhile she concluded, "It must have been because our employers bribed the editors." "Couldn't the employers of the bricklayers have bribed the editors?" She had never thought of that. Most people never do think; they see one thing totally unlike another, but the person who stops to inquire into the cause that produces the one or the other is the exception. So this young Irish girl was simply not an exception, but followed the general rule of people, whether men or women; she hadn't thought. In the case of the bricklayers, no editor, either Democrat or Republican, would have accepted the proffer of a bribe, because he would have known that if he denounced or ridiculed those men, not only they but all the trade union men of the city at the next election would vote solidly against the nominees advocated by that editor. If those collar laundry women had been voters, they would have held, in that little city of Troy, the "balance of political power" and the editor or the politician who ignored or insulted them would have turned that balance over to the opposing party.

My friends, the condition of those collar laundry women but represents the utter helplessness of disfranchisement. The question with you, as men, is not whether you want your wives and daughters to vote, nor with you, as women, whether you yourselves want to vote; but whether you will help to put this power of the ballot into the hands of the 3,000,000 wage-earning women, so that they may be able to compel politicians to legislate in their favor and employers to grant them justice.

The law of capital is to extort the greatest amount of work for the least amount of money; the rule of labor is to do the smallest amount of work for the largest amount of money. Hence there is, and in the nature of things must continue to be, antagonism between the two classes; therefore, neither should be left wholly at the mercy of the other.

It was cruel, under the old regime, to give rich men the right to rule poor men. It was wicked to allow white men absolute power over black men. It is vastly more cruel, more wicked to give to all men— rich and poor, white and black, native and foreign, educated and ignorant, virtuous and vicious—this absolute control over women. Men talk of the injustice of monopolies. There never was, there never can be, a monopoly so fraught with injustice, tyranny and degradation as this monopoly of sex, of all men over all women. Therefore I not only agree with Abraham Lincoln that, "No man is good enough to govern another man without his consent;" but I say also that no man is good enough to govern a woman without her consent, and still further, that all men combined in government are not good enough to govern all women without their consent. There might have been some plausible excuse for the rich governing the poor, the educated governing the ignorant, the Saxon governing the African; but here can be none for making the husband the ruler of the wife, the brother of the sister, the man of the woman, his peer in birth, in education, in social position, in all that stands for the best and highest in humanity.

I believe that by nature men are no more unjust than women. If from the beginning women had maintained the right to rule not only themselves but men also, the latter today doubtless would be occupying the subordinate places with inferior pay in the world of work; women would be holding the higher positions with the big salaries; widowers would be doomed to a "life interest of one-third of the family estate"; husbands would "owe service" to their wives, so that every one of you men would be begging your good wives, "Please be so kind as to 'give me' ten cents for a cigar." The principle of self-government can not be violated with impunity. The individual's right to it is sacred—regardless of class, cast, race, color,

sex or any other accident or incident of birth. What we ask is that you shall cease to imagine that women are outside this law, and that you shall come into the knowledge that disfranchisement means the same degradation to your daughters as to your sons.

Governments can not afford to ignore the rights of those holding the ballot, who make and unmake every law and law-maker. It is not because the members of Congress are tyrants that women receive only half pay and are admitted only to inferior positions in the departments. It is simply in obedience to a law of political economy which makes it impossible for a government to do as much for the disfranchised as for the enfranchised. Women are no exception to the general rule. As disfranchisement always has degraded men, socially, morally, and industrially, so today it is disfranchisement that degrades women in the same spheres.

Again men say it is not votes, but the law of supply and demand which regulates wages. The law of gravity is that water shall run down hill, but when men build a dam across the stream, the force of gravity is stopped and the water held back. The law of supply and demand regulates free and enfranchised labor, but disfranchisement stops its operation. What we ask is the removal of the dam, that women, like men, may reap the benefit of the law. Did the law of supply and demand regulate work and wages in the olden days of slavery? This law can no more reach the disfranchised than it did the enslaved. There is scarcely a place where a woman can earn a single dollar without a man's consent.

There are many women equally well qualified with men for principals and superintendents of schools, and yet, while three-fourths of the teachers are women, nearly all of them are relegated to subordinate positions on half or at most two-thirds the salaries paid to men. The law of supply and demand is ignored, and that of sex alone settles the question. If a business man should advertise for a book-keeper and ten young men, equally well qualified should present themselves and, after looking them over, he should say, "To you who have red hair, we will pay full wages, while to you with black hair we will pay half the regular price," that would not be a more flagrant violation of the law of supply and demand than is now perpetrated upon women because of their sex.

And then again you say, "Capital, not the vote, regulates labor." Granted, for the sake of the argument, that capital does control the labor of women, Chinamen and slaves; but no one with eyes to see and ears to hear, will concede for a moment that capital absolutely dominates the work and wages of the free and enfranchised men of this republic. It is in order to lift the millions of our wage-earning women into a position of as much power over their own labor as men possess that they should be invested with the franchise. This ought to be done not only for the sake of justice to the women, but to the men with whom they compete; for, just so long as there is a degraded class of labor in the market, it always will be used by the capitalists to checkmate and undermine the superior classes.

Now that as a result of the agitation for equality of chances, and through the invention of machinery, there has come a great revolution in the world of economics, so that wherever a man may go to earn an honest dollar a woman may go also, there is no escape from the conclusion that she must be clothed with equal power to protect herself. That power is the ballot, the symbol of freedom and equality, without which no citizen is sure of keeping even that which he hath, much less of getting that which he hath not. Women are today the peers of men in education, in the arts and sciences, in the industries and professions, and there is no escape from the conclusion that the next step must be to

make them the peers of men in the government—city, State and national—to give them an equal voice in the framing, interpreting and administering of the codes and constitutions.

We recognize that the ballot is a two-edged, nay, a many-edged sword, which may be made to cut in every direction. If wily politicians and sordid capitalists may wield it for mere party and personal greed; if oppressed wage-earners may invoke it to wring justice from legislators and extort material advantages from employers; if the lowest and most degraded classes of men may use it to open wide the sluice-ways of vice and crime; if it may be the instrumentality by which the narrow, selfish, corrupt and corrupting men and measures rule—it is quite as true that noble-minded statesmen, philanthropists and reformers may make it the weapon with which to reverse the above order of things, as soon as they can have added to their now small numbers the immensely larger ratio of what men so love to call "the better half of the people." When women vote, they will make a new balance of power that must be weighed and measured and calculated in its effect upon every social and moral question which goes to the arbitrament of the ballot box. Who can doubt that when the representative women of thought and culture, who are today the moral backbone of our nation, sit in counsel with the best men of the country, higher conditions will be the result?

Insurrectionary and revolutionary methods of righting wrongs, imaginary or real, are pardonable only in the enslaved and disfranchised. The moment any class of men possess the ballot, it is their weapon and their shield. Men with a vote have no valid excuse for resorting to the use of illegal means to fight their battles. When the masses of wage-earning men are educated into a knowledge of their own rights and of their duties to others, so that they are able to vote intelligently, they can carry their measures through the ballot box and will have no need to resort to force. But so long as they remain in ignorance and are manipulated by the political bosses they will continue to vote against their own interests and turn again to violence to right their wrongs.

If men possessing the power of the ballot are driven to desperate means to gain their ends, what shall be done by disfranchised women? There are grave questions of moral, as well as of material interest in which women are most deeply concerned. Denied the ballot, the legitimate means with which to exert their influence, and, as a rule, being lovers of peace, they have recourse to prayers and tears, those potent weapons of women and children, and, when they fail, must tamely submit to wrong or rise in rebellion against the powers that be. Women's crusades against saloons, brothels and gambling-dens, emptying kegs and bottles into the streets, breaking doors and windows and burning houses, all go to prove that disfranchisement, the denial of lawful means to gain desired ends, may drive even women to violations of law and order. Hence to secure both national and "domestic tranquility," to "establish justice," to carry out the spirit of our Constitution, put into the hands of all women, as you have into those of all men, the ballot, that symbol of perfect equality, that right protective of all other rights.

"THE NECESSITY OF WOMAN SUFFRAGE"
1896

During the California suffrage campaign of 1896, Susan B. Anthony wrote dozens of articles on topics relating to woman suffrage for the *San Francisco Examiner*. In this essay, published in 1896, she reacts to a reporter's conclusions about women in politics in Colorado, which are stated in the excerpt that follows (see the *San Francisco Examiner*, May 17, 1896, in *Papers*).

The elevating influence of woman has not yet completely purified the Republican party in Colorado. The County Convention of Arapahoe county in which Denver is situated, rivaled a Barbary Coast picnic in its effort to disgust and intimidate its female Chairman and the other women who ventured to participate in its proceedings. Ribaldry, profanity and wild disorder were resorted to in the attempt to prove that only men were fit to cope with the stern duties of politics. Perhaps the intended effect may have been produced, but six months in the County Jail would have been an appropriate reward for the statesmen who achieved it.

When the editor wrote that did he realize what a new feature he had introduced into social economics? It is safe to say that the vast majority of newspapers in the country will deduce from the Colorado incident the conclusion that because of the action of these ruffians, women should retire from the political field. From one end of the country to the other the cry will go up: "This proves that women have no business in politics." We shall watch for any general expression, in fact for any further expression, to the effect that the men who were guilty of such conduct should be rewarded with "six months in jail."

There is a class of men in every State who use all the means in their power, who scruple at nothing, to prevent women from obtaining the franchise. Having failed in this, it is but natural that this rough and hoodlum element should endeavor to drive women out of politics. In all probability these reports are greatly exaggerated, but from what we know of the element which occasionally gets hold of a convention in other States besides Colorado, the proceedings very likely were of a nature to disgust men even who regard decency. The thing to do, as "The Examiner" says, is not to drive women out and leave this class in control, but to rally the respectable men of the State and see that such a scene never occurs again. I have recently attended three State Conventions in California, and during the entire proceedings there was not an incident that could offend or annoy a woman. The fourth, doubtless, will be no exception. This occurrence in Colorado emphasizes the necessity for taking politics out of the unworthy hands of the men who have brought it to its low estate. Too much honor cannot be given to the brave Colorado women who refused to be driven from the position to which they were as much entitled as any man in the convention. It is gratifying to know that the women of Arapahoe county are clothed with that authority which alone is able to overcome such men as disgraced the convention. While, perhaps, there is no law which can give them the six months in jail, they probably will be allowed to serve a long term in private life.

From time immemorial the rule has been not to punish the male offender, but to get the victim out of his way. If a little girl is bullied and abused by a little boy while out in the yard at play the girl is taken into the house while the boy is left in full possession of the yard. If women are insulted on the street at night the authorities, instead of making the streets safe for them, insist that they remain indoors. Some places have gone so far as to make it a finable offense for women to be out after a certain hour. Even in the matter of woman's dress men have arrogated to themselves authority, and whether it was a Mother Hubbard wrapper or a bloomer costume, have taken legislative action prohibiting it. At Huntington, Long Island, the School Board forbade the women teachers to ride to school on bicycles, "as it

produced immorality among the pupils," but the men teachers were not interfered with. In many places school boards have forbidden women teachers to ride a bicycle, and a number of ministers, including Bishop Coxe, have preached against it. These are but the expressions of the old idea that the man has dominion over the woman and that she should be subject to his authority in all things.

There has been no royal road for woman, but every step of the way into freedom has been as hard as it was possible to make it. One would suppose that teaching always had been considered a proper avocation for women, but in the early history of the United States only men were employed. Fifty years ago women were considered competent to teach only summer schools which boys did not attend, and for this were paid six dollars a month, while men holding similar positions and not so well educated received thirty dollars a month. At present there are only two States in the Union where men and women teachers receive equal pay for equal work, and in most vocations the same holds true. In every occupation which woman enters she is at first treated with discourtesy and opposition, and in many instances she is never able entirely to overcome the prejudice.

The opposition to woman suffrage, strong as it is in many quarters, is not so bitter as was the determination to prevent women from speaking in public. The delighted crowds which, during the past few weeks, have listened to the many able women speakers here in California could hardly believe the story that might be told of the first attempts of women to speak in public in this country. In 1853 Antoinette L. Brown, a beautiful and eloquent woman, went to New York as a delegate to a world's temperance convention. Although women at that time were doing a great work for temperance, and although she was armed with the proper credentials, the men refused to let her speak. For three hours she stood on the platform without wavering, while the men of the convention, a large proportion of them ministers, yelled, howled, hissed, cheered and drowned her voice every time she attempted to use it. At last, when they were so thoroughly exhausted they could make no more noise they took a vote and ruled her out.

When Lucy Stone graduated at Oberlin in 1849, a coeducational college, she was not allowed to read her essay because it was so unwomanly for a woman to appear on a platform. Afterward, when in her gentle, modest way she began to speak for the cause of woman, the men in her audience turned the hose on her, and one of them threw a book and hit her head. Similar accounts could be given of many of the women who attempted to speak in public forty years ago.

Women who have studied for the ministry have been accorded no better treatment because the students with whom they were associated were preparing to spread the gospel of Christ. At the theological schools they have been ignored, snubbed and insulted, usually without protest from the faculty. While possibly five hundred are now preaching in the United States, their path is not one of roses, and they are far from receiving the attentions and adulations that are so abundantly showered upon the masculine preacher.

Perhaps the way was hardest of all for the women of the early days who wished to study medicine. When women first entered the medical department of the University of Pennsylvania, about 1868, they were followed on the streets by the male students, insulted and reviled and finally mobbed, and had to seek protection. When women were first admitted to the clinics in the hospitals of New York, the lecturing physicians made their lectures and their illustrations so obscene that Elizabeth Cady Stanton and other distinguished women of that city were obliged to accompany girl students and remain with them. While such occurrences as these would not now be tolerated, the woman physician still finds herself at a disadvantage, no matter what her qualifications, because of the deep-seated, ancient prejudice against the enlargement of what had been marked out as woman's sphere. . . .

Even in the coeducational colleges the girls are dubbed "co-eds," and made to feel in many ways by the male students that it is a great condescension and tolerance on their part to permit them to share in the advantages of the institution. It will be found in all such cases that the students reflect the sentiments of the Faculty in this regard, and the position of the latter may be accurately judged by the actions of the body of the students. The Faculty creates the atmosphere of respect or disrespect by which the girls are surrounded.

Upon no one of these progressive movements—not upon all of them together—was there such adverse criticism as when it was proposed to amend the laws so as to permit married women to hold property in their own name. The flood of billingsgate was opened. It was declared on the floor of Legislatures that if women owned a pocketbook they would forsake their homes and children; they would run away with other men; families would be broken up; general chaos would take the place of peaceful households. There was a long and bitter fight, extending through many years, before this privilege was secured for women. And yet where now is the man who would advocate the repeal of this law?

These are not pleasant subjects to dwell upon, but it is necessary to study the history of the past in order to apply its lessons to the problems of the present. Wendell Phillips said, "To talk of freedom for the black man without the ballot is mockery." O. B. Frothingham declared, "Though a man have everything which the world deems desirable, without the ballot he has nothing, because he has not the power to protect that which he has." The ballot, the right protective of all other rights, which woman should have had equally with man from the foundation of the republic, is the last to be placed in her hands. But the opposition, which has fought every progressive step, still blocks the way, still interposes the same old arguments, still sounds the same notes of alarm and waves the same old scarecrows—abandoned husbands, neglected children, forsaken homes, the loss of all womanly charms, a general upheaval of social conditions.

One would think that when each and all of these prophecies had been made of every progressive step taken by women during the last fifty years, and not one had been fulfilled, that even the dullest and narrowest would realize their utter shallowness and absurdity. Everything that woman has done for herself, all that has been done for her by others, to enlarge her sphere of usefulness and influence, has been not only of inestimable advantage to herself, but also to her husband, her children, her home and society. Far beyond the benefits derived from the privileges already granted will be those which shall result in making her absolutely free in the exercise of every civil and political right.

CHRONOLOGY

1820   Susan Brownell Anthony born in Adams, Massachusetts, the second child of Daniel and Lucy Read Anthony.

1822   Daniel Anthony builds and operates his own cotton textile mill in Adams.

1826   Anthony family moves to Battenville, New York, where Daniel assumes the management of a cotton mill.

1827   Following the Great Separation of 1827, U.S. Quakers divide into two groups. Daniel Anthony and his family concur with the majority and become part of the more liberal Hicksite faction.

1833   Accepted as a member of the Quaker Meeting in Easton, New York.

1834   Sister Eliza Anthony dies at the age of two years from scarlet fever.

1835   Begins her first teaching job, instructing young children in the summer session at her father's home school.

1836   Leaves home to teach and board with a family in Easton, New York. Earns $1 a week.

1837   Enrolls in Quaker Deborah Moulson's female seminary in Pennsylvania, where her sister Guelma is already a student. Meets Lydia Mott, who becomes a lifelong friend and colleague.

1838   Hears Lucretia Coffin Mott lecture while a student at Moulson's school.

Daniel Anthony's businesses fail as a result of the Panic of 1837. Susan and Guelma must withdraw from school and return to Battenville. Susan attends a local school and helps support her family by teaching.

1839   Anthony family forced to sell their home in Battenville and move to the neighboring village of Hardscrabble. Susan teaches at Eunice Kenyon's Quaker boarding school in New Rochelle, New York. Guelma marries Aaron McLean, a close friend of both Guelma's and Susan's.

1845   Susan moves with her family to a farm in Rochester, New York.

1846   Susan's sister Hannah marries Eugene Mosher, a businessman from Easton, New York. Daniel and the rest of the Anthony family become friends with a community of Hicksite Quakers who are dedicated to radical social reform, particularly abolitionism. Susan accepts a job as a teacher and headmistress of female students at Canajoharie Academy, in Canajoharie, New York, where her uncle Joshua Read is a trustee.

1848   Begins her career in reform. Joins the Canajoharie chapter of the Daughters of Temperance. Chosen to act as "Presiding Sister," or secretary of the organization. Learns the details of the second woman's rights convention held in Rochester from her sister Mary and her parents, who attended.

Chronology   *303*

1849 Delivers her first public speech at a Daughters of Temperance gathering. Resigns from her post at Canajoharie Academy and returns home to Rochester, where she joins that city's chapter of the Daughters of Temperance. Becomes increasingly interested in the abolitionist movement through her Rochester Hicksite Quaker connections.

1850 Attracted to the women's rights movement after reading a speech in the *New York Tribune* that had been delivered by abolitionist and women's rights activist Lucy Stone at the First National Woman's Rights Convention in Worcester, Massachusetts.

1851 Meets abolitionists Abby Kelley Foster and Stephen Symonds Foster in Rochester and accompanies them on a lecture tour of northern New York. Develops an intense interest in the abolitionist movement. Meets Elizabeth Cady Stanton. Meets Lucy Stone at a meeting to discuss coeducational colleges. Intensifies her temperance activism.

1852 Forms the Woman's State Temperance Society and travels throughout the state to encourage women to organize temperance societies. Circulates petitions and campaigns in support of legislation that would prohibit most retail alcohol sales. Attends her first woman's rights convention, the Third National Woman's Rights Convention in Syracuse, New York, where she meets leaders of the women's rights movement Lucretia Coffin Mott, Antoinette Brown (Blackwell), Gerrit Smith, Martha Coffin Wright, Matilda Joslyn Gage, Paulina Wright Davis, and Ernestine Potowski Rose. Makes the difficult decision to begin wearing the Bloomer costume.

1853 Withdraws from leadership of the Woman's State Temperance Society when conservatives assume power and oust Cady Stanton from the presidency. Transfers activism to the women's rights movement. To encourage women teachers to demand equal pay and an equal role in their profession, attends state teachers' convention. Participates in a successful temperance lecture tour with Antoinette Brown (Blackwell) and Amelia Jenks Bloomer.

1854 Accompanies Ernestine Potowski Rose on a women's rights lecture tour of Washington D.C., and southern cities. After observing and being horrified by the institution of slavery, she deepens her commitment to abolitionism. Plans and begins a campaign to expand the Married Women's Property Law of 1848 in New York state.

1855 Executes and completes her first winter of work on the New York Married Women's Property Law campaign. Anthony is dismayed when Lucy Stone announces that she will marry and mourns the loss of her activism. Suffers from severe back strain and exhaustion, and decides to recuperate at a water-cure spa in Worcester, Massachusetts. Her time in New England gives her the opportunity to visit and become closer to New England abolitionists and reformers.

1856 Continues campaign for women's property rights. Accepts position as New York general agent of the American Anti-Slavery Society (AASS). Serves as principal organizer of the Seventh National Woman's Rights Convention.

1857 Writes and delivers her "What Is American Slavery?" speech, which protests the *Dred Scott* decision. After developing a commitment to disunionism, Anthony organizes and directs a "No Union with Slaveholders" tour of AASS field lecturers throughout New York state. Anthony cannot carry out a national woman's rights convention because Cady Stanton, Antoinette Brown Blackwell, and Lucy Stone are all consumed by their domestic responsibilities. Begins planning and writing her speech "The True Woman," which she works on until 1859.

1858 Spends the winter months directing groups of male and female AASS lecturers across New York state. Lectures on the benefits of coeducation. Organizes a protest meeting against capital punishment in the case of Ira Stout, a man condemned to hang for murder. Receives news from Wendell Phillips that she has been named a trustee of the Jackson Fund, to benefit the women's rights cause. Organizes the Eighth National Woman's Rights Convention.

1859 Faces mobs nearly everywhere that she and her troupe of AASS lecturers speak as antiabolitionist fervor intensifies. Directs the Ninth National Woman's Rights Convention. Advises executors of the Hovey Fund on how to allocate appropriations intended to support abolitionist and women's rights reform. Holds a memorial for the executed John Brown in Rochester in December. Sends the proceeds to his widow and children.

1860 Continues to shepherd AASS lecturers during the winter months. Lobbies New York state legislators for six weeks prior to the legislature's vote enacting the expanded Married Women's Property Law. Organizes and executes the Tenth National Woman's Rights Convention, the last held until after the Civil War. Challenges Wendell Phillips's and William Lloyd Garrison's critique of Cady Stanton's resolutions about divorce reform that were presented at the convention. Assists in the rescue of a woman tyrannized by her husband and brothers in the face of Garrison's and Phillips's opposition.

1861 Conducts the "No Compromise with Slaveholders" tour of New York state. Confronts the most violent audiences of her experience as many northerners blame the impending national crisis on the actions of the abolitionists. Must cancel the Eleventh National Woman's Rights Convention because her colleagues insist that agitation, whether for women's rights or abolition, will harm the Union cause. Returns to Rochester to work on the farm and spend time with her family.

1862 Meets and begins a close friendship with the abolitionist orator Anna Elizabeth Dickinson. Lectures on abolition and the abuses of northern racial prejudice throughout New York state. Mourns the loss of her father, Daniel Anthony, who dies in November.

1863 After Lincoln announces the Emancipation Proclamation, Anthony and Cady Stanton establish the Woman's National Loyal League (WNLL) in New York City and lead the WNLL's petition drive to persuade Congress to pass a Thirteenth Amendment guaranteeing the freedom of African Americans. Anthony protests publicly the failure of Lincoln's Emancipation Proclamation to protect African Americans.

1864 The Senate passes the Thirteenth Amendment in April. By August, the WNLL collects more than 400,000 signatures supporting the amendment. Senator Charles Sumner assures Anthony and Cady Stanton that the House will soon pass the amendment. They close the New York City WNLL office in the fall when the amendment's passage seems imminent. They campaign on behalf of Republican presidential candidate John C. Frémont.

1865 The House passes the Thirteenth Amendment in January, and it is sent to the states for ratification. Anthony travels to Leavenworth, Kansas, during the final weeks of the war to visit her brother, D. R. Anthony. Observing the pressing needs of emancipated African Americans who have flooded into Kansas, she organizes freedmen's relief. Encourages African Americans to combat racial prejudice and discrimination by helping them to form their own equal rights league. Lectures

1865
cont.
throughout Kansas on the evils of Lincoln's and Johnson's reconstruction policies. Returns east by late summer to protest the wording of a proposed version of the Fourteenth Amendment that endangers women's claim to their rights and citizenship.

1866 Plans and executes the Eleventh National Woman's Rights Convention with Cady Stanton. Helps found the American Equal Rights Association (AERA), an organization dedicated to securing universal suffrage.

1867 Conducts an unsuccessful campaign to persuade New York legislators to alter language in the state constitution barring women from the suffrage. Travels to Kansas on behalf of a woman suffrage referendum, where she campaigns with the racist Democrat George Francis Train. Following the failure of the Kansas campaign, Anthony tours and lectures in midwestern and eastern cities. She returns home to face the outrage of fellow AERA members over her association with Train and is accused of misusing AERA funds.

1868 Establishes *The Revolution* with Cady Stanton, with money provided by Train. Persuades Senator Samuel Clarke Pomeroy and Representative George Washington Julian to propose a Sixteenth Amendment resolution in both houses of Congress. After organizing the Working Women's Association (WWA), attends the National Labor Union Congress as a WWA delegate. Becomes estranged from old friends and colleagues Lucy Stone, Henry Blackwell, Wendell Phillips, William Lloyd Garrison, and other Republican abolitionists because of their exclusive focus on gaining the ballot for African Americans. Realizes the need for a national woman suffrage association.

1869 Organizes the first woman suffrage convention, as part of her and Cady Stanton's Woman Suffrage Association of America. Attends explosive final

meeting of the AERA in May and, shortly thereafter, founds the National Woman Suffrage Association (NWSA) with Cady Stanton and other women's rights activists. They dedicate the NWSA to obtaining a Sixteenth Amendment guaranteeing women's right to vote. Anthony convinces employers to start a typesetters' school for unskilled women during a typesetters' strike. Accused of strikebreaking at the National Labor Union Congress and is forced to withdraw her membership. Attends the founding convention of Stone and Blackwell's American Woman Suffrage Association (AWSA) in Cleveland, Ohio, in November. Asks AWSA members to join forces with her and the NWSA to demand that Congress pass a Sixteenth Amendment. Wyoming's territorial legislature enacts woman suffrage in December.

1870 Utah territorial legislature extends the suffrage to women. Anthony terminates publication of *The Revolution* for financial reasons. Cady Stanton refuses to help settle debt, so Anthony assumes full responsibility of the paper's remaining $10,000 debt. Theodore Tilton attempts to unite the NWSA and the AWSA, with Anthony and Cady Stanton's cooperation. Merger efforts fail when the AWSA rejects his proposal. Anthony embarks on a woman suffrage tour of the Midwest to begin to pay *The Revolution* debt.

1871 Participates in a suffrage lecture tour of California with Cady Stanton, then tours and lectures throughout Oregon and Washington Territory with Abigail Scott Duniway. Meets Victoria Claflin Woodhull and is impressed. Anthony is encouraged by the possibilities of the "New Departure" strategy, which declares that the Fourteenth and Fifteenth Amendments already give women the right to vote.

1872 Prevents Victoria Claflin Woodhull from taking over the NWSA convention. To earn money to pay off *The*

Revolution debt, continues to tour as a lyceum lecturer. Focuses NWSA activities on broadcasting the "New Departure" theories. Campaigns for Ulysses S. Grant, Republican presidential candidate. After voting with other women in the 1872 presidential election in Rochester, Anthony is arrested by a U.S. marshal for having committed the federal "crime" of voting. The newspapers' coverage of the Beecher-Tilton Scandal erroneously associates suffragists with the free-love movement.

1873   Anthony is indicted, tried, and convicted of voting illegally in the case *United States v. Susan B. Anthony*. Prior to the trial, she and Matilda Joslyn Gage lecture throughout Monroe and Ontario Counties in New York to publicize the constitutional arguments upholding her right to vote. Nurses older sister Guelma Anthony McLean through her final fatal illness.

1874   Besieged by reporters demanding information about the Beecher-Tilton Scandal, Anthony bemoans the scandal's effects on the NWSA and the woman suffrage movement. Continues lecturing throughout the country on the lyceum circuit to repay *The Revolution* debt.

1875   In the wake of the Supreme Court's adverse decision in the case of *Minor v. Happersett,* Anthony and her fellow suffragists abandon the "New Departure" strategy and urge the NWSA to refocus efforts to achieve a Sixteenth Amendment. Anthony pays the remainder of *The Revolution* debt. Lectures throughout Iowa in support of a woman suffrage bill. When her brother D. R. is seriously wounded by a rival publisher, Anthony rushes to Leavenworth to help care for him. Anthony is bereft when her closest confidante and adviser, Lydia Mott, dies.

1876   With Cady Stanton and Matilda Joslyn Gage, writes the *Declaration of the Rights of Woman* and delivers this manifesto at the Centennial Exposition, held in Independence Square in Philadelphia. Anthony and Cady Stanton begin to discuss their plan to write a history of the women's rights and woman suffrage movements.

1877   Cares for her dying younger sister Hannah Anthony Mosher through the final days of her illness. Anthony worries that she will succumb to tuberculosis, as did Guelma and Hannah. Campaigns in the Colorado suffrage campaign, which she declares is the most arduous of her career thus far.

1878   Spends nine months of the year traveling and lecturing for woman suffrage. In her absence, Cady Stanton persuades Senator Aaron Augustus Sargent to propose her newly worded version of the Sixteenth Amendment to Congress.

1879   Anthony meets with President Rutherford B. Hayes to ask that he persuade Congress to protect women's civil and political rights. Continues to pursue the Sixteenth Amendment campaign. Meets Rachel Foster, a young Quaker woman, who becomes devoted to suffragism.

1880   Launches a massive program to persuade political party leaders to include woman suffrage in their party platforms. With Cady Stanton and Joslyn Gage, actively engages in the writing of the *History of Woman Suffrage (HWS).* Remains in the Rochester area during the final months of her mother Lucy Read Anthony's life. Lectures widely on woman suffrage. Rejoices that Frances Willard, president of the Woman's Christian Temperance Union, is recruiting temperance women to fight for the "Home Protection Ballot" and woman suffrage.

1881   Volume 1 of the *History of Woman Suffrage* is published. Anthony and Cady Stanton begin work on volume 2.

1882   The Senate finally responds to the
        NWSA's demand that a Senate Select
        Committee on Woman Suffrage be
        organized. Volume 2 of the *HWS* is
        published. Susan helps Rachel Foster
        lead the Nebraska suffrage campaign.

1883   Tours Europe with Rachel Foster and
        meets with European feminists. In
        England, discusses plans for an Interna-
        tional Council of Women (ICW) with
        Cady Stanton. Develops a warm,
        intimate friendship with Foster while
        in Europe.

1884   Initiates planning for the first ICW, to
        be held in 1888 in Washington, D.C.
        Spends months working on volume 3
        of *HWS* with Cady Stanton.

1886   Volume 3 of *HWS* is published.
        Anthony delivers her annual address to
        Congress on behalf of a woman
        suffrage amendment.

1887   Anthony and NAWSA suffragists
        protest the federal Edmunds-Tucker
        Act, which disfranchises Utah women
        who had been voting since 1870. The
        Senate votes against the Sixteenth
        Amendment, but Anthony is encour-
        aged that more senators support it than
        ever before. Stone proposes a meeting
        with Anthony to discuss the possibility
        of a merger of the AWSA and the
        NWSA. Anthony and Foster meet with
        Stone and Alice Blackwell in Boston
        for the first merger meeting. Anthony
        welcomes temperance women and
        religious conservatives into the ranks of
        the NWSA, though many of her first-
        generation suffrage colleagues fear that
        conservative women will alter the
        NWSA's mission and agenda.

1888   Helps lead the International Council of
        Women (ICW). Meets and enlists
        orator Anna Howard Shaw as an
        NWSA lecturer. Merger negotiations
        between NWSA and AWSA proceed.
        Susan, disturbed by Rachel Foster's
        marriage to Cyrus Avery, intensifies her
        search for a future top suffrage leader.

1889   Travels to South Dakota to help state
        suffragists commence their planning
        for that state's woman suffrage cam-
        paign. As merger negotiations proceed,
        Anthony is forced to handle protests
        against the merger from dissenting
        NWSA leaders Olympia Brown, Joslyn
        Gage, Lillie Devereux Blake, and others.

1890   Supervises the first convention of the
        National American Woman Suffrage
        Association (NAWSA), the new
        merger organization of the NWSA and
        the AWSA, and successfully struggles to
        have Cady Stanton elected its first
        president. Travels to South Dakota for
        its state suffrage campaign. After
        working on the campaign with
        NAWSA activists Carrie Chapman
        Catt and Anna Howard Shaw, Anthony
        becomes aware of their strong leader-
        ship potential.

1891   Establishes a permanent home with her
        sister Mary Anthony at the family
        home in Rochester. Cady Stanton
        declines Anthony's invitation to live
        with her, to her deep disappointment.

1892   Anthony is elected president of
        NAWSA. She struggles to have
        women's achievements made a
        prominent part of the upcoming 1893
        World's Fair.

1893   Attends the World's Fair and the ICW
        in Chicago. Attends many national
        political conventions in the hope that a
        political party will add a woman
        suffrage plank to its platform, but none
        complies. Lucy Stone dies. Anthony
        supervises the Colorado suffrage
        campaign from the East. Colorado
        becomes the first state to enact woman
        suffrage by a popular referendum,
        thanks to the efforts of a rising power
        in NAWSA, Chapman Catt.

1894   Spends the year campaigning in two
        long, grueling suffrage battles in Kansas
        and New York. Both efforts fail.

1895   Travels to California to prepare state
        suffragists to lead an 1896 campaign for

woman suffrage. Cady Stanton's publication of *The Woman's Bible* embroils Anthony in controversy and protests.

1896 NAWSA leads a successful suffrage campaign in Idaho, and the state votes to enfranchise women. Spends eight months working on the California suffrage campaign, the most extensive state struggle of its time. Ida Husted Harper agrees to write her biography. NAWSA leaders vote to censure *The Woman's Bible,* which enrages Anthony.

1897 Compiles her two-volume biography with Husted Harper in Rochester. (A third volume is written and published in 1908, after Anthony's death.)

1898 Husted Harper's two-volume biography, *The Life and Work of Susan B. Anthony,* is published.

1899 Leads the U.S. delegation to the ICW in London. She focuses attention on selecting a leader to succeed her as president of NAWSA.

1900 Resigns as president of NAWSA but remains active in the organization. Carrie Chapman Catt is elected NAWSA president with Anthony's support. Anthony is instrumental in securing the admission of women to the University of Rochester. Her youngest sibling, Jacob Merritt Anthony, dies unexpectedly.

1901 Spends months recovering from a stroke suffered in 1900. Works on compiling and completing volume 4 of the *History of Woman Suffrage* with Husted Harper.

1902 Makes final appearance before the Senate Select Committee on Woman Suffrage. Grieves for Cady Stanton, who dies at the age of 87. Volume 4 of *HWS* is published.

1903 Distributes hundreds of volumes of *HWS* to public schools, colleges, and libraries. Attends the NAWSA convention in New Orleans.

1904 Travels to Europe to attend the ICW and the first convention of the International Woman Suffrage Alliance in Berlin. Rushes to Leavenworth, Kansas, for final visit with her dying brother, D. R. Anthony. Persuades Anna Howard Shaw to become president of NAWSA when Chapman Catt steps down.

1905 Anna Howard Shaw becomes president of NAWSA. Anthony crosses the country to attend the NAWSA convention in Portland, Oregon. Meets with President Theodore Roosevelt in Washington to ask him to urge Congress to support a woman suffrage amendment.

1906 Attends her last NAWSA convention and enjoys her last birthday celebration. Dies at home in Rochester, New York on March 13, with Shaw and her sister Mary by her side. Ten thousand mourners arrive in Rochester to pay her homage.

BIBLIOGRAPHY

Anthony, Katharine. 1954. *Susan B. Anthony: Her Personal History and Her Era.* Garden City, N.Y.: Doubleday.

Aptheker, Bettina. 1982. *Woman's Legacy: Essays on Race, Sex and Class in American History.* Amherst: University of Massachusetts Press.

Aptheker, Herbert. 1989. *Abolitionism: A Revolutionary Movement.* Boston: Twayne Publishers.

Arling, Emanie Sachs. 1928. *"The Terrible Siren": Victoria Woodhull (1838–1927).* New York: Harper and Bros.

Bacon, Margaret Hope. 1980. *Valiant Friend: The Life of Lucretia Mott.* New York: Walker.

———. 1985. *The Quiet Rebels: The Story of the Quakers in America.* Philadelphia: New Society Publishers.

———. 1986. *Mothers of Feminism: The Story of Quaker Women in America.* San Francisco: Harper and Row.

Barry, Kathleen. 1988. *Susan B. Anthony: Biography of a Singular Feminist.* New York: New York University Press.

Bartlett, Irving H. 1961. *Wendell Phillips: Brahmin Radical.* Boston: Beacon Press.

Beeton, Beverly. 1986. *Women Vote in the West: The Woman Suffrage Movement 1869–1896.* New York: Garland Publishing.

———. 1991. "How the West Was Won for Woman Suffrage." In *One Woman, One Vote: Rediscovering the Woman Suffrage Movement,* ed. Marjorie Spruill Wheeler. Troutdale, Oreg.: New Sage Press.

The Biographical Record of the City of Rochester and Monroe County, New York. 1902. New York and Chicago: S. J. Clarke Publishing.

Blackwell, Alice Stone. 1930. *Lucy Stone: Pioneer of Women's Rights.* Boston: Little Brown.

Blake, Katherine Devereux, and Margaret Louise Wallace. 1943. *Champion of Women: The Life of Lillie Devereux Blake.* New York: Fleming H. Revell.

Blassingame, John W., Mae G. Henderson, and Jessica M. Dunn, eds. 1980–1984. *Antislavery Newspapers and Periodicals.* 4 vols. Boston: G. K. Hall.

Blocker, Jack S., Jr. 1989. *American Temperance Movements: Cycles of Reform.* Boston: Twayne Publishers.

Blockson, Charles L. 1987. *The Underground Railroad.* New York: Prentice Hall.

Blodgett, Geoffrey. 1971. "Blackwell, Alice Stone." In *Notable American Women 1607–1950: A Biographical Dictionary,* ed. Edward T. James, Janet Wilson James, and Paul S. Boyer. Cambridge, Mass.: Belknap Press of Harvard University Press, 1:156–158.

Bogin, Ruth. April 1974. "Sarah Parker Remond: Black Abolitionist from Salem." *Essex Institute Historical Collections* 110:2.

Bordin, Ruth. 1981. *Woman and Temperance: The Quest for Power and Liberty, 1873–1900.* Philadelphia: Temple University Press.

———. 1986. *Frances Willard: A Biography.* Chapel Hill: University of North Carolina Press.

Bovée, Warren G. 1986. "Horace Greeley and Social Responsibility." *Journalism Quarterly* 63, no. 2 (summer):251–259.

Boyd, Melba Joyce. 1994. *Discarded Legacy: Politics and Poetics in the Life of Frances E. W. Harper, 1825–1911.* Detroit: Wayne State University Press.

Boydston, Jeanne, Mary Kelley, and Anne Margolis. 1988. *The Limits of Sisterhood: The Beecher Sisters on Women's Rights and Women's Sphere.* Chapel Hill: University of North Carolina Press.

Brown, Olympia. 1917. *Democratic Ideals: A Memorial Sketch of Clara B. Colby.* n.p. A Federal Suffrage Association Publication.

Buckmaster, Henrietta. 1941, 1992. *Let My People Go: The Story of the Underground Railroad and the Abolition Movement.* Columbia: University of South Carolina Press.

Buechler, Steven M. 1990. *Women's Movements in the United States: Woman Suffrage, Equal Rights, and Beyond.* New Brunswick, N.J.: Rutgers University Press.

Buhle, Mary Jo, and Paul Buhle, eds. 1978. *A Concise History of Woman Suffrage: Selections from the Classic Work of Stanton, Anthony, Gage, and Harper.* Urbana: University of Illinois Press.

Burton, David Henry. 1995. *Clara Barton: In the Service of Humanity.* Westport, Conn.: Greenwood Press.

Cain, William E., ed. 1995. *William Lloyd Garrison and the Fight against Slavery.* New York: Bedford Press.

Campbell, Karlyn Kohrs. 1993. *Women Public Speakers in the United States, 1800–1925: A Bio-Critical Sourcebook.* Westport, Conn.: Greenwood Press.

Catt, Carrie Chapman, and Nettie Rogers Shuler. 1926. *Woman Suffrage and Politics: The Inner Story of the Suffrage Movement.* New York: Charles Scribner's Sons.

Cazden, Elizabeth. 1983. *Antoinette Brown Blackwell: A Biography.* Old Westbury, N.Y.: Feminist Press.

Clark, Clifford E., Jr. 1978. *Henry Ward Beecher: Spokesman for a Middle-Class America.* Urbana: University of Illinois Press.

Collier-Thomas, Bettye. 1997. "Frances Ellen Watkins Harper: Abolitionist and Feminist Reformer 1825–1911." In *African American Women and the Vote, 1837–1965,* ed. Ann D. Gordon. Amherst: University of Massachusetts Press.

Cott, Nancy F. 1987. *The Grounding of Modern Feminism.* New Haven, Conn.: Yale University Press.

———, ed. 1994. *The History of Women in the United States.* 21 vols. New York: K.G. Saur.

Cromwell, Otelia. 1958. *Lucretia Mott.* Cambridge, Mass.: Harvard University Press.

Davis, Angela Y. 1983. *Women, Race, and Class.* New York: Vintage Books.

Davis, Paulina W. 1871. *A History of the National Woman's Rights Movement for Twenty Years.* Republished 1970. New York: Source Book Press.

Derbyshire, Lynne. 1993. "Paulina Kellogg Wright Davis." In *Women Public Speakers in the United States, 1800–1925: A Bio-Critical Sourcebook,* ed. Karlyn Kohrs Campbell. Westport, Conn.: Greenwood Press.

Dillon, Mary Earhart. 1971. "Frances Elizabeth Caroline Willard." In *Notable American Women 1607–1950: A Biographical Dictionary,* ed. Edward T. James, Janet Wilson James, and Paul S. Boyer. Cambridge, Mass.: Belknap Press of Harvard University Press, 3:613–619.

Dorr, Rheta Childe. 1928. *Susan B. Anthony: The Woman Who Changed the Mind of a Nation*. New York: Frederick A. Stokes.

Douglass, Frederick. 1955. "Woman and the Ballot." In *The Life and Writings of Frederick Douglass*, Vol. 4, ed. Philip S. Foner. New York: International Publishers, pp. 235–239.

———. 1994. *Frederick Douglass Autobiographies*. New York: Library of America.

DuBois, Ellen Carol. 1978. *Feminism and Suffrage: The Emergence of an Independent Women's Movement in America 1848–1869*. Ithaca, N.Y.: Cornell University Press.

———. 1987. "Outgrowing the Compact of the Fathers: Equal Rights, Woman Suffrage, and the United States Constitution, 1820–1878." *Journal of American History* 74, no. 3 (December):836–862.

———. 1991. "Making Women's History: Activist Historians of Women's Rights, 1880–1940." *Radical History Review*, no. 49:61–84.

———. 1995. "Taking the Law into Our Own Hands: Bradwell, Minor, and Suffrage Militance in the 1870s." In *One Woman, One Vote: Rediscovering the Woman Suffrage Movement*, ed. Marjorie Spruill Wheeler. Troutdale, Oreg.: New Sage Press.

———. 1997. *Harriot Stanton Blatch and the Winning of Woman Suffrage*. New Haven, Conn.: Yale University Press.

———, ed. 1992. *The Elizabeth Cady Stanton–Susan B. Anthony Reader: Correspondence, Writings, Speeches*. Boston: Northeastern University Press.

DuBois, Eugene E. 1994. *The City of Frederick Douglass: Rochester's African-American People and Places*. Rochester: Landmark Society of Western New York.

Duniway, Abigail Scott. 1971. *Path Breaking: An Autobiographical History of the Equal Suffrage Movement in the Pacific Coast States*. New York: Schocken Books.

Dunn, Mary Maples. 1979. "Women of Light." In *Women of America, a History*, ed. Carol Ruth Berkin and Mary Beth Norton. Boston: Houghton Mifflin.

Earhart, Mary. 1944. *Frances Willard: From Prayers to Politics*. Chicago: University of Chicago Press.

Edwards, G. Thomas. 1990. *Sowing Good Seeds: The Northwest Suffrage Campaigns of Susan B. Anthony*. Portland: Oregon Historical Society Press.

"Ernestine Potowski Rose." In *Women Public Speakers in the United States, 1800–1925: A Bio-Critical Sourcebook*, ed. Karlyn Kohrs Campbell. Westport, Conn.: Greenwood Press.

Flexner, Eleanor. 1971a. "Shaw, Anna Howard." In *Notable American Women 1607–1950: A Biographical Dictionary*, ed. Edward T. James, Janet Wilson James, and Paul S. Boyer. Cambridge, Mass.: Belknap Press of Harvard University Press, 3:274–277.

———. 1971b. "Catt, Carrie Clinton Lane Chapman." In *Notable American Women 1607–1950: A Biographical Dictionary*, ed. Edward T. James, Janet Wilson James, and Paul S. Boyer. Cambridge, Mass.: Belknap Press of Harvard University Press, 1:309–313.

———. 1975. *Century of Struggle: The Woman's Rights Movement in the United States*. Cambridge, Mass.: Belknap Press of Harvard University Press.

Foner, Eric. 1988. *Reconstruction: America's Unfinished Revolution, 1863–1877*. New York: Harper and Row.

Fowler, Robert Booth. 1986. *Carrie Catt: Feminist Politician*. Boston: Northeastern University Press.

Friedman, Lawrence J. 1982. *Gregarious Saints: Self and Community in American Abolitionism, 1830–1870*. New York: Cambridge University Press.

Frost-Knappman, Elizabeth. 1994. *ABC-CLIO Companion to Women's Progress in America*. Santa Barbara, Calif.: ABC-CLIO.

Giele, Janet Zollinger. 1995. *Two Paths to Women's Equality: Temperance, Suffrage, and the Origins of Modern Feminism*. New York: Twayne Publishers.

Gifford, Carolyn De Swarte. 1995. "Frances Willard and the Woman's Christian Temperance Union's Conversion to Woman Suffrage." In *One Woman, One Vote: Rediscovering the Woman Suffrage Movement,* ed. Marjorie Spruill Wheeler. Troutdale, Oreg.: New Sage Press.

Gordon, Ann D., and Tamara Gaskell Miller, eds. 1997. *The Selected Papers of Elizabeth Cady Stanton and Susan B. Anthony*. Vol. 1. New Brunswick, N.J.: Rutgers University Press.

Graham, Sara Hunter. 1996. *Woman Suffrage and the New Democracy*. New Haven, Conn.: Yale University Press.

Graves, Lawrence L. 1971. "Brown, Olympia." In *Notable American Women 1607–1950: A Biographical Dictionary,* ed. Edward T. James, Janet Wilson James, and Paul S. Boyer. Cambridge, Mass.: Belknap Press of Harvard University Press, 1:256–258.

Green, Norma Kidd. 1971. "Colby, Clara Dorothy Bewick." In *Notable American Women 1607–1950: A Biographical Dictionary,* ed. Edward T. James, Janet Wilson James, and Paul S. Boyer. Cambridge, Mass.: Belknap Press of Harvard University Press, 1:355–357.

Griffith, Elisabeth. 1984. *In Her Own Right: The Life of Elizabeth Cady Stanton*. New York: Oxford University Press.

Gurko, Miriam. 1974. *The Ladies of Seneca Falls: The Birth of the Woman's Rights Movement*. New York: Macmillan.

Harper, Ida Husted. 1899, 1908. *The Life and Work of Susan B. Anthony*. 3 vols. Indianapolis: Bowen-Merrill (vols. 1 and 2) and Hollenbeck Press (vol. 3).

Hays, Elinor Rice. 1961. *Morning Star: A Biography of Lucy Stone 1818–1893*. New York: Harcourt, Brace and World.

———. 1967. *Those Extraordinary Blackwells: The Story of a Journey to a Better World*. New York: Harcourt Brace.

Hersh, Blanche Glassman. 1978. *The Slavery of Sex: Feminist-Abolitionists in America*. Urbana: University of Illinois Press.

Hewitt, Nancy A. 1984a. "Amy Kirby Post." *The University of Rochester Library Bulletin* 37:4–21.

———. 1984b. *Women's Activism and Social Change: Rochester, New York, 1822–1872*. Ithaca: Cornell University Press.

Hinck, Edward A. 1991. "The *Lily*, 1849–1856: From Temperance to Women's Rights." In *A Voice of Their Own: The Woman Suffrage Press, 1840–1910,* ed. Martha M. Solomon. Tuscaloosa: University of Alabama Press.

Hine, Darlene Clark. 1993. "Harper, Frances Ellen Watkins." In *Black Women in America: An Historical Encyclopedia,* ed. Darlene Clark Hine, Elsa Barkley Brown, and Rosalyn Terborg-Penn. Brooklyn, N.Y.: Carlson Publishing, pp. 532–537.

Hine, Darlene Clark, Elsa Barkley Brown, and Rosalyn Terborg-Penn, eds. 1993. *Black Women in America: An Historical Encyclopedia*. 2 vols. Brooklyn, N.Y.: Carlson Publishing.

History of Woman Suffrage, vol. 1, 1881, ed. Elizabeth Cady Stanton, Susan B. Anthony, and Matilda Joslyn Gage; vol. 2, 1882, ed. Stanton, Anthony, and Gage; vol. 3, 1886, ed. Stanton, Anthony, and Gage; vol. 4, 1902, ed. Anthony and Ida Husted Harper; vols. 5 and 6, 1922, ed. Ida Husted Harper. Reprint. New York: Arno Press, 1969.

Hoffert, Sylvia D. 1993. "New York City's Penny Press and the Issue of Woman's Rights, 1848–1860." *Journalism Quarterly* 70, no. 3 (autumn):656–665.

————. 1995. *When Hens Crow: The Women's Rights Movement in Antebellum America.* Bloomington: Indiana University Press.

Hoganson, Kristin. 1993. "Garrisonian Abolitionists and the Rhetoric of Gender, 1850–1860." *American Quarterly* 45, no. 4 (December):558–595.

Holland, Patricia G., and Ann D. Gordon, eds. 1992. *The Papers of Elizabeth Cady Stanton and Susan B. Anthony.* (Microfilm edition.) Wilmington, Del.: Scholarly Resources.

Huggins, Nathan Irvin. 1980. *Slave and Citizen: The Life of Frederick Douglass.* Boston: Little Brown.

Humez, Jean McMahon. 1992. "Sarah P. Remond." In *Notable Black American Women,* ed. Jessie Carney Smith. Detroit: Gale Research.

Huth, Mary M. 1995. *Upstate New York and the Women's Rights Movement.* Online. University of Rochester Library. Available at http://www.lib.rochester.edu/rbk/women/women.htm.

Huxman, Susan Schultz. 1991. "The *Woman's Journal,* 1870–1890: The Torchbearer for Suffrage." In *A Voice of Their Own: The Woman Suffrage Press, 1840–1910,* ed. Martha M. Solomon. Tuscaloosa: University of Alabama Press.

Iverson, Joan. 1990. "The Mormon-Suffrage Relationship: Personal and Political Quandaries." *Frontiers* 12, nos. 2–3:8–16.

James, Edward T., Janet Wilson James, and Paul S. Boyer, eds. 1971. *Notable American Women 1607–1950: A Biographical Dictionary.* Cambridge, Mass.: Belknap Press of Harvard University Press.

Jerry, E. Claire. 1991. "Clara Bewick Colby and the *Woman's Tribune,* 1883–1909." In *A Voice of Their Own: The Woman Suffrage Press, 1840–1910,* ed. Martha M. Solomon. Tuscaloosa: University of Alabama Press.

Johnson, Allen, and Dumas Malone, eds. 1964. *Dictionary of American Biography.* New York: Scribner's.

Johnson, L. C. 1971. "Duniway, Abigail Scott." In *Notable American Women 1607–1950: A Biographical Dictionary,* ed. Edward T. James, Janet Wilson James, and Paul S. Boyer. Cambridge, Mass.: Belknap Press of Harvard University Press, 1:531–533.

Jones, Beverly. 1993. "Terrell, Mary Eliza Church." In *Black Women in America: An Historical Encyclopedia,* ed. Darlene Clark Hine, Elsa Barkley Brown, and Rosalyn Terborg-Penn. Brooklyn, N.Y.: Carlson Publishing, 2:1157–1159.

Karcher, Carolyn L. 1994. *The First Woman in the Republic: A Cultural Biography of Lydia Maria Child.* Durham, N.C.: Duke University Press.

Kerr, Andrea Moore. 1992. *Lucy Stone: Speaking Out for Equality.* New Brunswick, N.J.: Rutgers University Press.

————. 1995. "White Women's Rights, Black Men's Wrongs: Free Love, Blackmail, and the Formation of the American Woman Suffrage Association." In *One Woman, One Vote: Rediscovering the Woman Suffrage Movement,* ed. Marjorie Spruill Wheeler. Troutdale, Oreg.: New Sage Press.

Kimmel, Michael S., and Thomas E. Mosmiller, eds. 1992. *Against the Tide: Pro-Feminist Men in the United States, 1776–1990: A Documentary History.* Boston: Beacon Press.

Kovnat, Denise Bolger. 1995. "Dear, Blessed Susan B." *University of Rochester Review* (fall):16–22.

Kugler, Israel. 1987. *From Ladies to Women: The Organized Struggle for Woman's Rights in the Reconstruction Era.* Westport, Conn.: Greenwood Press.

Lasch, Christopher. 1971. "Avery, Rachel Foster." In *Notable American Women 1607–1950: A Biographical Dictionary,* ed. Edward

T. James, Janet Wilson James, and Paul S. Boyer. Cambridge, Mass.: Belknap Press of Harvard University Press, 1:71–72.

Lasser, Carol, and Marlene Deahl Merrill, eds. 1987. *Friends and Sisters: Letters Between Lucy Stone and Antoinette Brown Blackwell, 1846–1893.* Urbana: University of Illinois Press.

Lewis, W. Davis. 1971. "Bloomer, Amelia Jenks." In *Notable American Women 1607–1950: A Biographical Dictionary,* ed. Edward T. James, Janet Wilson James, and Paul S. Boyer. Cambridge, Mass.: Belknap Press of Harvard University Press, 1:179–181.

Logan, Rayford W., and Michael R. Winston, eds. 1982. *Dictionary of American Negro Biography.* New York: W. W. Norton.

Lutz, Alma. 1959. *Susan B. Anthony: Rebel, Crusader, Humanitarian.* Boston: Beacon Press.

———. 1968. *Crusade for Freedom: Women in the Antislavery Movement.* Boston: Beacon Press.

Mabee, Carleton. 1970. *Black Freedom: The Nonviolent Abolitionists from 1830 through the Civil War.* Toronto: Macmillan.

Magdol, Edward. 1986. *The Antislavery Rank and File: A Social Profile of the Abolitionists' Constituency.* New York: Greenwood Press.

Marilley, Suzanne M. 1996. *Woman Suffrage and the Origins of Liberal Feminism in the United States, 1820–1920.* Cambridge, Mass.: Harvard University Press.

Massey, Mary Elizabeth. 1966, 1994. *Women in the Civil War.* Lincoln: University of Nebraska Press.

McBride, Genevieve G. 1993. *On Wisconsin Women: Working for Their Rights from Settlement to Suffrage.* Madison: University of Wisconsin Press.

McFeely, William S. 1991. *Frederick Douglass.* New York: W. W. Norton.

Merrill, Marlene Deahl, ed. 1990. *Growing Up in Boston's Gilded Age: The Journal of Alice Stone Blackwell, 1872–1874.* New Haven, Conn.: Yale University Press.

Merrill, Walter M. 1963. *Against Wind and Tide: A Biography of William Lloyd Garrison.* Cambridge, Mass.: Harvard University Press.

"Miss Phoebe Couzins." 1893. In *A Woman of the Century,* ed. Frances E. Willard and Mary A. Livermore. Buffalo, N.Y.: Charles Wells Moulton, p. 211.

Mitchell, Catherine. 1993. "Historiography: A New Direction for Research on the Woman's Rights Press." *Journalism History* 19, no. 2 (summer):59–63.

"Mrs. May Wright Sewall," 1893. In *A Woman of the Century,* ed. Frances E. Willard and Mary A. Livermore. Buffalo, N.Y.: Charles Wells Moulton, pp. 643–645.

"Mrs. Rachel Foster Avery." 1893. In *A Woman of the Century,* ed. Frances E. Willard and Mary A. Livermore. Buffalo, N.Y.: Charles Wells Moulton, pp. 37–38.

Oates, Stephen B. 1984. *To Purge This Land with Blood: A Biography of John Brown.* Amherst: University of Massachusetts Press.

———. 1994. *A Woman of Valor: Clara Barton and the Civil War.* New York: Free Press.

Oatman, Eric F. 1985. "Pillsbury, Parker." In *American Reformers,* ed. Alden Whitman. New York: H. W. Wilson.

Painter, Nell Irvin. 1994. "Difference, Slavery, and Memory: Sojourner Truth in Feminist Abolitionism." In *The Abolitionist Sisterhood: Women's Political Culture in Antebellum America,* ed. Jean Fagan Yellin and John C. Van Horne. Ithaca, N.Y.: Cornell University Press.

———. 1996. *Sojourner Truth: A Life, a Symbol.* New York: W. W. Norton.

Pease, Jane H., and William H. Pease, eds. 1972. *Bound with Them in Chains: A Bio-*

graphical History of the Antislavery Movement. Westport, Conn.: Greenwood Press.

Peck, Mary Gray. 1944. *Carrie Chapman Catt.* New York: H. W. Wilson.

Pellauer, Mary D. 1991. *Toward a Tradition of Feminist Theology: The Religious Social Thought of Elizabeth Cady Stanton, Susan B. Anthony, and Anna Howard Shaw.* Brooklyn, N.Y.: Carlson Publishing.

Phillips, Clifton. 1971a. "Harper, Ida A. Husted." In *Notable American Women 1607– 1950: A Biographical Dictionary*, ed. Edward T. James, Janet Wilson James, and Paul S. Boyer. Cambridge, Mass.: Belknap Press of Harvard University Press, 2:139–140.

———. 1971b. "Sewall, May Eliza Wright." In *Notable American Women 1607–1950: A Biographical Dictionary*, ed. Edward T. James, Janet Wilson James, and Paul S. Boyer. Cambridge, Mass.: Belknap Press of Harvard University Press, 3:269–271.

Porter, Dorothy Burnett. 1982a. "Remond, Charles Lenox," In *Dictionary of American Negro Biography*, ed. Rayford W. Logan and Michael R. Winston. New York: W. W. Norton.

———. 1982b. "Remond, Sarah Parker." In *Dictionary of American Negro Biography*, ed. Rayford W. Logan and Michael R. Winston. New York: W. W. Norton.

———. 1985. "The Remonds of Salem, Massachusetts: A Nineteenth-Century Family Revisited." *Proceedings of the American Antiquarian Society* 95, no. 2:259–295.

Pryor, Elizabeth Brown. 1987. *Clara Barton: Professional Angel.* Philadelphia: University of Pennsylvania Press.

Quarles, Benjamin. 1969. *Black Abolitionists.* New York: Oxford University Press.

———. 1982. "Robert Purvis, Sr." In *Dictionary of American Negro Biography*, ed. Rayford W. Logan and Michael R. Winston. New York: W. W. Norton, pp. 508–510.

Renehan, Edward J., Jr. 1995. *The Secret Six: The True Tale of the Men Who Conspired with John Brown.* New York: Crown Publishers.

Ripley, C. Peter, ed. 1993. *Witness to Freedom: African American Voices on Race, Slavery, and Emancipation.* Chapel Hill: University of North Carolina Press.

Robbins, Peggy. 1990. "Where Do You Stand Horace Greeley?" *Civil War Times Illustrated* 29, no. 5:50–55.

Robertson, Stacey Marie. 1994. *Parker Pillsbury, Antislavery Apostle: Gender and Religion in Nineteenth-Century U.S. Radicalism.* Ph.D. diss., University of California at Santa Barbara.

Robinson, David. 1985. *The Unitarians and the Universalists.* Westport, Conn.: Greenwood Press.

Rosenberg-Naparsteck, Ruth. 1984. "A Growing Agitation: Rochester Before, During, and After the Civil War." *Rochester History* 46, nos. 1–2:1–39.

Rossbach, Jeffrey. 1982. *Ambivalent Conspirators: John Brown, the Secret Six, and a Theory of Slave Violence.* Philadelphia: University of Pennsylvania Press.

Rugoff, Milton. 1981. *The Beechers: An American Family in the Nineteenth Century.* New York: Harper and Row.

Schulze, Suzanne. 1992. *Horace Greeley: A Bio-Bibliography.* New York: Greenwood Press.

Sears, Hal D. 1977. *The Sex Radicals: Free Love in High Victorian America.* Lawrence: The Regents Press of Kansas.

Sewall, Richard H. 1976. *Ballots for Freedom: Antislavery Politics in the United States, 1837– 1860.* New York: Oxford University Press.

Shaw, Anna Howard. 1915. *Story of a Pioneer.* New York: Harper and Bros.

Sherr, Lynn. 1995. *Failure Is Impossible: Susan B. Anthony in Her Own Words.* New York: Times Books.

Shriver, Phillip R. "Upton, Harriet Taylor." In *Notable American Women 1607–1950: A Biographical Dictionary*, ed. Edward T. James, Janet Wilson James, and Paul S. Boyer. Cambridge, Mass.: Belknap Press of Harvard University Press, 3:501–502.

Smith, Jessie Carney, ed. 1992. *Notable Black American Women*. Detroit: Gale Research.

Solomon, Martha M., ed. 1991. *A Voice of Their Own: The Woman Suffrage Press, 1840–1910*. Tuscaloosa: University of Alabama Press.

Stange, Douglas C. 1977. *Patterns of Antislavery among American Unitarians, 1831–1860*. Cranbury, N.J.: Associated University Presses.

Stanton, Elizabeth Cady. 1898, 1973. *Eighty Years and More: Reminiscences of Elizabeth Cady Stanton*. New York: Source Book Press.

Stanton, Theodore, and Harriot Stanton Blatch, eds. 1922. *Elizabeth Cady Stanton as Revealed in Her Letters, Diary and Reminiscences*. 2 vols. New York: Harper and Bros.

Sterling, Dorothy. 1984. *We Are Your Sisters: Black Women in the Nineteenth Century*. New York: W. W. Norton.

———. 1988a. "Ida B. Wells." *Black Foremothers: Three Lives*. New York: Feminist Press.

———. 1988b. "Mary Church Terrell." *Black Foremothers: Three Lives*. New York: Feminist Press.

———. 1991. *Ahead of Her Time: Abby Kelley and the Politics of Antislavery*. New York: W. W. Norton.

Stewart, James Brewer. 1976. *Holy Warriors: The Abolitionists and American Slavery*. New York: Hill and Wang.

———. 1986. *Wendell Phillips: Liberty's Hero*. Baton Rouge: Louisiana State University Press.

———. 1992. *William Lloyd Garrison and the Challenge of Emancipation*. Arlington Heights, Ill.: Harlan Davidson.

Stoehr, Taylor. 1979. *Free Love in America: A Documentary History*. New York: AMS Press.

Stoneburner, Carol, and John Stoneburner, eds. 1986. *The Influence of Quaker Women on American History: Biographical Studies*. Vol. 21 of *Studies in Women and Religion*. Lewiston, N.Y.: Edwin Mellen Press.

Suhl, Yuri. 1990, 1959. *Ernestine Rose: Women's Rights Pioneer*. 2nd ed. New York: Biblio Press.

Taylor, William R. 1971. "Blake, Lillie Devereux." In *Notable American Women 1607–1950: A Biographical Dictionary*, ed. Edward T. James, Janet Wilson James, and Paul S. Boyer. Cambridge, Mass.: Belknap Press of Harvard University Press, 1:167–169.

Terrell, Mary Church. 1940. *A Colored Woman in a White World*. Washington, D.C.: Ransdell.

Thomas, Dorothy. 1971. "Couzins, Phoebe Wilson." In *Notable American Women 1607–1950: A Biographical Dictionary*, ed. Edward T. James, Janet Wilson James, and Paul S. Boyer. Cambridge, Mass.: Belknap Press of Harvard University Press, 1:390–391.

Tyler, Alice Felt. 1971a. "Davis, Paulina Kellogg Wright." In *Notable American Women 1607–1950: A Biographical Dictionary*, ed. Edward T. James, Janet Wilson James, and Paul S. Boyer. Cambridge, Mass.: Belknap Press of Harvard University Press, 1:444–445.

———. 1971b. "Hooker, Isabella Beecher." In *Notable American Women 1607–1950: A Biographical Dictionary*, ed. Edward T. James, Janet Wilson James, and Paul S. Boyer. Cambridge, Mass.: Belknap Press of Harvard University Press, 2:212–214.

———. 1971c. "Rose, Ernestine Louise Potowski." In *Notable American Women 1607–1950: A Biographical Dictionary*, ed. Edward T. James, Janet Wilson James, and Paul S. Boyer. Cambridge, Mass.: Belknap Press of Harvard University Press, 3:195–196.

Underhill, Lois Beachy. 1995. *The Woman Who Ran for President: The Many Lives of Victoria Woodhull*. Bridgehampton, N.Y.: Bridge Works Publishing.

Van Voris, Jacqueline. 1987. *Carrie Chapman Catt: A Public Life*. New York: Feminist Press.

Venet, Wendy Hamand. 1991. *Neither Ballots nor Bullets: Women Abolitionists and the Civil War*. Charlottesville: University Press of Virginia.

Walker, S. Jay. 1983. "Frederick Douglass and Woman Suffrage." *The Black Scholar* 14 (September–October):18–25.

Waller, Altina L. 1982. *Reverend Beecher and Mrs. Tilton: Sex and Class in Victorian America*. Amherst: University of Massachusetts Press.

Warbasse, Elizabeth B. "Gage, Matilda Joslyn." In *Notable American Women 1607–1950: A Biographical Dictionary,* ed. Edward T. James, Janet Wilson James, and Paul S. Boyer. Cambridge, Mass.: Belknap Press of Harvard University Press, 2:4–6.

Wells-Barnett, Ida B. 1970. *Crusade for Justice: the Autobiography of Ida B. Wells*, ed. Alfreda M. Duster. Chicago: University of Chicago Press.

Wheeler, Leslie, ed. 1981. *Loving Warriors: Selected Letters of Lucy Stone and Henry B. Blackwell, 1853–1893*. New York: Dial Press.

Wheeler, Marjorie Spruill, ed. 1995a. *One Woman, One Vote: Rediscovering the Woman Suffrage Movement*. Troutdale, Oreg.: New Sage Press.

———. 1995b. *Votes for Women! The Woman Suffrage Movement in Tennessee, the South, and the Nation*. Knoxville: University of Tennessee Press.

Whitman, Alden, ed. 1985. *American Reformers*. New York: H. W. Wilson.

Willard, Frances E., and Mary A. Livermore, eds. 1893. *A Woman of the Century*. Buffalo, N.Y.: Charles Wells Moulton.

Wrench, Susan Bleiweis. 1985. "Upton, Harriet Taylor." In *American Reformers*, ed. Alden Whitman. N.Y.: H. W. Wilson, pp. 820–821.

Yacovone, Donald. 1991. *Samuel Joseph May and the Dilemmas of the Liberal Persuasion, 1797–1871*. Philadelphia: Temple University Press.

Yee, Shirley J. 1992. *Black Women Abolitionists: A Study in Activism 1828–1860*. Knoxville: University of Tennessee Press.

Yellin, Jean Fagan, and John C. Van Horne, eds. 1994. *The Abolitionist Sisterhood: Women's Political Culture in Antebellum America*. Ithaca, N.Y.: Cornell University Press.

Young, James Harvey. 1971. "Dickinson, Anna Elizabeth." In *Notable American Women 1607–1950: A Biographical Dictionary,* ed. Edward T. James, Janet Wilson James, and Paul S. Boyer. Cambridge, Mass.: Belknap Press of Harvard University Press, 1:475–476.

ILLUSTRATION CREDITS

INDEX

Note: The general headings below such as "European travel" and "Years of struggle" refer to the life of Susan B. Anthony. Headings that cite page numbers in bold refer to main encyclopedia entries or subsections of entries devoted to the topic in question.

AASS. *See* American Anti-Slavery Society
Abolitionist movement, **3–7**
    African-American women activists, 3–4, 105, 168, 224–226
    Anthony family role in, 14, 15, 16–17, 26
    Anthony's activities, 4–7, 8, 26, 27, 70, 83
    Brown, John, **60–61**
    Civil War's effect on, 69
    emancipation issues, 70
    Emancipation Proclamation, **87–88**
    financial support for, 112
    friendships in, 5–6, 27
    hardships endured by abolitionists, 5–6, 123–124, 128
    Harpers Ferry raid, 60, 61
    illustration of members, 6
    and the Kansas-Nebraska Act, **120–121**
    lecturers, 27, 70, 79–80, 91, 92, 99, 123–124, 128, 156, 167, 168, 224
    Liberty Party, 3
    Lincoln as viewed by, 70–71
    "moral suasion," 3
    Phillips, Wendell, **152–156**
    publications supporting, 81, 123–124, 149
    Quaker involvement in, 4, 14
    Underground Railroad, **227–228**
    violent tactics, 60–61
    and woman suffrage, 8–9, 28–29, 155–156, 259–260
    Woman's National Loyal League (WNLL), 7, 70, 88, 191, **257–259**
    women activists, 3–4, 7–8, 99, 105, 130–132, 159–160, 189–190, 224–226
    as women's rights movement precursor, 7–8, 190, 264–265
    See also American Anti-Slavery Society; Garrison, William Lloyd; Garrisonians; Racial prejudice
Activism. *See* Male reformers; Political activism; Women reformers
AERA. *See* American Equal Rights Association
African-American male suffrage
    disenfranchisement in the South, 55–56, 246, 249–250, 257
    and the Enforcement Act, 230
    in New York State, 9
    woman suffrage movement rejected in favor of, 10, 48–49, 81–82, 91, 93, 112, 118, 120, 140, 153–155, 166, 172
    women activists for, 257–258
    See also Fifteenth Amendment; Fourteenth Amendment
African-American woman suffrage, opposition to, 245
African-American women
    in the abolitionist movement, 3–4, 105, 168, 224–226
    civil rights activism, 246–247
    suffrage for, 245
    in the woman suffrage movement, 11, 105–106, 168, 219–221, 224–226, 237–239, **245–248**
    in the women's rights movement, 264
African Americans
    activists, 3–4, 11, 80–82, 105–106, 160–161, 167, 168
    citizenship of, 82–83, 238, 257–258
    civil rights activism, 237–239, 246–248, 257–258
    emancipation issues, 70–72